Impersonality

Impersonality

SEVEN ESSAYS

Sharon Cameron

THE UNIVERSITY OF CHICAGO PRESS

Chicago and London

SHARON CAMERON

is the William R. Kenan, Jr., Professor of English
at Johns Hopkins University. Among her
publications are, most recently, *Thinking in Henry
James, Choosing Not Choosing: Dickinson's Fascicles*,
and *Beautiful Work: A Meditation on Pain.*

The University of Chicago Press, Chicago 60637
The University of Chicago Press, Ltd., London
© 2007 by The University of Chicago
All rights reserved. Published 2007
Printed in the United States of America

16 15 14 13 12 11 10 09 08 07   1 2 3 4 5
ISBN-13: 978-0-226-09131-0 (cloth)
ISBN-13: 978-0-226-09132-7 (paper)
ISBN-10: 0-226-09131-7 (cloth)
ISBN-10: 0-226-09132-5 (paper)

Library of Congress Cataloging-in-Publication Data

Cameron, Sharon.
Impersonality : seven essays / Sharon Cameron.
p. cm.
Includes bibliographical references and index.
ISBN-13: 978-0-226-09131-0 (cloth : acid-free paper)
ISBN-10: 0-226-09131-7 (cloth : acid-free paper)
ISBN-13: 978-0-226-09132-7 (pbk. : acid-free paper)
ISBN-10: 0-226-09132-5 (pbk. : acid-free paper)
1. American literature—History and criticism.   2. Self in
literature.   3. Identity (Psychology) in literature.   4. Persona
(Literature)   5. Emerson, Ralph Waldo, 1803–1882—Criticism
and interpretation.   6. Eliot, T. S. (Thomas Stearns),
1888–1965—Criticism and interpretation.   7. Melville, Herman,
1819–1891—Criticism and interpretation.   8. Edwards, Jonathan,
1703–1758—Criticism and interpretation. I. Title.

PS169.S425C36 2007
814'.3—dc22   2006008930

Contents

Preface

This is a collection of essays on impersonality in the writings of major figures in American literature—Jonathan Edwards, Ralph Waldo Emerson, Herman Melville, T. S. Eliot—and of major figures of international modernism, Simone Weil and William Empson, included because of the intensity of their engagement with this topic. A genetic study of influence and association among these authors might observe cultural and biographical links, expressed most dramatically in the tradition pointed out by Perry Miller's celebrated "From Edwards to Emerson." A more modest connection is illuminated through Eliot's interest in Simone Weil, which led him to write the preface to her posthumously published *The Need for Roots* (1949, 1952). It was from D. T. Suzuki's 1927 *Essays in Zen Buddhism (First Series)* and his 1933 *Essays in Zen Buddhism (Second Series)* that Simone Weil learned about Buddhism,[1] but Suzuki's first publication was an "Essay on Emerson."[2] Edwin Arnold, who published *The Light of Asia* (1879), a late nineteenth-century account of the Buddha's life and teachings, called his son "Emerson" after the man he admired, who in fact baptized Arnold's child (B 180–81). The connection between Emerson and Weil (mediated by Arnold's popular study) also reaches in another direction: Eliot's involvement with Buddhist texts had its origins in his childhood reading of Arnold's book.³ In 1844, having assumed the editorship of the *Dial* at Emerson's urging, Elizabeth Peabody published her translation, from the French, of the Lotus Sutra, thereby introducing Buddhism to America.⁴ For accounts of Buddhist theories and practices both Eliot and Empson relied on the expertise of Masaharu Anesaki (1873–1949), the foremost scholar of Japanese religion in the first half of the century: Empson consulted him in the 1930s on his theory of incompatible features of Buddha faces; earlier, in 1913–14, Anesaki gave a series of lectures on Mahayana Buddhism in the Harvard Philosophy Department, on which Eliot took extensive notes.⁵ Yet these sometimes tangential and fascinating biographical connections, which could of course be elaborated, are not the focus of the following pages. Rather, my essays are concerned with the uncompromising nature of writing about the precariousness of personal identity measured at the moment of its disintegration. In this preface I indicate some of the theoretical and philosophical connections that link the writers I consider as they address the making and *un*making of personality.

The word *person* confers status (designating a rational being in distinction to a thing or an animal), value, even equality; it establishes intelligibility within a political and legal system, indicating a being having legal rights or representing others' rights, either because he is a human being or *natural* person or because he is a corporate body or *artificial* person. (For Hobbes an artificial person must also be a natural person.) It does not, however, presume anything of substance, nor did the word *persona* from which it derived. A persona was never essential, since a persona is not an actor but the mask which covers the actor, or the character who is acted. In the same way the *three-personed God* is a mechanism for thinking about the Trinity, indicating how God is represented through the idea of modes, how the parts go together. The designation legitimates the relation of these parts; it does not presume essence. For Hobbes, the definition of a person (or agent) is what we agree to treat as a person; a being is determined human not by philosophical definitions or by man, but by law.⁶ To be a person or agent, according to Hobbes, it is not sufficient to consider yourself a person; you must also be considered as possessing agency. In distinction, *personality* stresses self-ownership, the *of* or possessive through which individuality is identified as one's own.

Impersonality is an idea that Eliot made commonplace. But whereas Eliot coined the word narrowly to indicate the extinction of personality that defines the artist, this extinction (if not the word *impersonality* itself, which is absent from Edwards's writing) has different contours in the works I consider, contours which are in each case mysterious, since personality and impersonality do not stand in a binary relation. The point of my essays is to get at the particularity of those understandings. Weil indicates the elusiveness of the distinction between personality and impersonality when she provides a shocking example of what can be destroyed without endangering personality: "If it were the human personality in [every man] that was sacred to me, I could easily put out his eyes. As a blind man he would be exactly as much a human personality as before. I should have destroyed nothing but his eyes."[7] One way of approaching impersonality is to say it is not the negation of the person, but rather a penetration through or a falling outside of the boundary of the human particular. Impersonality disrupts elementary categories we suppose to be fundamental to specifying human distinctiveness. Or rather, we don't know what the *im* of impersonality means. I shall argue it means different things for different authors.

Representations of impersonality suspend, eclipse, and even destroy the idea of the person as such, who is not treated as a social, political, or individual entity. Such writing repels social and personal aggrandizement, rather establishing a momentum and an ethos which is disintegrative. We see disintegration in the dissociation of Emerson's sentences; in Weil's unmaking of the "I," a practice she called "de-creation";[8] in Empson's halving of photographs of Buddha faces in order to demonstrate the incompatibility of the two sides; in Melville's identification of antipodes which cannot be separated from each other, but which cannot be integrated either; in Eliot's constitution of voices in terms of singularities that do not add up to personal identities. The writing of these authors is epigrammatic (Emerson and Weil); even explicitly fragmentary (in Eliot's *Four Quartets* prosodic distinctions register as disruptive). The splintered features in much of the writing correspond to a discovery (differently manifested in Edwards, Emerson, Weil, and Eliot) that being itself is momentary. For Melville's *Billy Budd* the mercurial quality of being is dramatized by the instantaneousness with which a character defined as a peacemaker becomes a killer. For Emerson, Eliot, Weil, and Empson the recognition of momentariness which renders impersonality visible requires training,[9] while for Edwards training is irrelevant, since no amount of training could perfect the ideal of impersonality (an ideal Kant would rewrite into the aesthetic), as it is for Melville's fiction, which represents impersonality as a pressing inevitability whose manifestations are inescapably everywhere.

The writing of the authors I consider is uncompromising because it *must* be practiced (Emerson, Weil, Eliot) or because it *cannot* be practiced (Edwards). It is equally uncompromising because of the way in which the impersonal is marked by the nonhuman, and even the inanimate, most dramatically exemplified by Jonathan Edwards's insistence that to imagine the nothing that is beyond the nothing "of you and me" is as difficult as to imagine what "sleeping rocks dream of";[10] by Simone Weil's idea that the self must become "dead wood" (*FL* 220) or "a chlorophyll conferring the faculty of feeding on light" (*N* 1:223); by Schopenhauer's supposition, exemplified in Melville's writing, that the essence of a stone and the essence of a mind are the same (not just the same kind of) thing; by Emerson's equation of "the wild man, and the wild beast and bird"—the globe itself—all shown by "molecular philosophy" to be composed of "astronomical interspaces betwixt atom and atom."[11] In Emerson one manifestation of the trait of externality—"the world is all outside: it has no inside" (E 481)—that equally marks everything is impenetrability. The person is a surface—nothing that *can* be penetrated, something that does not even register contact—is impervious as a stone would be.

This hardness which comes about because there is no inside (nothing in which an inside might be situated) is a state without exception for Emerson. "Nothing is of us" (E 483), Emerson remarks. The nothing equally applies to all phenomena, which, nonunique, are swept together by a "vast flowing vigor" of imparticularity (E 486). In Melville's *Billy Budd* a category crossing between the human and the nonhuman results in characters possessing the same plastic and contradictory features of the universe to which the characterological is irrelevant. This has a corollary in Eliot's *Four Quartets* in the erosion of distinction between animate and inanimate entities—in a face and a street which transiently share the same properties of disfigurement. While for Emerson there is a category crossing between the impersonal and the inhuman (persons "melt so fast into each other, that they are like grass and trees," like "a rack of clouds, or a fleet of ripples which the wind drives over the surface of the water"),[12] such effacements of distinction also sweep across systems, states, beings that are not even grammatically comparable—as on the first page of "Nature," where Emerson says he will explain "language, sleep, madness, dreams, beasts, sex,"[13] even as it remains unclear how these manifestations of inexplicability could be identified with each other.

For Simone Weil the blunting of distinction first requires a hardening of the self to its own exceptionality ("dead wood"), which can be cultivated by attention that is more inclusive than an "I" and more inclusive than "thought," both of which are limits. The goal of attention is to see there is no difference between a glass of water ("God's 'I love you'") and the dryness in the throat after two days in the desert with nothing to drink (also "God's 'I love you'") (*FL* 128). The goal is to have no preference, to see from no point of view—a breakthrough experience in which the de-creation of an "I" is categorically inseparable from the de-creation of a God. For Jonathan Edwards existence is created anew in each successive moment. Thus there is no personal identity to be undone, since no identity ever existed in the first place: no more identity "than the sound of the wind that blows now, is individually the same with the sound of the wind that blew just before" (*W* 3.403). Therefore Edwards begins with the premise at which Emerson and Weil arrive. In *Four Quartets*, Eliot, from another vantage, opens up a space that is not distinction-driven, in which it is not possible to separate being and unbeing, the living and the dead, which have the same ontic status, and which are given substance only in relation to the other. As these examples imply, the elision of the impersonal and the nonhuman suggests more expansive category crossings, exemplified in Empson's obsessive focus on contradictory elements allocated to opposite sides of the Buddha face but imperceptibly diffused throughout the whole countenance (an emblem writ small of antipodes that morph into each other) and equally illustrated in the sweep of Melville's equation of a violence inherent in a "goodness beyond virtue" with a violence inherent in a "wickedness beyond vice."

The phrases are Hannah Arendt's,[14] elucidating *Billy Budd*'s relation to the French Revolution: The absolute—"and to Melville an absolute was incorporated in the Rights of Man—spells doom to everyone when it is introduced into the political realm" (A 84). For Arendt, the absolute implicit in a natural innocence is every bit as lethal as the absolute implicit in a natural depravity, because both eschew argumentative reasoning, politics, and law for swift, unmediated action (A 87). What interests me about Arendt's discussion of the equivalence of a "goodness beyond virtue" and a "wickedness beyond vice" is her astonishing conclusion: In *Billy Budd* Melville reverses the "legendary crime, Cain slew Abel" (A 87), a reversal that follows from the French Revolution's substitution of the proposition of original goodness for the proposition of original sin: "It is as though [Melville] said: Let us suppose that from now on the foundation stone of our political life will be that Abel slew Cain. Don't you see that from this deed of violence the same chain of wrongdoing will follow, only that now mankind will not even have the consolation that the violence it must call crime is indeed characteristic of evil men only?" (A 87–88).

Thus while Arendt italicizes the violence inherent in any revolution and its absolute ("Cain slew Abel, and Romulus slew Remus; violence was the beginning and, by the same token, no beginning could be made without using violence, without violating" [A 20]), her compelling words also emphasize another point: *Melville's* violence implicit in reversing the social assessment of categorical opposites like good and evil. In *Billy Budd* the transgression of a goodness beyond virtue which exceeds the transgression of an evil beyond vice could be construed only as violent, since it plays havoc with ethical and evaluative hierarchies. In the writings I consider, the propensity to equate phenomena that are socially incommensurate (the self, dead wood), and then to reverse understandings of the values of these phenomena (so that dead wood is superior to self) and of their dangers (so that a goodness beyond virtue is more perilous than an evil beyond vice), is, in its indifference to social judgment, itself a violent act—or could be so construed if indifference could be viewed as violent and if violence could be viewed as tacit.

We see violence in Jonathan Edwards's refusal to assign ultimate value to the ethical, which in his universe could never constitute "true virtue." We see it in Weil's insistence that "truth" is not "compatible with social life and its labels" (*N* 1:217). We see it in Empson's demotion of persons, whom he regards as ethically inferior to creatures called Wurroos, whose superiority derives from the fact that they have no human culture and, specifically, no Christian religion. We see it in Emerson's cool assessment that "persons [are] a conveniency in household matters," but "the divine man does not respect them" (NR 580). Thus one source of the violence in these writings is that they carve out images of perfection that have no social foundation, as in Empson's stunning understanding that the highest ideal is a rationality devoid of cruelty and a mildness devoid of sentimentality—an ideal which is not, and implicitly could never be, incarnated by persons.

The renderings of violence implicit in these writings are not, however, comparable. For the Edwards of *The Nature of True Virtue* violence inheres in the bizarre notion that amounts of love must be calculated in relation to amounts of being—bizarre because it would seem that classifying and calculating amounts are not operations intrinsic to love: a benevolence derived mathematically is opposite to a benevolence which is felt. Yet Edwards tells us that the only thing which could constitute impersonal love (being's consent to Being without particularity)[15] would be knowing how to make such quantifications. Although Weil would agree that feeling is no compass (nothing is more deceptive), what must more fundamentally be abolished is the entire personality, "what the animals in the soul ... [call] the 'me'!" (*FL* 232–33), since it is not only feelings that distort the real in Weil's apocalyptic vision, but also, Weil asserts, even a person's gaze, whose capacity to mar what is seen derives merely from its individuality: "Let me disappear in order that those things which I see may become, owing to the fact that they will then no longer be things which I see, things of perfect beauty" (*N* 2:383).

For Emerson, in a different register, violence is visible in the dramatization of the slide of the personal to the impersonal, when the dissociation of a particular, personal experience (grief at the death of his five-year-old child) becomes the spectacularly undifferentiated common denominator of *all* experience— the mirror in which the features of all experience can be read. In Eliot's *Four Quartets* violence is a consequence of the reduction of voice to a manifestation which is particular without being personal—a reduction relentlessly reiterated across four poems until its heuristic understandings are made conclusive. In *Billy Budd* violence lies in the fact that the characterological distinctions essential to the plot of *Billy Budd* are irrelevant to the metaphysical imperatives essential to the workings of its prose, through whose equivocations differences which specify no longer make any difference by specifying. Through the calibrations of the prose, ostensibly distinct characters and ostensibly distinct regions (the natural, the providential) assume a ghostly relation.

Something—an excess that does not pertain to character—nonetheless passes through it, making characters permeable to attributes that are not uniquely theirs and that are even antithetical to their attributes, as, for instance, a murderous impulse passes through Billy. Melville's writing thus engages in an arduous effort to take attributes and characterizations and, by making them applicable to what they weren't initially attached to, to deprive them of the capacity to mean again in a social way. Character remains intact but inconsequential—not transcended but surpassed. Moreover, what is in excess of personality is not only an action, and not even a content, but also a set of expressions. In this way Melville renders individuality and its undoing coterminous. The effect is not a neutralization but a bafflement or haunt. One could thus speak about the violence Melville visits on the reader in asking him to conciliate metaphysical and characterological imperatives that contradict each other, without so much as a word about how shocking such a directive is.

It will have become apparent that while certain propositions loosely pertain to all of the writers I consider—an unbinding from the personal manifested as an unbinding from the human; category crossings that disregard, even disdain, social discrimination; violence—the particular propositions that can be made about these writers are not in fact equivalent. This is partly because, for instance, although all the writings I discuss might be considered religious, Jonathan Edwards's Calvinism—with its absolute commitment to scripture as the highest authority—is not commensurate with Simone Weil's Catholicism. Specifically, Edwards's Calvinism is not equivalent to the Catholicism from which Weil, born a Jew, excluded herself, on the basis of *its* exclusions ("Nothing gives me more pain than the idea of separating myself from the immense and unfortunate multitude of unbelievers"; "I love God, Christ, and the Catholic faith;...But I have not the slightest love for the Church").[16] Weil carves a place for herself outside of and parallel to religious affiliation. Thus, she writes that it was while she was reciting Herbert's "Love (III)" that "Christ himself came down and took possession of me" (*WG* 69). But she also equates the words of the Bhagavad Gita—not the words of biblical scripture—with "an incarnation of God" (*WG* 70).

In distinction, Edwards, a celebrated preacher, "spent years shepherding parishioners through awakenings and declines" and in defining "the role of the Church in a town and region that were making the transition from a Puritan heritage toward a revolutionary destiny."[17] Simone Weil's idea of reducing the self to "vegetative energy" (*FL* 220) and her interest in attention owes much to Buddhist thinking. Buddhism could not have influenced Jonathan Edwards, because it was not a presence in America until the nineteenth century, although Edwards's insistence on a person's nonautonomy ("dependent being") is as unequivocal as any Buddhist assertion of that premise.[18]

While Edwards and Weil would have agreed that subjective experience alone has no authority to determine whether religious affection is genuine, Edwards fastened on biblical rules for "what true affections ought to look like," and in *Religious Affections* he insisted on a commitment to Christian practice as the only reliable sign of a keeping of God's commandments.[19] Weil's understandings of practice are consistently idiosyncratic in form if not in content: "Almsgiving when it is not supernatural ... buys the sufferer" (*WG* 147). But sometimes they are *also* idiosyncratic in content: "The presence of God in us has as its condition a secret so deep that it is even a secret from us" (*WG* 151). Therefore Weil could never adhere to the prescriptiveness arising from biblical rule which Edwards made foundational. Moreover, Weil's linking of religion to attention ("Religion is nothing else but a looking"

[*WG* 199]) resulted in formulations ("Creative attention means really giving our attention to what does not exist" [*WG* 149]) Edwards would have found outrageous.

Emerson's transcendentalism rejected the triune God of Edwards and Weil. He disdained "the personality of the deity" (the "soul knows no persons"), rather discovering manifestations of deity everywhere, which throughout his essays he variously called "the Over-soul," "the moral sentiment," "virtue," law," and "nature." His pantheism depended on the liquidity of foundational terms like "God," "Nature," and "self," terms which—offering no resistance to each other—were permeable. For Emerson the infusion whereby man is "made sensible that . . . earth and heavens are passing into his mind; that he is drinking forever the Soul of God," results in continuous ecstasy.[20] Although the world of Melville's *Billy Budd* is similarly haunted by the presence of God, the result is not a blessing but a torture. In a letter to Nathaniel Hawthorne—which could even be construed as a rebutting of Emerson's enthusiasms[21]—Melville enumerated the same elements (me, God, nature) whose confluence Emerson saw everywhere in the "influx of the Divine mind into our minds"[22] as a condition with a different outcome. For Melville, "As soon as you say *Me, a God, a Nature,* so soon you jump off from your stool and hang from the beam. Yes, that word is the hangman."[23] These foundational terms are deadly because they are not lived realities. They are not permeable to each other, or insofar as they are permeable, the result is catastrophic. Thus in *Billy Budd,* God is identified as a cause of evil (Claggart is "like the scorpion, for which the Creator alone is responsible"),[24] but a cause with no single manifestation (since if God is responsible for the scorpion he is also responsible for everything else), an "influx of the Divine mind into our minds," whose calamity is all-pervasive. While in Eliot's *Four Quartets* Anglicanism and Buddhism confront each other tacitly (in Eliot's poem only perception—not doctrine and not memory—counts as valid), for William Empson the features of impersonality made visible in Buddha faces offer an explicit contrast to the "torture" God of Christianity.[25]

It is not only different religious traditions which prohibit neat summary statements about these writings, it is also that their genres (*The Nature of True Virtue* is a treatise; Emerson wrote essays; *Billy Budd* is a novella; Simone Weil's most powerful formulations are distributed across essays, books, and notebook writings; *Four Quartets* is a poem; Empson's commentary on Buddha faces derives from published articles and from unpublished manuscript drafts) invite different kinds of consideration. Moreover, Emerson's,

Weil's, and Empson's discursive writing admits of explicit summary while the meaning of Edwards, Melville, and Eliot must be gleaned obliquely. In this preface, I have not omitted observations which pertain only to some of the authors. However, because of these and like distinctions, what follow are essays rather than chapters with an overarching argument. In addition, while there is nothing arbitrary about the authors included in this study, other American writings (for instance, Henry Thoreau's *Journal,* about which I have written elsewhere)[26] might have been examined here. Yet what inflects the writings I consider—as it does not, for instance, Thoreau's *Journal*—is a *resistance* to impersonality or the marshaling of strenuous arguments which anticipate others will resist it—as in Edwards's exorbitant demonstrations that ethics and common morality are irrelevant to true virtue. We see resistance in the form of equivocality in Emerson's "Experience," when subjectivity is marked as unique at the moment of its disappearance as unique. Thus when in "Experience," in yet another erosion of the distinction between the impersonal and the inhuman, Emerson triumphantly embraces the "constitutional necessity of seeing things under private aspects" ("yet is the God the native of these bleak rocks" [E 490]), we are offered an image of subjectivity ("bleak rocks") that does not look like subjectivity because it is indistinguishable from natural elements.

It may seem peculiar to gloss a seafaring tale by a classic text on urban modernity. But in "The Metropolis and the Mental Life," Georg Simmel's description of the metropolis and the money economy which generates "the blasé attitude ... an indifference toward the distinctions between things[,] not in the sense that they are not perceived, as in the case of mental dullness, but rather that the meaning and the value of the distinctions between things, and therewith of the things themselves, are experienced as meaningless," throws into relief a different relation between indistinction and affect in Melville's *Billy Budd.* In *Billy Budd* the hollowing out of "the core of things, their peculiarities, their specific values and their uniqueness and incomparability in a way which is beyond repair" does not lead to the blasé attitude, but rather leads to the sensational quality—the thrill—of Melville's prose.[27] However he might try ("This is to be wondered at. Yet not so much to be wondered at" [*BB* 86]), the narrator can't negate the sense of the marvelous he is continuously introducing by the penetrations of the prose which bore through facile impressions to something "deeper ... to the understanding of the essential in certain exceptional characters, whether evil ones or good" (*BB* 75). In addition, when Billy kills Claggart—when Billy departs from his own character in a Schopenhauerian annulment of individuality—there is a thrill for the reader in the sublime of Billy's not being intelligible as Billy. Thus it could be said that Billy's fist is like a stone flying through air—like "the flame from a discharged cannon at night" (*BB* 99)—exerting a will that is alien to his character in the sense that it can't be attributed to a form of knowingness, but not alien to his character in the sense that its force supplants intention and agency, arising in the place where agency was expected to be.

A thrill emerges in another context of near sublimity in Emerson's "Experience" when the most painfully intense property of a particular personal experience—dissociation ("it does not touch me")—migrates so that it is recognizable as the property of *all* experience independent of particularity. Thus what looked to have a set of determinants that arose specifically from a child's death becomes reunderstood as determinants with no exceptionality. For Weil, the thrill arises from the fact that attention could liberate being from personality—a thrill at the heart of Empson's fascination with Buddha faces.

How the alien characteristics of the personal and the impersonal conceptually come together in discrete representations is the subject of the following pages, which I call essays—because they are "provisional."[28] I begin with an introduction by way of William Empson—the literary critic whose lifelong fascination with contradiction had an intense and enduring focus in his writings on Buddha faces. Empson's capacity to anatomize countenances based on the human particular but simultaneously moving beyond its limits, marking a person's features so they are recognizable as discrete and also the point at which this recognizability is effaced—at once crystallizing individuality and the flow that undoes it—gives a face to the paradox whose features inflect the writings I consider. The second essay, on Jonathan Edwards's *The Nature of True Virtue*, considers a limit case in the other direction, since for Edwards no person could reflect self-transcendence. Essays on Emerson come next: the first is on "Experience," which identifies the recognitional moment when the elements characteristic of the most excruciating personal experience are discovered to be the elements characteristic of all experience; the second essay examines the idea of impersonality coincident with that discovery, as it differently arises in Emerson's other essays, in relation to the claim "If in the hours of clear reason, we should speak the truth, we should say that we had never made a sacrifice. In these hours...nothing can be taken from us that seems much. All loss, all pain, is particular; the universe remains to the heart unhurt."[29] Essays on Simone Weil's practice of impersonality and on T. S. Eliot's insistence in *Four Quartets* that experiences, reflections, voices become particularized to consciousness by not belonging to anyone at all, follow.

My book concludes with an essay on Melville's *Billy Budd*, the most taxing representation of impersonality and the culmination of my analysis. *Billy Budd* hollows out the core of individuality "in a way beyond repair" not because character is a linguistic concept and not because personal identity (in distinction to other phenomena) is understood as discontinuous, or interpretively illegible: these would be the deconstructive claims of *The Confidence Man* and *Benito Cereno*, respectively. Rather, in *Billy Budd*, the force beyond the social world of persons, unlike Arendt's absolutes—either the antipodes of a goodness beyond virtue and a wickedness beyond vice or the "radical evil" she located in a region beyond forgiveness and punishment alike[30]—is not specially circumstanced. The wonder of this force is its banal all-pervasiveness. In *Billy Budd* a neutral phenomenon like light, which is unremarkable, even unnoticeable, comes to be spellbinding not because of its essence, but rather because of its pervasiveness. This same pervasiveness also arises in relation to phenomena that are not naturally diffusive. The force in *Billy Budd* which engages "the realm of human affairs" but also transcends its distinctiveness, which cries out for judgment and disables any meaning judgment might have—represents the other extreme of Empson's Buddha faces, in that Empson saw incongruents like the personal and impersonal reconciled in a human image, and Melville did not.

Acknowledgments

"Representing Grief: Emerson's 'Experience' is reprinted from *Representations* 15 (Summer 1986): 15–42; "'The Way of Life by Abandonment': Emerson's Impersonal" is reprinted from *Critical Inquiry* 25 (Autumn 1998): 1–31; "The Practice of Attention: Simone Weil's Performance of Impersonality" is reprinted from *Critical Inquiry* 29 (Winter 2003): 216–52. "'The Way of Life by Abandonment': Emerson's Impersonal" was given as a lecture at Boston University, Dartmouth College, Stanford University, UCLA, and the University of Arizona. Under a different title, "'Lines of Stones': The Unpersonified Impersonal in Melville's *Billy Budd*" was given as a lecture at Barnard College, Johns Hopkins University, Princeton University, UCLA, the University of Arizona, the University of Michigan, the University of Notre Dame, and the University of Utah. I am grateful to the generous audiences for their questions and criticisms in the discussion periods and I would particularly like to thank Gregg Crane, Joseph Dimuro, Jeff Nunokawa, David O'Connor, and Fred Rush, for pressing me to clarify certain ideas in the Melville lecture.

I must also express my gratitude to readers whose thoughts about revision inform every page of the essays that follow: Amanda Anderson, Lindsley

Cameron, Elizabeth Falsey, Frances Ferguson, Allen Grossman, Deborah Kaplan, David Lawrence, Janet Malcolm, Walter Benn Michaels, Michael Moon, Ross Posnock, Christopher Ricks (for vigorously arguing with me about an early draft of the Eliot essay, which would still dismay him), Peter Sacks, Jerome Schneewind, Martin Stone, and Larzer Ziff. The manuscript is changed many times over in large and small ways by their suggestions. I owe a special acknowledgment to those who read the whole manuscript: to my colleague and friend Jonathan Goldberg, whose lucid mind repeatedly sharpened my way of seeing and saying things; to George Kateb, for bracing engagements with these essays; to Joan Dayan, for conversations about Melville which reoriented my thinking; to Eric Sundquist, for suggestions about the book's beginning; to Barry Weller, for his impeccable gift of lighting up error and imprecision; to Neil Hertz, whose associations to certain passages in the texts deepened my understanding of them. Finally, I thank Johns Hopkins University for granting me leave time, and my colleagues there over the years, whose commitment to intellectual life remains the gold standard.

Introduction by Way of
William Empson's Buddha Faces

i

Writing on the "fantastic" slowness of the Noh theatre, William Empson, who had lived in Japan and China during the 1930s, differentiated the "music of the Far East" from that of European music in these astonishing terms:

> Now the scientists seem to agree that we feel differently about rhythm according as it is slower or faster than a heartbeat, and nearly all European music goes faster than a heartbeat....I think it is true to say that European music is a much larger creature than Far Eastern music; it is the fresh air. But the fundamental difference in all these things goes back to the view taken of God and of the individual man. A rhythm quicker than the heartbeat is one that you seem to control, or that seems controlled by some person; the apparently vast field of our music is always...the individual speaking up. Music based on rhythms slower than the heartbeat...remains somehow impersonal. I only want to say here that you must take the music seriously as something that fits in with the whole story, and the story may well be the other half of the truth about the world.[1]

I begin with William Empson's characterization of impersonality as "the other half of the truth about the world" because of its largeness of outlook. Empson's fascination with Buddhism as "a viable alterative to the Christian-Sacrificial ethic of the West that he so deeply scorned"[2] did not arise from Buddhism's pessimism but from its credence in impersonality—the fact that Buddhist doctrine "does not believe in the individual" (*A* 534). Though Empson was quick to interject "I naturally would not want to present myself as a believer by mistake," his "respect," even admiration, for "the basic position" of Buddhism—which advocates self-abandonment—"needs to be remembered," Empson insisted, "when one tries to survey what the human mind could think about a subject" (*A* 600). Empson's own passion for that subject is manifested in his placement of the Fire Sermon[3] at the front of the *Complete Poems*; in his study of Buddhist iconography, which culminated in the completion of a monograph, *Asymmetry in Buddha Faces*;[4] and—in response to what he called the Buddhist "version of a death wish," based on the supposition that "no sort of temporal life whatever can satisfy the human spirit" and that "therefore...we must work for an existence outside time in whatever terms"—in Empson's rational assessment: "I doubt whether any process of analysis could show it to be wrong" (*A* 537). What appealed to Empson about Buddhism's denunciation of existence was its nonsentimental inclusion of "all existence...even in the highest heaven." "The coolness of Buddhism towards heaven, and towards the supernatural in general" (*A* 599)—specifically Buddhism's capacity "to remove *all* doctrinal props about immortality and still claim that death is somehow of the highest value" (*A* 536)—"gave fruit to millions of men" (*CP* 151). Empson elaborated:

> And this is what [the Fire Sermon] said, and it said, "Death, there is no other possible good thing but death," and it said that very clearly. The facts about the behaviour of men are very much stranger than they seem to us. And so it is important to say...that almost all the effects of the Fire Sermon were good effects. For example, hundreds of thousands of men have been burned while still living in the name of Jesus, and probably no man has been so burned in the name of Buddha. But the Buddha said things that gave much more reason for burning, much more hate of common living, much more poison, if you are looking at the simple words, than the words of Christ. But in fact they did no damage. As a question of history, where these words came they did good. (*CP* 151)

Empson's writings on the Far East also express enthusiasm at the idea of karma (the lawfulness of cause and effect minus the oppression of a "personal lawgiver" [A 598]); at the paradoxical notion that pleasure is not the antithesis of pain but is inseparable from it; at the nonexclusiveness of the Buddhist religion ("everyone might now aim at becoming a Buddha" [RB 37], in distinction to a Christian church which claimed to be "the only source of salvation" [RB 36]); and, most especially, as I have begun to discuss, at the idea of impersonality. In "Mr. Eliot and the East," Empson argued that Eliot's "stress on society and tradition rather than the individual...is not an argument for Christianity but for Buddhism" (A 568). When Empson remarked that death wishes in Buddhist doctrine are "trivial by comparison with the values which grow in their shadow" (A 544), it was ideas like these he had in mind.

Empson's capacity to make available his persistent sense of both the strangeness and the seduction of impersonality, as he encountered it in the music and doctrines of the Far East ("This is the teaching that went across all the east of Asia and by only touching a country made it strong" [CP 151])—his ability to contemplate its foreignness without domesticating, assimilating, or, conversely, rendering it exotic—is even more visible in the mixture of curiosity and powerful sympathy that vitalizes his descriptive analyses of Buddha faces, on which I pause in the following pages:

> The drooping eyelids of the great creatures are heavy with patience and suffering, and the subtle irony which offends us in their raised eyebrows...is in effect an appeal to us to feel, as they do, that it is odd that we let our desires subject us to so much torment in the world. The first thing to say about the Buddha face...is that the smile of superiority can mean and be felt to mean simply the power to help.
>
> The next thing, I think, about the stock type, is that it is the simplest conception of high divinity the human race has devised; people say it is monotonous, but there is a sort of democracy about its repetition....Anyone who cares about the Lord Buddha can do his face in a few ignorant strokes on sand or blotting paper, and among all the crude versions I have walked past I do not remember one that failed to give him his effect of eternity. It is done by the high brow, soaring outwards; by the long slit eye, almost shut in meditation, with a suggestion of a squint, that would be a frighteningly large eye if opened; and by a suggestion of the calm of childhood in the smooth lines of the mature face—a certain puppy quality in the

long ear helps to bring this out. If you get these they carry the main thought of the religion; for one thing the face is at once blind and all-seeing…so at once sufficient to itself and of universal charity. This essential formula for the face allows of great variety and is hardly more than a blank cheque, but one on a strong bank, so to speak. To my feeling a quite unrealistic Buddha is far more ready than a European head of Christ to be conceived as a real person in the room; as you sink into it you seem to know what it would feel like to have those extraordinary hands. (*A* 574)

The formula, which does not require skill to master, lingers on and, from successive vantages, penetrates the Buddha's eyes ("terrible," Empson remarks, "when the Buddha…once fully opens his eyes, as he takes his last look at his wife" [*A* 574]). What compels Empson's attention shifts from the "drooping eyelids…heavy with patience and suffering," to the raised eyebrows ("an appeal to us to feel" as he does), to "the long slit eye, almost shut in meditation," to the almost parenthetical speculation that the eye would be too large if opened, to Empson's reading in these half-closed eyes "the main thought of the religion." Although Empson does not immediately gloss the thought for which the paradox "blind and all-seeing" stands as foundation, the point is its comprehensiveness—at once "sufficient to itself and [indicative] of universal charity"—which would seem an inclusiveness that is an end point, but which marks two further forms of expansiveness not indebted to totality per se. There is first a shift from Empson's gaze at the figure's half-closed eyes to a presumptive seeing that those eyes see, a vision which has the effect of suffusing the icon with vitality so that it is like "a real person in the room." The second is a shift from seeing that the figure sees to penetrating what is seen, not as a vision but as a proprioceptive presence which sinks into the body, experienced from within. In "you seem to know what it would feel like to have those extraordinary hands," Empson intuits an animism which, in lieu of particularization, harks back to earlier articulations of the "extraordinary"—whether this is instantiated in the power of contentment, or which might be "simply the power to help," but which is first the capacity to feel "so much torment in the world" (*A* 574)—and which is also drawn forward into subsequent characterizations of the "extraordinary": "the archaic fixed smile" an "effect both of secure hold on strength and peace and of the humorous goodwill of complete understanding" (*A* 575). "What it would feel like to have those extraordinary hands" thus becomes a synecdoche for the manifestation of sentience everywhere—the antithesis of the lifelessness

Empson claims is conveyed by the stereotype (the "misunderstandings of a man in the street: that the Buddhas have no expression at all…or else that they all sneer" [*A* 573])—for an impersonality that, deriving from a formula, breathes being into the whole.

In the Pali suttas, whose doctrine I now examine briefly, the sentience Empson prized in Buddha faces is systematically uncoupled from individuality. Though Empson does not dwell on this aspect, the impersonality he idealized does not just come about; rather, it must be practiced. The practice prescribed by the suttas is a disidentification with perception and sensation. This disidentification, expressed most starkly in the imperative, *You will not be by that*, erodes the foundation of personal identity, since the relentless teaching of the suttas is that perception and sensation, though experientially inescapable, do not constitute a self.

In the Mahaparinibbana Sutta (The Great Passing, or The Buddha's Last Days),[5] which both William Empson and T. S. Eliot read in the translation by Henry Clarke Warren,[6] Ananda, the Buddha's servant,[7] gives voice to a grief that is also disseminated everywhere: "The Teacher is passing away, who was so compassionate to me!" (*DN* 265). But this narrative, which draws on conventions of mourning that mark the passing of a sacred figure[8]—descriptions whose punctuation is intelligible to us from other miraculous death narratives—grows perspectivally uncanny in the clarification of the Buddha's final instruction. The content of that teaching ("You should live as islands unto yourselves, being your own refuge…with the Dhamma…as a refuge" [*DN* 245]) is not "be self-sufficient," but rather a prescription to cultivate isolated conditions of practice in which to contemplate the four foundations of mindfulness[9]—the body, feelings, mind states, and objects of mind: "How does a monk live as an island unto himself,…with no other refuge?….A monk abides contemplating the body as body, earnestly, clearly aware, mindful…and likewise with regard to feelings, mind and mind-objects" (*DN* 245).

In the absence of distraction, one is able to discern the changing nature of bodily sensation and the contingent (nonautonomous) nature of bodily sensation (to see that nothing can arise alone without the support of other things on which its existence depends)[10]—that is, the nonsubstantive nature of bodily sensation. And similarly of feelings, mind states, and objects of mind.[11] Experienced rather than conceived, all are empty phenomena, whose insubstantiality could not constitute individuality. What body, feelings, mind states, and mind objects are empty of is personal identity. The reduction to sensation without thoughts that appropriate it (or a seeing through such thoughts) unsocializes perception so that its objects are particles—like driving rain, or snow on the television screen—nothing that could have meaning: "When…regarding things seen, heard, sensed, and cognized by you, in the seen there will be merely the seen, in the heard there will be merely the heard, in the sensed there will be merely the sensed, in the cognized there will be merely the cognized, then…you will not be 'by that.' When…you are not 'by that,' then you will not be 'therein.' When…you are not 'therein,' then you will be neither here nor beyond nor in between the two. This itself is the end of suffering" (*SN* 1175–76). Merely the seen, merely the heard, merely the thought deconstructs individuality so that a man, a woman, a living being might be a conventional or legal reality, but no longer an essential one, an extremity which reiterates its lack of compromise in "you will not be 'by that'…you will not be 'therein.'" Such an imperative declares the illegitimacy of identifying with, of assuming a possessive relation to, any sensation or perception, which, however experientially inescapable, is not self-constituting. Thus when the Buddha says about the four foundations of mindfulness, "This is the direct path for the purification of beings" (*MN* 155), he is advocating an immediate experience which demolishes the perception "I am" or "This is mine." Practice consists of repeating this disidentification over and over again. To be "your own island" is to discern virtually infinitesimal phenomena whose transience renders vacant such grammatical constructions.

Moreover, when in the Mahaparinibbana Sutta the Buddha consoles Ananda, saying, "Enough, Ananda, do not weep and wail! Have I not already told you that all things…are changeable, subject to separation and becoming other? So how could it be, Ananda—since whatever is born, become, compounded is subject to decay—how could it be that it should not pass away?" (*DN* 265), he seems to refer only to his impending death. But the instruction to "contemplate the body as the body"[12] so that "in the sensed there will be merely the sensed, in the heard…merely the heard" (Empson, commenting on such repetitions, wrote "If you put in all [of them]…it is a pretty appalling experience")[13] amplifies the reference to which "all things…are subject to change" pertains. After the Buddha's death, the refrain is echoed:

Those monks who had not yet overcome their passions wept and tore their hair, raising their arms, throwing themselves down and twisting and turning, crying…"the Well-Farer has passed away…the Eye of the World has disappeared!" But those monks who were free from craving endured mindfully and clearly aware, saying: "All compounded things are impermanent—what is the use of this?"...

There are sky-devas whose minds are earth-bound; they are weeping and tearing their hair...earth-devas...they do likewise. But those devas who are free from craving endure patiently, saying: "All compounded things are impermanent. What is the use of this?" (*DN* 272)

The reiteration, "All compounded things are impermanent," expresses not only an *ultimate* manifestation of the insubstantiality of self at death, but also, more unnervingly, an *immediate* manifestation of it revealed in the explanation of what it means to "comprehend" the impersonal nature of experience. In every moment of clear awareness, "You will not be 'by that'" (*SN* 1176).

The point of Buddhist doctrine—to which I return only briefly in the essay on Eliot—is its extremity as a model. But not a contrasting one. Although it might seem the case that passages from the suttas derive not only from a foreign culture, but also from a foreign vantage far exceeding any alienation of a Western analogue, the writing discussed in my essays argues to the contrary. Empson's fascination—congruent with his lifelong engagement with contradiction in general—with the incompatibilities of the Buddha features has a special pertinence to my discussion of impersonality. Impersonality (as a practice, as an ethic, as a representation), since it is undertaken by persons, could only be contradictory by definition. Moreover, Empson's repeated attempts to capture the Buddha expression reveal, as a defining insight, that the power of these icons does not issue from a depth, an autonomy, an interior, but from a fully visible presence whose enigma, and whose value, does not lie in its uniqueness.

"In so far...as you know that two things are opposites, you know a relation which connects them," William Empson wrote in *Seven Types of Ambiguity* of the final type,[14] whose "criterion" is "psychological" as well as logical (*ST* 192). Empson's tense, even compromised analysis of the seventh type—an impossibility that is possible, opposites that are inseparable—was founded on his eccentric refusal to grasp the paradox of Christianity. At the same time Empson generalized his perception: "The way in which a person lives by these vaguely-conceived opposites is the most important thing about his make-up" (*ST* 221).[15] In Empson's examination of Buddha faces the opposites had a specific focus:

The experts have tended to avoid talking about the expressions of the great Buddha heads, partly because the whole subject of faces is so little understood by science that one can only assert a personal impression....But the faces are magnificent; it is a strange confession of helplessness if we have to keep mum for fear of talking nonsense. I think there is a clear point to be made here which has been neglected by Western critics, a point that lets you understand and enjoy the statues better. It will be agreed that a good deal of the startling and compelling quality of these faces comes from their combining things that seem incompatible, especially a complete repose with an active power to help the worshipper. Now of course the two things must somehow be diffused through the whole face, or it would have no unity; the whole business is very subtle. But the normal way of getting the effect in the great periods is a reliable and simple one; the two incompatible things are largely separated onto the two sides of the face.[16]

While Empson's seventh type contained less an ambiguity than an insoluble contradiction, in the short 1936 "The Faces of the Buddha" (the piece that anticipated the now-lost *Asymmetry in Buddha Faces*), and in draft fragments for the latter, of which the above is a first paragraph, Empson asserted that in Buddha faces he saw the possibility of obtaining a commensurability of incongruents. Buddha faces, in their representation of human features, both relied on the category of the person and, in the "magnificen[ce]" associated with the integration of global polarities,[17] simultaneously implied the transcendence of this category: a person who is like a person but not a person, what Weil would call an "impersonal person." What drew Empson to Buddha faces (as to the masks of the Noh stage to which Masaharu Anesaki suggested he compare them) was the way in which "the faces were constructed to wear two expressions" (in the case of the Noh masks) and to harmonize contradictory senses (in the case of the Buddha statues), contradictions made mysterious for being "diffused" into a "unity." Writing of the "after-dinner look of many Buddhas, and the rings of fat on the neck," Empson explained as follows: "An idea that you must be somehow satisfied as well as mortified before entering repose goes deep into the system, and perhaps into human life" (*A* 573).

In the following passage from the *Asymmetry* manuscript Empson moves from contemplation of human features to the contemplation of Buddha features (an inclusiveness that the previous quotation demonstrates in the reverse order). Describing the feature of the lips, with their "sharp (nearly rectangular) curved edges" as "the nearest thing in the body to the geometrical edges of the butterfly and the flower—that are their chief beauty," Empson marvels: "But what forces determine the actual curves, what conceivable convenience of biology made them exist and made us able to interpret them, I do not know that anyone has explained" (bMS). Shifting from general reflections on desire's manifestation[18] on the appearance of the lips to these embodied ones, the passage continues:

> Even the sense in which these forces can be called unconscious seems doubtful; a life driven by desire kept unconscious and therefore perverted produces dull lips, while a life tormented by desire consciously admitted as such but denied...produces a grey face with swollen dull-scarlet lips like a wound, not far from the purple bruised lips of the morning after drinking. This shocking effect is not on the typical monk's lips, red as they are, but I really cannot pretend to know the full effects on the human face either of the love of God or of the queerer forms of universal love sanctioned by Mahayana Buddhism. The normal late Buddha's lips of course are the plump but sharply defined lips of a full and well-organized satisfaction. (bMS)

The description of the Buddha's lips seems to isolate them as at once the most neutral embodiments of the generic features described in the paragraph, and, as a consequence of its placement at the end of a sequence which includes a range of representations of sensuality and its effacement—an effacement which the Buddha's contented expression implies he has passed through and passed beyond—also the most mysterious. Desire which is repressed, desire which is acknowledged but not indulged (however it might look like desire that has been sated: "swollen dull-scarlet lips...not far from the purple bruised lips of the morning after drinking"), and desire that has been evacuated ("the typical monk's lips, red as they are") each signal desire's negation—to which the Buddha's lips are described as the colorless antithesis. The Buddha visage is enigmatic because, against type, the Buddha has surrendered not desire as such, but rather the pain of its torment. His expression is an antidote to the singular appearances of desire requiring management. If the Buddha is an example, it is by his capacity to feel not less but rather more. The visage reflects desire's enlargement ("the queerer forms of universal love") or transmutation. This inclusiveness is extended in another direction by a formal echo[19] which connects the Buddha with the inhuman forms of beauty in the butterfly and flower. While "satisfaction" would seem a deepening of the personal, the implicit likening of the Buddha's appearance to nonhuman, geometrical forms of beauty is, rather, contributive to its erasure.

In the left margin of the page I have been discussing—and horizontally between its typed lines—Empson added in handwriting these elaborative details:

> The upper lip of the young seems to pass across a low ridge of fat that rises sideways along the zygomatic: any habitual "setting" of the muscles takes it away. One might say that the swelling above (lifted to suck) is infantile—vegetable creatures sucking through the stalk of the lotus, swelling below (sagging with overdevelopment) sensual, and that "the short but proudly breathed" lip...has a relic of the lift of the snarl, mixed inextricably with the raised curl of laughter and acceptance—The whole effect heart-centered as against the belly-centered mouth of pouting and repose. But here it is a matter of muscles: it is clear that muscles, whether conscious or not, do not shape the actual lip edge. I suspect that the "dimple" under the end of lips held back in conscious childishness is in part imitating with muscles what in itself is a more mysterious product of tissues. (bMS)

This passage, which at first seems to be working out the typology of a feature ("the upper lip of the young"), subsequently glosses the typescript: the lips are at once "infantile" and "sensual." In its further comparison ("the whole effect heart-centered as against the belly-centered mouth of pouting and repose"), the draft juxtaposes the lips of the representation Empson has been anatomizing to those of a second icon which is not fully discrete from it, in that both share a formula. In this passage, as typically in Empson's considerations, a figure's singularity is revealed through a comparison, even as it is hard to keep the contrasted expressions isolated, because the features of both—the lips—are characteristically distinguished by the same oppositional structure, which implies as included all the states between each of the poles.[20] Thus, in the shifting variations that constitute the type, there is an elasticity, even a mobility, attributed to a form that is in fact solid and fixed. In this way Empson treats as one expressions that are contrasted *within* the Buddha image to expressions that are constituted *among* the Buddha images. The representations in Empson's passages repeatedly suggest icons whose particularity does not constitute individuality and whose iconic status is not compromised by variation:

> The formula leaves much of the face free. The nose can do what it likes, and is used for anything between childishness, sensuality, and administrative power. The mouth can do what it likes, and varies from a rich sensual repose to the strained tight-lipped alert smile seen on flying aces and archaic Greek sculpture....The point about the archaic fixed smile, on Buddhas or elsewhere, is that it would be made by a pull on the main zygomatic, the muscle most under conscious control, leaving the others at rest; thus it is an easy way to make a statue look socially conscious, willful, alert. Many of the Chinese Buddhas from the Yun-kang caves, the earliest period, get a strong effect from using this quite flatly....But you have only to sink the ends into the cheeks to give it an ironical or complacent character, and my example from Yun-kang, almost winking as it is, gets, I think, with these simple means, an extraordinary effect both of secure hold on strength and peace and of the humorous goodwill of complete understanding....In the Chuguji [example], who will also when he is born bring a new revelation, it is rather the older convention for the mouth, toned down and with a couple of ripples in the smooth wood, that gives all that lightness and tenderness which will at any moment brush away the present universe as an unwise dream. (*A* 575)

Implicit, though not discussed, in Empson's passages is the idea that these representations in wood and stone of an impersonal presence could have meaning only if they were more than formal expressions, if their expressions were presumed to correspond, at a depth or within an interior, to practiced understandings. Thus although Empson acknowledges that "a face, granting it says something about character, may tell a lie" (bMS), such a disparity cannot apply to Buddha features, which could have value only if they were commensurate with a truth that was indisputable, incapable of mendacity. But if behind Buddha expressions Empson supposes a *person's* lived relation to a formal surface (though not a person's hypocrisy), the attainments indicated by those expressions transgress a *person's* limits. As a consequence of this contradiction, the closer Empson gets to the face he describes, the more distant he is from the mysteriousness of the presence—a discrepancy magnified by the fact that, however rigorously he might anatomize the features of the Buddha's lips, he has no access to the Buddha's eyes, which are closed to scrutiny. In the absence of access to the eyes, the mouth assumes the expressive crisis.[21]

I have dwelled so long on these passages of Empson's because their writing allows me to clarify—without prerehearsing the arguments specific to the essays that follow—a subjectivity that isn't a subjectivity, a person who is impersonal or who aims, though cannot will, to be so;[22] or who discovers the inevitability of being so; or who represents the inconsequence of personality before a force that leaves personality intact but, notwithstanding its persuasive outlines, in effect always trivial. But if Empson's Buddha faces expose certain elements in the representation of an impersonal person, they consistently omit this one: In the icons Empson describes, the "passive power" affiliated with the incompatibilities diffused throughout the Buddha face is never linked to violence. Buddha expressions bear no traces of violence—violence being the antithesis of, the one contradictory feature exempted from, the constellated peace of which the Buddha is the image. By comparison, as my essays indicate, when persons are represented in relation to a force that effaces what individuates them, their surrender to that power (which, in its destructive wake, lays bare inner states to which Buddha "expressions" are congruent) is directly linked to violence, as Weil and Melville most extremely demonstrate.

ii

One way of understanding the contradictory double-edged phenomenon of impersonality in the writings I consider is in terms of Terry Eagleton's *Ideology of the Aesthetic*, whose origins he locates in the Enlightenment project of "refashioning the human subject from inside" by a "law which is not a law"[23] because it is self-prescribed and self-legitimating, so as to give experience and perception autonomy from abstract universal reason. The aesthetic is a reunderstanding of subjectivity in that the individual obeys an inner law, not an external power, even as "the liberated subject is the one who has appropriated the law as the very principle of its own autonomy" (*IA* 19). Although Eagleton emphasizes the versatility of his formula—for Kant the aesthetic is a way of universalizing subjectivity;[24] for Schopenhauer it is a way of "demolishing subjectivity"[25]—Eagleton's "aesthetic," as with the training of ancient philosophers and Buddhist practitioners, is a term that consistently refers to the realm of perception, intuition, sensation, in distinction to the realm of abstract thought. The aesthetic "signifies a creative turn to the sensuous body, as well as an inscribing of that body with a subtly oppressive law; it represents on the one hand a liberatory concern with concrete particularity, and on the other hand a specious form of universalism" (*IA* 9). For the authors I consider, however, this ingraining of the impersonal—in its lived perception—would not make it specious.[26]

The difference between Eagleton's aesthetic and the imperative of a law that is understood to be empirically other is clarified by an essay of Kant's, "What Does It Mean to Orient Oneself in Thinking?" (1786),[27] in which Kant rehearses what it means to orient oneself geographically ("literally to find the sunrise...to use a given direction to find the other ones [8]...through a subjective ground of differentiation" [9]), mathematically (how to one orient oneself in space in a dark room [9]), and finally "logically...in thinking in general" (in relation to what *cannot* be experienced or known—the supersensible—where "there are no objects of intuition, only the space for intuition" [9]). Kant's idea of orientation makes difference as such inseparable from the subjective ground that perceives it. Thus he writes of orientation *within* the bounds of experience:

> Even with all the objective data of the sky, I orient myself *geographically* only through a *subjective* ground of differentiation; and if all the constellations, though keeping the same shape and position relative to one another, were one day by a miracle to be reversed in their direction, so that what was east now became west, no human eye would notice the slightest alteration on the next bright starlit night, and even the astronomer—if he pays attention only to what he sees and not to what he feels would inevitably become *disoriented*. But in fact the faculty of making distinctions through the feeling of right and left comes naturally to his aid...[and] he will be able not only to notice the alteration which has taken place, but in spite of it he will also be able to orient himself. (9)

Right and left are subjective differences for which no empirical marks can be given. The relative positions of the fingers on the right hand and on the left hand are identical, except that one points right and the other left. Yet we know right and left: we feel the difference between them. Therefore, for Kant orientation depends on the faculty of distinguishing difference "without the need of any difference in the objects" (8).

When orientation is required beyond empirical bounds, specifically in relation to the concept of limitlessness, to which no experience or intuition could be adequate, "There enters *the right* of reason's *need*, as a subjective ground for presupposing and assuming something which reason may not presume to know through objective grounds; and consequently for *orienting* itself in thinking, solely through reason's own need, in that immeasurable space of the supersensible, which for us is filled with dark night" (10). Kant's point is that the idea of a limitless being—a God—is the one necessary presupposition which would make sense of "all limited beings, hence of all other things" (11). Therefore "the concept of a first original being" (11), which cannot be known theoretically, is necessary for practical reason as a condition of the moral endeavor. When you orient yourself in thinking, as when you orient yourself in relation to objects of experience, you also rely only on a subjective feeling of difference, though in the first case feeling pertains to an empirical realm and in the second case feeling is induced a priori by the imperative of a moral law which precedes it.[28] That is what orienting oneself in thinking means for Kant. The moral feeling—the closest we can get to limitlessness—is subjective because nothing in perception corresponds to it. Yet the moral feeling allows us to find a difference between virtuous and vicious action—as the feeling of left and right, and of east and west, allows us to find our direction, even though there is no empirical difference between the two. Difference for us is a feeling, not a transcendent intuition of an objective or knowable opposition.

Nothing could be further from the orientation to difference in the writings considered in the following pages. For Edwards, Emerson, Melville, Weil, and Eliot there is no "dark night" that could be brightened by any subjective *feeling* of difference, or by any subjective pointer of moral feeling. In the writings of these authors, the subjective isn't a brightness. Rather, the perception of difference, of polarity—in its most extreme form, of contradiction—is a means of emerging from a point of view.

In the Empson Papers in Houghton Library are reproductions of Buddha faces on postcards and posters that Empson collected from Europe and the Far East. In the collection are photographs of Buddha statues that Empson—experimenting with the idea that "a good deal of the startling and compelling quality" of Buddha faces comes from their "combining things that seem incompatible"—doctored. Empson secured two photographic prints of each Buddha face—one reversed, the mirror image of the other. He cut these two faces down the center and arranged the matching halves so that the mirror halves formed a single image. From a single original photograph, he thus produced two images, now quite different from each other, each symmetrical, with the left and right sides of the face identical. Placed side by side, these two faces seem not only "constructed to wear different expressions" but also to derive from different countenances, from figures so unlike as to have no commonness between them. Then—illustrating that the two sides we might assume to be identical in the Buddha face are not in fact identical—Empson repeated this procedure with a second photograph of another Buddha face, which (splitting and duplicating its halves) he showed also to be self-different.

In one image of one of the doctored pairs (see figure 1),[29] a hand is raised; its thumb and index and middle fingers are lifted. The middle finger grazes the face to the side of the upper lip. But this stylized gesture—duplicated by Empson so that two hands frame each side of the face—transforms the impersonal mudra the gesture was meant to represent into a parody insinuating self-reference. The smile is full and handsome. (Empson wrote of a different figure that "its very subtle mouth" lent it "a somewhat foxy elegance" [*A* 575]). In the companion image (see figure 2)[30]—except for darkened eyebrows—the features are inconspicuous. The arms hang demurely downward. The cheeks are babyish. The mouth is thin and sweet. Among the Empson Papers, there is no representation of the original images from which Empson constructed these amalgamations.

In *First and Last Notebooks*, Weil wrote: "God has no word for saying to his creature: I hate you. But the creature has words for saying 'I hate you' to God. In a sense the creature is more powerful than God. It can hate God and God cannot hate it in return. This impotence makes him an impersonal Person. He loves, not as I love, but as an emerald is green. He *is* 'I love.' And I too, if I were in the state of perfection, would love as an emerald is green. I would be an impersonal person."[31] The representations I consider do not, however, depict impersonality in terms of a single element—not "as an emerald is green"—but rather in terms of oppositions. Harmony, Weil wrote, is entirely the product of contraries: "The things which are like and related are not in any need of harmony; but the things which are unlike and unrelated and of a different order necessarily require to be locked up together under the key of a harmony that is able to contain them."[32] For this reason, contradictions are "openings into the transcendent; they are like doors on which one must knock again and again" (*FL* 269). Unlike Kant's contraries (the feeling of left and right, the feeling of east and west, the feeling of virtuous and vicious action, the feeling

FIGURE 1. Untitled photograph, William Empson Papers (pf MS Eng 1401 [1151]). By permission of the Houghton Library, Harvard University.

of a limitless being induced a priori by the imperative of a moral law to make sense of limited beings)—the point being for Kant an orientation that arises contingent on the faculty of distinguishing difference without any need of difference in the objects—orientation in the authors I consider is not contingent on a set of oppositions that are subjectively generated. Yet to say this is not to predicate a formula whereby the origin or even the operative arena of such differences is readily perceptible. The most difficult case is that of *Billy Budd*. In *Billy Budd* the antithetical elements constitutive of the personal and the impersonal are not absolutely separated (as in Edwards's treatise), or eventually integrated (as in Emerson's "Experience"). And they are not

FIGURE 2. Untitled photograph, William Empson Papers (pf MS Eng 1401 [1151]). By permission of the Houghton Library, Harvard University.

related by that conversion Emerson called "ravishment"[33] (as Emerson, Weil, and Eliot differently exemplify it). They thus have the effect of suffusing each other without changing each other, as in Empson's faces.

In a passage from the 1937 article "Ballet of the Far East," in which Empson compared Western music ("faster than a heartbeat") to Far Eastern music ("slower than a heartbeat"), he also described Noh and Kabuki theater, which he understood as a form of dancing: "when you know the plot you can see the performance as ballet" (*A* 578). Of Kabuki drama he wrote:

The music tends to be quicker than in Noh…though it keeps getting back to the slow beat. The performance is made up of single scenes from enormous plays that everybody knows already…a quite different attitude to the stage from ours. It would be amusing to make up an evening from bits of *Hamlet*, *The Dynasts*, *School for Scandal*, *Oedipus* in Greek, and *Charley's Aunt*, but it would not go well. We would want to go on sympathising with particular characters; we would want to know the end of the story. The characters in a Far Eastern play are not even what we call "types," far less individuals. It is the situation that is typical. The situation often happens in real life, and a play about it is therefore real, and may be very moving. But in real life the situation ends in all sorts of ways, and you are not much interested in the way *this* one ended. Why should you be, when the individuals who happen to be in it are not the important thing? (*A* 579)

Contributing to the features that render individuals "not the important thing" are the miscellaneous quality of scenes which are arranged together without concern for unity, the grating effect the plays intentionally have on the nerves ("There are long squalling noises that hold you up during the wait for the next beat, and at last the beat comes with a snap, as if you had stretched an elastic till it broke" [*A* 578]), the presumed incommensurability of outcome to narrative and dramatic interest ("Japanese dance never finishes a story" [*A* 580]), a theory of tragedy shocking (for Westerners) to contemplate (in Noh plays "the tragic thing…is not being able to die enough" [*A* 579]), and a distribution of conditions in which "violent forces of life in the action" set against "the ideal of death…in the words" are also juxtaposed to steps "so near to actual casual movement" that they seem uncalculated (*A* 580). Such amalgamations (constellations of inequivalent elements assimilated to each other) were aggregates that both enticed and appalled Empson[34]—amalgamation or aggregation being an alternative not simply to individuality, but also to the oppositional logic of the contradictions he wrote about unceasingly.

Amalgamations were also forms Empson constructed. In his fable *The Royal Beast*, begun in 1937 (and never completed), contemporary with his writings on Buddha faces, Empson invented a race he called Wurroos—"a group of newly-discovered African mutants—rational creatures with the characters of sub-human primates" (*RB* 26), whose chief representative is named Wuzzoo. The Wurroos are not men, and they refuse to be classified as men even though George, the British official in the African colony to whom Wuzzoo appears, warns him: "If you are men a man cannot kill you for pleasure; but if you are not men, and you do not belong to some man, if you are not some man's animal, then any man can come and shoot you with a gun and kill you. And they will want your fur, because it is very nice fur.... They will all come with guns and kill you and take your fur.... And if you are not men nobody can stop them" (*RB* 145).[35]

The appearance of the Wurroos on the human planet "disturbs the cosiness of the universe," because "if there are other intelligent creatures...we can't feel it's all arranged for us" (*RB* 161). Although Empson's fable specifically challenges the "smugness" (*RB* 33) of the idea that earth is assumed "to be the only habitable planet so that Christ could be unique" (*RB* 161), I conclude my discussion of Empson with the examination of a passage in which a different concern arises: Is a Wurroo a person, a good person, that kind of person who is an angel (an epithet with which Mary, the superintendent's wife, compliments Wuzzoo), or some other kind of rational creature who, not a person at all, does not deserve rights?

The questions What is a person? and What are the assumptions of persons about one another? specifically, What are the implications of estimating a person to be "unique," individual (sufficiently—or insufficiently—like oneself)? echo throughout Empson's fable. When Mary, the British official's wife, calls Wuzzoo an angel, she has been regarding him as an "agreeable...large dog in the room." But then she tells Wuzzoo—speaking *to* him, but also *of* him as if he were *not* in the room—she has a flash of insight: "When you see the eyes suddenly, you jump because they are not less than human, they are much more. It is an angel in the room...that was what made me jump" (*RB* 164). Wuzzoo is in fact dismayed at the designation "angel." He calls it "real bad news." This is the bad news:

> "If you just call me an angel like you might call a spaniel an angel, I am very pleased to have people pat me on the head. Because that might be important. But you mustn't mean I have got spiritual heights. It really isn't just a matter of dogma. You have got all the spiritual heights in the human race and all the spiritual depths too; that is why you are so cruel....We are very flat kind of people beside you....And it is very frightening if you start to call us angels, that is just what we want to avoid.... Your eyes are frightening me at this minute quite as much as mine can have frightened you," he said steadily. "You feel I am unnatural, and you are a generous-minded girl so you turn it into calling me an angel....But I fancy I see a war of extermination behind the awe in your eyes." (*RB* 164–66)

In his writing of the 1930s Empson is deliberating the features of Buddha figures and of creatures like the Wurroo—who are like persons but not persons, and also not like one another. What the Buddha and the Wurroo put in question is a set of presumptions about identifying, judging, valuing—a set of beliefs about human value, about the value of being human. When persons elevate and demote other creatures ("angel…animal") or other human beings ("the kind of person who is an angel") or their own being—no less compromised by idealization—they are in the grip of "an unwise dream."[36] In the eyes of the Wurroo such a dream is an illusion, composed of imaginary "heights" and "depths" which, if disassembled—if, in Wuzzoo's language, flattened—would leave in its wake rationality without cruelty and, in the case of Buddhas, mildness without sentimentality ("the humorous good will of complete understanding"). It is the Buddha's eyes of course into which Empson can't directly see. But he can see into the eyes of his creature Wuzzoo, who, less than a person—as the Buddha is more than a person (such comparatives being virtually inseparable from thinking)—nonetheless sees, as the Buddha does, with even neutrality. If one looked into the eyes of such a "flat" creature when *he* was looking into the eyes of a person—as the undisclosed vision Mary has of Wuzzoo's eyes looking at her invites us to do—one would see not a vacancy but an omission: a gaze from which "the awe" and (behind it) the "extermination" were missing.

2

What Counts as Love:
Jonathan Edwards's *True Virtue*

Jonathan Edwards concludes the notes he titled "Of Being" with this remarkable passage:

> When we go about to form an idea of perfect nothing we must shut out all…things. We must shut out of our minds both space that has something in it, and space that has nothing in it. We must not allow ourselves to think of the least part of space, never so small, nor must we suffer our thoughts to take sanctuary in a mathematical point. When we go to expel body out of our thoughts, we must be sure not to leave empty space in the room of it; and when we go to expel emptiness from our thoughts we must not think to squeeze it out by anything close, hard and solid, but we must think of the same that the sleeping rocks dream of; and not till then shall we have a complete idea of nothing….
>
> When we go to inquire whether or no there can be absolutely nothing we speak nonsense….There is no other way, but only for there to be existence; there is no such thing as absolute nothing. There is such a thing as nothing with respect to this ink and paper. There is such a thing as nothing with respect to you and me. There is such a thing as nothing with respect

to this globe of earth, and with respect to this created universe....But there is no such thing as nothing with respect to entity or being, absolutely considered.[1]

Edwards had no more passionate subject than this concern with "Being" to which his writings persistently return. Only God has continuous Being; all else is "*dependent* identity."[2] So much is our being dependent on an "*arbitrary* constitution of the Creator" (*W* 3:403) that "God's *preserving* created things in being is perfectly equivalent to a *continued creation*, or to his creating those things out of nothing at *each moment* of their existence" (*W* 3:401). In Edwards's account, "the present existence" of any "created substance, cannot be an effect of its past existence....The prior existence can no more be the proper cause of the new existence, in the next moment, or next part of space, than if it had been in an age before, or at a thousand miles distance, without any existence to fill up the intermediate time or space" (*W* 3:400–401). With respect to persons (or, in Edwards's nondiscriminating examples, with respect to the body of the moon), which "can't be the effect of [their] existence at the last foregoing moment" (*W* 3:400), Edwards reiterates: "The *antecedent existence* is nothing....God produces the effect as much from *nothing*, as if there had been nothing *before*" (*W* 3:402).[3]

Assuming that this "nothing" is not just a figure of speech—and Edwards does assume that, since the hypothetical "as if there had been nothing *before*" pertains to the fact that the something the person mistakes for himself *did* exist before, not to the certainty of the annihilation and recreation—it is difficult to see the mechanics of existing and then being nothing. Specifically, it is not clear what being nothing means if you get to be the same after you are vitalized again, just as it is difficult to understand whether there is a space between moments of being nothing and moments of existing, or to know whether every moment of creation is also a moment of annihilation. These are nice distinctions which Edwards does not treat. But in saying that God creates persons out of nothing, Edwards is not contradicting his earlier claim in the sleeping-rocks passage that "there is no such thing as nothing with respect to entity or being, absolutely considered," for in both cases there is only nothing with respect to entities like you and me.[4]

Moreover, in an annihilation thought experiment, Edwards, in "The Mind," insists, contra Locke, that the same memory is not equivalent to the same identity: "It is possible without doubt...for God to annihilate me, and after my annihilation to create another being that shall have the same ideas in his mind that I have, and with the like apprehension that he had had them before in like manner as a person has by memory; and yet I be in no way concerned in it, having no reason to fear what that being shall suffer, or to hope for what he shall enjoy.... Will anyone say that he, in such a case, is the same person with me, when I know nothing of his sufferings and am never the better for his joys?" (*W* 6:386). In addition, God can regulate what belongs to personal identity—he can treat Adam as one with the generations that come after him,[5] just as he can treat you as identical with yourself from one successive moment to another—since identity is not a natural phenomenon, is not connected to an antecedent existence, but is rather arbitrarily constructed from without.[6]

The implications are radical: A person may seem continuous with himself, but he is not continuous. For if existence is created anew in each successive moment, he (or the newly created substance) is "absolutely considered, not the same with any past existence.... There is no identity or oneness in the case" (*W* 3:402–3). No more identity, Edwards elaborates, than wind which blows now is the same as that which blew a moment before, or than water which flows in front of us is the same as water which flowed past the moment before. No more is a person the same from one moment to the next—even though the Creator "*treats them as one*, by" each moment "communicating to them like properties, relations and circumstances" (*W* 3:403)—than images in a mirror are the same from moment to moment: "the colors constantly vanishing as fast as put on. And the new images being put on *immediately* or instantly, don't make 'em the same, any more than if it were done with an intermission of an hour or a day" (*W* 3:403).

But while, as these passages extravagantly illustrate, there is no such thing as personal identity constituted from within, the amount of being to which persons have access *can* be increased through "an enlargement of the heart," as Edwards crucially goes on to emphasize. In *Charity and Its Fruits* and *The Nature of True Virtue* (Edwards's last work),[7] Edwards called this "enlargement of the heart"—this capacity for more being—"happiness." What allows for the "enlargement of the heart whereby self takes in existence in general" (*W* 8:551) is a recognition of the limited nature of the personal and—with regard to one's being immediately produced out of nothing at each moment (*W* 3:402)—the illusory nature of the personal, a recognition that expresses itself, or would, were it possible, as love without particularity. *True Virtue* called such love being's consent to "Being in general" (*W* 8:540).[8] *Charity and Its Fruits* puts it in these terms:

You should not seek your own things only, for you are not your own. You have not made yourself, nor are you made for yourself; you are neither the author or end of your being. Nor is it you that uphold yourself in being nor is it you that provides for yourself; you are not dependent on yourself....If you do not seek your own but the things of Jesus Christ, the things of others, God will make your interest and happiness his charge....So that not to seek your own, that is, not to seek your private worldly interest, is the best way of seeking your own in another sense. It is the most direct course you can take to obtain your truest happiness. (*W* 8:268–69)

True Virtue elaborates:

Self-love may be taken for the same as...a man's love of his own happiness. Which is short, and may be thought very plain: but indeed is an ambiguous definition, as the pronoun "his own" is equivocal, and liable to be taken in two very different senses. For a man's "own happiness" may either be taken universally, for all the happiness or pleasure which the mind is in any regard the subject of...or it may be taken for the pleasure a man takes in his own proper, private, and separate good. And so "self-love" may be taken two ways. (*W* 8:575)

In the passages above Edwards seems to be distinguishing between the selfish and the altruistic. But to subordinate man's happiness "taken universally" to one's "private...good" is not merely to misread greater and lesser happiness. It is also to mistake the fact that one is an independent entity who could seek and love anything properly called one's own.

In the following pages I shall be examining not only what counts as being but also what counts as love in *True Virtue*. In that treatise these questions are not fully separable. Initially it looks as if, with reference to Edwards's claims about identity as supernaturally constructed, personal identity is nothing but an effect of God's continued creation, and hence could only be threatened by the latter's cessation. I shall suggest, however, that personal identity is as deeply challenged by ideal love (one's own happiness taken universally). On the one hand, in Edwards's claim that we have no identity independent of God's moment-by-moment recreation of us there is a kind of failure of personal identity. On the other hand, in the ideal of one's own happiness taken universally, which would constitute "true virtue," there is a transcendence of personal identity. For when Edwards claims that we can't love without particularity—the force of this claim is not that we are not up to loving a certain way (because it is difficult to imitate Christ), but that we can't love this way categorically, in principle because we are persons. Edwards is not only saying it is hard to love your neighbor as yourself or (with respect to Christ's dictate) to love others "as I have loved you." The truly hard part of Edwards's theory does not focus on a psychological problem (how can we have feelings for this one as well as for that one?) or an ethical problem (how can we have the same kinds of feelings for this one as for that one?), but on a metaphysical problem. To call the problem psychological or ethical is to see it as possible to rectify. To call the problem metaphysical is to see that "true virtue"—the very thing we are enjoined to cultivate—is unavailable to persons. For a person, to love all equally would be not to love at all.

In part 1 of the following pages I examine the criteria for valuing from an impersonal perspective—a perspective which Edwards describes in *True Virtue* as what is viewed through "the eyes of him that perfectly sees all things as they are" (*W* 8:561). When Edwards establishes criteria for valuing from an absolute perspective he posits two incompatible formulas: one in which beings are equal and one in which some beings have more value than others and hence deserve more love. Although Edwards is committed to an idealist perspective, he can speak only theoretically from such a perspective, because an absolute or impersonal perspective is no perspective at all. In part 2 I consider whether we can correct errors of valuing in which we confuse lesser with greater being and persons with real substances. In Edwards's other works one can rectify such mistakes, can see with self-transcendence. By distinction, *True Virtue* insists there is no access to impersonal love except deductively. Thus *True Virtue* can't acknowledge what Edwards's other works make overt: that self-transcendence has a "taste" and an "intuitive" sense. In wording it in terms of an imperative—Edwards can't acknowledge self-transcendence—I am pointing to a motivated impediment, for Edwards is committed to negating a freedom from delusion that would enable persons to emerge from category mistakes. Thus *True Virtue* repeatedly reduces all things to self-love and allows no things to altruism. To acknowledge an experiential ground for adequate love would be to renege on the diminished sense of what is possible for persons, a sense that underscores every part of this treatise.[9] In part 3 I argue that for the Edwards of *True Virtue* calculation demonstrates the ability to reveal absolute formulas that persons cannot figure juxtaposed to relative formulas which they figure incorrectly. Part 4 considers how *discriminating* (a signal feature that typifies perception in

Edwards's other writings) is connected to *calculating* in Edwards's last work. I conclude in part 5 by considering an uncharacteristic example of Edwards's perception of the value—hence of the beauty—of the person as such.

Before I proceed, however, I wish to return to the sleeping-rocks passage. How does Edwards know what sleeping rocks dream of ? How does he get his mind in a position to articulate that particular object of contemplation as a possible object, while insisting we acknowledge the contours of its negation? In posing that question I mean to suggest that Edwards's propensity to inhabit states of consciousness identified as mistaken creates an authority about something for which there can be no authority, in the sense that Edwards claims that what he would have us entertain is impossible to entertain. Such authority issues from the conjunction of imperatives ("we must not allow") aligned with certainties ("there is no other way…there is no such thing"), along with inhabited impossibilities and counterassertions ("there is such a thing as…such a thing as…") with their progressively expansive objects ("this ink and paper…you and me…this globe of earth" [*W* 6:206–7]), and from the disarming inclusion of writer and reader among the additive nothings. Moreover, Edwards charts stages of unimaginability, moving us from the point at which the idea of nothing could be countenanced to the point at which absolute blockage suggests it cannot. It is just this compilation of a set of instructions for emptying thinking of all existents (first dispensing with the body, then with empty space, then with emptiness itself in a fleetingly graphic suggestion of bodily elimination for accomplishing emptying, which, since what is being expelled is emptiness from thoughts, is simultaneously suggestive of nothing at all) that delivers us to a state in which we are prepared to think of the same thing that sleeping rocks dream of. It is Edwards's point to bring us up against the experience of this impossibility. Edwards is deliberately positing a condition contrary to any person's capacity to imagine it—rocks being inanimate (hence insusceptible of change of state, unable to sleep) and also lacking consciousness (hence unable to dream). Edwards makes the nothing that cannot be imagined available to imagining. But he makes it available through a limit case before which we must remain on the near side of the limit.[10]

Yet Edwards's promise to make available some elusive but provocative absolute ("perfect nothing"/"Being in general")—to provide a set of procedures for its realization—holds his readers in a balance of expectation. We are asked to suppose that rocks have consciousness (but only when they dream), that, outside of our conceptions of rocks as insentient, there is some plausible world, animated by God, in which rocks *could* dream. The appeal of this attribution of consciousness to rocks (which don't know they have consciousness) lies largely in the implicit analogy we are invited to make to our own state. We think we know what rocks are (that they don't have consciousness) as we think we know what we are (that our consciousness or our personal identity defines us), but it might turn out that we, like the rocks, are rather truly identified by a set of conditions properly *extrinsic* to anything we could know, to which Edwards's writing opens out. The intrigue of the writing is Edwards's capacity to inhabit both positions, what sleeping rocks dream of being at once a mistake about what can be said about rocks and what can be said about persons' capacity to imagine rocks, and a mistake fleetingly deliberated as susceptible to rectification by virtue of the very language that insists on its inevitability.

i

The error of private affection is that it supposes an essential difference among persons.[11] This is to imply that some persons are more worthy in their individuality to be valued than others. In distinction, "true virtue most essentially consists in benevolence to Being in general....It is that consent, propensity, and union of heart...that is immediately exercised in a general good will" (*W* 8:540). Although a particular incarnation of being will inevitably have specific characteristics, these are irrelevant as a first motive for love. Truly virtuous love would remain indifferent to any secondary attributes of being, into which category good or bad characteristics inevitably fall. What compels virtuous love is not a certain manifestation of being, and specifically, Edwards is at pains to indicate, not even being which is beautiful or benevolent. Unmotivated love looks like this:

> If virtue be the beauty of an intelligent being, and virtue consists in love, then it is a plain inconsistence to suppose that virtue primarily consists in any love to its object for its beauty....For that would be to suppose that the beauty of intelligent beings primarily consists in love to beauty; or, that their virtue first of all consists in their love to virtue. Which is an inconsistence, and going in a circle. Because it makes virtue, or beauty of mind, the foundation or first motive of that love wherein virtue originally consists, or wherein the very first virtue consists; or it supposes the first virtue to be the consequence and effect of virtue. So that virtue is originally the foundation and

exciting cause of the very beginning or first being of virtue: which makes the first virtue both the ground and the consequence, both cause and effect of itself....So that there must be the love of the love of the love of virtue, and so on *in infinitum*. For there is no end of going back in a circle. We never come to any beginning or foundation. For 'tis without beginning and hangs on nothing. (*W* 8:543–44)[12]

The momentarily tortuous prose derides expressively as well as logically the idea that virtue derives from love of virtue, that virtuous love is caused by any beauty or benevolence in its object. But while love should properly be indifferent to the *characteristics* of being, it should not properly be indifferent to the *amount* of being perceived in the object. Crudely put, in Edwards's theory, the more being there is, the more love there should be:

He that loves Being, simply considered, will naturally...other things being equal, love particular beings in a proportion compounded of the degree of being and the degree of virtue, or benevolence to being, which they have. And that is to love beings in proportion to their dignity. For the dignity of any being consists in those two things. Respect to Being, in this propor- tion, is the first and most general kind of justice; which will produce all the subordinate kinds. So that, after benevolence to Being in general exists, the proportion which is observed in objects may be the cause of the proportion of benevolence to those objects: but no proportion is the cause or ground of the existence of such a thing as benevolence to Being. (*W* 8:571)

Thus Edwards differentiates between the primary object of love, Being in general, to which one owes indiscriminate love, and the secondary object of love, benevolence *in* beings. The benevolence of a *particular* being (*its* manifestation of love, hence its beauty) plus the *degree* of that being (God has most) dictates the proportion of love owed to *it*. That exacts the "jus- tice" specified above. If these calculations seem unperformable (who is in a position to make such calculations?) and indecipherable (*how* would they be made?), not to mention mechanistic (can love be so calibrated?), such an assessment just points out how ill equipped we, as persons, are to compre- hend the system Edwards is expounding. Edwards is not proscribing what we can do. The impediment is part of the point. Edwards is too expert a stylist not to have full control over the infelicitous contortions which con- stitute the rigor of his prose.[13] Edwards's mathematics of affection produces no simple calculation, in that what is specified is a ratio into which must be factored being, its amount, benevolence, and its amount in order to figure how much love is properly owed. Although initially no being is more valuable than any other (another way of forming the proposition that there is no cause for love), ultimately other criteria affecting the amount of love owed to being are understood as variable. The formula seems prescriptively clear while baffling any conclusion about how to adhere to it:

> It must be noted, that the *degree* of the *amiableness* or *valuableness* of true virtue, primarily consisting in consent and a benevolent propensity of heart to Being in general, in the eyes of one that is influenced by such a spirit, is not in the *simple* proportion of the degree of benevolent affection seen, but in a proportion *compounded* of the greatness of the benevolent being, or the degree of *being* and the degree of *benevolence*. One that loves Being in general will necessarily value good will to Being in general, wherever he sees it. But if he sees the same benevolence in *two* beings, he will value it *more* in two than in one only. Because it is a greater thing, more favorable to Being in general, to have two beings to favor it than only one of them. For there is more being that favors being: both together having more being than one alone. So, if one being be as great as two, has as much existence as both together, and has the same degree of general benevolence, it is more favorable to Being in general than if there were general benevolence in a being that had but half that share of existence. As a large quantity of gold, with the same degree of preciousness, i.e., with the same excellent quality of matter, is more valuable than a small quantity of the same metal. (*W* 8:548–49)

The proposition resists the clarification its discriminations promise. While on the one hand Edwards primarily has in mind the virtue of the being who is *loved*, such a calculation is rhetorically tied to how value is assessed by the being who *loves*. The propensity to consider simultaneously the one who loves and the one loved, the fact that the one loving and the one loved are made rhetorically inseparable, is—once Edwards's system is understood—seen to be a requirement of that system. Hence no one "truly [can] *relish* this beauty, consisting in general benevolence, who has not that temper himself" (*W* 8:549). Such an affective connection between the two persons is tightened by the operations dictated (of halving, compounding, comparing), the effect of which, oddly, is to leave one at a loss about precisely how to measure. Not knowing how to measure underscores the connection between persons, because the calculation that—if completed—would suspend the operation which draws the persons together does not do so here. Although this is not the point of the passage, it is the implicit consequence of the unperformable reckonings. This confounding of the formula—for determining amount of value on the basis of amount of being in relation to amount of benevolence—is not really lessened by the elegant analogy of more or less gold with which the passage lucidly concludes. The analogy asserts only that what is more valuable is more valuable.

What is held up in the first part of *True Virtue* is something like a set of criteria for loving—criteria antithetical to *persons'* criteria for loving, valuing, and in general finding "amiable." While the first two chapters of the treatise expound principles of true virtue according to some unfathomable calculus that persons can only hypothesize, chapters 4–7 redefine calculations based on self-love[14] understood as "affection which is to the highest degree private" (*W* 8:583)—a redefinition made so inclusive that it pertains to categories of good will we conventionally associate with altruism. It follows, in Edwards's argument, that "a man's love to those that love him is no more than a certain expression or effect of self-love" (*W* 8:579). It less obviously also follows that man will generalize from those conditions that secure his limited benefit and harm, so that he will disapprove spiteful and malicious behavior and approve virtuous behavior, abstractly considered, even when he is not the explicit recipient of that behavior (*W* 8:586). In loving what secures benefit, and hating what secures harm, a person always imagines himself the potential recipient of benefit and harm, constructing rectitude out of the surmise that what is at issue could be *his* benefit, *his* harm.[15] Ideas of justice also issue from self-love. Even pity is based on self-love, notwithstanding the altruistic sentiments of "humanity, mercy, tenderness of heart, etc." (*W* 8:613) that attend it. Not pity, not justice, not the golden rule (which must be understood in terms of self-consistency with no principle of "enlargement"), and, of course, not conscience, with its substitutive framework, constitute true virtue. For that which we calculate (love to those that love us, love to others as we would have them love us), that which we refuse to calculate (love to enemies), and that which is beyond calculation (Christ's commandment: Love others as I have loved you) adhere to a comparative framework obsessed with consequences for what is owed the self.[16]

In distinction, true virtue, or motiveless love, is love that is blind to consequence, specifically, according to Edwards, and in refutation of Hutcheson, love that does not evolve into either gratitude or anger toward others. For if gratitude and anger were virtuous sentiments truly infused with public affection, why not extend these to natural phenomena, which produce benefit and harm as surely as persons do?

> They say that the reason why we are affected with gratitude and anger towards men, rather than things without life, is moral sense: which they say is the effect of that principle of benevolence or love to others, or love to the public, which is naturally in the hearts of all mankind. But now I might say, according to their own way of arguing, gratitude and anger cannot arise from love to others, or love to the public, or any sense of mind that is the fruit of public affection. For, how differently are we affected towards those that do good or hurt to the public from understanding and will...from what we are towards such inanimate things as the sun and the clouds, that do good to the public by enlightening and enlivening beams and refreshing showers; or mildew, and an overflowing stream, that does hurt to the public by destroying the fruits of the earth?...Gratitude and anger cannot arise from the united influence of self-love and public love, or moral sense arising from public affection. For, if so, why are we not affected towards inanimate things that are beneficial or injurious both to us and the public, in the same manner as to them that are profitable or hurtful to both on choice and design, and from benevolence, or malice? (*W* 8:580–81)

Self-love makes it "natural to us to extend something of that same kind of love which we have for ourselves to them who are the same kind of beings as ourselves" (*W* 8:581) and not natural to extend gratitude or anger to clouds or mildew. We, like beasts, are differently moved when we suffer from an agent that has will than when we suffer from wind, water or hail, which do not (*W* 8:581). But the natural—based on ideas of desert derived from calculations to which self-love is indirectly central ("loving and being loved, showing kindness and receiving kindness" [*W* 8:612])—depends on a sense of reciprocity or agreement, which true virtue transcends. Or, as Edwards puts it, "The inclination to agree with ourselves...is a natural principle....An agreement or union of heart to the great system and to God, the Head of it...is a divine principle" (W 8:590). When Edwards defines "virtuous love" as exempt from a private system, and defines a "private system," no matter how expansive, as anything less than what comprehends "the universality of existence"—when he insists moreover that all nonuniversal love "put in the scales with it, has no greater proportion to it" than love for a single person (W 8:554)—it is safe to say that any person's love is excluded from qualifying as virtuous. Thus while Edwards deliberates the differences between a private system and a common morality, with its ever-enlarging circumference, he finally lumps these together, drawing a line between love based on any sense of exclusion (all love had by all persons) and that extended without limit everywhere. The latter—specified in this treatise by opposition, negation, and inference—repeatedly defined as what persons cannot muster, constitutes the only non-trivial principle of justice.

ii

The state of affairs—in which Being subsumes personal identity—does not seem real to the reader Edwards assumes. "Real" is Edwards's characterization: "There is such a thing as an appearing real, that is a conviction of the reality of the thing, that is incommunicable, that cannot be drawn out into formal arguments or be expressed in words, which is yet the strongest and most certain conviction" (W 13:338). That is *True Virtue*'s subject: an unreality (personal identity) does not present itself as a delusion, while "Being in general," which is genuine, does. In "The Mind," it does not seem actual to Edwards's reader that "God and real existence are the same" (W 6:345). In *True Virtue*, "Men are so ready to...leave the Divine Being out of their view...as though he were not properly belonging to the system of real existence, but as a kind of shadowy, imaginary being. And though most men allow that there is a God, yet in their ordinary view of things, his being is not apt to come into the account, and to have the...effect of a real existence, as 'tis with other beings which they see, and are conversant with by their external senses" (W 8:611). Elsewhere in Edwards's writing experiential understanding erodes the line between unreal and real by dictating the perceptual grounds whereby one becomes the other. Thus in *Religious Affections* one difference between natural and gracious affections lies in the "taste" ("the sweet taste of honey") possessed by the spiritual man but *not* possessed by the "natural man," who without the sense of tasting "cannot experience what sweetness is."[17] In a related formulation spiritual light is distinguished from "a mere notional understanding, wherein the mind only beholds things in the exercise of a speculative faculty; and the sense of the heart, wherein the mind don't only speculate and behold, but relishes and feels" (W 2:272).[18] In the minds of the saints (those who have experienced conversion) "there is a new inward perception or sensation...entirely different in its nature and kind, from anything that ever their minds were the subjects of before they were sanctified" (*W* 2:205).

This inward sense is missing on principle from Edwards's last work. Although in *True Virtue* "the heart" is invoked as the object of consideration ("Virtue consists in love to Being in general" [*W* 8:541])—in instance after instance love to Being in general is just what persons *cannot* know affectively. Even when Edwards hypothesizes a disposition which might qualify as virtuous ("If love to a created being comes from that temper or propensity of the heart" to Being in general, "it is virtuous" [*W* 8:558]), that redemptive possibility is immediately revoked by the proviso that follows, where it is stipulated that one must love Being in general *in* the beloved without *intending* love of Being in general. Such an intention would render good will a mere instrument in the project of one's own perfectibility. Thus what constitutes the value of a particular person must be discerned without being dictated by any preemptive adherence to a hierarchy that would foreclose real assessment. In a created being one should love the manifestation of "Being in general" instinctively, as it were. Yet it is just this instinct of which Edwards declares us bankrupt. When Edwards implies throughout that, for exercises of our love to count as virtuous, they must also be coincident with the *manner* in which God himself exercises love to the creature, it is no longer questionable, even to the ambitious, that such love is outside of human capability. Therefore although what is being considered in *True Virtue* is "love" as a "disposition," what repeatedly replaces the taste or sense of that disposition is a didactic set of propositions and calculations.[19]

In distinction Edwards's earlier writings deliberate the recognitional moments which emerge from the endless mistakes *True Virtue* makes irremediable. The following marks the moment when words conceived as platitudinously true—that nonsensate life endures beyond one's own life, as well as beyond the lives of particular generations—become affectively true. The passage documents a sense of how words which have no immediacy come to have conviction and force when a suddenly experienced sense brings them to mind. While the capacity to distinguish the perdurability of the earth from which we are removed ("clean gone off from the face of...in sixty or seventy years' time") is not identical to the capacity to discern the being/Being distinction made by *True Virtue*, it nonetheless represents the same relativizing of being in relation to manifestations of Being whose substance is enduring.

The text that says, "One generation passeth away, and another cometh; but the earth abideth forever."...This, to one in a common frame of mind, seems insipid....What is it to the purpose, whether the earth remains the same or no?...But yet, when upon an occasion I was more than ordinarily affected with the passingness of one generation after another, how that all those who made such a noise and bluster now, and were so much concerned about their life, would be clean gone off from the face of the earth in sixty or seventy years' time, and that the world would be left desolate with respect to them, and that another generation would come on that would be very little concerned about them, and so one after another; it was particularly affecting to me, to think that the earth still remained the same through all those changes upon the surface, the same spots of ground, the same mountains and valleys where those things were done remaining just as they were, though the actions were ceased and the actors quite gone—and then this text came into my mind. (*W* 13:290)

Seeming real is what the words of *Ecclesiastes* 1:14 initially do not do for Edwards, but what they come to do when he perceives the discrepancy between the earth's being made desolate (barren of persons) and *not* made desolate (not included in the barrenness and also not affected by it). The passage implicitly documents an obliteration of the *value* of persons (as well as documenting the obliteration of the *presence* of persons) seen from a counterperspective of what *is* enduring, the "same spots of ground...just as they were." The disposition to experience the real as a sense rather than as a thought is not voluntary. One can't will it, one can't effectively conceive it, and one can't repeat it. The past is useless with respect to sensation. It is the moment-to-moment novelty of sensation—being inside sensation—that alone counts as real:

These spiritual ideas are of such a nature, that a person that has once had them in mind, having obtained them by actual sense, yet it may be impossible for him to bring the idea into his mind again distinctly, or indeed at all. We can't renew them when we please, as we can our ideas of colors and figures, but [only] at some times; and at no time, except when [the] mind is particularly adapted to the reception of that idea. I can't have in my mind the idea of benevolence, except the disposition of my mind is something benevolent, or agreeable to that idea. At other times, I have only a general idea of it by the effects of it, to wit, that 'tis an inclination to another's happiness, etc.; but those simple spiritual ideas, that are most essential and considerable in it, my mind is destitute of; and I have no more an idea of benevolence than a man has of a rainbow, that has lost the idea of the colors. So it is in the more complex spiritual ideas...that are to the mind as color to the eye, not to be obtained by description. (*W* 13:286)

In these passages spiritual ideas are consistently made mysterious. They are ours, but not governed by us. They are noncontinuous (emerging "only at some times") yet lacking reference to any temporality (emerging "at no time"). In the concluding analogy of the man who cannot see a rainbow because he has lost the sense of color, Edwards makes unequivocal the difference between an immediate sense (which alone counts as penetrative) and one that is notional (which doesn't count at all). Yet "a general idea of benevolence" that is not a disposition toward it produces a residue of the experience now unavailable. When Edwards underscores the absence of a spiritual idea, the "prototype of nonsatisfaction" is not "a hollow space."[20] That is, to be impoverished of the sense of benevolence does not entail a literal absence or concealment ("What could the Psalmist mean, when he begged of God to open his eyes? Was he ever blind? Might he not have resort to the law, and see every word and sentence in it when he pleased?").[21] Yet while the sensation of color could be renewed through an immersion in an impression of it—one could mentally dwell on a color even detached from a particular object—one couldn't correct a spiritual deficiency by adding this or subtracting that, for the very idea of such an adjustment implies substance, figure, and extension to what, in Edwards's immaterialism, has none:[22] "Our common way of conceiving of what is spiritual is very gross and shadowy and corporeal, with dimensions and figure, etc.; though it be supposed to be very clear, so that we can see through it. If we would get a right notion of what is spiritual, we must think of thought or inclination or delight. How large is that thing in the mind which they call thought? Is love square or round? Is the surface of hatred rough or smooth? Is joy an inch, or a foot in diameter? These are spiritual things" (*W* 6:338).

Spiritual things have features, but not *physical* features, have textures, but not the textures of objects, have pervasiveness without substance:

That is a gross and an unprofitable idea we have of God, as being something large and great as bodies are, and infinitely extended throughout the immense space. For God is neither little nor great with that sort of greatness, even as the soul of man; it is not at all extended, no more than an idea, and is not present anywhere as bodies are present, as we have shown elsewhere. So 'tis with respect to the increated Spirit. The greatness of a soul consists not in any extension, but [in] its comprehensiveness of idea and extendedness of operation…equally to all places. God is present nowhere any otherwise than the soul is in the body or brain, and he is present everywhere as the soul is in the body. We ought to conceive of God as being omnipotence, perfect knowledge and perfect love; and not extended any otherwise than as power, knowledge and love are extended; and not as if it was a sort of unknown thing that we call substance, that is extended. (*W* 13:334–35)

When Edwards writes "God is present nowhere any otherwise than the soul is in the body or brain, and he is present everywhere as the soul is in the body," the spatial equivocation has the same stress and point as Stanley Cavell's "The spirit of the wind is neither smaller nor larger than the wind; and to say it is *in* the wind is simply to say that it exists only where there is a wind,"[23] in that both formulations insist on a distinction without a separation. No separate set of characteristics comprises spirit or soul. If the spirit is always available to be seen but is not always actually seen as other than "an obscure representation," what makes the spirit (of the biblical text, of benevolence, of God's real existence, and, in the following passage, of the divine light) "appear…real" (*W* 13:338)? Edwards can't produce criteria that would answer such questions. The point of these passages is that there is no set of traits by which spirit could be certainly distinguished:

A mind not spiritually enlightened beholds spiritual things faintly, like fainting, fading shadows that make no lively impression on his mind, like a man that beholds the trees and things abroad in the night.…A man that sets himself to reason without divine light is like a man that goes in the dark into a garden full of the most beautiful plants, and most artfully ordered, and compares things together by going from one thing to another, to feel of them and to measure the distances; but he that sees by divine light is like a man that views the garden when the sun shines upon it. There is as it were a light cast upon the ideas of spiritual things in the mind of the believer, which makes them appear clear and real, which before were but faint, obscure representations. (*W* 13:470)

Nothing has been added to the garden to make the perception of it beautiful, as nothing has been subtracted from one's sight when the garden makes "no lively impression on [the] mind." There are no marks that would separate "real" from unreal. Moreover, to say that divine light accompanies the vision of the garden properly illuminated is falsely to imagine divine light as a phenomenon rather than a medium. Yet in the representation of the garden "faintly" beheld and the representation of the garden beheld "when the sun shines," Edwards is juxtaposing incomparable states of perception of a single image seen in different lights. Access to the real might arise through a coincidence of a set of words with an understanding (as in the biblical text, though it is not equivalent to that coincidence). Or it might arise as an inner stirring that precedes benevolence but is not yet its inclination. To see the garden adequately is to be immersed in a perception of it not by virtue of reason alone and not by virtue of experience alone; for Edwards there is ultimately no difference between experience and reason, in that to experience properly *is* to reason properly and to do so by the aid of spiritual light.

At the same time that Edwards insists on the distinction between speculative and immediate evidence—hence between real and unreal—the brilliance of his writing lies in its production of phenomenological descriptions for what, not yet properly experienced by persons, *could* be so experienced. The following explains how supernatural happiness is not less desirable than natural happiness, a correction which turns upon an account of how we can desire what we already have, can want what we in effect no longer want:

> When God brings a soul out of a miserable state and condition into an happy state in his conversion, he gives him happiness who before had none. But he does not at the same time take away some of his love of happiness. And so when a saint increases in grace, he is made still more happy. But his love of happiness and his relish of it do not grow less as his happiness itself increases; for that would be to increase in one way, and diminish it in another. But when God makes a soul happy which was before miserable, or makes a soul more happy than it was, he continues the same love of happiness. (*W* 8:255)

The passage seeks to correct the fear that supernatural happiness exacts a loss or a diminishment. We don't relinquish our desire for what we have been given because we have been given it. The experience of happiness doesn't produce the devaluation of happiness. Moreover, no excess of happiness could constitute an "inordinacy" (*W* 8:256). Thus supernatural happiness is made recognizable by an implicit comparison to natural happiness, made recognizable in terms of what can be assumed about an experience still only anticipated. In a corollary passage from the Miscellanies, Edwards renders this happiness—here called ecstasy—*un*recognizable in the radical shifts of perception that relativize time and redefine usefulness.

> As for the other thing that is said, that there may be a degree of devotion that may hinder one from being useful to the rest of the universe: I suppose they will not dislike devotion if it only hinders one for but a half a minute, and makes one much more useful ever after; I mean, if it only makes us useless during our life upon earth, and much more useful to eternity afterwards. Not that I believe that a man would be the less useful even in this world, if his devotion was to that degree, as to keep him all his lifetime in an ecstasy. (*W* 13:191)

If supernatural happiness can be reunderstood as *desirable* (for which "relish" would not grow less as happiness "increased") and if "ecstasy" can be reunderstood within a pragmatic of usefulness—in other words, if persons can be said to see in such corrective terms as these—why does *True Virtue* prohibit the possibility of adequate experiential understanding? This question can be asked because the distinctions entertained by Edwards's passages—natural/supernatural happiness, usefulness/ecstasy, speculative/immediate evidence, being/Being—are all ones of kind rather than degree.

Only once in passing does Edwards entertain the idea that some "fully enlightened" being might be "delivered from…a private sphere" (*W* 8:595). Untainted by personality, such a being would not have more benevolence for some than for others. He would know how to calculate, but not according to his own frame of reference. Rather, he would see, on the basis of calculations which constitute an escape from the personal and the psychological, what has most being (hence most beauty), therefore what deserves most love. Thus *True Virtue* implicitly posits two frames of reference, one intuitively recognizable, the other which can be known only analytically or numerically. To ask what enables Edwards to *describe* true virtue through "the eyes of him that perfectly sees all things as they are" (*W* 8:561), which could only be God's eyes, is in effect to ask what enables any theological philosophy (as distinct from moral philosophy) to know what can only be alien to it.[24] In the calculus of *True Virtue* a speculative continuum allows an apprehension of units exemplifying magnitude all the way to infinity: The proportion inherent in a polygon is less beautiful than the proportion of a human countenance, and that less beautiful than the proportion in natural justice, and each of these less beautiful than existence in its entirety.[25] In other of *True Virtue*'s formulations, we imagine what we don't know and can't intuit by explicit substitution:

> Thus, we have no conception, in any degree, what understanding, perception, love, pleasure, pain, or desire are in others, but by putting ourselves as it were in their stead, or transferring the ideas we obtain of such things in our own minds by consciousness, into their place;...And this is the only way that we come to be capable of having ideas of any perception or act even of the Godhead. We never could have any notion what understanding or volition, love or hatred are, either in created spirits or in God, if we had never experienced what understanding and volition, love and hatred are in our own minds. Knowing what they are by consciousness, we can add degrees, and deny limits, and remove changeableness and other imperfections, and ascribe them to God. Which is the only way we come to be capable of conceiving of anything in the Deity. (*W* 8:591–92)

True Virtue equivocates about whether persons must imagine God with reference to themselves (as in the "add[ing] degrees...deny[ing] limits") or whether even by inference arguing from the personal to the impersonal constitutes a mistake. In accord with one principle in *True Virtue*, we can calculate the impersonal with reference to a lack in ourselves which could be conceptually corrected. In accord with a second principle we can *only* calculate it (not intuit it), through the logic of mathematics. According to this second way of understanding the inaccessibility of true virtue, we might approve and desire true virtue, but "without seeing the true beauty of it" (*W* 8:595). For the true beauty could be seen only from a "fully enlightened state" in which, far from reasoning from the private sphere, one is delivered from that sphere.

However, in both ways of understanding, in Edwards's treatise, a person is legible as someone who can quantify. He can *calculate* what is present and what is absent ("A man may be much moved and affected with uneasiness, who yet would be affected with no sensible joy in seeing signs of the same person's or being's enjoyment of very high degrees of pleasure" [*W* 8:606]). Who can *compare* degrees of incommensurate affect ("If pure benevolence were the source of natural pity doubtless it would operate to as great a degree in congratulation, in cases of others' great prosperity, as in compassion towards them in great misery" [*W* 8:608]). Who can *equilibrate* and who understands how equilibration works ("Pity may…consist with true malevolence.…A man may have true malevolence towards another, desiring no positive good for him, but evil: and yet his hatred not be infinite, but only to a certain degree" [*W* 8:606–7]). Who can *distinguish* the ways conditions affect calculations ("Men may pity others under exquisite torment, when yet they would have been grieved if they had seen their prosperity" [*W* 8:607]). Most to the point, a person is legible as one *who can say when an effect counts as a manifestation* of a quality ("Some men…would be far from being uneasy at [another's] death.…Yet at the same time they are capable of pitying even these very persons if they should see them under a degree of misery very much disproportioned to their ill will" [*W* 8:607]).

Although the point of these calculations is consistently to refigure common morality in terms of a sum that trivializes it, calculation is more generally a sign of the personal. Calculation is how the personal instantiates itself as well as being the signal operation of the writer of this treatise. Or rather, in Edwards's last work, a deficient calculation is a sign of the personal, in that adding and subtracting are operations set in motion with reference to self-love. By light of Edwards's earlier work, however, even when persons are calculating the *right* thing (degrees of Being), their calculations differently have no validity, since spiritual authenticity depends on an intuition, not a calculation. With respect to the prescriptions of the early Miscellanies and "A Divine and Supernatural Light," the "real" can be apprehended only by a mind "spiritually enlightened," through a deep sense. With respect to the claims made in *True Virtue* such a sense could never be deep enough, and would in fact always be deficient precisely because, notwithstanding any depth, it would be *only* a sense. In Edwards's last treatise, for virtue to count as true, it must have reference to things as they *are*, not things as they are *sensed*. Edwards's management of prescriptions for what is imperative on the one hand (the sense) and irrelevant on the other (the sense) leads to the hairline distinctions that govern his work. By light of the passages in the Miscellanies, affective sense changes everything without, in *True Virtue*, changing anything. Yet while the two systems (true virtue, common morality based on self-love) are radically unlike—that is the point of equation after equation—Edwards's quantifications reveal a simultaneous disappearance of the person (for whom they exist synecdochically, as emblems of what he is and can do) *and* of the impersonal, which is differently blanked out in a vacuum of absolute value.

iii

I have argued that Jonathan Edwards's calculations—his numerical imaginings—which could only be adequate by being endless,[26] can be contrasted with passages whose discriminations are grounded in embodied perceptions. The distinction I am making between counting and discriminating is analogous to that made by Brian Rotman between the idea of counting that has endless iteration at its core and a non-Euclidean geometry he proposes, which posits a rewritten finite that relativizes truth by recognizing it as both artifactual and corporeal, no longer a "divinely apprehendable 'ideality'" but rather "the fragile, contingent, and disaster-prone condition of all human becoming and all signification in which this becoming takes place"[27] In Rotman's thesis what deforms classical mathematics is the idealization of a "Subject"—ahistorical, acultural, asocial—who issues imperatives or exhortations to an "Agent" within the mathematical code, as in "drop a perpendicular...reverse all functions...exhibit all real roots" (*AI* 71) which the predicated Agent obeys. In Rotman's thesis, as the Subject is a truncated version of a "Person," so the Agent is a truncated version of the Subject. The Agent, as a proxy, is an automaton without corporeality and hence without mortality, while the Subject, according to the imaginary splitting, *is* mortal. Rotman's critique of the ghostliness of the "nobody phantom" that haunts classical mathematics arises in relation to an infinite capacity to perform operations which no person could perform ("One could grant the Agent not one but several lifetimes in which to execute actions such as counting. But why not a thousand or a million lifetimes?" [*AI* 92]). Rotman therefore takes issue with the assumption that one could apply the same methods for ascertaining what is hypothetical as for ascertaining what is actual. (Why should we believe that the regularities of counting "that appear to hold for the numbers of our experience extend to the numbering of...things as yet unexperienced and...even unexperienceable?" [*AI* 121]). In other words, he attacks an idealism in which truth matters are settled through an infinite that depends on a forfeited lexicality (analogous to W. V. Quine's critique of settling truth values mechanically without reference to conditions).[28] Such idealizations in which calculations issue from no embodied vantage ("the *first* object of virtuous benevolence...the *second* object of a virtuous propensity of heart" [W 8:545–46]), in which quantities are unreferenced (the proportion for compounding the amount of benevolence in relation to the amount of Being), and in which the hypothetical is undiscriminated from the actual ("love to beings actually existing" compelling right feeling toward "love for beings possibly existing"), are just the kinds of propositions I have been examining.

Yet the idealism that Rotman critiques—in which endless procedures are performed through a mechanical manipulation of signifiers—could differently be understood in relation to Kant's mathematical sublime, which oppositely stipulates the same idealism as facilitative. In *The Critique of the Power of Judgment* a thing has magnitude either by intuition or number. When one can't take in magnitude "at a single glance," when the imagination is inadequate "to get the full emotional effect of the magnitude" (of the pyramids, "the stones piled on top of one another") all at once and all as one, the beholder perceives numerically with a series of numbers progressing toward infinity what can't be sensibly understood intuitively.[29] In Frances Ferguson's understanding of Kant's passage, "the Kantian account of regulative pattern makes it possible to see psychology less as the story of affect than as the deduction of possibilities not necessarily available to the senses."[30] While Kant's mathematical sublime differs from Edwards's calculation of true virtue (in that Kant is concerned with unspecified units of an infinite and Edwards with units of infinite love), what is in question in both systems is the contrast between the intuited and the calculated. Even though the units in Kant's series (a mile, an inch) are produced by regular intervals of measurement, whereas the units in Edwards's series are not (a polygon, a flower, countenance, justice), in both systems what is important is not the result of a calculation but "the pattern of our working."[31] Setting Rotman next to Kant raises the question of whether the sacrificed lexicality in Edwards's quantifications are enabling (as Kant specifies) or disabling (as Rotman specifies). The infinite gives one a concept or model with no empirical coordinates. For Rotman this is a problem, because it is not possible to embody the model. For Kant and for Edwards not being able to embody the model does not invalidate the concept but rather preserves it as an ideal. The infinite is preserved as an ideal not in spite of our being unable to arrive at it, but precisely because we can't empirically arrive at it.

Yet the decontextualized idealism of *True Virtue*'s calculations strangely constitutes a mistake from the vantage of Edwards's other writings, where a commitment to empiricism suggests nothing can be certainly concluded.

In texts like *Religious Affections*, "The Distinguishing Marks of a Work of a Spirit of God," and "A Divine and Supernatural Light," perceptions rotated toward determining the presence of the supernatural are like counting in the sense that determination lies at their core. But they are *not* like counting in the sense that any formula for discerning the presence of *this* rather than the presence of *that* is proven impossible certainly to determine. Therefore what looks like the establishment of evidence is really a calling of it into question ("A work is not to be judged of by any effects on the bodies of men; such as tears, trembling, groans, loud outcries";[32] "That persons have many impressions don't prove that they have nothing else" [*W* 4:235]; "All their love of Christian virtue...appears amiable to natural men; but no otherwise than silver and gold appears amiable in the eyes of a merchant" [*W* 2:277]). What is central to discriminating (and absent from counting) is the psychological density produced by epistemological problems, in distinction to the abstraction that underwrites quantification. For counting always proceeds according to a pattern, whereas discrimination is indeterminate and cannot be patterned: "Now I ask the question: of the different bodies in the world, why is this body in this place and not in that or some other; why is this body of such dimensions and not of others; why is this body of this figure and that of that?" (*W* 13:255). Such questions preempt an answer (and perhaps even a logical coherence), since they appear to be disarticulating, in the process of investigating, what makes a body what it is. Differently put, tautologies which cannot fully derive an interrogative from a formula of equivalence (why is this this?) convert the impulse of the "why" which could be determinately answered into an expression of wonder.

Edwards's earlier writing often establishes a phenomenology of questioning. Such a phenomenology, which can distinguish the experienced from the thought, one's own experience from another's, and *kind*s of experience, characterizes the dazzle—the virtuoso quality—of Edwards's writing, even as this writing underscores a propensity to rule out conclusions from logical deductions.[33] Edwards's ventriloquism of the deluded state is frequently equivalent to the representation of understandings inaccurately understood to be decisive:

> Let us suppose a person who has been for some time in great exercise and terror through fear of hell, and his heart weakened with distress and dreadful apprehensions...is all at once delivered, by being firmly made to believe, through some delusion of Satan, that God has pardoned him, and accepts

him as the object of his dear love, and promises him eternal life: as suppose through some vision…of a person with a beautiful countenance, smiling on him, and with arms open, and with blood dropping down, which the person conceives to be Christ…or perhaps by some voice or words coming as if they were spoke to him, such as those, "Son, be of good cheer, thy sins be forgiven thee," or, "Fear not, it is the Father's good pleasure to give you the Kingdom." (*W* 2:149)

In the passage above a mistake—not a miscalculation—is not a matter of quantifying incorrectly, or a question of quantifying according to the wrong rule (adding degrees of self-advantage rather than degrees of being). A mistake is a question of being in error when you think you are not in error. What makes Edwards a great stylist with respect to moments that ventriloquize a mistaken position—equivalent as it were to the person's position—is the way in which his representations underscore the overlapping of enticement and delusion. Thus, for example, the comedic misperception in the passage cited above in which a person sees himself redeemed—"Son,…thy sins be forgiven thee…it is the Father's good pleasure to give you the Kingdom"— represents the thrill of being singled out and chosen. But it also represents the delusion of being singled out and chosen. It is Edwards's capacity to be simultaneously inside the mistake (for only inside it can he exemplify how it compels) and outside the mistake (for only outside the mistake, from a vantage that isn't personal, can the mistake be recognized *as* a mistake). Edwards discriminates a mistake from the inside; he reproduces the landscape of an inside in the conviction of hearing voices ("Son…") just as hearing voices ("Son…") grounds that conviction in an auditory hallucination.

In distinction to the propositional language of *True Virtue*, which rehearses the deficiencies of the personal from a perspective so pure it is no perspective at all, the essence of the mistake in the passage above can't be identified. In "Son,…thy sins be forgiven thee…it is the Father's good pleasure to give you the Kingdom," where is the mistake? Not in the idea of forgiveness. Or (from Edwards's point of view) in the idea of eternal life. Or in the fear of hell. Or in the man's ascertaining a personal relation to a God. These features are at the heart of Edwards's understanding of a theology. They are not what undermines that theology. Nor does the mistake derive from being compelled by the *sense* of a conviction, since only through sense is conviction made real. Nor is the mistake attributable to the imaginability of the person's conversing with Christ. The mistake can't be pinned on the imagination, or on sensing, or on the content of what is imagined and sensed. Rather, the passage produces a picture of an error without its being possible to identify its source. (Here one thinks of Wittgenstein's idea that one could recognize the correction of a mistake even if one did not understand the rule which it violated or the language in which the mistake occurred.)[34] In Edwards's writing a reader constantly discovers himself recognizing what a mistake looks like without recognizing criteria to which the mistake (or its recognition) could be ascribed. (Designating devils, or Satan, as marking the man's delusion does not constitute a criterion—devils being a kind of redundancy for what constitutes a mistake, a reiteration of the thing that requires explanation.) A mistake is such because Edwards says it is. A nonmistake would look exactly the same but for the correction marking the difference between the two. The complexity of Edwards's representations thus arises from the impulse to constitute a mistake in relation to a constellation of its elements. In the implicit irony of "Son,…thy sins be forgiven thee" Edwards recognizes the fact of the mistake, while recognizing that its source could precisely *not* be reduced to a miscalculation.

In contrast to such representations, mistakes in *True Virtue* are transposed into miscalculations, deluded persons being represented as those who quantify according to self-reference rather than according to degrees of being. And this assessment of a mistake—and its rectification understood in terms of substituting a different object of calculation (degrees of being compounded as distinct from degrees of self-love) seems thin or dimensionless—not registering as a credible representation of what persons do or are, outside of Edwards's prescriptive stance. Not seeming credible might precisely be understood as a *function* of the truth—whereby counting could be seen as a pure form of discriminating—form stripped of inessentials, reductive in the sense of pure, rather than reductive in the sense of inadequate. Reductiveness is a function of the absolute *difference* between counting and discriminating—a difference so irremediable that counting (in distinction to discriminating) looks deficient from the perspective Edwards triumphantly describes as flawed. Thus in *True Virtue* Edwards arrives at his real by the very formulas his other work derides.

If absolute standards govern Edwards's account of a deficient empiricism, empirical standards govern Edward's logic of an absolute—as in the passage below, written on May 12, 1743, where Edwards provides an account of how God equilibrates the legal and the evangelical principle: "When love is high, and the soul full of it, we don't need fear. And therefore a wise God has so ordered it that love and fear should rise and fall like scales of a balance, when one rises the other falls, as there is need."[35] Such ideas of counting, of measuring what can't be counted, and of weighing (a form of measuring) govern Edwards's *True Virtue*, even though it might be supposed with respect to the previous passage that God would be free of our calculations, even when engaged in negotiations with us.

There is a vertiginous moment in *True Virtue* when a "spiritual sense" is briefly entertained as an ontological possibility that could be intuited rather than counted or measured. In section 8 Edwards incongruously speaks of a "spiritual and divine sense, by which those that are truly virtuous and holy perceive the excellency of true virtue, [which] is in the Scriptures called by the name of light, knowledge, and understanding, etc." (*W* 8:622).[36] The passage continues: "And it being so, hereby persons have that true knowledge of God, which greatly enlightens the mind in the knowledge of divine things in general, and does (as might be shown, if it were necessary to the main purpose of this discourse) in many respects assist persons to a right understanding of things in general.... Whereas, the want of this spiritual sense, and the prevalence of those dispositions that are contrary to it, tends to darken and distract the mind, and dreadfully to delude and confound men's understandings" (*W* 8:623).

Up to section 8 the treatise had been committed to nonempirical understanding: to divorcing calculating from sensing. But in the paragraph above Edwards momentarily compromises his hard-line distinctions and introduces the possibility of right understanding as a "spiritual *sense*." Such a "sense" is said to be possible (even said to be necessary in that the want of this spiritual sense deludes), though the inevitability is contradicted by the evidence marshaled by the treatise as a whole, and though it is immediately dismissed as not "necessary to the main purpose of this discourse" by the paragraph's conclusion. Thus in the last chapter of *True Virtue* the language of "immediate perception" enters the discourse. But it enters the discourse as a *logical* imperative in order to prove that God's creation is, in all respects, consistent, in agreement with itself. By this logic, those who perceive the beauty of true virtue "by the frame of their own minds" do so because God does not act arbitrarily: rather, he gives the sense of true virtue to a created mind so that the creature's temper agrees with his own temper; only through this agreement can created beings agree with each other, and, with themselves (*W* 8:620–21).

In this way an "inward sense" (*W* 8:620) has been immediately translated to an ideal condition and a logical imperative. Thus the treatise concludes by arguing a coincidence between perception by measurement (scales, number) and perception by "immediate evidence" (sense) that its previous sections had been at pains to make diverge. "Sense" is introduced as a logical necessity almost as if it were an entity or quantity—important in being accounted for, though said to be unnecessary to elaborate in the treatise, and emphatically at odds with its centrally reiterated claims.

iv

Although *True Virtue* claims that one with a benevolent disposition "should be more disposed than another to have his heart moved with…affection to particular persons" (*W* 8:541–42), that is, although there are supposed to be consequences for benevolence, in Edwards's last treatise love doesn't look like love because there are no human instantiations of it. In Edwards's other writings self-love inspires self-castigation: "[I desire that God should] make me to know how that I deserve to be cast away, as an abominable branch and as a vessel wherein there is no pleasure".[37] In the Miscellanies such emptying of the self is called "hating our own life" (*W*: 13:215). To his fifteen-year-old daughter (reflecting on the possibility of a "dangerous sickness that should issue in death," where "you might probably be in your grave before we could hear of your danger"), Edwards writes:

> Though you are at so great a distance from us, yet God is everywhere. You are much out of the reach of our care, but you are every moment in his hands. We have not the comfort of seeing you, but he sees you.…And if the next news we should hear of you should be of your death (though that would be very melancholy), yet if with all we should hear of that [we should] hope that you had died in the Lord, how much more comfortable would this be (though we should have no opportunity to see you, or take leave of you in your sickness), than if we should be with you in all your sickness…and after all have reason to apprehend that you died without God's grace and favor! (*W* 16:289)[38]

This substitutive economy ("out of [our] reach…, but…in his hands"; a person's truth against a higher truth) runs through Edwards's writings. That economy has a corollary in Edwards's letters, visible in the breathtakingly indistinguishable line between the truth values he invoked and what his opponents regarded as deformations of truth, which, during Edwards's life, set him repeatedly at odds with his parishioners and friends, for whom he cared perhaps too rigorously to leave any space for what might be called affection.[39] Edwards's letters at the time of the communion controversy[40] are uncompromising with respect to alternative logics he cannot make coincide: "I have many enemies abroad in the country, who hate me for my stingy principles, enthusiasm, rigid proceedings....I seem as it were to be casting myself off from a precipice; and have no other way, but to go on, as it were blindfold, i.e., shutting my eyes to everything else but the evidences of the mind and will of God, and the path of duty" (May 24, 1749 [*W* 16:284]). Edwards's letters are litigious with respect to how those two logics are to be adjudicated. Thus Edwards admonishes his parishioners on the delicate question of whether he should be separated from them, a separation which they desired, and he did not: "You would call a council to judge...and yet would tell them at the same time that you have decided this matter already....And this is, in effect, to tell the council, at the same time you call them, that you do not need them....You are not only inconsistent with yourselves but...with reason and justice....And I desire you impartially to consider whether, if you should persist in these conclusions, it would be doing as you would be done by?" (*W* 16:305). In Stockbridge, where the arguments focused on the question of how Indian children were to be educated,[41] a report was filed against Edwards in the Massachusetts House of Representatives, which, by his own account, describes him as attempting "to criminalize, contradict, oppose, and counteract the measures...pursued by the Committee in conformity and obedience to the General Court's orders" (*W* 16:567). Such complaints typically lodged by Edwards against his parishioners (though in the last instance lodged by the parishioners against Edwards) are not simply a theme of the letters; they are the dominant strain of the letters, a counterpoint, in the case of the letters written from Stockbridge, to Edwards's *The Nature of True Virtue*, composed at the same time.

In "Heaven Is a World of Love" (the last sermon of the series Edwards preached on First Corinthians 13, in 1738, fifteen years before *True Virtue*), Edwards described heaven as "the palace, or presence-chamber, of the Supreme Being" (*W* 8:369). Disappointingly, it might be said, the presence-chamber preserves worldly inequities: "Though all are perfectly free from pride, yet...some will have greater degrees of divine knowledge than others"

(*W* 8:376); although all the saints are not equally loved, God "loves all the saints far more than any of them love each other" (*W* 8:377); although everyone is completely satisfied and full of happiness, having as much as he is capable of enjoying and desiring, some are capable of enjoying more happiness than others (W 8:375); "seeing the superior happiness" of some is no "damp" to the others (*W* 8:376). Yet in the presence-chamber there are these perfections: There will be no "fading of the beauty of the objects beloved, or any decaying of love in the lover, [or] any satiety in the faculty which enjoys love" (*W* 8:385). Moreover, love will be visible to all "as much as if there were a window in all their breasts, that they could see each other's hearts" (*W* 8:378).

But although Edwards asserts the necessity of correspondences between the presence-chamber and the world ("As heaven is a world of love, so the way to heaven is the way of love" [*W* 8:396]), he is unable to imagine an instance of earthly love that would count for anything. The idealism of the sermon therefore throws into relief a mundane countervision "of pride and malice and contention and perpetual jarring and strife, a world of confusion, a wilderness of hissing serpents, a tempestuous ocean where there is no quiet rest, where all are for themselves, and self-interest governs....[In a world of such] injustice...[this] abundance of opposition and cruelty [is] without any remedy" (*W* 8:393). "Without any remedy" is what occasions the violence of the charismatic "Sinners in the Hands of an Angry God" composed—it is surprising to remember—after "A Divine and Supernatural Light." Given the disalignment of Edwards's presence-chamber and world, delight in one requires pain in the other, an inverse economy serenely explicated as follows: "If intelligent beings are to be annihilated, there are some of God's works which it is impossible for the intelligent being to take delight in, yea, which 'tis necessary that he should have pain in the view of: even His constituting the creation so that the intelligent being, in so short a time, must be annihilated....The more perfect and intelligent he is, the more pain will the consideration give him" (*W* 13:267).

When Edwards was dying, he instructed his daughter, "Give my kindest love to my dear wife, and tell her, that the uncommon union, which has so long subsisted between us, has been of such a nature, as I trust is spiritual, and therefore will continue forever."[42] Edwards on his deathbed is translating personal love into its spiritual register, calculating on an occasion where one might have expected mere feeling. In the Miscellanies he more spectacularly corrects a misperception about whether love for particular persons is figured in Christ's sacrifice. Specifically at issue is whether Christ had "dying love" for "every particular believer" or whether he had impersonal love for *all* believers taken corporately. Edwards concludes that Christ did not "die with any view to particular persons that he loved, only from a love to the race of mankind in general." He adds for emphasis: "with a view to them as a race without any regard to particular persons" (*W* 13:212).

That only God is "real" is not only a doctrinal claim for Edwards, but, outside of *True Virtue*, also a "conviction." Edwards continues: "This seeming real" is "the testimony of the Spirit, and is a sort of seeing rather than reasoning the truth of religion" (*W* 13:338). By virtue of that seeing Edwards has access to "knowledge of the existence of an universal mind," which is visible in "actions of the world," just as knowledge "of the existence of a particular mind" would be visible "in a gesture, look and voice" (*W* 13:288): "There wants nothing but a comprehensive view, to take in the various actions in the world and look on them at one glance, and to see them in their mutual respects and relations, and these would as naturally, as quick, and with as little ratiocination, and more assuredly, intimate to us an universal mind, than human actions do a particular" (*W* 13:288). From what could be called a common perspective, "want[ing] nothing but a comprehensive view" would of course be wanting everything. But Edwards grasps "the comprehensive" with more facility and intimacy than he grasps "a gesture, look and voice." The world described outside of the "comprehensive" does not constitute Edwards's "real." The "gesture, look and voice" are not for him "real."

There is, however, a memorable passage in the Miscellanies when Edwards dwells on a person's features vivified from within: "The sweet disposition and joy of the heart will sometimes almost make the face to shine without a miracle. And how differently doth the face appear in the different extremes of the dispositions and affections!" (*W* 13:325). This is an ecstatic moment in which a person's face is beheld with interest, even wonder, testimony to its value, despite its particularity. Edwards's sentence occurs in a larger meditation on whether "man's body before the fall shone or no" ("I believe his flesh looked glorious, and appeared with a beautiful cast and a sort of splendor" [*W* 13:325]). Edwards in this passage on the shine of the face is recalling Paul in Second Corinthians, who is himself recalling Exodus.[43]

When Moses comes down from Mt. Sinai "the skin of his face shone because he had been talking to God" (Exodus 34:30)[44] and Moses's face continues to shine while he relays God's commandments to the Israelites. Paul in Second Corinthians (3:7–4:7) rewrites the story of the "shine" of Moses's face as "a brightness that is fading." Exodus says nothing about any bright-ness fading. But Paul's strategy for insisting that this "splendor" (the old covenant) "has come to have no splendor at all" compared to "the splendor that surpasses it" (the splendor of God revealed in Jesus), is to revise Exodus in relation to a "fading" he *introduces*. And it is not just the idea of splendor fading which is introduced by Paul. What is also introduced is the idea of splendor that is veiled, for Paul insists there are two kinds of seeing, the one had by the Israelites "when Moses put a veil over his face" so they "might not see the end of the fading splendor" and the one had when we, "with unveiled face beholding the glory of the Lord, are changed into His likeness."[45] In the distilled amalgamation of both biblical passages, Edwards is deliberating what makes the flesh look "glorious...with a beautiful cast...and a sort of splendor"—"what makes the face to shine"—and what effaces its splendor. Can shine *be* reflected in the human face (so we "are changed into His like-ness")? Or does the natural person's face always only veil splendor ("so that they could no longer bear to see themselves, or be seen by God or each other" [*W* 13:325])?

Edwards is also recalling *this* moment in Paul's reclaiming of the gen-esis of the shine: "It is the God who said, 'Let light shine out of darkness,' who...has shone in our hearts to give the light of the knowledge of the glory of God in the face of Christ"—a revision that at once interiorizes the radiance and relocates its emanation from Moses's face to Christ's. Edwards retains the inwardness as an origin but he transposes the manifestation of splendor from Moses's face *and* Christ's, so that "the joy of the heart some-times almost makes the face to shine without a miracle." In Edwards's rewriting of Paul's rewriting, it is the *human* face which shines—or almost shines. Here, for a moment, what Paul calls "this transcendent power [that] belongs to God and not to us" emanates, without being compromised by—or compromising—the person's incarnated particularity.

Edwards studied the difference between absolute Being—"being's consent to Being without particularity" (which could not be imagined)—and absolute or "perfect nothing"—what "sleeping rocks dream of" (which momentarily almost could be). He mined the contours of both impossibilities, without actually inhabiting them, by something like a sense. Like a sense, but not a sense. We can't sense those states. In the sleeping-rocks passage, sense is transposed from what *we* might have to what *rocks* might have, but not know that they had (and only when they dream), as in *True Virtue* sense is transposed from what we might have to what we *can't* have, "love to Being in general" being not our sense. The sleeping-rocks passage and *The Nature of True Virtue* exemplify the opposite of personification in that human attributes are everywhere evacuated from a world in which rocks have consciousness and love is bereft of it. And if Edwards can't relinquish "sense" as a primary term that animates all his writing, in *True Virtue* he comes to conceive of it outside an experiential register and, except in passing, outside a logical register. Edward has the peculiar ability to write of a state whose first proposition is that "There is such a thing as nothing with respect to you and me," a negation that renders visible, one might almost say available, some impersonal universe in which thought and affect (though not our thought and not our affect) are made at once unrecognizable and intelligible. In the sleeping-rocks passage, as in the treatise on true virtue, nothing and everything are almost made perceptible, if perception could be reinscribed as a fully alienable phenomenon, as something not ours.

3

Representing Grief:
Emerson's "Experience"

"Where do we find ourselves?" Emerson's "Experience" begins,[1] implicitly answering a question raised seven years earlier in and about "The American Scholar": "Let us inquire what light new days and events have thrown on his character, and his hopes."[2] This time the question implies its own answer. The place Emerson finds himself is one where no light is ("night hovers all day in the boughs of the fir-tree"). And it is more oppressive than that because he can't see where he is and he can't see his way out. What he attests to is stupor:

> We wake and find ourselves on a stair; there are stairs below us, which we seem to have ascended; there are stairs above us, many a one, which go upward and out of sight. But the Genius which, according to the old belief, stands at the door by which we enter, and gives us the lethe to drink, that we may tell no tales, mixed the cup too strongly, and we cannot shake off the lethargy now at noonday. Sleep lingers all our lifetime about our eyes, as night hovers all day in the boughs of the fir-tree. All things swim and glitter. Our life is not so much threatened as our perception. (E 471)

Perhaps the most striking part of the testament is the disavowal of the very feeling that pervades these pages. For feeling survives the complaints of its being canceled. Emerson is conceding with one part of himself what he is disputing with another.

If vertigo for Emerson is occasioned by being in a mid-world from which vision is occluded, for the reader vertigo is occasioned by assertions that only half successfully cancel each other:

> The only thing grief has taught me, is to know how shallow it is....Grief too will make us idealists. In the death of my son, now more than two years ago, I seem to have lost a beautiful estate,—no more. I cannot get it nearer to me....This calamity...does not touch me: some thing which I fancied was a part of me, which could not be torn away without tearing me, nor enlarged without enriching me, falls off from me, and leaves no scar. It was caducous. I grieve that grief can teach me nothing. (E 472–73)

These insistent denials of feeling—on the occasion of which each time feeling suffers a resurgence—are curious. For the Emerson of the essay's beginning *cannot* get grief nearer him. He cannot acknowledge grief any way but this. Still, what is interesting about the acknowledgment is its absolute adequacy. The acknowledgment, in fact, culminates in perhaps the essay's most frequently cited passage: "I take this evanescence and lubricity of all objects, which lets them slip through our fingers then when we clutch hardest, to be the most unhandsome part of our condition" (E 473).

True to the double pattern of assertion thus far, the grammatical reference for "this evanescence" is not only the life of the child but also the evasiveness of the grief occasioned by the child's death. This puts us in no danger of mistaking the reference. Why then does Emerson mistake it, seeming to mourn the loss of his affect more than the loss of his son? Partly because he has asserted "opium is instilled in all disaster." Hence disaster can be voiced only if the voice is then denied. What, though, is the connection between the articulation of grief and the inability to experience grief ("I cannot get it nearer to me") and a second, more critical dissociation between the meditation on grief at Waldo's death in these relentless first few pages and the enumeration of general, impersonal dissatisfactions with which the rest of the essay is concerned?

All critics of Emerson have commented on the contradictory feature of the essays—namely on the fact that Emerson fails to take account of his own discrepant statements. O. W. Firkins explains unaddressed discrepancies in Emerson's essays by suggesting that disparate phenomena do not need to be admitted because Emerson perceives their ultimate unity: "The whole fascination of life for him lay in the disclosure of identity in variety, that is, in the concurrence, *the running together,* of several distinct images or ideas....No man ever breathed...who found more pleasure than Emerson in the disclosure of hidden likeness."[3] Firkins thus maintains that Emerson treats differences as likenesses because that is what they will become. In an opposite spirit, R. A. Yoder argues that in Emerson's essays disparate phenomena must be understood as instantiating the dialectical trinity of thesis/antithesis/synthesis. While Firkins implicitly suggests that Emerson need not admit differences because, properly seen, they must be construed as features of a nuanced but single entity, and while Yoder claims differences are ultimately recognized, other critics—Stephen Whicher, Barbara Packer, Eric Cheyfitz—argue that discrepant statements cannot be registered as such because Emerson can never separate the half of the antithesis to be repudiated from the half of the antithesis to be embraced.[4] I want in my own discussion to examine the two suppositions: "not able to" (Packer, Cheyfitz, Whicher) and "not necessary to" (Firkins and Yoder). Why in one instance is acknowledgment prohibited, and why in the other instance is acknowledgment found gratuitous? My interest in these questions is neither structural nor rhetorical. I rather wish to investigate the way in which dissociation reflects a self's relation to its own divergent claims.

Why are there frequently two voices in an Emerson essay? Why two voices that seem deaf to each other's words?[5] In an essay like "Experience" are claims voiced, repudiated, and differently iterated so that the self that can say words and the self that can hear them may be brought into relation and implicitly reconciled with each other? If so, is the idea of "integration," and the appropriateness of a psychoanalytic context which that word suggests, validated by the essay? What disables the psychoanalytic and philosophical explanations that the idea of dissociation and schism inevitably invites? In "Experience"— which, I shall argue, bears a special relation to the problem of discrepancy in Emerson's essays—an admission of grief is soon contested, first by the denial of grief and second by the disappearance of the subject of grief from the essay's subsequent pages. It is true that the two parts of "Experience" are not explicitly discrepant or contradictory. They are implicitly so, for—to specify the contradiction in terms that restate the problem—the initial pages of the essay claim that grief over Waldo's death does not register, while the body of the essay shows the pervasive ranges of that register. Why should Emerson not acknowledge the relation between the loss of the child and the perception of daily losses when one generates the other?

In the discussion that follows, addressing these questions, I contest the critical categories in which "Experience," in particular, and Emerson's essays in general, have been spoken of. So doing, I propose another set of terms, for "synthesis" and "contradiction" are not useful to describe Emerson's "Experience."[6] These terms are inadequate partly because "Experience" is different from Emerson's other essays (in it, for example, dissociation is considered as well as enacted). But they are also inadequate in a deeper sense. Specifically, to speak of the split between experience and idealism (which is the superficial form contradiction takes in "Experience") is to appropriate the essay by a logic it resists. My discussion will suggest that what is at stake in the essay is not a question of logic but rather a question of the elegiac. In "Experience," I shall argue, the elegiac has a logic of its own—not one of working through (not one of synthesis) and not one of explicit conflict. It may seem along the way as if I am describing, or as if Emerson is portraying, a condition of "melancholia." Instead, I argue, he is creating a powerful and systematic representation of grief. I shall get hold of the terms of this representation by coming at it several times and from different angles. In section 2, I delineate the dissociated elements that "order" the essay. Because I relinquish explanations of synthesis or contradiction, it may look as if the essay's subjects have an arbitrary hierarchy, or as if I have introduced the arbitrariness by a poststructuralist critique of conventional ways of reading Emerson that could apply as well to a representation of any subject as to a representation of grief. To the extent that concerns in "Experience" are all governed by Emerson's relation to the dead child, this arbitrariness is illusory—a claim I elaborate in section 3, when I examine passages that establish grief as the essay's determining focus. Finally, in 4, I consider the problem of an adequate vocabulary for Emerson's essay. For although it is the task of "Experience" to extricate grief from the numbness to whose spell consciousness has consigned it in the essay's first few pages and to represent, if not to see, what it looks like, it is not immediately clear how we are to understand the dynamic represented.

ii

It is almost inconceivable that after the initial pages of Emerson's "Experience," in which the mind is apparently successful in its attempt to render itself unconscious of the grief occasioned by the death of Emerson's five-year-old son, the essay, with no transition, should abandon this subject, abstractly turning its attention to the annoyance of daily vagaries. One explanation for the disjunctiveness of the shift is that the man who insists upon an imperviousness to grief ("This calamity…does not touch me") is so devastated by the subject from which he claims himself exempt that he can say no more about it. And in fact it is the case at the beginning of "Experience" that "all things swim and glitter" because dissociation replaces tears and because the man who writes these words knows that tears are the particular experience from which dissociation will protect him.

Emerson had said, "Our life is not so much threatened as our perception." In the context of the initial pages, the nature of the threat seems to be the inability to see at all, the stupor of dissociation. In the context of the body of the essay, the nature of the threat is that *all* ways of seeing are informed by Waldo's death. No vision is exempt from being dissolved by a grief that is causally unrelated to it. All things swim and glitter because everything is transient, either a loss in its own right or subject to loss—and these ordinary losses are governed by the extraordinary one with the bare statement of which the essay begins. Although it may seem, then, that Waldo's death is set forth and set aside, in fact the essay is a testament to the pervasiveness of a loss so inclusive that it is inseparable from experience itself.

What the initial pages of "Experience" hope for and despair of is a testament to grief's reality—its felt manifestations. "There are moods in which we court suffering, in the hope that here, at least, we shall find reality, sharp peaks and edges of truth. But it turns out to be scene-painting and counterfeit. The only thing grief has taught me, is to know how shallow it is. That, like all the rest, plays about the surface, and never introduces me into the reality, for contact with which, we would even pay the costly price of sons and lovers" (E 472–73). "Contact" with grief—its absolute inseparability from every conceivable aspect of experience—is just what is being courted in the essay's initial pages and just what is achieved in the pages that follow. Thus, "Where do we find ourselves?" elicits, on balance, an answer whose shock we are not initially in a position to appreciate: "In a series of which we do not know the extremes, and believe that it has none" (471).

What is extreme is the predication of a series—of consequences, of things touched by Waldo's death here emblematized by the particular range of subjects considered in the essay—that has no regress (Emerson, after the first three pages, never directly returns to talk of Waldo's death), and that has no terminus either. Moreover, the connection between the grief over Waldo's death and the grief that characterizes the daily losses and incompletions is all the more terrible because it goes without saying. It goes without saying, and any understanding of the relation between the first few pages and the rest of the essay depends upon its being assumed.

In fact, although the essay's initial pages describe the feeling of grief as a deficient one ("The only thing grief has taught me, is to know how shallow it is"), the body of the essay revises that assessment, calling into question Emerson's expectation (and ours) of what grief is. For ideas of depth, integration, internalization, perhaps acknowledgment, too (ideas anathema to the notion of grief and experience as both are here defined), suppose a contact with experience equivalent to its mastery. Grief—"that, like all the rest, plays about the surface, and never introduces me into . . . reality"—withholds contact with a reality that does not equivocate with experience, because unlike death, to which Emerson compares it, grief does not end experience. What is being redefined, then, is the idea about our relation to experience—about whether that relation is one of surface or depth.

At one level the connection between the two parts of the essay could not be simpler: Emerson's response to Waldo's death informs his responses to all other experiences. The two are related as cause and effect. But Emerson also implicitly proposes that we construe the connection in equative as well as causal terms. Grief and experience are equivalent because the characteristics of grief are identical to the characteristics of experience, as each is separately defined. Specifically, they are equal to each other because dissociation impersonally defines both. With respect to grief, the manifestation of dissociation is stupor, the inability to feel. Four years after the death of his wife Ellen in 1831, Emerson writes in his journals: "I loved Ellen, & love her with an affection that would ask nothing but its indulgence to make me blessed. Yet when she was taken from me, the air was still sweet, the sun was not taken down from my firmament."[7]

On February 4, 1842, a week after the death of his child, in a letter to Caroline Sturgis: "Alas! I chiefly grieve that I cannot grieve; that this fact takes no more deep hold than other facts, is as dreamlike as they; a lambent flame that will not burn playing on the surface of my river. Must every experience—those that promised to be dearest & most penetrative,—only kiss my cheek like the wind & pass away? I think of Ixion & Tantalus & Kehama."[8]

These figures borrowed from Greek mythology, in the case of Ixion and Tantalus, and from Robert Southey's *The Curse of Kehama*, in the case of

Kehama, are crossbred so that what the emergent figure suffers is to perceive in perpetuity the existence of a feeling he is deprived of experiencing—like Tantalus condemned to stand always in water up to his chin, with fruit-laden branches above his head and both water and fruit receding from his reach at each attempt to eat or drink.

The passage from "Experience," drawing on the despair if not the actual words of these earlier notations, specifies its hopelessness in comparable—not identical—terms. For one way to talk about the relation between journal, letter, and essay is in terms of reverberation. Voices not in dialogue pick up each other in oblique ways: "The Indian who was laid under a curse, that the wind should not blow on him, nor water flow to him, nor fire burn him, is a type of us all. The dearest events are summer-rain and we the Para coats that shed every drop" (E 473). It is in the context of such invulnerability that Emerson a few lines earlier in the essay had remarked: "Grief too will make us idealists."

Emerson is not only saying: Because grief tells us we are deprived of what we love, we must therefore reflect on what we no longer experience. He is also saying: Because grief tells us nothing, because we are in its presence without feeling our relation to it, we must imagine even it. We must hypothesize the sorrow, and the source of the sorrow, we are unable to feel. It is, of course, true that the opposite could be argued: Since grief is an affect, Emerson is positing a feeling he cannot take back as quickly as I suggest. Yet it is not that Emerson retracts or takes grief back. It is rather that he seems never to acknowledge the consequences of having allowed it direct expression. When Emerson offers up prospectively (to gain "contact" with grief) "the costly price of sons and lovers" that he has already paid, it is to illustrate what it feels like to be deprived of proper affect. What it feels like is to imagine you are in a position to relinquish (are therefore still in possession of) what you have already lost. And the disparity between the man's offer and his ignorance of its illegitimacy is all the more shocking when we remember that the sacrifice being contemplated is of a wife and a child. If we recoil from the brutality of this assault, what we recoil from is the fact that to the man who voices these words they do not seem brutal because they do not seem real. There could be no more harrowing testimony to the terror of idealism than this example of a self forced prospectively to imagine the loss it retrospectively refuses to feel.

Dissociation is also apparent in Emerson's itemization of the essay's subjects (in the poem that precedes the essay and yet again in a paragraph that is placed toward its close) as these designations seem divorced from, and seem only arbitrarily to apply to, discrete portions of the essay. In fact, although Emerson provides us with a gloss of the essay's subjects, he simultaneously calls attention to the gloss's inadequacy: "Illusion, Temperament, Succession, Surface, Surprise, Reality, Subjectiveness,—these are threads on the loom of time, these are the lords of life. I dare not assume to give their order, but I name them as I find them in my way" (E 490–91). It is not, moreover, clear where the arbitrariness indicated above comes from, whether the lack of order is in the threads or in Emerson's ability to specify the order of the threads. As the language of the passage implies, the distinction blurs in the making.

In fact the second part of the essay demonstrates the unsuccessful attempt to understand phenomena, much as the first part of the essay demonstrated an unsuccessful attempt to feel them. If the sentence whose import dominates the essay's initial pages is "Grief too will make us idealists," the sentence whose meaning dominates the remainder of the essay is "Life has no memory" (E 484). The stupefaction is so extreme that we see in the sentence's verbal displacement the self attribute to life its own disputed amnesia. What it would dissociate itself from is not the incoherence of the tragic (on which the initial pages turned their back) but rather the confusion of the everyday. For despite the mind's efforts to wrestle phenomena into comprehensible shape, to ascribe meanings to experience in which it can believe, our thoughts lose their grip. We betray our convictions, or they betray us.

In "Experience" the particular form this betrayal takes is that our ambivalence leads us to advocate antithetical beliefs, and, as if that ambivalence were not bad enough, we cancel the distinction between the opposite beliefs ostensibly being contested. Thus Emerson asserts that our lives are fixed because the succession of moods is limited by temperament. But he then disavows this claim, suggesting that to believe in such limitations is to "house with the insane" (E 476). Yet both assessments amount to the same thing because although hope tells us our moods and life must change, Emerson's exemplification of that change ("I have had good lessons from pictures, which I have since seen without emotion or remark" [E 476]) is purely pejorative. Change is possible/Change is not possible/If change is possible we stand only to lose by it. Because at best these formulations are only contradictory, Emerson dismisses the turns of this particular thought and dismisses the efficacy of thought in general: "But what help from these fineries or pedantries? What help from thought? Life is not dialectics" (E 478).

Since there is no help from thought, Emerson will rise above his ruminations to consider actions and surfaces. Once he does so, terms like "betrayal" and "the plaint of tragedy" (E 477), which were initially suggested by the death of the child, seem empty and abstract: "The whole frame of things preaches indifferency. Do not craze yourself with thinking, but go about your business anywhere. Life is not intellectual or critical, but sturdy.... To fill the hour,—that is happiness; to fill the hour, and leave no crevice for a repentance or an approval. We live amid surfaces, and the true art of life is to skate well on them" (E 478).

The praise of the transitory in which "we must set up the strong present tense," since life "is a flitting state, a tent for the night" (E 481), culminates in the assertion "We thrive by casualties. Our chief experiences have been casual" (483). The association of the casual with the casualty (an association in which the latter is inevitably particularized as Waldo's death)—like the earlier comparison of Waldo's death with the loss of an estate—is shocking, for in each case phenomena psychically divorced from each other (the property and the child, the casual and the casualty) are made categorically comparable. The vulgarity of alluding to these losses as if they were comparable is meant to replicate the vulgarity of experience's obliviousness to any niceties of human perception. The man who must sacrifice not simply his child but also his belief that the sacrifice has a uniquely personal meaning replicates the failure of discrimination by which he sees himself victimized. The vengeance of experience lies in the way it gives and takes away as if its losses were equivalent. The vengeance of response lies in its adherence to this fiction. Vengeance is involved because losses are not equal. In positing their equivalence, Emerson preserves the sanctity of his feeling, preserves by keeping hidden or unconscious (that is, dissociated) his sorrow for the child, as if hidden the feeling escapes the words that debase it, and, as I have noted earlier about this same passage, escapes acknowledgment of its actuality and, perhaps, therefore too its fact. Emerson brings together the loss of the child and the loss of the estate, then, to preserve a crucial disparity between the feeling and the words which degrade it that has crucially been violated on another—the disparity between a trivial and a consequential loss. Alternatively, he undermines our supposition that the casual and the casualty are only etymologically related. In that enigmatic "We thrive by casualties. Our chief experiences have been casual," he suggests that the accidental is the incidental on which meaning has been conferred. Events assume meaning (that is, connection) in the present, then, at tremendous cost. For our relation to meaning, at least with the recollection of Waldo in mind, is in the form of fatality.

Of course things can mean, retrospectively ("The years teach much which the days never know" [E 483]), but then they have no relation to us. Wisdom, divorced from any memory of how we came to possess it, is likewise divorced from any actual experience of it. The bottom line of this separation is absolute subjectivity—unconsciousness that separates existence from our thoughts about it; thoughts from action; action from agency; temporal units from each other. "That which proceeds in succession might be remembered, but that which is coexistent, or ejaculated from a deeper cause, as yet far from being conscious, knows not its own tendency" (E 484). Throughout the essay the complaint seems to be that you can endure loss but not suffer it; you can gain wisdom but not experience the gain because at any given moment you are oblivious to what you are experiencing. As a consequence, events have significance as fatalities, or they have no significance at all. You can know and you can have, but you cannot know what you have, because you cannot connect the two, for connection—between experience and its register in feeling (in the first part of the essay) or experience and the understanding of it (in the second part of the essay)—is just what seems impossible.

The word "experience" itself, associated with empiricism and therefore with one half of the conventional philosophical dichotomy of which "idealism" is the complement, has been painstakingly dislodged from the neatness of this dialectic and redefined as a mere middle, standing between what we desire and what we get, what we recall and what we expect. No longer part of a known opposition, experience stands between such oppositions, but—as Emerson will note, altering the spatial understanding—connected to them obliquely. Insofar as "experience" seems to designate the self's relation to its present, it redefines personal identity by disengaging the self from both past and future. But the self's relation to the present is similarly defined by disengagement, for if "experience" indicates those phenomena that happen to the self, it also, definitionally, implies that such phenomena are alien to the self. Thus the idea of a self is first made to forfeit its connection to a past and a future (it is made temporally discontinuous), and then made to reconceive its connection to a present as a relation, not an identity (it is made spatially discontinuous).[9] "You will not remember…and you will not expect" (E 483), the imperative issued by the negative conditions that govern, respectively, the inability to feel or understand, is really a dictate that disallows connection between the serial and the significant, the casual and the casualty.

The present may be the privileged moment that best survives the charges made against it, for, to recapitulate a thematic of the essay, if loss is always figured as the loss of the present moment, the redress of that loss will always be figured as the immediacy of the present. Indeed it could be argued that insofar as the essay thematizes a solution to the dissociation it describes, it does so by valorizing the idea of a present over which discontinuity fails to hold sway. If one were describing the progression of the essay, adhering to the logic of this thematic, the description would read as follows. First Emerson laments the absence of contact with the child. Or rather, as the child is incidental to his lament, the man grieves numbness, grieves the loss of contact with feelings occasioned by the child's death. Then he revalues the importance of such contact, finding it undesirable. In conclusion, he proposes a substitution for contact. Namely, while at the essay's beginning Emerson mourns the lack of binding—of temporal moments to each other, of spatial connections—at the conclusion he celebrates the force of unbinding; he celebrates the primacy of the present moment, dissociated from all other moments. He rejoices in the power of the self to outdistance its need for connections. He finds wholeness gratuitous.

The trouble with this thematic, or with this interpretation of the thematic, is that it supposes the loss of affect rather than the loss of the son to be the primary object mourned. The thematic implies that what was mourned at the essay's beginning was not the child but rather the man's feeling. (Hence, without much adjustment, if feeling is lost, it can also be recuperated.) That assessment seems to me to mistake the subject of many of the essay's passages, much as the man in the essay could be said to exemplify the problem of mistaking the subject of his own words. I shall discuss these passages whose power comes from the fact that they challenge the thematic, that they are antagonistic to it, providing a crucial countermovement against it. Specifically, they suggest that mastery is not in a real present, not in any moment, but rather in a psychic state or space. If the temporal terms urged by the thematic suggest a cure to the curse of experiences that are ever present and never present—and specifically suggest a cure to the loss of the man's affect—the spatial terms of the essay suggest that what is at stake is not the recuperation of affect but rather the recuperation of the child.

For despite the charges made in the essay, it does not present us with a theory of tragedy, and it does not present us with a facile accommodation to loss. It rather presents us with a theory of "power," which is importantly related to the way in which Emerson comes to terms with the death of his son.[10] This theory posits itself between the conditions staked out in the essay's first half (you must suffer grief without feeling it) and those staked out in the second half (you must live life without understanding it), staked out, in other words, between the casualty and the casual, between the cataclysmic and the everyday.

At the essay's beginning obliquity is impotence: "Nature does not like to be observed.... Direct strokes she never gave us power to make; all our blows glance, all our hits are accidents. Our relations to each other are oblique and casual" (E 473). By the middle of the essay obliquity is power: "A man is like a bit of Labrador spar, which has no lustre as you turn it in your hand, until you come to a particular angle; then it shows deep and beautiful colors. There is no adaptation or universal applicability in men, but each has his special talent, and the mastery of successful men consists in adroitly keeping themselves where and when that turn shall be oftenest to be practised" (E 477).

Having discussed the ways in which the essay's unfolding concerns can be considered, in the remaining two sections I shall focus on the essay's beginning and end, as well as on the subject of grief that connects the two. So doing, I wish to expose the "turn" Emerson "practices" in "Experience," for it is through that turn that the dissociation attached to death is converted to the dissociation that facilitates power. I shall have more to say specifically about the question of power at the end of my discussion. First, however, I wish to address the conversion I have described. As this conversion depends on understanding Emerson's equivocal expression of grief (and his ultimately unequivocal relation to it), I shall press hard on certain passages, some of them introduced earlier in my discussion.

iii

The centrality of Waldo's death for Emerson is attested to in journal entries contemporaneous with the event. That centrality is reiterated in the following extraordinary passage of July 8, 1857, also from the journals: "This morning I had the remains of my mother & of my son Waldo removed from the tomb of Mrs. Ripley to my lot in 'Sleepy Hollow.' The sun shone brightly on the coffins, of which Waldo's was well preserved—now fifteen years. I ventured to look into the coffin" (*JMN* 14:154). In that flatly declarative last sentence Emerson records his sense of the risk associated with looking for the child, or of looking at the child's remains, or of looking into the space where the child is or was. If the journal entry shies away from specifying what is looked for and what is seen, the essay "Experience" does not.

"Experience" is an elegy, an essay whose primary task is its work of mourning, and, in light of that poorly concealed fact, it is surprising that critics have consistently spoken of the child as only one of several causes equal in their provocation of listlessness and despair. In those few discussions in which Waldo's death is acknowledged to have special status, it is still not seen as it crucially must be: the occasion that generates in a nontrivial way all other losses that succeed it. For Waldo's death is not just one of a number of phenomena equally precipitated and having parity with each other. Raising itself above the evasively identified "series of which we do not know the extremes, and believe that it has none" of the essay's second sentence, and enunciating itself outside of Emerson's itemization of the essay's ostensible subjects ("Illusion," "Temperament," "Succession," "Surprise," "Reality," "Subjectiveness") from whose abstraction it is definitionally exempt, the grief occasioned by the death of the child is the essay's first cause; it begets the other subjects, the consideration of which—Emerson's and ours—depends on our understanding their relation to Waldo's death. Mourning does its work in that the loss and grief initially attached to a single experience ultimately, impersonally, pervade the perception of all experience so that everything is susceptible to the same disappointment.

Freud in "Mourning and Melancholia" characterizes such grief as accompanied by "loss of interest in the outside world—insofar as it does not recall [the dead one] . . . the . . . turning away from any activity that is not connected with thoughts of him."[11] And although Emerson does not explicitly enumerate connections between the loss of the child and the perception of daily losses (of power, of wholeness, of will, of possession), he implicitly insists we recognize the connection in a central remark: "It is very unhappy, but too late to be helped, the discovery we have made, that we exist. That discovery is called the Fall of Man. Ever afterwards, we suspect our instruments. We have learned that we do not see directly, but mediately. . . . Perhaps there are no objects" (E 487). We are invited to take this declaration two ways. One emphasizes subjectivity ("We do not see directly, but mediately"). The other emphasizes loss—the death of the child calling into question the reality of all other phenomena ("Perhaps there are no objects"), with separation (the man from the child) preceding the subjectivity with which the paragraph seems exclusively concerned.

The discovery "that some thing which I fancied was a part of me, which could not be torn away without tearing me, nor enlarged without enriching me, falls off from me, and leaves no scar. It was caducous"—this discovery, or this account of the discovery, anatomizes in visceral terms the severed connection it claims cannot be felt. Emerson describes a *vision* of loss that registers on the body—mutilating, scarring, rending. And nothing about the negations in that same sentence, which manifestly contradict the vision of mutilation, in fact contradicts it at all. It is a case of displacement because although Emerson claims he is mourning the loss of feeling, in fact what he is mourning is the lack of feeling's effects. Loss does not touch him not because he does not feel it but rather—he says—because the feeling has no palpable consequences. Here "consequences" seem imagined not only as a bodily manifestation but also as that particular bodily manifestation that affects the body of the mourner. Loss does not injure the mourner's bodily integrity, although the primitiveness of supposing it could establishes the fantasy connection between the man and the child whose absence is lamented. The mind anatomizes the loss as a severed connection with part of itself. And the graphic terms of the wish that it could be so (for if it were so there would be a correspondence between the feeling in the body and its representation *by* the body, its exaction *from* the body—an eye for an eye, a pound of flesh) remains unsavaged by death's actual effects.

Another way to regard the displacement I have described might be to say that because Emerson is here focusing on the discrepancy between the feeling of bodily violation and the fact of bodily intactness, he has displaced his attention from the loss of the child to the absence of the corporeal violation he would have the loss register. Thus there is some sense in which grief "does not touch" him. And that is not only the content of the complaint (that he has no contact with it, no bodily relation to it) but also its point (that grief does not touch him, that it has no effect on him). Emerson cannot "experience" the child's death. Cannot and does not wish to. Because to mourn the child in the only way mourning can be done is also to relinquish him. Thus from one point of view the deficiency of reality—or our deficient relation to it—protects not only the self (from the same fate as the dead child) but also the self's relation to the dead child.

Though in the mind the death of the child is equivalent to the death of the self—at least to its mutilation—the world belies the corporeality (hence the completeness) of that equivalence: "Marriage (in what is called the spiritual world) is impossible, because of the inequality between every subject and every object" (E 487–88). A passage from the essay's first three pages italicizes the point: "Nothing is left us now but death. We look to that with a grim satisfaction, saying, there at least is reality that will not dodge us" (E 473).

Satisfaction so conceived illustrates a particularly brutal version of the conclusion to which Emerson comes: The only way for him to have access to the child's death is to experience his own. Yet if experience gives the lie to conception because the death of the child is not equivalent to the death of the man, and because insofar as it affects the man it affects the man's mind or his heart (not rending or scarring his body), if in these ways death is less than the mind imagined, in its uncompromising equivalence with every other aspect of experience, that same loss is more than the mind imagined—it is displaced from the specific catastrophe to the general understanding.

If "effects" are being measured, we see that there is no more apocalyptic one than that in which the death of the son leads to this conclusion: "the discovery we have made, that we exist," a discovery contextualized unambiguously as follows: "That discovery is called the Fall of Man." Thus what was different from what the mind imagined becomes more than what the mind imagined, Emerson turning away from the death of the son whom he struggles not to mourn, converting grief to analysis, experience to reflection, loss of the son to perception of death. Although the subject of Waldo's death may appear to be abandoned after the third page of the essay, then, it is the moving force without which the philosophical split between experience and idealism can only be trivial. Death removes things from the immediate to the abstract. It always marks the limits of the experienced. Indeed the essay demonstrates a kind of enactive stylistics. What is never said is that it is the son who can no longer be experienced. Instead of lingering on the enormity of that fact, Emerson deflects his attention to experience itself, specifically to that "evanescence and lubricity of all objects, which lets them slip through our fingers then when we clutch hardest." Once we understand the deflection we see it is pointless to ask, Why does Emerson never allude to the son again? To take up the son's death as a displacement—to deflect the discussion of the son into miscellaneous experiences that "second" the son's loss, that reiterate or duplicate it—is to talk about the son the only way he can be talked about: at the remove at which death has placed him.

Our complaint about Emerson's dismissal of the subject of Waldo's death (for it is as a dismissal or abandonment that we first experience the displacement I have been describing) is akin to Emerson's own disappointment that grief does not do to the body what it does to the mind, and to a corollary disappointment, noted in a passage I cited earlier which observes that grief is superficial. Grief is superficial because it has no depth and because it is not penetrative. That grief is not penetrative means that the self cannot be pierced through by it. If the self could be pierced through by grief, the self would be equivalent to grief, hence not required to feel it. If we consider the two notions—of depth and penetration—we see that "depth" (or its absence) has to do with outsides and that "penetration" has to do with insides. The conjunction of the two (and of the self's inadequate relation to each) implied by the essay treats the self as a double surface.

Such a way of figuring it still leaves the self separate from what it contemplates. It is this separateness Emerson attempts to rectify when he complains that grief is "shallow...like all the rest, plays about the surface, and never introduces me into...reality." In the context of the hope implied by the sentence (that grief could be equal to all that is external to it), "introduces" is an interesting verb, for, negotiating the difference between self and reality, it suggests, not incidentally, that the two could come together. Another of the metaphors differently extended by this hope implies the self could attain reality as a palpable achievement: "There are moods in which we court suffering, in the hope that here, at least, we shall find reality, sharp peaks and edges of truth" (E 472).

The theatricality of the spatializations is repudiated when Emerson recognizes them as such: "But it turns out to be scene-painting and counterfeit." Although grief affects us, it is neither one with experience nor one with our own experience. Our relation to it is skittish, inconsequential. As Emerson moves from equating grief with "sharp peaks and edges" to associating it with "depth" and then with "surface," we see the spatializations per se—of height, depth, and, in the last resort, surface—ultimately dismissed as illusory. The images that presuppose access to grief belie the dissociation that characterizes it in fact: "Was it Boscovich who found out that bodies never come in contact? Well, souls never touch their objects. An innavigable sea washes with silent waves between us and the things we aim at and converse with....In the death of my son, now more than two years ago, I seem to have lost a beautiful estate,—no more. I cannot get it nearer to me" (E 472).

In Emerson's essay grief becomes a trope for experience because the self's relation to experience, like its relation to grief, is oblique, angled, contingent, dissociated. Thus the point I want to insist on with respect to the obliquity and dissociation in "Experience" is that these features of discourse are inevitable. Once the self understands its relation to experience, what it understands is that something has been removed. Death is the source of that understanding, teaching us our relation to *every* event.

As I have noted, then, after the essay's first three pages we see that what appears to be a displacement from the subject of Waldo's death is no displacement at all. It is rather a reiteration of the child's death, which ostensibly has been displaced, for the only way the dead son can be recalled is in a delegatory and impersonal way. We see how this reiteration works in the passage from the letter cited earlier from 1842, when a week after Waldo's death Emerson writes: "Alas! I chiefly grieve that I cannot grieve; that this fact takes no more deep hold than other facts, is as dreamlike as they; a lambent flame that will not burn playing on the surface of my river. Must every experience—those that promised to be dearest & most penetrative,—only kiss my cheek like the wind & pass away?" The image above is not here a trope for the passing of all experience. It is rather a metaphor for the son reincarnated as a trope. So too in Emerson's essay: Although grief is a trope for experience, it is always the particular experience, the death of the son, that is being simultaneously evoked and evaded. In the passage just cited, the child is evoked because the image of the wind kissing the man's cheek recalls the child even as it acknowledges his absence in the substitution of personification for person. In the passage from the essay which corresponds to that in the letter, contradictory imperatives similarly characterize a discourse in which grief is expressed and disavowed by the same words.

When writing of "the Indian who was laid under a curse, that the wind should not blow on him, nor water flow to him, nor fire burn him," who is "a type of us all," Emerson laments his own imperviousness to grief, his inability to register it. Yet although he mourns that "the dearest events are summer-rain, and we the Para coats that shed every drop"—although the man claims he is deficient of feeling—the trope rather suggests feeling so extensive that it overwhelms the bounds of the personal, becoming absorbed by the universe in an externalization: the shedding of the rain expressing the man's grief for him. In addition, the passage insists on a confusion between mourning and the thing mourned. Drops as rain (emblematizing the child who is lost) become drops as tears (emblematizing grief at that loss). Thus the expression of loss is made inseparable from its source, and equally inseparable from the man who asserts obliviousness to it. For even as grief is externalized as rain, the man also owns up to its source in himself. Thus one way of reading "and we the Para coats that shed every drop" is to see the phrase as connoting the evanescence of grief when the self repels and exteriorizes what it will not feel. An opposite way of reading the same sentence—bitter either way we understand it—is to note its depicting grief so inseparable from the self that identity is defined by the man's emphasized claim to it: "The dearest events are summer-rain, and we the Para coats that shed every drop." In the implicitly italicized pronoun of that sentence, Emerson is reiterating the idea of his bodily connection to the son whose body, in some similarly mysterious way, came from his own—a connection that in the sentences "[It] falls off from me and leaves no scar. It was caducous," he had contested. Underscoring the ambiguity of rain and tears, grief that is delegated and grief that is owned, the essay remains unclear as to whether "the dearest events," which the man says he cannot feel/which the man says he does feel, signify the child or the child's death—"events" being a word that is purposively evasive. The point to be made about this ambiguity is that it is a representative one. The child cannot now be experienced apart from his death, and, as the essay in its entirety is at pains to inform us, it is just in his death that he cannot be experienced at all.

If contradiction is at the heart of the passages I have described, this is in keeping with the strategy of the essay, which never concedes ultimately (the absence of grief) what it concedes initially (the absence of grief); hence the triumph of its ending. Grief is never given in to and therefore is never given up. To this end—the savoring of grief; the reenactment of the man's relation to it—there is a repetitiveness to the instances and examples of it in the essay, as if each one were employed to replicate the conflict whose doubleness I have described. Once we see that the figure of the son appears everywhere in the essay, we no longer wish to ask: Why is the subject introduced so as to be dismissed? We rather wish to ask an opposite question: Why does the man's grief need to be repeated, mirrored in all aspects of experience, indiscriminately, as if there were no end to it? The point of this repetition in psychological terms is to continue to place in apposition the contradictory impulses—the refusal to mourn/the imperative to mourn—that I have been describing. For if it is the case that the child must be relinquished, this is how he is to be relinquished, by what Freud calls a "struggle." Because— paraphrasing Freud—although the testing of reality shows that the loved object no longer exists, people never willingly abandon a libido-position: "[This struggle] is now carried through...under great expense of time and cathectic energy, while all the time the existence of the loved object is continued in the mind....Why this process of carrying out the behest of reality, bit by bit, which is in the nature of a compromise, should be extraordinarily painful is not at all easy to explain in terms of mental economics. It is worth noting that this pain seems natural to us" (*Standard Edition*, 14:245).

Repetition in "Experience" dramatizes the partiality of experience—the "bit by bit" to which Freud refers. Also its fleetingness. The man can mourn the same indirect relation to experience and to grief ten times because each time—every single time—what he says is both fleeting and partial. Thus the parts of the essay and the expressions of grief that they represent are not disparate and they are not integrated. They are continuous, but as a series of continuous displacements.

iv

One could describe the problem of contradiction that characterizes Emerson's essays as one of dissociation created by his disinclination to comment on the relation between contradictory assertions—his unwillingness first to admit them and second to instruct us on how we are to proceed in light of them. "Experience," I have claimed, bears a special relation to the problem of dissociation. It does so for several reasons, which I am now prepared to elaborate.

First, of all of Emerson's essays it is the only one to thematize dissociation, conceiving it initially in terms of death and ultimately in terms of power. Therefore, to the extent that it addresses itself to the source (death) and the consequence (power) of dissociation—the central concern in all of Emerson's essays—it has something to tell us about the questions that arise in them. Here I should reiterate that in "Experience" the dissociation precipitated by death and that connected to power are not in fact the same. I shall shortly amplify this point.

Second, "Experience" bears a special relation to the question of dissociation because, in the split between the essay's first three pages and its body, it exemplifies the most severe instance of dissociation in Emerson's oeuvre—a severity whose consequences have determined critics' inability coherently to locate the dominant subject in the essay. As I have noted, if they do see the death of the child as central, they have viewed it as the first of a number of phenomena to which Emerson has an equally contingent relation rather than understanding its generative connection to all else that follows. As a consequence, to the extent that they have observed that the essay is dominated by the problem of discrepancy or contradiction or dissociation they have done so in terms that invoke the dichotomy between idealism and experience without simultaneously understanding that the very ability to conceptualize division in these abstract terms is in "Experience" presented implicitly as a consequence of the child's death.

Third, "Experience" bears a special relation to the question of dissociation in Emerson's essays because, as its title suggests, its status is different from that of the rest of Emerson's essays. Though the title itself is an abstraction, the essay refers to things as experienced, not as abstracted.[12] To explain my distinction: Although the essay does not have a different kind of disorder from Emerson's other essays, it has a different relation to its own disorder. One way of understanding this difference is to observe that "Experience" does not contest the reality it describes. It does not have a confrontational relation to the experience of which it renders an account. In characterizing the early essays (like "The Divinity School Address," "Self-Reliance," *Nature*) as confrontational, I mean to suggest that they challenge experience, offering alternatives to it: the primacy of soul in "The Divinity School Address" and of the involuntary in "Self-Reliance." In characterizing the late essays (like "Fate") as differently confrontational, I mean to suggest that although these essays appear to accept the terms of experience, because they do so in a formal dialectic that concludes in a synthesis, the synthesis mitigates or dissolves the acceptance to which Emerson—in an essay like "Fate"—initially concedes. (Needless to say, these generalizations ideally ought to be substantiated by readings of the essays in question.) Distinguishing itself from the strategies of early and late essays, "Experience" neither stands in opposition to experience nor synthesizes the oppositions in experience that it recognizes and makes explicit. Rather, it situates itself in the midst of the issues it is considering, taking no "position" on its announced topic. An analogy may help to elucidate the way in which I wish to characterize "Experience" as different from the essays that precede and follow it. In "Fate" Emerson will recognize the beautiful as the contingent, codifying that recognition in the directive: "Let us build altars to the Beautiful Necessity."[13] "Beautiful Necessity" is a trope for the oxymoronic recognition in whose grip Emerson finds himself in "Experience" before he has learned to stand outside of the perception and, coolly, to find a figure for it.

Moreover—to explore my analogy—if we investigate the source of power in the two essays ("Fate" and "Experience") we see how it differs. The power of "Fate" lies in the antagonism between its concluding image—altars built to Beautiful Necessity—and the rest of the essay. The idea of a sacrifice, and the particular terms of its valorization here, occur *after* the argument (fate includes all and therefore fate includes freedom) has been successfully conducted. The image clinches the argument by changing its terms. Establishing a distance between the conclusion and the dialectic that precedes it, Emerson suggests that what is at stake is neither fate nor freedom, but rather the simpler question of whether the world is to be conceived as incoherent or meaningful: "If we thought men were free in the sense, that, in a single exception one fantastical will could prevail over the law of things, it were all one as if a child's hand could pull down the sun. If, in the least particular, one could derange the order of nature,—who would accept the gift of life?" (F 967). It is a question with no contest, and its brilliance lies in its dismissive relation to everything that has preceded it, as much as announcing: Forget previous arguments and previous ways of positioning the argument, however logically persuasive; this is the real issue.

In "Fate" we see where the essay becomes empowered—in the juxtaposition of the image of "Beautiful Necessity" to the previous exposition. Yet if in "Fate" power comes in the adjacency of the image to the argument, in "Experience" the obliquity of power saturates the essay; power comes from the inability to nail it down anywhere. Power pervades the essay in the multiple instances of dissociation, as these succeed each other in a series "of which we do not know the extremes, and believe that it has none." Although some change occurs between the stupor of the essay's beginning and the determined energy of its final pages, this change does not take place prospectively in the essay's last sentence, though that is where Emerson speaks of a potential "transformation of genius into practical power," and though that is where the critics, following Emerson's signpost, have located it—albeit with bewilderment at what would be its precipitous expression, were it really to emerge for the first time in that sentence.

Although I want to insist on our inability to say where the essay's transformation takes place, the change can be described by pointing to the man's altered relation to his own grief as this is expressed at the essay's beginning and end. At the essay's beginning, the man disavows grief—disavows and preserves it in the ways that, as I have suggested, specifically have to do with the idea that loss makes the body of the mourner deficient. At the conclusion of the essay, grief has become a gratitude, specifically expressed at the intactness of the man's body. In fact grief is entirely absent from the passage cited below, which, as a consequence, may look disconnected from earlier passages considered, though, as I shall explain, a figurative subtext relates them: "When I receive a new gift, I do not macerate my body to make the account square, for, if I should die, I could not make the account square. The benefit overran the merit the first day, and has overran the merit ever since. The merit itself, so-called, I reckon part of the receiving" (E 491).

Granted, the word "macerate," which describes the wasting away of flesh by fasting, presents a different image of bodily loss than that in the earlier passages (which depict loss as a scarring of the body, or as a tearing of the body, or simply as an expenditure of the body—as in tears or other vital fluids). Yet to the extent that all of these passages are concerned with getting and spending, with things given and taken away, with what is and can be lost—and with loss as something that affects the body—I believe we are required to see these passages as related. Specifically, we are required to ask: What has happened between the initial passages and the later ones—between passages that do not admit to loss (but which describe its toll on the body) and passages that talk openly about getting and losing (and which show the body intact)?

Before I address this question, I want to call attention to two other pertinent points that suggest a connection between the passage cited above and the earlier passages that address the child's death explicitly. One is the monetary imagery that governs the description of the child's death analogized initially to "the bankruptcy of my principal debtors, the loss of my property" (473); in the passage above such imagery seems reinvoked to describe compensation: "mak[ing] the account square." The second point of connection between this passage and earlier ones is that since the death considered in the essay has pertained to the child, not the man, and since, moreover, death has been actual not prospective, the subjunctive "if I should die," at this point in the essay, is affectively indistinguishable from the retrospective "since he has died" of the essay's opening pages, and this substitution matters because the conclusion that follows is a conclusion about the child's death.

In the spectacularly understated end of the essay, the subject of death is not absent from consideration; rather it is reiterated. But, as the initial pages of the essay put grief at a remove because the man had no access to it, the concluding pages of the essay put grief at a remove because there is no reason for it. In these pages grief is not inaccessible—grief is gratuitous. Gifts are not taken away; rather they are received. The body is not macerated; it is nourished at great cost; the subject considered is not the death of the child but rather the death of the self. As a consequence of the double displacements I have described, loss is nowhere conceded in Emerson's "Experience"—not at the beginning where grief is deemed inaccessible; not at the end where it is deemed gratuitous. Yet it marks every page less the first three—if in no other way than in the sacrifice of the subject stated in direct terms. In fact while the inability to mourn becomes a refusal to mourn, as we have seen, this conversion detracts attention from the essay's most salient fact—that the child who is banished from most of its pages nevertheless affects those pages as an incompletely displaced presence.

Several observations may clarify the transformation I have described. In psychoanalytic terms the man is able to move from images of bodily loss to ones of bodily wholeness because he has internalized the child—introjected him—and, so doing, he has simultaneously conceded the child's absence from the world. This explanation—on which one understanding of the end of the essay crucially depends—is simultaneously challenged by aspects of the essay that contest the idea of "integration" implicit in it, for the essay invites kinds of explanations that it then repels as inadequate. In asserting that the Freudian explanation might be inadequate—because the work of mourning needs to be repeated; because there are no conclusions to the repetitions in the essay (hence the child never returns to the essay's consideration); because insofar as the lost object is introjected, that introjected object is inaccessible to the man (hence the evasion of the subject of Emerson's essay "Experience")—I want immediately to acknowledge that my own understanding of the process of mourning in the essay depends on a Freudian model. Moreover, one could argue that the psychoanalytic model seems inadequate because Emerson subverts a real working through of grief. But it could also be argued that the model seems inadequate because, insofar as Emerson does give us a picture of mourning that is accomplished, we see that the way in which it is accomplished is not, as Freud suggests, in terms of integration, introjection, completion, or accessibility.

In this connection, Jacques Derrida's account of Nicolas Abraham and Maria Torok's distinction between incorporation and introjection is of interest to me, for they resist the idea that mourning is a process that can be completed, and—directly relevant to the question of the dead child's "place" in Emerson's essay—they therefore also call into question the problem of how spatially to represent the introjected object.[14] I am specifically interested in their notion that introjection is a process that takes place secretly—that the object introjected is kept in a secret place—and I am interested in Derrida's elaboration of this theory: that the consequence of secrecy is a cryptic text. The theoretical understanding of introjection as a phenomenon that occurs in such a way as to leave the introjected object both unavailable and invisible to the self in which it is encrypted offers a means to picture the way in which Waldo dominates the essay from which he has disappeared.[15]

If we assume for a moment, though, the usefulness of the psychoanalytic perspective, we see that it is impossible to say where the internalization has occurred. The introjection has been completed in the "bit by bit" that Freud describes as the process of mourning. The primary transformation, Emerson's claim notwithstanding, is not of genius into practical power. It is rather of the loss of the child into the loss of the man's affect and then, again, of the loss of the man's affect into the recuperation of that affect. Thus it would seem that mourning eschewed at the beginning of the essay becomes mourning that is completed at the end of the essay—but for the fact that the subject of the child never returns to these pages. To put this another way: The thematic of the essay may imply power for those present moments over which disso-ciation and, therefore, death do not preside. But this thematic is blocked by a countermovement in the essay (emblematized by the child's incompletely banished presence) that predicates power not in any actual moment, not in a time, but rather in a fantasized psychic space.

Two pages before the conclusion of the essay Emerson writes: "Life wears to me a visionary face. Hardest, roughest action is visionary also" (E 491). This assertion resumes the meditation begun by the sentence "Grief too will make us idealists" (473), as if it had not been broken off some eighteen pages earlier. Grief will make us idealists because grief will make the man imagine the child who can no longer be experienced. But if action as well as grief is in need of being imagined, then the distinctions between thought and action, the imagined and the experienced, the child and the recollection of the child—between all those oppositions the essay has worked to preserve—are inconsequential. To put this another way: In the fact that the second sentence appears to echo the first and also to contradict the exclusivity of its claims—hence to amplify them—it seems that action and the visionary now exist on the same plane. But as this is an essay entitled "Experience," the plane on which they exist is outside the essay.

Although there is a local meaning, then, to "Hardest, roughest action is visionary also" (namely that if "hankering after an overt or practical effect" is "apostasy" we must envision the effect we are prevented from experiencing), in the context of the issues that govern the whole meditation, the sentence "Hardest, roughest action is visionary also" has a broader, subversive mean-ing. What it subverts is the distinction between idealism and experience on which the discriminations in the essay consistently depend. It does this not so as to unite the two inside the essay (the essay has repeatedly demonstrated the impossibility of such a union) but rather to unite them in some hypo-thetical outside. If the child, who must now be imagined, exists at a remove, and if action (the most palpable characteristic of experience) exists at that same remove, then although both have been evacuated from the observations made by the essay (from what it purports to be able to talk about) in the parity of the essay's treatment of them—ousting each, as it does, from what it insists can be experienced—they are somewhere related. Although spatializing the issue this way personifies and gothicizes it, repeated metaphors of spatialization (apparent, for example, in the paragraph that describes grief in terms of depth, surface, peaks, edges) have invited just this kind of analysis. They have done so for a reason.

Dissociation in "Experience," and differently in Emerson's other essays, always seems resorted to so as to sustain at a remove what cannot be sustained in immediacy. In other essays this adjacency exists for the purpose of relegating qualifications to the margins when these conflict with the essay's polemical thrust. In "Self-Reliance," for example, the idea of the tyranny of the unconscious is exorcised to a sideline where it can contest but not come in contact with the essay's dominant voice, which wishes to stipulate conflict between the self and the social world undisturbed by the complications of any division in the former.[16] The legislative and repressive task assigned to obliquity in Emerson's essays is therefore, not surprisingly, the source of power. Obliquity sweeps aside objections, makes them tangential, disabling their ability to interfere with the essay's claims. In essays that characteristically desire into existence the prospective and the hypothetical, this legislative strategy is absolutely central. Power is not so much a consequence of obliquity per se, then, as it is a consequence of the driving force that marginalizes objections to primary claims without ever emasculating those claims. The metaphor is intended, for Emerson's primary claims are always at risk of having their potency threatened. If power, in general, is rapacious and anarchic ("Power keeps quite another road than the turnpikes of choice and will" [E 482]), man can only resist the force that itself resists control. Thus the tension of Emerson's essays is a consequence of keeping ideas that challenge central premises, however imperfectly, at a remove.

In "Experience" power is no less characterized by the tension I have described, but it is differently sourced. The essay introduces grief over the child's death only to usher it out of the text to some liminal place (for the essay's beginning suggests that grief is not only marginalized but will also frame what follows), some statutory nowhere where, undisturbed by the resolutions the essay records, Emerson preserves the loss he will not directly address. In "Experience," obliquity exists not to prevent what is dismissed to the periphery from disturbing what is said on the page; obliquity rather exists to preserve what is dismissed from anything that might threaten it—specifically, it exists to empower the grief that the essay has marginalized.[17]

Thus, although Emerson in "Experience" disavows spatializations that depend on ideas of integration, he relies on spatializations that depend on ideas of proximity. The essay inverts the central and the peripheral, the margin and the page, as well as the relative values implicitly attributed to each, and the triumph of its ending depends upon the inversion. "It does not touch me," Emerson says of grief at the beginning of the essay, but the lament turns to defiance at the end of the essay, where grief is the subject that cannot be touched. If the conversion I am describing savages the idea of reconciliation—to the child's death, to everything death represents—this is in keeping with the rest of the essay, which, like some science-fiction manifesto, insists, impersonally, on the isolated, the alien, the rootless, the excluded:

> We fancy that we are strangers, and not so intimately domesticated in the planet as the wild man, and the wild beast and bird. But the exclusion reaches them also.... Fox and woodchuck, hawk and snipe, and bittern, when nearly seen, have no more root in the deep world than man, and are just such superficial tenants of the globe. Then the new molecular philosophy shows astronomical interspaces betwixt atom and atom, shows that the world is all outside: it has no inside. (E 480–81)

In assertions like these, of which "Experience" is elemented, the idea of a depth psychology which conceptualizes mourning as a "task carried through" seems all but phantasmal.

4

The Way of Life by Abandonment:
Emerson's Impersonal

"Most of us have false beliefs about our own nature, and about our own identity, over time," Derek Parfit writes in *Reasons and Persons,* a book that challenges commonsense ideas about personal identity, and whose conclusions,
I shall suggest, pertain directly to the writings of Ralph Waldo Emerson.[1]
The false view, according to Parfit, centers on the idea that we are separately
existing entities. We hold such a view because we mistake the psychological
continuity of consciousness for the continued existence of a separately existing self in whom that consciousness inheres. But since experience gives no
proof of this premise, we ought, Parfit writes, to reject it. We ought to accept
the reductionist claim that "the existence of a person just consists in the existence of his brain and body, and the doing of his deeds, and the occurrence of
various other physical and mental events" (*RP* 225). In other words, we ought
to see there is no identificatory extra essence, distinct from our brains or bodies, on which a discrete or personal identity could be founded. I shall return
to this characterization, described by Parfit as "impersonal," at the end of
my discussion, but before leaving it, I want to underline Parfit's understanding of the radical implications of his theory. Granting that personal identity
does not matter is equivalent to, or has the consequence of, supposing that

"if tomorrow someone will be in agony [it is] an empty question whether this agony will be felt by *me*," to seeing that "if I am about to lose consciousness, there may be no answer to the question 'Am I about to die?'" (*RP* 280). What would it mean not to care if pain were *your* pain, to find the question empty? To find unanswerable the question of whether the loss of consciousness would mean *your* death? These are the central questions raised, I shall argue, obliquely, one might even say unconsciously, by the centrally recurring idea of the impersonal in Emerson's essays, to which I now turn.[2]

In the middle of "Nominalist and Realist" Emerson articulates *his* disillusion with the conventional idea that persons are separate and integral entities: "I wish to speak with all respect of persons, but sometimes I must pinch myself to keep awake, and preserve the due decorum. They melt so fast into each other, that they are like grass and trees, and it needs an effort to treat them as individuals."[3] The essay equivocates between belief in individuals and disbelief in them ("Though the uninspired man certainly finds persons a conveniency in household matters, the divine man does not respect them" [NR 580]), seeing this equivocation as a matter of shifting moods. But in the end Emerson's point of view is unambiguous, in favor of acknowledging what in "Montaigne" he names the "catholic sense," the "larger generalizations,"[4] in effect the impersonal, called by him "the Over-soul" in the most famous example: "In youth we are mad for persons. Childhood and youth see all the world in them. But the larger experience of man discovers the identical nature appearing through them all. Persons themselves acquaint us with the impersonal."[5] Impersonality is the antidote for the egotistical, the subjective, the solipsistic. It is so specifically because it refutes the idea that the mind is one's "property," that one's relation to being is that of ownership, on the one hand, and separate identity, on the other (O 390). From the perspective of the truth Emerson advocates in "The Over-soul," subjectivity and egotism are delusions about personal identity. From the vantage of the truth Emerson advocates in "The Over-soul," what defines "thoughts" as well as "events" is "alien energy," not "the will I call mine" (O 385). Thus the private will is overpowered by a force—variously named in this essay a "common heart" (O 386), and in others a "universal mind," an "identical nature"—that inhabits all.[6] By light of this identical nature, ownership is nonsensical; it is a mistake to call a talent, an idea, an achievement, or even a heart (and therefore a body) one's own, as it is a mistake to entertain the more abstract idea that persons have discrete identities. When Emerson in "The Over-soul" writes "We do not yet possess ourselves" (O 391), he means that we live out of synch with the truth of this impersonality. Yet to live *in* synch with it is to become indifferent to any fate one might conceivably call "mine" (the point ultimately made by the essay "Fate").

In part 1 of the following I examine formulations which elaborate the mechanics of impersonality, an examination necessary to specify how persons come in contact with the impersonal; in the second half of part 1 I examine Emerson's analysis of the way in which body and mind, counterintuitively, exemplify attributes of impersonality, as well as the way in which that "law," outside of body and mind, is equally said to epitomize it (M 708).

In part 2, I consider the features of the person who is expounding impersonality. I argue there is a connection between the anonymous voice of the speaker, the essays' stylistic singularity, and the compensating features of the erasure of personality. Throughout this and the following section I consider a series of concerns that threaten to produce a devastating critique of Emerson in any serious reading of him. Someone might reasonably feel that Emerson's idea of the impersonal is ethically illegitimate if not indeed simply delusional. If it is neither of these, what keeps it from being so? I understand such a question to mean: From what vantage *could* one relinquish the personal perspective one inevitably has as a delimited self? At the heart of the question is the issue of what licenses the abdication of a perspective one can't in some sense abdicate—what licenses it for oneself and what sanctions such a claim when it is made on another's behalf. For when, for instance, Emerson makes the following astonishing assertion, "If, in the hours of clear reason, we should speak the severest truth, we should say, that we had never made a sacrifice. In these hours the mind seems so great, that nothing can be taken from us that seems much. All loss, all pain, is particular; the universe remains to the heart unhurt....It is only the finite that has wrought and suffered; the infinite lies stretched in smiling repose," this seems the sort of claim that cannot be made by one person for another (SL 305).

In part 3 I turn to "The Poet," the practitioner of impersonality—the poet being he who relinquishes the "jailyard of individual relations," who lays aside his private self so as to draw on "great public power...by unlocking, at all risks, his human doors."[7] Although public power appears to require an indifference to persons, specifically to the distinction among persons, and especially to the particular status of the person who is writing, I argue that it does so at the peril of calling its own authority into question. Thus I claim that the deficiency in Emerson's representation of the impersonal lies peculiarly in the missing sense of a person.

How one gains access to the impersonal (in distinction to the inevitable access conferred by grief in Emerson's "Experience") is a question that precedes all others in Emerson's essays. In "The Divinity School Address" it receives an explanation that initially differentiates what "the preacher" is to do from what others are to do. The preacher is to decline any secondary relation to God: "to go alone; to refuse the good models...and dare to love God without mediator or veil." Disavowing custom and authority, the preacher is "to live with the privilege of the immeasurable mind." He is to become visible to himself. The ocular image is Emerson's (in that the "immeasurable mind" is what the preacher will see when fashion, custom, authority, pleasure, money "are not bandages over [his] eyes"). When the preacher is visible to himself, he is enjoined to make himself visible to others, so that they will have a model. ("Let their doubts know that you have doubted, and their wonder feel that you have wondered.") What they will have a model *for* is precisely autonomy, which leads, in turn, to their ability to look within themselves, to do what the preacher does: like the preacher, "to go alone." From the preacher's point of view what is advocated is a theory of interpenetration: the self with "the immeasurable mind" and consequently with others. In this formulation inspiration turns inward and outward at once: To be visible to yourself is to make yourself visible to others, which will make visible the fact that what is in you is also in them. Such visibility will bequeath to them the autonomy that Emerson in his sermon is arguably bequeathing to the young students.[8]

The paradigm for access is somewhat different in "The American Scholar," where the self "going down into the secrets of his own mind...has descended into the secrets of all minds." The American scholar has access to others *by* having access to himself, unlike the "Divinity School" preacher who, having access to himself, consequently (as opposed to identically) has access to others, and who therefore can show others how to have access to themselves. But the difference is without ultimate significance, since (disappointingly from a pedagogic vantage) the lesson in both cases is that "the man has never lived that can feed us ever. The human mind cannot be enshrined in a person."[9]

In context this is an astonishing statement. It does not mean that no man is an exemplary, in the sense of adequate, incarnation, because each is partial (what it would mean in *Representative Men* or "Nominalist and Realist"). Nor does it precisely suggest that you should look to yourself rather than to others, though, like "The Divinity School Address," it also counsels autonomy, but for slightly different reasons. The American scholar become autonomous will discover that no person (not even his own person) is adequate to enshrine the human mind. Thus while other persons produce a barrier to what "The Divinity School Address" calls "the immeasurable mind," so does one's own self understood in any conventional way. In effect, then, what self-reliance turns out to mean for Emerson is a strong recognitional understanding of the inadequacy of any person: other persons *or* this person.[10] And what the preacher and the American scholar know how do is to break out of the tyranny of egotistical self-enclosure.

But what is meant by a person? And what is the alternative to supposing that the human mind can be "enshrined in a person"? "Compensation" provides one answer to the second of these questions. In the essay Emerson has been arguing the need for recompense ("Each thing is a half, and suggests another thing to make it whole"), on the one hand, and, on the other hand, the means *of* recompense ("We can no more halve things...than we can get an inside that shall have no outside").[11] In this way a theory of dualism turns into a theory of ultimate totality. But the essay also wishes to illustrate some fact "deeper than" recompense which does not therefore require it: "The soul is not a compensation, but a life. The soul *is*. Under all this running sea of circumstance, whose waters ebb and flow with perfect balance, lies the aboriginal abyss of real Being. Essence, or God, is not a relation, or a part, but the whole" (C 299). Not part of the system of compensation (not necessitating it, not contributing to it), the soul is free of the drama of "More and Less" which is also the drama of "*His* and *Mine*" or, put differently still, free of the drama of the "inequalities of condition" and circumstance (C 301).

In "Compensation," then, the soul is free of particulars, good or bad; impersonality is a consequence of that liberation. The following paragraph from "Self-Reliance" elaborates the nature of this freedom. It does so by identifying the features of "real Being" (the name "Compensation" gives it), a state so stripped down that it is defined by negations. In such a state, characterized in the following passage as intuition without an object, one lives impersonally, that is, "in the present, above time" and "with God":

> And now at last the highest truth on this subject remains unsaid; probably cannot be said; for all that we say is the far-off remembering of the intuition. That thought, by what I can now nearest approach to say it, is this. When good is near you, when you have life in yourself, it is not by any known or

accustomed way; you shall not discern the foot-prints of any other; you shall not see the face of man; you shall not hear any name;—the way, the thought, the good, shall be wholly strange and new. It shall exclude example and experience. You take the way from man, not to man. All persons that ever existed are its forgotten ministers. Fear and hope are alike beneath it. There is somewhat low even in hope. In the hour of vision, there is nothing that can be called gratitude, nor properly joy. The soul raised over passion beholds identity and eternal causation, perceives the self-existence of Truth and Right, and calms itself with knowing that all things go well. Vast spaces of nature, the Atlantic Ocean, the South Sea,—long intervals of time, years, centuries,—are of no account. This which I think and feel underlay every former state of life and circumstances, as it does underlie my present, and what is called life, and what is called death.[12]

In the state Emerson describes, immediate experience is incomparable, not contingent on others' experience or on one's own experience. But what does it mean to get beyond others' and one's own experience? What is one *beyond*?

The answer offered by the passage has something to do with extrication from emotion, including all those emotions like hope, gratitude, joy, which one might suppose Emerson to wish to cultivate. Hope is understood to be "low" presumably because, by definition, it supposes the inadequacy of the present state; "gratitude," which is inspired by the sufficiency of the present, presumes, albeit implicitly, some alternative state that *wouldn't* be adequate. In effect it assumes a discrimination between the actual and an alternative to the actual. "Joy" especially implies the possibility of its opposite; moreover, the very meaning of joy, and the experiential sense of joy, presupposes an excess, a going beyond the bounds of bare awareness to which the soul has penetrated. Joy is a reaction, albeit a pleasant reaction. But the state Emerson describes is empty of reaction. That is its beneficence, its great gift. Vision undistracted by passion (by hope, gratitude, joy) is vision that is equanimous; Emerson calls it "calm." The passage asserts no reliable distinction between what underlies this present state of mind and what underlies either of those states supposed to be categorically other, between "what is called life, and what is called death."

If "this which I think and feel" is also foundational—is the *same* foundation—for "what is called life, and what is called death," then the all-substantial present, the present made substantial by the clairvoyance of one's seeing of it ("the hour of vision"), is the predicative ground for what we suppose to be different in both magnitude and category. That is what we see when we see the present as it is: without passion, and without comparison, as if it alone were real.

Though it might seem surprising, the impersonal, as instantiated in the passages I have touched on, *leads* to the social in its highest form. In Emerson's words, the consciousness of divine presence "makes society possible" (O 392). Thus in Emerson's account the impersonal enables the social world it appears to eradicate. "The Over-soul" offers a rigorous analysis of how the impersonal is incarnated. The Over-soul makes itself manifest through particular properties within particular persons, who act as its conduit. This Over-soul is not an entity, nor is it a property. Call it a manifestation, even always a particular manifestation, though not always the same particular manifestation:

> All goes to show that the soul in man is not an organ, but animates and exercises all the organs; is not a function, like the power of memory, of calculation, of comparison, but uses these as hands and feet; is not a faculty, but a light; is not the intellect or the will, but the master of the intellect and the will; is the background of our being, in which they lie,—an immensity not possessed and that cannot be possessed. From within or from behind, a light shines through us upon things, and makes us aware that we are nothing, but the light is all. A man is the façade of a temple wherein all wisdom and all good abide. What we commonly call man, the eating, drinking, planting, counting man, does not, as we know him, represent himself, but misrepresents himself. Him we do not respect, but the soul, whose organ he is, would he let it appear through his action, would make our knees bend. When it breathes through his intellect, it is genius; when it breathes through his will, it is virtue; when it flows through his affection, it is love. And the blindness of the intellect begins, when it would be something of itself. (O 386–87)

The passage is precise in its analysis of how this power (not an organ, like Descartes's gland; not a function; not a faculty) becomes embodied *by* organs, by functions, by faculties. The Over-soul inhabits, vivifies, or traverses the mind, the will, the heart, but it is *not* the mind, the will, the heart. The Over-soul can be seen in those incarnations through which it "breathes": "genius," "will," "virtue," "love," and "action." Not separate from and also not equal to any particular trait, but also manifesting itself only through recognizable particularities—through actions, emotions, properties, only through what is actual and even at times visible (action would be visible, and genius, will, virtue, love might be so). In "Nature" transparency cancels being. But the Over-soul animates and makes being palpable. It is precisely this palpability which compels tribute: "Would [a man] let it appear through his action, [it] would make our knees bend." In fact, it could be argued that it is the Over-soul's visibility *in* action, function, property, and person that permits us to mistake action, function, property, person for the manifestational power which animates them.

The Over-soul, then, *is* associated with the individual, though one can have no proprietary relation to it. (From "Illusions": "The notions, '*I am*,' and '*This is mine*,' which influence mankind, are but delusions of the mother of the world.")[13] The trouble begins when the mind falsely identifies with the powers that inhabit it. The mistake lies in associating the Over-soul with the self and particularly with the voluntary self. It *is* associated with the person, but not as his property and not through his will (therefore not through "eating, drinking, planting, counting"). These activities misrepresent the person not because they are palpable and also not because they are functional or social. Rather, because they are limited.

In pointing to something other than the experiential world of the fragmentary (a world whose piecemeal nature he would describe most eloquently in "Experience"), Emerson is not mystically gesturing to an alien nature which he domesticates, converting the not-me into something with recognizable contours. The Over-soul always remains other, while all the time being all-accessible (O 394). In fact it is precisely the point that we cannot relinquish our difference from it. No procedure is performed that would cancel the egotistical person, the person with interests, needs, desires, will. It is not a matter of willing to be better than we are or different than we are. It is a matter of not-willing, of seeing what we are when the will stops executing its claims. When we give ourselves up to the involuntary, "the walls are taken away. We lie open on one side to the deeps of spiritual nature, to the attributes of God" (O 387). I take Emerson's spatial image as testifying to the necessarily divided nature of our allegiance to the egotistical and the impersonal. On one side there is access, on the other there is not.

In seeing one's true alliance is not with will or desire, not with anything piecemeal, but rather with the totality, the personal becomes impersonal. But to put it like this still implies a conventional choice, and I take Emerson to be insisting that at such a moment there is no real choice, no other way to be in *proper* relation. If what's given up by the isolate self is a deluded sense of its power, what's given back is what Emerson, silently quoting Plotinus, calls innocence, that to which the "religious" cedes when it stops being an idea: "The soul gives itself, alone, original, and pure, to the Lonely, Original, and Pure, who, on that condition, gladly inhabits, leads, and speaks through it. Then is it glad, young, and nimble. It is not wise, but it sees through all things. It is not called religious, but it is innocent" (O 400). Thus in acceding to the impersonal, one is "beyond" emotions, beyond the idea that identity is fixed. But not beyond the social or the recognizable. We are continuously enjoined to see we can recognize the impersonal (called "the Over-soul" or, in "Spiritual Laws," the "homogeneous" [SL 321]), though not in the familiar terms by which we customarily mistake it: not connected to sequence, not in relation to the voluntary, and not as an anomaly.

The interest of Emerson's essays lies in moments when the impersonal *emerges*. To put this in different terms: While it has frequently been noted that Emerson's essays dramatize contradiction, the *content* of the contradiction can repeatedly be specified by the process through which the personal becomes the impersonal, as in "Nominalist and Realist," where the science of universals alternates with the science of parts, and where nature (one of Emerson's ways of denominating the whole) rises up against persons, specifically against "each person, inflamed to a fury of personality" (NR 581). In the following examples, differently epitomized—by the eyes, by moods, by moral law—the impersonal is set against the "fury of personality." This contest takes the place of narrative or *is* the narrative of Emerson's essays.

In the essay "Behavior" allegiance to the universal is immediately articulated by a glance of the eyes. Interestingly, unlike in "Culture," where an adherence to the universal needs to be *learned,* the eyes confess the truth, from one perspective, and penetrate to it, from another, immediately and involuntarily. ("The communication by the glance is in the greatest part not subject to the control of the will. It is the bodily symbol of identity of nature.") What the eye reveals is the degree of discrepancy between the "generous and universal" and the "fury of personality":

> There are asking eyes, asserting eyes, prowling eyes; and eyes full of fate,— some of good, and some of sinister omen. The alleged power to charm down insanity, or ferocity in beasts, is a power behind the eye.... 'Tis very certain that each man carries in his eye the exact indication of his rank in the immense scale of men, and we are always learning to read it. A complete

man should need no auxiliaries to his personal presence. Whoever looked on him would consent to his will, being certified that his aims were generous and universal. The reason why men do not obey us, is because they see the mud at the bottom of our eye.[14]

Although the beholder reads the eye with respect to an index of behaviors (that pertain to action, to speech, to hospitality, to security), the standard for assessing each remains an alliance of the personal with the universal. The personal is the "mud at the bottom of our eye." The eyes give the lie first to what the person would want to be believed, indicating a discrepancy between what is asserted and what is true; second, they reveal that when there is not in fact harmony between one person and another—hence not harmony between the person and the universe—the "bodily symbol of identity of nature" (Emerson's presumptive ideal) stands degraded and betrayed. Thus the eyes reveal the personality and reveal *beyond* it. One way of understanding such a divided revelation is to see the "fury of personality" as a mere part of being which inherently also reflects something extrinsic to it. The eyes reveal an impersonal register of value identically legible to all.

Emerson's representation of the transience of moods further erodes the commonplace idea that mental states are personal and that we govern what occurs "within." "Circles" radically tells us that our moods determine *us*. Further, "Our moods do not believe in each other....I am God in nature; I am a weed by the wall."[15] In "Experience" life is described as a flux: "a succession of moods."[16] In "Nominalist and Realist" the very propensity to believe in universals over particulars or vice versa is a consequence of shifting moods. Thus so-called fixtures (like "truth" in "Circles," like perspective in "Nominalist and Realist," but also like temperament in "Experience") are subject to alteration. That there is no security against moods in effect calls into question the idea of any fixture legislating what is thought, believed in, felt, experienced. If every insight, like every mood, is, as Emerson implies, partial, fleeting, and mediate, then we are merely inhabited by these truly extrinsic (hence impersonal) mental states which we host without controlling. They are events in our history without being properly identified as ours. Harry Frankfurt writes: "A person is no more to be identified with everything that goes on in his mind...than he is to be identified with everything that goes on in his body."[17] Emerson goes more than a step further, suggesting, it would seem, that there is *no* mental experience with which we are to be identified; for there is no permanence to any mood, perception, or belief ("Permanence is a word of degrees" [Ci 404]) and, further, no ability to determine when, affected by these moods, one experiences the self as "God in nature" or, oppositely, as a "weed by the wall."[18] This extrinsicality even of those determinations that most apparently define us is underscored and—from one point of view outrageously—extended in "Uses of Great Men" where Emerson asserts: "The power which [great men] communicate is not theirs. When we are exalted by ideas, we do not owe this to Plato, but to the idea, to which, also, Plato was debtor." Such erasure of identity, such a consistent dramatization (in "Circles," "Experience," "Nominalist and Realist," "Uses of Great Men") of moods as constitutive of belief and even of personality and temperament suggests that moods exist "irrespective of persons," that "moods" like the forces described in "Uses of Great Men" become "power[s] so great, that the potentate is nothing." Moods, like those forces, are presented as "destroying individualism."[19]

Thus, to say, as I did earlier, that mental states are things we host without controlling, are "events in our history," is still to suppose a personal identity inhabited by moods extrinsic to it, just as to imply an alien physical state (like the "broken sleep" described below) is to suppose an essence to which that physical state is contrastively other. But this sense of contrast is only rhetorical (has no significant application). While it looks like such formulations presume something stable on which identity could be pinned (our body, our history), the formulations are stable only by contrast; they are something which contrast—the next formulation—shifts. Nothing is "ours" except rhetorically, or positionally. In that rhetoric a person lays claims to some elusive property which he cannot really own.

One way of understanding the impersonal, then, is as something that appears through *bodies* (as visible in the eyes) as a critique of the personal (also visible there), that which shows up its limits, as in the passage from "Behavior." A second way of understanding the impersonal is in terms of moods and *mental states:* The very moods that we might suppose to define our individual persons, when scrutinized in Emerson's representations, rather contradict the idea of the personal (though not necessarily the idea of the individual, since one could be individuated by mental states that were not properly one's "own"). Thus if in "Behavior" the impersonal speaks *through* the self (is visible in the eyes), in an essay like "Nominalist and Realist" the impersonal calls into question the very idea of a self as a stable or predictable entity, for the moods which define our perceptions, beliefs, thoughts are in effect only contingent on circumstance (in "Montaigne," even principles—opinions on right and wrong, on fate and causation—are "at the mercy of a broken sleep or an indigestion" [M 704]). In yet a third example the impersonal is associated not with the body and not with the affective life of the mind but rather with a law (alternatively called "the moral sentiment") to which the "self" adheres, disregarding as it were the conditions of body and mind: "All moods may be safely tried, and their weight allowed to all objections: the moral sentiment as easily outweighs them all.... This faith avails to the whole emergency of life and objects" (M 708). So much does the ideal of law prevail against body and mind that the ideal survives the degradation of it, passionately represented in the penultimate passage from "Montaigne":

> Charles Fourier announced that "the attractions of man are proportioned to his destinies"; in other words, that every desire predicts its own satisfaction. Yet, all experience exhibits the reverse of this; the incompetency of power is the universal grief of young and ardent minds. They accuse the divine providence of a certain parsimony. It has shown the heaven and earth to every child, and filled him with a desire for the whole; a desire raging, infinite; a hunger, as of space to be filled with planets; a cry of famine, as of devils for souls. Then for the satisfaction,—to each man is administered a single drop, a bead of dew of vital power, *per day*,—a cup as large as space, and one drop of the water of life in it. Each man woke in the morning, with an appetite that could eat the solar system like a cake; a spirit for action and passion without bounds...but, on the first motion to prove his strength,—hands, feet, senses, gave way....In every house...this chasm is found,—between the largest promise of ideal power, and the shabby experience. (M 708)

Despite the hyperbolically exampled discrepancies between the ideal and the experienced, the conclusion of the essay adheres to the ideal, though without Fourier's illusions. The personal (what is experienced by the hands, the feet, the senses, and epitomized by an "appetite that could eat the solar system like a cake") is cast aside, not afforded weight, in favor of "the moral sentiment." It is not cast aside because its presence is immaterial, because it does not affect the person. From one point of view it *constitutes* the person's desire, his aspiration, his endeavor, his voraciousness and registers the thwarting of these. But if such frustration defines the *personal*, from another point of view, it does not define the *person*, who rather "resist[s] the usurpation of particulars," so as to "penetrate to their catholic sense" (M 709). Here body and mind are subordinated to a manifestation of the impersonal which cannot be assigned to a will or a desiring self. And this impersonal force (called in "Montaigne" as in "The Divinity School Address" the "law") also becomes the object of our affirmation, against the evidence of the personal and, even more to the point, against the interests of the person.

ii

In Emerson's writing, style functions as a validation of propositions in lieu of logic or as a supplement to logic, as I shall explain. This distrust of formal argument originates in Emerson's critique of the commonplaces of prayers and sermons. In "The Divinity School Address," against the deadliness of the formalist preacher, who substitutes "doctrine" for life, Emerson posits what is impossible to formulate:

> The child amidst his baubles, is learning the action of light, motion, gravity, muscular force; and in the game of human life, love, fear, justice, appetite, man, and God, interact. These [divine] laws refuse to be adequately stated. They will not be written out on paper, or spoken by the tongue. They elude our persevering thought; yet we read them hourly in each other's faces, in each other's actions, in our own remorse....This sentiment [the perception of lawfulness] is the essence of all religion. (DSA 76)

In the passage Emerson gets his reader to accede to an important experience which only subsequently is characterized as *religious*, as "the essence of all religion." Religious experience is *integral* to ordinary experience, but because it is not separable from ordinary experience, it is not knowable in terms of easily detachable criteria. Nor can it be articulated, though it cannot help but be intuited. Moreover, arising out of concrete experience, such laws are nonetheless "out of time, out of space, and not subject to circumstance" or summary account (DSA 76). They are within and without particular experiences; embodied by experience to which they are nonetheless not reducible. Such "laws," elsewhere cumulatively called "the religious sentiment," are by definition impersonal and in "The Divinity School Address" are repeatedly juxtaposed to the person of Jesus. Such law can be analogized to a natural phenomenon ("It is a mountain air....The silent song of the stars is it" [DSA 78]); it is knowable *in* nature, and often *as* nature. It is also knowable as *depth*. Thus Jesus's name "is not so much written as ploughed into the history of this world." That name is said to be an "infusion" (DSA 79).

In "Self-Reliance" the impersonal (which alone has depth and thus ultimate reality) is associated with "*Whim*," with the "involuntary," with "genius," and with "intuition" (S 262, 269, 260, 271). In "The Divinity School Address" the impersonal (which alone has depth) is associated with "the soul." My point here is that, unlike a systematic thinker, Emerson makes no attempt to confer consistency on his designations, or even to establish connections among terms that occupy the same structural position in different essays. Intuition has depth; as the soul has depth; as Jesus's name (in "The Divinity School Address"), which is "ploughed into the history of this world," has depth; but whether these are different terms for the same phenomenon remains, I believe, intentionally unaddressed. The consequence for a reader is to encounter phenomena which clearly overlap without being clearly identical. And this nonidenticality seems a purposeful block to the summarizing definition which could characterize the impersonal, but which cannot do so here because the experiences in which it is shown to be situated eschew logical "comparative" relations.

If in "The Divinity School Address" Emerson preaches the soul against the religion of the person, in "The Over-soul" this entity is recognizable as what is "public and human" (O 400). Though incarnated in form, it always points inward to some identical "nature," some "centre of the world," some "influx of the Divine mind into our mind" (O 389, 392). That "influx" is characterized in one passage as coming on condition of an "entire possession"; it is also characterized, sequentially, as coming as "insight," as coming as "serenity," and conclusively (but always nondefinitively) as coming as "grandeur" (O 396, 397). Thus again we note the asymmetry of terms by which manifestations of the impersonal defy systemization: they are connected in this discourse, but not logically so. Their originality lies in their deliberately unexplained relations often perceptible as mere contiguity.

But if the designations for the soul keep us off balance through a nonalliance, and if we are commensurately enjoined to renounce description of the soul for habitation within it—are enjoined to reside in that "influx of the Divine mind into our mind" (called at this moment "the religious sense")—Emerson does characterize the experience of such an influx consistently as "enthusiasm," as "ecstacy," as "trance," or as "inspiration," and, "in the case of...remarkable persons" like Socrates, Plotinus, George Fox, Jakob Behmen, as what he calls "ravishment" (O 392–93). In fact "ravishment" (that proprioceptive sense of what occurs at that moment when the personal is annihilated by the influx of the impersonal) is what the essays attempt to dramatize.

What replaces philosophical logic is something like the representation of ravishment, a phenomenon all the more difficult to recognize because it occurs in relation to experiences that seem at last, as at first, categorically different from each other (the name of Jesus ploughed into the history of the world; the baubles of the child's play ingrained as law; innocence which results when the "soul gives itself, alone, original, and pure, to the Lonely, Original, and Pure"). There is, moreover, another reason that the representation of moments of ravishment is disorienting. In narrating such moments, Emerson assumes a stance and a voice above and beyond the personal, for his authority in these essays with respect to the "religious sentiment" (elsewhere "innocence," the "soul," "laws that refuse to be adequately stated") is the authority of one who has access to principles of organization that are conferred beyond individual experience.[20] Hence, for instance, the difficulty in attributing individuality to the voice which says "the soul gives itself, alone, original, and pure."

This is not Emerson's voice, because it is Plotinus's.[21] But it is not Plotinus's either, because *in* Emerson it is legible as no one's voice at all. And that this anonymous voice, which is not a recognizable voice, because not legible as a single person's voice, should tell of ravishment—ravishment being the precise moment marked in extraordinary persons at "the influx of the Divine mind into our mind"—is remarkable, given the fact that if the imperative for someone's voicing the impersonal is access to experience that transcends his own, the imperative for someone's voicing ravishment is to inhabit the very experience whose particularity must be owned (and experienced as such) before it is annihilated, if the experience is to register as one of ravishment. Thus the experience being described ("the Divine mind into our mind," the obliteration of the personal—call it, as Emerson does, ravishment) reveals a weird absence, the opposite of which is stylistic mimesis, since nothing counts or registers as "personal" even prior to the epiphanic moment of its proclaimed disappearance.

The voice of no private person, Emerson's voice in his essays is public and is engaged in a performance. What is being performed is something like "ravishment" as a consequence of self-abandonment. In Emerson's essays the personal is most marked at the moment of its obliteration—or it would be so if it were initially established, as it is, rarely, in instances like the following. In the most celebrated example, from *Nature,* the self that is lost is briefly first owned: "Standing on the bare ground,—my head bathed by the blithe air, and uplifted into infinite space,—all mean egotism vanishes....I am part or particle of God."[22] In this example the person is forfeited for "Universal Being," whereas in "Experience" what is forfeited is something like personal affect—"In the death of my son, now more than two years ago, I seem to have lost a beautiful estate,—no more. I cannot get it nearer to me....This calamity...does not touch me" (E 473)—and, ultimately, personal connection—"The longest love or aversion has a speedy term. The great and crescive self, rooted in absolute nature, supplants all relative existence" (E 487).

In "Circles," self-abandonment is theorized as that philosophically necessary position that makes ravishment possible: "The one thing which we seek with insatiable desire is to forget ourselves, to be surprised out of our propriety, to lose our sempiternal memory, and to do something without knowing how or why; in short, to draw a new circle....The way of life is wonderful: it is by abandonment" (Ci 414). Typically, however, while the impersonal is ostensibly represented at the moment of its emergence in Emerson, and though this emergence is ostensibly performed, there is characteristically vacancy in the place where we might expect to find a person.

Thus although the essays perform the task of ravishment—that process through which the person is annihilated by the impersonal—no sacrifice is customarily really exacted, because rarely is it the case that a discrete or particularized self initially occupies the subject position. What is great about nature, Emerson argues in an early essay, "The Method of Nature," is "that there is...no private will, no rebel leaf or limb, but the whole is oppressed by one superincumbent tendency, obeys that redundancy or excess of life which in conscious beings we call *ecstasy*."[23] We could say that what occupies the subject position of Emerson's essays—how the voice we call Emerson's implicitly comes to be defined—is a rhetorical construction, the most enduring feature of which impedes or staves off any apparent individuality, any representation of a "private will." That is the sine qua non of the Emersonian "I," ostensibly styled without either point of view or idiosyncrasy. (Of course voices in writing are always rhetorically constructed, but the rhetorical construction of Emerson's "I" can be characterized by its fetishized universality, its obsessively constructed anonymity.) The platitudes that often seem stunning in an Emerson essay—stunning that a writer who displays so much expertise in crafting powerful sentences could also write so vapidly—well serve this goal of voicing words whose particular source is undiscoverable. It precisely serves Emerson's purpose to rehearse commonplace remarks which could be spoken by anyone. In "Intellect," we are told that "silence is a solvent that destroys personality, and gives us leave to be great and universal."[24] In Emerson's essays contradictory propositions (along with the abstracted "I," constructed at once, as if indiscriminately, out of original, vital images and empty enervated ones) are the solvent that dissolves personality.

There is a hypnotic and vertiginous momentum to the (much-discussed) contradictory drift of these essays, which advocate, on the one hand, self-trust and, on the other, self-abolition. Precisely because of this self-contradiction, the essays implicitly promise an overall logic or an argumentative progression which would make sense of and therefore rectify the self-canceling propositions. In lieu of this context—one could say in defiance of it—the propositions, like the self who voices them, are constructed as momentary: good for the moment, but again and again cast off and recreated. The "endless seeker, with no Past at my back" (Ci 412)—one of Emerson's most wishful self-descriptions—staves off perspective, duration, and therefore questions about limit. The "person" that Emerson represents himself as being is one with no situational givens—one who, like the poet's language in "The Poet," is "fluxional," "vehicular," "transitive," therefore a man indifferent to needs (P 463). This Emersonian self, the "I" of the essays, can invoke the impersonal, purporting to be embodied by or fed to it (and this without sacrifice, or with "nothing...that seems much"), the celebration of which process is said to produce excess, ecstasy, and, alternatively, ravishment, because his own being is so spectacularly unconstituted by anything *physical*. The Emersonian speaker who celebrates the impersonal is something like the "soul" he frequently catechizes. Or if not a soul, then "a method, a progressive arrangement; a selecting principle" (in "Spiritual Laws," these explicitly constitute the definition of "a man" [SL 311]). Or he is an intellect ("Intellect goes out of the individual, floats over its own personality" [I 417]). Or a force like love, which we are told "must become more impersonal every day."[25]

In view of these peculiarities—speech that is unsituated, unreferenced to a body; constituted by contradiction and by nonsummatory arguments; conciliatory with respect to loss ("Nothing that can be taken from us seems much"); and delegating away various properties like love, like intellect—I wish to ask: What is the appeal of the impersonal; what makes it attractive?

The context that might explain the enticement of the impersonal above what Henry Ware, Jr., in 1838, writing against Emerson, called "the happiness of human life" is the heroic—a model, or an ideal, that, it could be argued, Emerson shares with Kant.[26] Thus for example when Emerson advocates dismissing "the eating, drinking, planting, counting man" for the Over-soul, what is being distinguished is personal interest in an entity aspiring to be "something of itself" for the sake of interest in "an immensity not possessed and that cannot be possessed" (O 387).[27]

When Kant distinguishes the categorical from the hypothetical by saying that in the case of the former "all interest is renounced, which is the specific criterion of categorical as distinguished from hypothetical imperatives,"[28] this self-abnegation sounds peculiarly like Emerson, although Kant is talking about what constitutes the basis of proper (ethical) action and Emerson is talking about what constitutes the basis of proper identification (since the interested or partial man "does not...represent himself, but misrepresents himself"). For Kant—at least in regard to ethical action—the worth of rational beings lies in their capacity to adhere to "a mere idea" which serves as "an inflexible precept of the will" (in other words, dignity is the result of the autonomy of man's will from "the physical law of [the self's] wants"). I call this "heroic" because it presupposes a contact with the real that is not contingent on this or that condition. For Kant "personal worth" consists in adhering to the requirements of pure practical reason independently of inclination (FP 81). Hence, what is involved is choice of nobility. According to the *Fundamental Principles of the Metaphysics of Morals* only in the moral world "is [a person] his proper self (being as a man only the appearance of himself)" (FP 91). For Emerson, as for Kant, a higher interest and identification with something higher presuppose a person's access to a real stripped of inessentials. Thus in "Worship": "We are never without a hint that these powers [of sense and understanding] are mediate and servile, and that we are one day to deal with real being,—essences with essences."[29] The promise of the essays is access to "real being," to being further irreducible (at the end of "Worship" called "the superpersonal Heart," the "nameless Power"),[30] to contact with the real—a sudden often apocalyptic encounter with it ("I am nothing; I see all" [N 10]) in comparison with which contingent or personal identity not only misrepresents the self but also is in effect trivial. Emerson dismisses the Eucharist—the conventional trope for figuring such an encounter—in order to reinvent the necessity of some way of representing unmediated, face-to-face contact with this reality ("real being,—essences with essences") whose fundamental nature must each time be gleaned anew.

It is an unmediated "face-to-face" which the essays again and again retrieve. They can do this "again and again" precisely because there is no rite, no symbol or authorized entity—not Christ, not the moral sentiment, not the Over-soul—nothing *repeatable* to be apprehended in these essays. It is precisely Emerson's point that an encounter with the real cannot be repeated. Hence there is no single name for it, and often only negative attributes. Contact is mystified because it is irreducible to anything but style and to the idiosyncrasies of style. What is performed is idiosyncrasy. At the emergence of the idiosyncratic formulation, conventional features of the prose—the sententious exhortation ("Trust thyself" [S 260]), the apostrophe ("O my brothers, God exists" [SL 309]), the aphoristic and pedantic formulation ("The soul's emphasis is always right" [SL 312]), the propositional banality ("We must go alone" [S 272])—drop away. The point about the revelatory language which replaces such banal formulations is to dramatize the heuristic often in arcane images which thwart *understanding* of the exact relation ostensibly being adduced.

One could argue that the ultimate prestige in an Emerson essay depends upon the direct discrepancy between a straightforward claim and the eccentric, sometimes grotesque, and often mysteriously physical trope in which it is enveloped—as in the following passage, where at one level the experience is recognizable, and at another level it cannot be recognized. The "surprise" part of the following passage from the second essay "Nature" and the climactic finish in which it is couched are key to the Emersonian formula. Such a moment cancels the person's servitude to particulars, in effect by illuminating that everything outside of the self is constituted of the same elements:

Man imprisoned, man crystallized, man vegetative, speaks to man impersonated. That power which does not respect quantity, which makes the whole and the particle its equal channel, delegates its smile to the morning, and distils its essence into every drop of rain. Every moment instructs, and every object: for wisdom is infused into every form. It has been poured into us as blood; it convulsed us as pain; it slid into us as pleasure; it enveloped us in dull, melancholy days, or in days of cheerful labor; we did not guess its essence, until after a long time. (N 555)

This is a signature Emersonian paragraph. It has all the recognizable components I have been considering: at issue is "essence," in the Emersonian world not only startling when ascertained but also violent, as the verbs imply;

a power that affects physical being through pain (as the word "convulsed" reiterates), but also through pleasure (as the word "slid" reiterates), raising an irrelevant question about a potentially confused relation between pleasure and pain, and about conferred physicality in general ("is infused...has been poured"). It is easy to forget the *subject* of such a passage. (What is difficult about the passage is the constant drifting of reference and a syntax that can't be sustained because this would keep persons in their place.) Most immediately, that subject is "wisdom," the antecedent of "it." But it is wisdom about "power," and if we read back further still, it is wisdom about the power of the *general*—the ability to see that what is said to "exist in the mind as ideas" in nature is forever embodied (N 554). The ultimate discovery, then, concerns a perceived *identity* among animal, vegetable, mineral; between mind and nature. And the specific gesture accomplished by style here (as well as by the asymmetry of terms such as "moments" and "objects," which are given syntactical equality, both being subjects of "instructs") is to make such identity unmistakable. There would be a discrepancy between container (the human body) and thing contained (the blood) because of the latter's source in the world, which we could assume to be substantial, were it not the case that all aspects of the passage are at work to critique a term like "discrepancy" as referring to a phenomenon the confrontation of which—the seeing it face-to-face—cancels any distinction between "the whole and the particle." Therefore essence can be spoken of in terms of "drops of rain" *and* essence can be spoken of in terms of human "blood." Nature is not outside of us. If we can't oversee nature, that is not because it is alien but is rather because it is internal. These half-implicit propositions are enacted by style. They could never be made in logical form, because such terms would subvert the "originary" impulse of these essays, which generate endless text in order to dramatize the essayist's encounter with "the catholic sense" of things, a sense that is best discoverable again and again at the core of one's own being.[31] Being in all cases what the essays have worked toward (often in explicit and trite formulation), the tenor of such a passage and its denotative meaning are all but unmistakable—they are never in doubt—while the vehicle, as well as the statement's residue, characteristically prohibits easy, or even intelligible, formulation (as in the indecipherable relation between "man impersonated" and "man imprisoned").

Thus oddly enough, although the goal of these essays *is* generality (however it is called) and although the style is often inimitably general—Emerson writing in no man's voice—the point of the essays' climactic figures is the representation of an encounter whose truth is somehow tied to its stylistic or rhetorical singularity. The untransmissible trope, irreducible to symbol or rite and buried in unmistakable, often clichéd figuration, counts as evidence in lieu of evidence that the author of the essay—in distinction to the reader whose tutelage the author implicitly takes on—has knowledge of an encounter with ultimate reality. In this way Emerson's banal assertions combine with his solecisms to produce a style whose inimitability serves a logical function.

I have argued that in Emerson's essays what is dramatized is the fact that the impersonal speaks despite us, though *through* us (it is visible in the eyes); even as it perpetually (in the transformation of moods) calls the idea of a fixed self into question; or it is otherwise seen as an alternative to moods (in the fixture of the "moral sentiment"), something having a stability no experiencing self could have. But this impersonality is not, for Emerson, abstractly dissociated from the idea of self. It is viscerally represented as what must be "owned" by the very self with which it is understood not to be identical.[32]

When Emerson recommends "own[ing]" what is other, this endorses a logic equivalent to Hegel's idea that the single individual is incomplete Spirit. But, readers commonly object, while Emerson has the right to sacrifice his personal interest—the interest of *his* person—to that universal spirit, he does not have the right to sacrifice another's personal interest to or for something higher. He can neither ethically approve such a sacrifice for others, nor ethically recommend it to them. Nor can he define interest (whether higher or lower) for another. Moreover, he cannot define *his* interest as equivalent to another's. He cannot assume that *his* higher interest is precisely *theirs*. He has no authority to do so. Although this complaint is posed by readers who object to Emerson's social conservatism (as discussed below), such a question about authority is in my view also raised by a more theoretical question about what kind of alliance to, and difference from, other persons a speaker must acknowledge or prove to speak on their behalf. The subject of authority and legitimacy with respect to another's interest raises the odd question of whether Emerson speaks on his own behalf.

iii

The subject of authority might be usefully examined in relation to William Ellery Channing. When Channing writes, "We conceive that the true love of God is a moral sentiment" and "We see God around us because he dwells within us," such sentences sound like Emerson's. But they are not in fact comparable, for what authorizes Channing's assertions is his position as a minister—specifically, it is as a minister that he has authority to create analogies between the human and the divine, and to show they are *only* analogies. For Channing the source of divinity is not the impersonal, but is rather the *person* of "God the Father and quickener of the human mind."[33]

To make statements about the divinity of the soul without authority is to make them *casually,* to construct or imagine them. No tradition is being explained in such statements; rather, something is being composed and invented against tradition. But why trust this invention about a universal that demands the same sacrifice as conventional religion without any of its compensations? Moreover, although Emerson proclaims a nonsectarian universal, we have only to look at Emerson's distinctions—and his dismissal of those distinctions—to see that persons are not always the undifferentiated beings constructed by the prose. The great shame of Emerson, as his detractors observe, is his callous indifference to the very social distinctions he occasionally recognizes.

"Compensation" of course *denies* social distinction by immediately trivializing it: "In the nature of the soul is the compensation for the inequalities of condition....The heart and soul of all men being one, this bitterness of *His* and *Mine* ceases. His is mine" (C 301). But except in the verbal world of the essay there is no impersonality of ownership. *His* is not *mine.* Nor do "we all take turns at the top" as "Nominalist and Realist" would have it (NR 582). This barbarous idealism infects all of the writing. Emerson's capitalist economic theory, his proprietary individualism, sanctions the drama of social injustice by denying its existence (as in the citations above), or by *justifying* its existence as in the following from *Nature:*[34] "Debt, grinding debt, whose iron face the widow, the orphan, and the sons of genius fear and hate;—debt, which consumes so much time, which so cripples and disheartens a great spirit with cares that seem so base, is a preceptor whose lessons cannot be forgone, and is needed most by those who suffer from it most" (N 26–27). In writing that *denies* the differences of persons, that *justifies* those differences, or that *deprecates* the acknowledgment of difference as petulant, finally, in writing that, as above, sees "grinding debt" as moral and as imposing a moral which some require and others, differently, do not—how, but as barbarous, shall we read "All loss, all pain is particular. The universe remains to the heart unhurt"? For it looks suspiciously as if what is being made light of is someone else's pain. What one wants, given the dissonance in Emerson's writing between an impersonality that enables by providing access beyond one's own limited self-interest and an impersonality that imperiously dismisses others' interest, is something like the Kantian acknowledgment of happiness. For Kant does not deny the legitimacy of either happiness or interest; he merely specifies that neither may be consulted as motivation for moral action. And while the categorical imperative is the same for all—unlike things, all beings have unconditional value and must be treated as ends in themselves—one function of that imperative is to prescribe certain duties, among them beneficence. But if one has a duty to promote another's happiness, this involves the recognition that there are different specifications of that general end. In other words, the Kantian universal or categorical imperative does not preclude the idea of individuals at variance with each other; in fact it presupposes that difference. The Kantian universal does not presuppose impersonality. What one wants in Emerson is the acknowledgment of the legitimacy of material self-interest. In addition, one wants something to separate those statements which enlarge the idea of (one's own) interest from those which annihilate the idea of (another's) interest.

It is in the context of Emerson's failed acknowledgment of material difference in a social world that I return to the subject of the heroic, for the acknowledgment of singularity, and so of difference, is conceptually central to the idea of the heroic and therefore to the Emersonian impersonal, from which it may seem so dissociated. I refer here to something like a reinvented American heroic (reinvented in the sense that its emphasis on the face-to-face confrontation with the divine is originally Homeric as well as Old Testament), a heroic as it is reimagined by Whitman, Dickinson, Melville, and Thoreau. When Whitman, in "Crossing Brooklyn Ferry," says, "Floodtide below me, I see you face to face!…you furnish your parts toward the soul";[35] when Dickinson's speaker is stopped dead in "Our journey had advanced—" by "Eternity's White Flag Before— / And God—at every Gate—";[36] finally when Melville in *Moby-Dick* constructs tragedy, and in *Pierre* and *The Confidence Man* the parody of tragedy, upon the *masking* of a face, these pivotal moments recall exactly the logic of Emerson's impersonal. In so doing, they also, indirectly by counterexample, reveal the source of its deficiency.

What deprives Emerson of the authority to speak of the soul's manifestations of divinity is not after all—or, precisely, not *at* all—that his pronouncements are personal rather than ministerial. Conversely, what deprives Emerson's voice of authority is that his statements are *insufficiently* personal, except in the passages I have discussed, and there only by inference. That is, their authority is neither functional *nor* personal. The *content* of Emerson's impersonal implies a heroic *context*: an encounter with the real, however indecipherable its name, the "owning" of that encounter, as well as an acknowledgment of the real or, in the language of "Character," the "*know[ing of] its face.*" But the heroic implies a *person's* contact with the real. This source and this source alone gives it authority, as Dickinson, Whitman, Melville, and, of course, Thoreau knew. Emerson, strangely, *doesn't* know this. He invents a mode of discourse dissociated from the institutionally religious. He produces a discourse that has access to the real prior to the mediating symbol or rite whose necessity it obviates. The legitimacy of that discourse therefore depends on the visibility of the person speaking. It depends on the fact that an epiphanic encounter occurs to someone *in particular* who, by virtue of that particularity, is in a position to describe it. But except in the essay's climactic moments—moments that, as I've argued, are typified by their idiosyncrasy—Emerson then erodes the representation of any self-articulated distinction which would make his discourse legible and meaningful. Not able to countenance or represent what differences himself, he similarly betrays the differences of others, which he either denies or denigrates. Thus Emerson is unable to represent the encounter for the sake of which his discourse exists—for there is ultimately no one to whom that encounter happens. The deficiency in Emerson's representation of the impersonal lies peculiarly in the missing sense of the person. The power of such an encounter could therefore only be rhetorical. The "person" of Emerson—by which I mean something like the invented persona, Michel Foucault's author-function—is not visible, except through style, and except perhaps in "The Poet," one essay where a person comes frontally into view.

In "The Poet," we are offered serial descriptions of what imprisons us ("the custody of that body in which [we are] pent up" [P 460]), of "the inaccessibleness of every thought but that we are in" (P 463), of our phlegmatic nature, and of how the poet—"a beholder of ideas, and an utterer of the necessary and causal" (P 450)—can liberate us. Among his many skills, he invites us "into the science of the real" (P 452). In other words, the poet makes our birthright discoverable to us. Significantly, he can do this because beside "his privacy of power as an individual man, there is a great public power, on which he can draw, by unlocking, at all risks, his human doors" (P 459). ("Public" here means something like "universal.") The poet is, therefore, a transformer: he is free and he makes us free (see P 462). The mechanism for escape, called here "true nectar," is "the ravishment of the intellect by coming nearer to the fact" (P 460). (Such immanence is marked by a talismanic naming precisely coincident with the poet's liberation from "the custody of that body," and from the "jailyard of individual relations in which he is enclosed.") "Ravishment" is a word we encountered before—in the context of "the influx of the Divine mind into our mind." In "The Poet" the "fact" occasioning ravishment is a man's "passage out into free space" (P 460). As elsewhere, ravishment signals the transformation whereby the person vanishes into what is "owned" as other. But one difference between this and the other essays is the fixture of "The Poet" at the nexus of transformation, the act and iteration of which is as it were diffused throughout the essay. There is no climactic moment at which the transformation could be said to be performed.

Power, a "*dream*-power ... transcending all limit and privacy" "intoxicates" the poet (P 467, 461). But it does not intoxicate thoroughly enough. For though the essay tirelessly dramatizes the poet in relation to his liberating task, this very repetition produces a felt sense of *what* is being transformed, specifically of the person prior to his emergence from the private and the individual, therefore of a person locked in his thought, limited by self-identification and excluded from full expressiveness. In "The Poet" the transformation from the personal to the impersonal does not occur. The essay ends by resorting to a promissory note on what will be performed but is *not yet* performed ("I look in vain for the poet whom I describe" [P 465]). While the poet is not visible, the one who calls him into being is precisely visible as a presence whose rhetoric fails. If we ask, with Foucault, What are the modes of existence of this discourse? Who can assume these various subject functions? a response would gesture toward the crossed viewpoints that the essay inevitably expresses. For, on the one hand, the reference for the speaking voice is the *un*emancipated person who anticipates the poet. But, on the other, the poet being evoked also seems referenced to the subject position we call "Emerson." The one who calls for the poet, who calls the poet forth, is the one who knows enough of bondage not to be wholly or even mainly defined by freedom. Thus the essay charts two positions and has a double voice. The all-consuming frenzy ("ravishment") epitomized at the essay's end by the figure of "transparent boundaries" (P 468) is repeatedly contested by the essay's enumerated impediments (caves, cellars, prisons, drifts, chains, pans and barrows, stuttering and stammering, jailyards) which the frenzy can't vanquish. These movements, or subject positions, are inseparable in

Emerson's "The Poet." In the space of their negotiation a person is almost legible, making credible, as well as meaningful, an idea of the impersonal again and again in the space of this essay incompletely realized.

Modern criticism shows the point at which the idea of the impersonal is completely detached from religion, which initially gave it life (either traditionally defined as sourced by a God or Law, or alternatively defined—as Whitman, Dickinson, Melville define it—as sourced by a spectacle of the real apprehended by a person). Emerson proleptically marks the moment when the idea of the person is evacuated from the scene of the impersonal. The discourse which remains exhibits an apparently unrecognized nostalgia for the idea of the person on whom the impersonal is imagined to register. This is how I understand the odd pathos of the summary accounts which make a gesture of dramatizing the impersonal even as they retreat from actualizing such a confrontation in the climactic or figural moments whose style I discussed in the passage about "man impersonated."[37] Yet as I have suggested, something is deficient in Emerson's representations, and this deficiency directly pertains to the understood relation between impersonality and individuation. I conclude by elaborating the contours of this relation as it is made visible by two sets of reflections upon it.

In *Time and the Other* Emmanuel Levinas posits a state of impersonality that *precedes* individuation; in *Reasons and Persons* Parfit posits a state of impersonality that *constitutes* individuation. I want briefly to consider these two notions for the light that, albeit differently, they shed on Emerson's relation to his central construct of impersonality. Levinas distinguishes between existing and an existent, between an anonymous and impersonal "there is" and a state of consciousness "where an existent is put in touch with his existing," hence with his materiality and solitude. In Levinas's account the anonymous, impersonal state precedes the formation of a material "I" for whom suffering is a direct consequence of being imprisoned in the experience of personal identity. Thus, "solitude is not tragic because it is the privation of the other, but because [the self] is shut up within the captivity of its identity, because it is matter." The experience of the "I am" is, therefore, what Levinas calls "enchainment."[38] Parfit also argues that the idea of personal identity enchains. But for Parfit that idea is understood to be *false*:

> We are not separately existing entities, apart from our brains and bodies, and various interrelated physical and mental events. Our existence just

involves the existence of our brains and bodies, and the doing of our deeds, and the thinking of our thoughts, and the occurrence of certain other physical and mental events. Our identity over time just involves...psychological connectedness and/or psychological continuity. (*RP* 225)

In this reductionist view there is no deeper fact—no spiritual substance (or soul), no purely mental construct (a Cartesian pure ego), no separate physical entity, "of a kind that is not yet recognized in the theories of contemporary physics," nor any other ineffable essence—to which we can ascribe identity (*RP* 210). (The consequence of this, Parfit argues, is that there is no distinct entity that constitutes identity; that the unity of consciousness and the unity over time need not be accounted for by the claim that "the experiences in this person's life are had by this person" who is a separately existing entity [*RP* 210]. Such unities can rather be explained by the relations of psychological connection and continuity; we can therefore understand our life in an impersonal way; and the reductionist view has radical moral consequences.)[39]

What strikes me, it might seem randomly, is the subject of resistance, even "suffering" (Levinas's term), which attends both discussions of impersonality. For Levinas personal identity is the *cause* of suffering, while for Parfit, at least initially, the absence of personal identity has central afflictive power. (Ultimately Parfit will claim that the impersonal view is not only the more beneficial but is also personally consoling: "It makes me less concerned about my own future, and my death" [*RP* 347].) There is, however, a compelling moment in a chapter entitled "Is the True View Believable?" in which Parfit, who has been arguing against the absence of some deep fact beyond physical and psychological continuity—no soul, no pure ego, no extrapolated physical presence which would testify to a person's unique, unreplicable identity— exemplifies, shockingly, the practical implications of his austere theory. In relation to a science fiction fable that Parfit invents to preface his analysis of the *absence* of any extra identificatory essence on which discrete personhood could be founded, he asks whether the idea of being replicated (physically and psychologically) and teletransported to Mars produces someone who "would *be* me" or "someone else who has been made to be exactly *like* me" (*RP* 200, 201; italics mine). The question here is whether if the replica is qualitatively identical with me, but not numerically identical with me, the replica is the same person as I am (see *RP* 201). Parfit concludes his discussion by arguing that there is nothing extra which would define me (like a soul or a cogito) that could make such a question intelligible:

> When I fear that, in Teletransportation, *I* shall not get to Mars, my fear is that the abnormal cause may fail to produce this further fact. As I have argued, there is no such fact. What I fear will not happen, *never* happens. I want the person on Mars to be me in a specially intimate way in which no future person will ever be me. My continued existence never involves this deep further fact. What I fear will be missing is *always* missing. Even a space-ship journey would not produce the further fact in which I am inclined to believe.
>
> When I come to see that my continued existence does not involve this further fact, I lose my reason for preferring a space-ship journey. But, judged from the standpoint of my earlier belief, this is not because Teletransportation is *about as good as* ordinary survival. It is because ordinary survival *is about as bad as,* or little better than, Teletransportation. *Ordinary survival is about as bad as being destroyed and having a Replica.* (RP 279–80)

Ordinary survival is as bad as being destroyed and replicated because ordinary survival does not presuppose anything that would distinguish a self as a discrete separate entity whose personal identity matters. What the truth about ordinary survival destroys is the idea of the person and the personal.

I mark these moments in Levinas and Parfit because, albeit to different ends, they represent a *person's* resistance to the idea of impersonality nonetheless being expounded.[40] Suffering is occasioned by the friction of *feeling* oneself a person (Levinas's "I am") where such a feeling is shown to be unfounded. There cannot help but be resistance to the idea of the impersonal, since the consequences of the impersonal destroy being in the only form in which we think we know it.

But Emerson's accounts of the impersonal exist without such acknowledgment, uncontaminated by resistance and free of any hint of the registration of suffering whose expression might taint them. It is as if the perspective from which Emerson's words are voiced is an imaginary perspective, purified of unideal motivation. Emerson's perspective does not take into account what thwarts the ideal; or how it might affect the voice which is propounding it. The plea for impersonality has been evacuated of religious content. Yet there is something evasive, incomplete, and empty about the fact that Emerson does not acknowledge what replaces the idea of a God, as if the idea of God had not actually been dismissed but had rather been transferred to the omniscient speaking voice. (Hence Nietzsche's valorization of Emerson.) That is, Emerson does not take the responsibility a person should take for his words, and therefore betrays the complexity of a person's response to their desirability. But can there be real knowledge of the impersonal if its consequences, and even its constitutive terms, remain unintelligible? If one tries to answer the question What is a person? no answer with any coherent substance can be produced with reference to Emerson's writing.

One of the reasons Emerson fails to acknowledge others' suffering, which is never very real to him, is that he fails to acknowledge his own suffering, which is never very real to him. I don't mean to suggest that suffering, or any other displayed affect, is a criterion for successful theorization. But I do mean to repeat one last time that Emerson's words are iterated in a register unmarked by the ambivalence which, one might suppose, would challenge a wholehearted endorsement of a machine as undiscriminated as a superpersonal heart, an immeasurable mind, or an Over-soul. For ambivalence about the impersonal is the one contradiction Emerson successfully resists. Yet, as Parfit makes clear, if we assume the truth of the impersonal, "ordinary survival is about as bad as being destroyed and having a Replica." Thus Emerson does not become accountable for the implication of his words, which are voiced without penetrating. It is as if, in his sentences, his life failed to be experienced as his own. If this is a supreme fulfillment of the imperative of impersonality—to speak without the registration of any affect that would contest the *construct* of impersonality—it nonetheless leaves undisclosed the *experience* of impersonality (ravishment), to which the essays, from first to last, seductively promise access.

5

The Practice of Attention:
Simone Weil's Performance of Impersonality

The principal claim we think we have on the universe is that our personality should continue. This claim implies all the others. The instinct of self-preservation makes us feel this continuation to be a necessity, and we believe that a necessity is a right. We are like the beggar who said to Talleyrand, "Sir, I must live," and to whom Talleyrand replied, "I do not see the necessity for that."[1]

Attention is what creates *necessary* connections. (Those which do not depend upon attention are not necessary.)[2]

Headaches are a persistent subject in Simone Weil's spiritual autobiography: "In 1938 I spent ten days at Solesmes, from Palm Sunday to Easter Tuesday, following all the liturgical services. I was suffering from splitting headaches; each sound hurt me like a blow." But "by an extreme effort of concentration I was able to rise above this wretched flesh, to leave it to suffer by itself, heaped up in a corner, and to find a pure and perfect joy in the unimaginable beauty of the chanting and the words" (*WG* 68). In this instance, concentration is a mechanism for casting oneself outside the pain. Weil rises to a sphere in which the pain is left behind. In another passage from her notebooks, Weil imagines expelling the pain of the headaches "into the universe," though with a compromised result: "less pain…but an impaired universe."[3] But whether Weil projects the pain into the universe or projects herself out of the universe of pain, attention is focused to a point of concentration, which fastens on one thing and dismisses another.

Elsewhere, however, concentration (which specifies the degree of attention) is that state in which objects are relinquished. In "Reflections on the Right Use of School Studies," to which I shall return, Weil writes: "Attention consists of suspending our thought.…Our thought should be in relation to all particular and already formulated thoughts, as a man on a mountain who, as he looks forward, sees also below him, without actually looking at them, a great many forests and plains. Above all our thought should be empty, waiting, not seeking anything, but ready to receive in its naked truth the object that is to penetrate it" (WG 111–12). Thought, as we ordinarily understand it, is not quite the word Weil means, for thought implies the very focus that is intentionally suspended in this description of attention. At issue is the distinction between fastening the attention around a single phenomenon and leaving the attention open, a difference immediately understood by Weil in terms of larger freedoms and constraints: "If one desires a particular thing one becomes enslaved to the series of conditions. But if one desires the series itself, the satisfaction of this desire is unconditioned" (FL 143).

These two forms of attention, focused on an object and released from all objects ("empty, waiting, not seeking anything"), as well as the specific practices Weil associates with attention, indicate the range and subtlety of a topic to which Weil continually returned. In the following pages I shall examine this phenomenon of attention—in her spiritual autobiography Weil identified its discovery with the overcoming of a despair so severe that it led her to contemplate suicide[4]—in order to inquire how it became a discipline for forfeiting personality and consequently came to be associated with the affliction and violence requisite for such a renunciation. I am interested in examining how an ostensibly neutral phenomenon like attention could require violence, and I am especially interested in considering a person's relation to such a requirement. I am also concerned with how we might understand someone who attempted to separate personality from being—that is, with how we might value someone who herself valued impersonality at such tremendous cost. My own understanding arises from the consideration of Weil's assertions beyond the pathology of self-hatred or cruelty. My essay will examine the frictive relations within Weil's writing on self-annihilation—she called it "de-creation" (*N* 1:279)—as well as the relation between Weil's didactic imperatives for the achievement of that state and her representation of a person who lived such a reduced life. The resistance between these positions is what makes Weil's writing interesting; resistance registers her uncompromising understanding of the difficulty of her own project. Weil's contemplations of impersonality indicate a depth perception about a matter so alien to us that we barely have concepts for it, so quick are we to find any attempt to eradicate egotism in terms this extreme repellent. Yet unlike writers who treat impersonality as desirable but impossible (Jonathan Edwards, for instance) or desirable and inevitable, something without cost or consequences (Ralph Waldo Emerson, for instance), Weil represents a middle ground, one could almost say a normative case, in which impersonality is seen as desirable and possible. Her work describes the cultivation of a practice for its attainment.

Throughout these pages I shall be suggesting that although the point of losing all personal being might be to produce a void that could receive supernatural grace ("produce" being a word that would be flawed for Weil because of its sense of agency), the cultivation of attention is a *naturalistic* process. For "while virtue is a supernatural thing," attention, for Weil, is a natural one; she crucially describes attention as "possibly without an analogue among natural phenomena" (*N* 1:96). In fact, "a rational creature is one that contains within itself the germ, the principle, the vocation of de-creation." In Weil's cosmology, attention makes the void or de-creates the "I" so that there is a forfeiture of personality, in the absence of which "supernatural grace [might] descend." Yet if "the void serves for nothing except grace," it is not itself dependent on grace (*FL* 159). In other words, there are "two annihilations, annihilation in nothingness and annihilation in God" (*N* 2:463). For Weil, the first precedes the second, as a training or a practice.[5] In addition, although God is central to Weil's practice of attention (as its object or its point) doctrine doesn't matter to her. My understanding would be consonant with Weil's own distinction that, for instance, "the Gospel contains a conception of human life, not a theology" (*FL* 147). That understanding would be consonant in turn with her explicit repudiation of Christian dogma as at once antagonistic to individual spiritual practice and bound to exclusions that render any incarnation of Christianity impossible: "I remain beside all those things that cannot enter the Church…on account of…two little words," namely, "*anathema sit*" (*WG* 77). She elaborated: "In my eyes Christianity is catholic by right but not in fact. So many things are outside it, so many things that I love…so many things that God loves, otherwise they would not be in existence. All the immense stretches of past centuries, except the last twenty are among them; all the countries inhabited by colored races; all secular life in the white peoples' countries;…all the traditions banned as heretical, those of the Manicheans and Albigenses for instance; all those things resulting from the Renaissance, too often degraded but not quite without value" (*WG* 75).[6] In the following pages, I shall argue that it is necessary to locate Weil's practice of impersonality with reference to procedures of disidentification or with reference to what she elsewhere called "*a philosophy of Perception,* of a practical and experimental nature" (*N* 1:313). My examples range across Weil's essays, notebook writings, and *The Need for Roots*; however heterogeneous the contexts, these examples raise the question of what kind of interest is generated by the destruction of a personality—a destruction so captivating that it seems to occur on the reader's behalf yet is ultimately useless for the reader,[7] a topic touched on in the essay's last pages.

i

A minimalist economy governs Weil's notebook prose. Thus when Weil writes, "Denude oneself of everything that is above the vegetative life" (*FL* 294), this idea of denuding—which necessitates sacrificing and stripping bare—not only refers to the abandonment of an "I" or, as I shall suggest, to the erosion of imagination but also characterizes the style of the prose fragments, which have integrity, but without extraneous connection, as if topics were only manifest to Weil in discontinuous bits. Thus, while one might have supposed that the severed, epigrammatic quality of the prose in *Gravity and Grace* came from being excerpted, to return to the notebooks in their entirety is to see the same aphoristic fragments devoid of personal reference and generative occasion—no dates for given entries; no situating event; no proper names; minimal elaboration of ideas, which are often set forth in short, juxtaposed paragraphs—as if context has been torn away, ideas revealing themselves whole but in isolation. (Such desituating is not characteristic of Weil's factory notebooks, where the goal is to historicize the conditions of work.)

Although the "I" figures in this prose, it has been deprived of particularity; it is positional rather than substantive, an abstraction, an "I" that *is* a figure. Thus, for instance, Weil writes: "God created me as a non-being which has the appearance of existing, in order that through love I should renounce this apparent existence and be annihilated by the plenitude of being….The 'I' belongs to non-being. But I have not the right to know this. If I knew it, where would be the renunciation? I shall never know it" (*FL* 96–97). Despite the theatricalization of the concluding sentence, the self's loss or preservation is not being dramatized, for what would be preserved and sacrificed are not the same entities. These subject positions aren't commensurate in the sense that an error which sees existence where there is only nonbeing is a mistake of self-aggrandizement, whereas an error that sacrifices a presumptive existence is an error of generosity. The mistake might technically be the same; in the one case you impute being where it is absent and in the other you sacrifice being that isn't there. But the second mistake isn't equal to the first because the first has the motivation of preserving a self, and the second has the motivation of relinquishing it. Weil is constantly dramatizing the relation between these two positions—preserving an "I" that is nothing at all, renouncing an "I" that never existed—that are nonequivalent, since to relinquish something you think you have is to correct a mistake, whereas to confuse nonentity with being is to make the mistake that needs to be corrected. Moreover, neither the "I" that claims existence nor the "I" that theoretically abdicates it is equal to the "I" that writes, which occupies a territory that is neither deluded nor free from delusion. "I shall never know it" is posited by one who *does* know the nonbeing of "I," yet without having the conviction of efficacious knowing. Thus what remains after Weil's prose has been "denuded" of the apparatus of personality, situation, and any other limiting specific is just these negotiations, activated in a realm where nothing conceals their stark outline.

But if the "I" is by definition excluded from Weil's sentences—or if the "I" is a category to be defaced and "denuded"—so too God occupies a symmetrical position. God is a category equally inhospitable to anything that could identify him. Thus de-creation pertains to the construct of a God as much as it does to the construct of a self. For instance, "We should do every sort of work, make every sort of effort for God *while* thinking that he does not exist" (*N* 1:142); "One mode of purification: to pray to God…while thinking that God does not exist" (*N* 1:136); "There are two sorts of atheism, one of which is a purification of the notion of God" (*N* 1:126). As a consequence of such a purification, the traditional consolations that attend the notion of a God are equally invalidated: "Not to believe in the immortality of the soul, but to look upon the whole of life as destined to prepare for the moment of death" (*N* 2:469). The passages in Weil's notebooks unfeature the "I," render it faceless, and simultaneously unfeature the idea of a God:[8]

"We have to believe in God who is like the true God in everything, except that he does not exist, for we have not reached the point where God exists" (*N* 1:151). God's not-yet-existing requires attention to the object properly gazed at, the unidolatrous object, which should be explained as a natural phenomenon.

If, in Weil's mental cosmology, one can't rule out thoughts of an "I"—thoughts held in place by a point of view and a reference—one can, in compensation, refuse to identify the thought with the truth. Weil specified: "'Know yourself,' means: 'Do not identify yourself with your thoughts.'"[9] To posit a split between the thought and the truth is to see what thought can't accommodate.

> God...plants [suffering] in the soul as something irreducible, a foreign body, impossible to digest, and constrains one to think of it. The thought of suffering is not of a discursive kind. The mind comes slap up against physical suffering, affliction, like a fly against a pane of glass, without being able to make the slightest progress or discover anything new, and yet unable to prevent itself from returning to the attack....
>
> To turn suffering into an offering is a consolation, and it is thus a veil thrown over the reality of suffering. But the same applies if we regard suffering as a punishment. Suffering has no significance. There lies the very essence of its reality. We must love it in its reality, which is absence of significance. (*N* 2:483–84)

Suffering is a "thought" that enables one to see the meaninglessness of anything one could say about it. To be "up against" "suffering...like a fly against a pane" is to note that accurately seen, suffering is insusceptible to what Weil calls "reading." To see suffering like this is to see that suffering merely *is*, that it expresses nothing. Suffering is not neutral with respect to its afflictive power (there it is compelling), but it resists explanatory procedures that would align it with any system of compensation or point of view. This effacement of point of view, this breaking it off or unmaking of it, equally suspends the "I," even as it leaves the experience intact—indigestible—something "foreign," that retains its sting. In this way, we are up against what harms, without grasping the harm and also without escaping it.

If thought is insufficient to penetrate "reality" (the discursive being unequipped to penetrate the real), affect is understood to be equally incompetent. As with the assessments "consolation" and "judgment," which warp an event by assigning meaning from a relative vantage to which the event is indifferent, affect incorrectly draws conclusions with reference to the well-being of an "I," that is, to the well-being of something illusory. Hence, "there are imaginary sufferings; imaginary efforts also. As for the inner feeling, there is nothing more deceptive" (*N* 1:320). Affect equates a true state of affairs with a pleasurable state. Weil contests this:

> Because we live in falsehood, we are under the illusion that happiness is unconditionally important. If someone says: "How I would like to be rich!," his friend may answer: "Why? would it make you any happier?," but if someone says "I want to be happy," no one will answer "Why?" Tell me your reasons for wanting to be happy. (*FL* 311)

Weil insists that "happiness is not a thing to be desired without reason, unconditionally; for it is only the good that is to be desired in this way" (*FL* 311). Therefore, What are your reasons for wanting to be happy? should not be a question to which an answer is deemed obvious or gratuitous. Moreover, this demotion of happiness does not depend on any compensatory theological counterstructure that would render indifference to happiness conventionally legible. In fact "the same criticism [also] applies to happiness when it is glorified as eternal felicity, eternal life, Paradise, etc. Happiness of every kind should be criticized" (*FL* 311). Thus Weil's indifference to happiness—an indifference essential to her naturalist cultivation of attention—has more in common with Franz Kafka's insistence that "real consolation does not exist"; Wallace Stevens's attempt to fix his gaze on "nothing that is not there and the nothing that is"; and, as I shall illustrate, Paul Valéry's approbation of "difficulty"; in short, more in common with modernist conceptions of an unblemished neutrality in the face of difficulty than with any devotional practice. But if the consolations of theology are not being juxtaposed to the impoverishments of a human range, what is being juxtaposed to an "I" propped up and held in place by both thought and affect? And how to slip free of these? For Weil, escape looks like this:

> It is at those moments when we are, as we say, in a bad mood, when we feel incapable of the elevation of soul that befits holy things, it is then that it is most effectual to turn our eyes toward perfect purity. For it is then that evil, or rather mediocrity, comes to the surface of the soul and is in the best position for being burned by contact with the fire.

It is however then that the act of looking is almost impossible. All the mediocre part of the soul, fearing death with a more violent fear than that caused by the approach of the death of the body, revolts and suggests lies to protect itself.

The effort not to listen to these lies, although we cannot prevent ourselves from believing them, the effort to look upon purity at such times, has to be something very violent; yet it is absolutely different from all that is generally known as effort, such as doing violence to one's feelings or an act of will. (*WG* 193)

The passage presents a strong picture of constraint against freedom: the solace of the bad mood that, however unpleasant, can be continued effortlessly; the feeling of powerlessness; and the absence of apparent resource. Moreover, insofar as the passage produces a directive against the mood and the powerlessness, it is unclear how to follow it. From *within* the bad mood, one is to look on purity (whatever that might be); not listen to what one believes (as if one could *un*hear or render moot what one was simultaneously acceding to); and submit to violence, but not to a violence that negates either feeling or will (notwithstanding the fact that both feeling and will constitute the mood from which one is enjoined to turn away). Examining the contradictory imperative—to submit to the feeling, but not to adhere to it; to look elsewhere than the mood when one is "incapable of doing so"; to overcome resistance but without recognizable effort—is to see how Weil dictates an action that she simultaneously renders unimaginable. Thus to focus on one of the coordinates (not to listen to what we believe) is to see the cross-purposes in which consciousness would be caught.[10] For though listening to lies logically precedes believing them, in Weil's account *not* listening undoes any prior believing in the sense that something thought to be true is simultaneously not a thought that's then credited or heeded. In the narrow space between believing and not listening to believing freedom is defined. Thus the violence that effects change is discoverable in a disalignment—of listening from believing—that relativizes believing and throws its efficacy into doubt.

ii

In Weil's lexicon attention is the operative phenomenon that allows one to move from believing to not listening to believing the motivated thought. (One way to understand attention is as regard without motive: "What we call 'I,'" Weil wrote, "is only a motive" [N 1:97].) Weil repeatedly posits a tension between moments of attention and what she calls "personal thoughts," which subject one "to the compulsion exercised by…the mechanical play of forces." If one believes that personal thoughts are not mechanical, one "is mistaken."[11] Attention not only turns the gaze away from the "I," but also commensurately "turn[s] it on to that which cannot be conceived" (N 1:179). In other words, automaticity lies in the range of personal thought and in the determinacy of what *can* be thought. Like the bad mood, thought is a limit. Attention penetrates the limit: "Attention is what seizes hold of reality, so that the greater the attention on the part of the mind, the greater the amount of real being in the object" (N 2:527). Weil's claim here is that real being is constituted (as opposed to being merely registered) by attention. A related distinction is rephrased in the following specification: "Reality is never given. Something is given, but what is given is not real.…The real is that which has a certain relationship to what is given. Yes, but what is that relationship?" (N 1:84). In the notebook entry, where Weil's question is recorded, these sentences follow: "Valéry: 'The proper, unique and perpetual object of thought is that which does not exist.'—'A thing understood is a thing falsified.'—'A difficulty is a light. An insuperable difficulty is a sun'" (N 1:84).

I take Valéry's first sentence to imply that the proper object for thought must be seen as undiscoverable, thought being always in excess of any object that could satisfy it. In view of Weil's own sentence ("Reality is never given"), the passage she cites from Valéry reiterates the idea of something not itself present that is nonetheless ceaselessly sought, as if associating the incessantly evasive nature of both "object" and "reality." What constitutes the "object" of thought in one instance is nowhere discoverable, as what constitutes "reality," in the second instance, is located in a relationship rather than in an essence. With reference to Valéry's sentence that equates "understanding" with "falsifying," the claim is that "understanding" cannot in *truth* exist. The alternative to understanding, which strives to be true but that can only be false, is perception, which can be neither true nor false. The sentences thus unravel anything definitive, fixed, or grasped, as if Valéry's point were to disengage an object *seen* from one merely *understood* and, implicitly, by Weil's juxtaposition of this to her own construction, to distinguish the conferral of attention—the quality of its givenness—from the fashioning of objects to which it is given. Attention brings into being without determining the nature of this being. In this way, the value term (Valéry's "sun," Weil's "reality") is produced by the difficulty that, from a heuristic point of view, frustrates it. The difficulty is not one of perceiving, but rather one of arriving at an orientation that, once you arrive at it, eliminates difficulty, but not through understanding. Seeing like this—without identification—is seeing that resists "reading." But such a state is virtually unimaginable, for the only way for signs not to be seen as signs, or to avert conception without averting discernment, would be for the process of recognizing to have no origin from which to arise, no owned point of view, for there to be no perceived entity from which to make distinctions.

Weil calls this undoing of vantage "being dead"—"One has to be dead to be able to see things in their nakedness" (N 2:554)—and she equates such a state of "extreme attention" with "the creative faculty" and even with "genius" (N 2:441). Assuming it is not always possible to see from such a ruined perspective, Weil wants to say it is sometimes possible to do so, and she wants to make being dead more than an abstraction. In Weil's topography one can arrive variously at being dead, which is not a physical state but which nonetheless relies on the depletion of the body's energy. Therefore "physical labor is a daily death" in that it transforms "a being who loves and hates, hopes and fears, wants and doesn't want, into a little pile of inert matter" (NR 286), a reduction approvingly regarded. "To face death with a...violent fear" ties one to "the bad mood" to which one clings as protection against the recognition that all moods (and affect generally) are irrelevant to true perception. Therefore a recognition of the immateriality of affect—its failure to count for anything—also secures the state of being dead, as does the separation of energy from desire. The point is to "tear the energy away from its object" (N 1:203), so that one preserves the energy but extricates it from both object and motivation alike. In another context still, to see as "truth...that one is composed of human material" produces an experience Weil calls being "anonymous" (N 1:217), a form of being dead. In these instances what is worn down variously—by labor, materiality, energy made aimless—is a reference point: a vantage from which to regard occurrences for which there is this or that preference.

Genius inheres in the brilliance of seeing outside of one's perspective and outside of perspective generally, in "that attention which is so full that the 'I' disappears" (N 1:179).[12] It is "creative" to see this way precisely because it is characteristically not deemed possible to do so. To see outside a point of view is to inhabit a stance outside oneself and, notwithstanding the inhospitality of such a space, to reside there: "Genius is—perhaps—nothing other than the ability to go through 'dark nights.' Those who have not got any, when on the edge of the dark night, become discouraged and say to themselves:

I cannot; I am not made for that; it is all incomprehensible to me....That is why talent is generally—almost always—in practice always—a condition of genius" (*N* 1:131). Genius, on this account, is defined by the inclination to do what seems both impossible and undesirable, and talent the resourcefulness that sees this inclination through. In such a condition good could only be unrepresentable because one would be in its midst without knowing where one was. Only genius could tolerate such a position without seeking to orient itself. Only genius, indifferent to outcome, could regard this vertiginous state as a foundation.

Given the difficulty of cultivating such a vertiginous state, one needs practice. "Reflections on the Right Use of School Studies with a View to the Love of God" supplies the rudiments. School studies—the geometry problem, the Latin lesson, any elementary but difficult intellectual exercise—are models that offer training in the cultivation of attention whose proper, if ultimate, use is crucial for prayer. Attention is at once said to be necessary for prayer ("Warmth of heart cannot make up for it" [*WG* 105]) and also its defining characteristic ("Attention...is the substance of prayer" [*WG* 108]). School studies teach us to regard failure without being daunted by this failure. Failure is irrelevant because even when there is no favorable result in the school exercise, there could be a compensatory result that cannot now be measured. For instance: "The useless efforts made by the Curé d'Ars, for long and painful years, in his attempt to learn Latin bore fruit in the marvelous discernment that enabled him to see the very soul of his penitents behind their words and even their silences" (*WG* 108). We are therefore to see no contradiction between the absence of proof and the inevitability of results. Weil explains: "Certainties of this kind are experimental. But if we do not believe in them before experiencing them, if at least we do not behave as though we believed in them, we shall never have the experience that leads to such certainties" (*WG* 107). In this way the attainment, though not reducible to the training, must infuse the training with its presumptive conviction.

On the one hand, school studies are said to be merely preparatory. If attention to the mathematical problem is preparatory to attention in prayer (or, less ambitiously, to "grasping the beauty of a line by Racine more vividly" [*WG* 107]), what is developed is a skill that can be transferred to any context. In view of this understanding, the "intrinsic interest" (*WG* 106) of a particular discipline (geometry or Greek, say) is subordinate to the cultivation of a habit.[13] On the other hand, the preparatory lesson is deemed to be correspondent to the thing being prepared for. Specifically, the proper attitude toward the geometry problem is identical to the proper attitude for prayer; in both, students must see the difference between "stiffening their muscles" and "paying attention" (*WG* 109). "Will power" and "muscular effort" are "entirely barren" as instruments of success. They might help one to pass examinations, but (in distinction to joy) they have "practically no place in study" (*WG* 110). In teaching the pupil how to decline exertion, the geometry lesson is "a little fragment of particular truth," hence is a "pure image of the…very Truth that once in a human voice declared: 'I am the Truth.'" Conceived in these terms, Weil concludes, "every school exercise…is like a sacrament" (*WG* 112). What makes the school exercise like a sacrament is its capacity to frustrate the student, while teaching him the gratuitousness of "contracting [his] brows, holding [his] breath" (*WG* 109)—efficaciously instructing him that attention, "the greatest of all efforts," is "a negative effort" (*WG* 111) that has nothing to do with tiredness or suffering.

What also makes the school exercise a sacrament is that it—and not something else—is before one. In light of this recognition the student should cultivate indiscrimination; he should be blind to the difference between school problems that seem important and those that seem trivial. "School children and students who love God should never say: 'I like mathematics'; 'I like French'; 'I like Greek.' They should learn to like all these subjects" (*WG* 106).[14] That is, they should learn to place value in paying attention itself, regardless of the subject. Attention is what they should learn to like. For desire—"There is a real desire when there is an effort of attention" (*WG* 107)—and attention here have the "significance" Weil denies to suffering.

The exercise in Latin translation teaches us our lack of agency. When we wait "for the right word to come of itself at the end of our pen…we merely reject all inadequate words" (*WG* 113). We are thus conduits, required only to dismiss choices that are erroneous, but never to be mistaken about the fact that we could compel a choice that could be either right or satisfactory. Thus what the geometry lesson and the Latin translation teach us is how to efface ourselves. In this way, stripped of instrumentality, imagination, and preference for outcome, attention becomes regard that looks through (eschews) listening to believing, and looks through (eschews) "fear of being dead."

In passages like the ones I have been citing, the value of attention is its capacity to free us from limitation. Yet there is a moment impossible to anticipate in "School Studies" when attention stops being neutral, when it seems in fact compelled, and when the freedom to look turns to enslavement.

(A comparable shift in "The Love of God and Affliction" puts it thus: "As for us, we are nailed down to the spot, only free to choose which way we look, ruled by necessity" [*WG* 124].) As the student of school studies is to attend to his task (most valuable when it lies outside of his ability to complete it, hence when it frustrates and pains him), so the student of God is to attend to his bondage. Bondage looks like this:

> [Spiritual guides] should bring out in a brilliantly clear light the correspondence between the attitude of the intelligence in each one of these exercises and the position of the soul, which, with its lamp well filled with oil, awaits the Bridegroom's coming with confidence and desire. May each loving adolescent, as he works at his Latin prose, hope through this prose to come a little nearer to the instant when he will really be the slave—faithfully waiting while the master is absent, watching and listening—ready to open the door to him as soon as he knocks. The master will then make his slave sit down and himself serve him with meat. (*WG* 113)

No amount of equivocating about Weil's appropriation of conventions explains what Weil has added in her passage.[15] Weil echoes the reciprocity Herbert literalized before her in which the master becomes the slave of his servant, in which being captivated by God becomes a captivation of God. The original part that Weil adds, however, lies in the curious position occupied by attention in the reversal of this master-slave dialectic. In other words, in making attention first instrumental, and then fundamental, two things happen: Waiting for the moment when the Latin passage becomes intelligible is made integral to (not only preparatory for) and therefore equivalent to waiting for God ("come a little nearer to the instant" implying only one goal), and hence attention is made integral to captivation and bondage. Weil insists on this interpretation:

> Only this waiting, this attention, can move the master to treat his slave with such amazing tenderness. When the slave has worn himself out in the fields, his master says on his return, "Prepare my meal, and wait upon me." And he considers the servant who only does what he is told to do to be unprofitable. To be sure in the realm of action we have to do all that is demanded of us [but]…what forces the master to make himself the slave of his slave, and to love him, has nothing to do with all that.…It is only watching, waiting, attention.

Happy then are those who pass their adolescence and youth in developing the power of attention. (*WG* 113–14)

But if bondage is the point of attention, this radically shifts our understanding of how attention is to be valued in Weil's economy. For while it is possible to see effacement (to become something without a human face) and being dead as an enlargement and a liberation from the constriction of an "I," bondage is difficult to interpret as bearing any positive inflection, unless as a salutary giving-up of agency. Yet it matters whether attention is a value because it leads out of the prison of the "I" to what Weil calls the real or whether attention rather differently first leads to—and then constitutes—imprisonment and slavery. From the vantage of the set of passages considered at the beginning of this essay (and at the beginning of "School Studies"), attention frees one from thought, from the bad mood, from limited effort and ability, from the personality, while from the vantage of the set of passages that upholds the figure of master and slave, attention *establishes* the bondage. I shall return to the question of how these claims are related, but I first wish to examine what enslavement looks like.

iii

In "The Love of God and Affliction," Weil explains affliction as follows:

> Affliction is a marvel of divine technique. It is a simple and ingenious device which introduces into the soul of a finite creature the immensity of force, blind, brutal, and cold. The infinite distance separating God from the creature is entirely concentrated into one point to pierce the soul in its center.
>
> The man to whom such a thing happens has no part in the operation. He struggles like a butterfly pinned alive into an album. But through all the horror he can continue to want to love. There is nothing impossible in that, no obstacle, one might almost say no difficulty. (*WG* 135)

"Affliction" is a technical term which Weil defines as the coincidence of "physical pain, distress of soul, and social degradation, all at the same time" (*WG* 134). While "pain" and "suffering" seem to have miscellaneous origins, with greater and lesser degrees of intensification, "affliction" cannot be mitigated, in that its source—distance from God—is irremediable. Yet this infinite distance is incorporated in the person ("introduce[d] into the soul"), internalizing distance from God as something only imperceptibly different from the experience of him. Thus affliction is at once an intensification of pain and suffering and that specific pain or suffering that, inexplicably but insistently, converts the person's *separation* from God to his *inseparability* from God.

Where then does the "love" come in? One must ask this because Weil's appreciation of "technique" in the "butterfly" passage could imply a causal connection between affliction and love, as there would be in any ordinary understanding of masochism. Yet love is generated in spite of the pain and by what the pain can't touch—"the greatest suffering" being insufficient to disturb "the acquiescent part of the soul, consenting to a right direction." Thus the relation between pain and love really evades the causality that might have inflected an interpretation of it. Relish, so understood, would be for what escapes pain's jurisdiction; it is for the separability of the love from the pain. Affliction and love are thus made to coexist—that is *their* "marvel"—without being constitutive of each other. The man has "no part in the operation" of being pinned alive, but he does have a part—a "possibility"—of choosing to love anyway. The passage produces a representation of what such a love would look like when it renders affliction and captivity in terms that are devastating ("pinned alive") but restricted—in which a limit is revealed that the devastation can't transgress.

In the "affliction is a...divine technique" passage, pain, though still pain, is consequentially mitigated. In the following passage, however, pain (seen to be inseparable from beauty) is first a lure and then a trap ("the trap God most frequently uses" [*WG* 163]), and this trap, which both enthralls and ensnares, does not simply resist being interpretively neutralized but is also, in addition, explicitly made fatal. Yet, far from leading Weil to turn against what ensures her own destruction, when peril is at an extremity, it enlists Weil in its service, making her no longer complicit only in her own destruction but also colluding with what destroys her to secure the ruin of others:

The beauty of the world is the mouth of a labyrinth. The unweary individual who on entering takes a few steps is soon unable to find the opening. Worn out, with nothing to eat or drink, in the dark, separated from his dear ones, and from everything he loves and is accustomed to, he walks on without knowing anything or hoping anything, incapable even of discovering whether he is really going forward or merely turning round on the same spot. But this affliction is as nothing compared with the danger threatening him. For if he does not lose courage, if he goes on walking, it is absolutely certain that he will finally arrive at the center of the labyrinth. And there God is waiting to eat him. Later he will go out again, but...he will have become different, after being eaten and digested by God. Afterward he will stay near the entrance so that he can gently push all those who come near into the opening. (*WG* 163–64)

In the stages marked by this passage there is first privation; then disorientation; then endurance (called here "courage") in the absence of any apparent justification for it; then, but not finally, bondage. Then being devoured by God. Thus being captivated turns to bondage and bondage to a fate that, in the reversal of the Eucharist, suggests and displaces cannibalism. To be consumed by God is to perish in an incorporation that transforms the victim into an agent who captures others and secures their perishing. So God's victim becomes God's agent. Why is masochism, and then sadism, not the right word for this?

Such a question is underscored by the terms in which the passage represents with complacency the menace it chronicles as a repeating danger: "the mouth of a labyrinth," the mouth of God, the "opening" that is a mouth into which others will be "push[ed]," as if the only existent structure, albeit with permutations, were one that swallowed up. A question about masochism is reiterated by the following passage where attention is assigned the role that allows bondage to thrive:

The attitude that brings about salvation is not like any form of activity....It is the waiting or attentive and faithful immobility that lasts indefinitely and cannot be shaken. The slave, who waits near the door so as to open immediately the master knocks, is the best image of it. He must be ready to die of hunger and exhaustion rather than change his attitude. It must be possible for his companions to call him, talk to him, hit him, without his even turning his head. Even if he is told that the master is dead, and even if he believes it, he will not move. If he is told that the master...will beat him when he returns, and if he believes it, he will not move. (*WG* 196)

The slave in the above passage is impervious to conditions that are neutral. He is also impervious to conditions that are lethal. He is equally deaf to any logic that might obviate the extremity of his discipline, even to a logic that would invalidate its necessity: "If he is told that his master is dead...he will not move." Thus it rather seems that attention has the function of obliviousness, as if it were stupefying its recipient into behavior that is senseless. Given this interpretation, one wonders if the inclination to accept Weil's gloss of being dead as "genius" and freedom in some of the passages considered earlier should be read less benignly. How can it be the case that attention can facilitate freedom in one set of circumstances and bondage in another? And if it is thus versatile, what kind of empty space—what kind of blind mechanism—is attention?

One way to understand the double agency of attention is to see that Weil is not choosing servitude when she could be choosing freedom. Rather, she is seeing the difference between an imaginary freedom (the "I") and a necessary bondage to the real. Given such a construction, one couldn't have freedom simply by looking away from bondage. One could only have illusion. Thus attention frees one from imaginary confinement. But it simultaneously reveals the impossibility of being free from the conditions of the real. Attention does not then deceive one into equating the real with what is desirable. Rather, what is illuminated is a contradiction: "When the attention fixed upon something has revealed the contradiction in it...a sort of unsticking process takes place....Each thing that we desire is in contradiction with the conditions or the consequences attaching to that thing....Contradiction is our wretchedness, and the feeling of our wretchedness is the feeling of reality. For our wretchedness is not something that we concoct. It is something truly real. That is why we must love it. All the rest is imaginary" (*N* 2:411). The specific contradiction that attention embodies is the clarification of what is left to value after the imagination is dispelled, that is, after the "I" is abandoned. According to Weil what is left to love is nothing. That is what we are bound to. It is that which demands fidelity.[16]

What it might take to sustain attention in the presence of "nothing possible to love" (*N* 1:200) is associated by Weil with a "door": "When a contradiction is impossible to resolve except by a lie, then we know that it is really a door" (*FL* 269)—contradiction here is how to sustain attention when it seems ludicrous to do so. The wall becomes a "door" because the person who has relinquished hope consents to see the contradiction, however excruciating, as irremediable. Thus the door is not something one passes through; rather, the door is an opening around an obstacle seen to be immovable. The opening is only revealed when attention to abhorrent conditions is not accompanied by the attempt to dispel them. Insofar as contradiction is repellent to what would make the world intelligible, resting in contradiction (indistinguishable from resting in attention) implies relinquishing under-standing, along with the recognition that understanding is an operation that can only be performed in a vacuum isolated from the real, as on a plaything. Thus attention is regard that is innocent of desire or aspiration, hence inno-cent of either masochism or sadism, and not to be explained by a psycholo-gizing vocabulary.

But under what conditions can attention, defined like this, be maintained? This question is reiterated by a passage in which "to look" and "to eat" are said to be mutually exclusive ways of cherishing: "Here below, to look and to eat are two different things. We have to choose one or the other. They are both called loving. The only people who have any hope of salvation are those who occasionally stop and look for a time, instead of eating" (FL 286).

With reference to the labyrinth passage where to look is not only to be deprived of food ("nothing to eat or drink") but is also to be consumed by God, the alternative to look or to eat really amounts to eat or to be eaten.

When Weil was taken to the Middlesex Hospital in wartime London to be treated for tuberculosis, having been discovered lying unconscious in her room (her doctor, according to the Simone Pétrement biography, claimed "she had let herself starve in an attic" [quoted in SW 526]), she refused food, and then a pneumothorax (which her doctor construed as "the clearest sign yet that she wanted to die" [SW 532]). When Weil did in fact die, her death was ruled a suicide by the coroner: "The deceased did kill and slay herself by refusing to eat whilst the balance of her mind was disturbed" (quoted in SW 537). Yet a day earlier she is reported to have spoken willingly about taking nourishment. According to a letter written by Mme. Jones, one of Weil's last visitors, "she was intelligent enough" to try to eat, "to absorb more and more.... She also asked me if I could find a French cook and, also, to let her have a little butter roll in the morning—both impossible things to procure! When I had spoken to her about...mashed potatoes she had said: 'Yes, if they are done the French way by a Frenchwoman.'" Pétrement concludes: "This letter seems to indicate that Simone was trying to eat and refused most foods only because she thought she could not tolerate them" (SW 538).

The impossibility of attributing Simone Weil's actions at the end of her life to any single motivation is governed by Weil's statements about them. She spoke matter-of-factly of her refusal of the pneumothorax: "She won-dered whether it was a good idea to sacrifice one lung when the other, already stricken, could...end up in very bad condition" (SW 532). Only a month earlier (she was thirty-four), Weil expressed defeat in terms divorced from any physical condition: "I am finished, broken, beyond all possibility of mending, and that independent of Koch's bacilli. The latter have only taken advantage of my lack of resistance, and, of course, are busy demolishing it a little further" (quoted in *SW* 531). Although Weil is silent about the source of her despair, it could contextually be explained by her thwarted project for the formation of frontline nurses, dismissed by De Gaulle as madness, and by a subsequent failed attempt to get herself "sent [back] to France with a special mission" (*SW* 514). Thus, while the language of the coroner's report will always raise the question of suicide by starvation, Weil's wish to be sent on a special mission (or the plan for the formation of frontline nurses) differently asks to be interpreted in a communal (rather than individual) context of sacrifice. Weil took pains to differentiate these contexts: "[I cannot avoid] difficulties, hardship, fatigue, and suffering…without betraying myself." Commenting sharply on her natural distaste for self-abnegation, she added: Without such an inner and outer imperative, "I haven't in me the energy to undergo pain and suffering" (*SW* 433). But if asceticism (or masochism) and sacrifice can plausibly be differentiated in the contexts enumerated above, a passage from the New York notebook interlineates these explanatory possibilities:

Example of prayer.
Say to God:
Father, in the name of Christ grant me this.
That I may be unable to will any bodily movement, or even any attempt at movement, like a total paralytic. That I may be incapable of receiving any sensation, like someone who is completely blind, deaf and deprived of all the senses. That I may be unable to make the slightest connection between two thoughts, even the simplest, like one of those total idiots who not only cannot count or read but have never even learnt to speak. That I may be insensible to every kind of grief and joy, and incapable of any love for any being or thing, and not even for myself, like old people in the last stage of decrepitude.
Father, in the name of Christ grant me all this in reality.
May this body move or be still, with perfect suppleness or rigidity, in continuous conformity to thy will. May my faculties of hearing, sight, taste, smell and touch register the perfectly accurate impress of thy creation. May this mind, in fullest lucidity, connect all ideas in perfect conformity with

thy truth. May this sensibility experience, in their greatest possible intensity and in all their purity, all the nuances of grief and joy....May all this be stripped away from me, devoured by God, transformed into Christ's substance, and given for food to afflicted men whose body and soul lack every kind of nourishment. And let me be a paralytic—blind, deaf, witless and utterly decrepit....

Father, since thou art the Good and I am mediocrity, rend this body and soul away from me to make them into things for your use, and let nothing remain of me, for ever, except this rending itself, or else nothingness. (*FL* p243–44)

Even though it is the case that Weil suggests in the sixth paragraph that the laming, blinding, paralyzing, mutilating, and cretinizing of the fourth paragraph should exist so as to enable her to see, hear, taste, smell, touch everything accurately, in perfection, "with the fullest lucidity," such causality does not mitigate the passage's extremity. And when Weil adds, "One does not voluntarily ask for such things. One comes to it in spite of oneself. In spite of oneself, yet one comes to it. One does not consent to it with abandon, but with a violence exerted upon the entire soul by the entire soul" (*FL* 244), asceticism, masochism, sacrifice each (and all in conjunction) seem inadequate categories for an imperative that reiterates its own conflicted motivation ("One comes to it in spite of oneself...yet one comes to it"), an imperative that is first asserted in opposition to one's will, but subsequently willed—in an iteration that crosses back and forth between imploring conditions and resisting those same conditions; between a surrender made on behalf of others ("given up for food to afflicted men" who "lack every kind of nourishment") and an aimless supplication in the sentence following this implored sacrifice, in which self-annihilation seems a redundant afterthought. For when Weil writes, "And let me be a paralytic—blind, deaf, witless and utterly decrepit," it must be noted that "And" is not "therefore." No necessity governs this plight. In other words, Weil's prayer ends with a fate that, though implored, is not any longer motivated or required.

The difficulty, we could say the conflict, of Simone Weil's writing, is emphasized by a passage like the previous one. Difficulty does not lie merely in understanding how something resisted could turn into something willed (sacrifice, masochism, asceticism, and even the idea of "training" all complexly address such a conversion).[17] Difficulty also lies in the relation between "be[ing] *in*sensible to every kind of grief and joy" and being sensible to "*all the nuances* of grief and joy" (italics mine). The passage asks us to see a juxtaposition as predictive of an ostensible causality in which the negation of one state of affairs produces the affirmation of another state of affairs. Hence the parallel syntax. But the passage then undoes the apparent significance of the causality by a reiteration that is a pure functionless negation. ("And let me be a paralytic" implores incapacities after they have been recompensed.) It is almost as if sequence (between one position and its antithesis) and any other logical relation among two such discrete positions—sacrifice that is motivated and sacrifice that is meaningless—is rendered absurd in Weil's writing. One can't produce a linkage between witless(ness) and lucidity because the voices articulating the desire for either of them apparently have no knowledge of each other. Thus, to return to the passage in which "believing" and not listening to believing accompany each other, or to return to the passage in which "the 'I' belongs to non-being" precedes "I have not the right to know this....I shall never know this," we see that Weil's passages are exemplary precisely for their theatricalizing of kinds of knowledge (and points of view) that cannot be assimilated to each other, even though they might be presented as combinatory. One explanation for the multiple instances in which attention absorbs implications as antithetical as freedom and bondage requires seeing the connotative instability of attention as a consequence of the fact that it is being registered from discrete perspectives. Therefore, in looking at instances of attention in Weil's writing, a reader does not see uniformly, but rather sees something like the "structure" of one of Empson's "complex words."[18] With respect to attention in its broadest manifestations the properties of an "I" in Weil's passages could be described as migratory or nomadic—not something situated or continuous—even within a single passage. Moreover, if one can't unify subject positions, one also cannot precisely separate them. Thus it might seem one can abstract the figures who populate Weil's passages to the one who *resists,* the one who *succumbs,* and (with respect to the labyrinth passage) the one who *pushes others in.* Who could say, however, whether a dreamy will-lessness that characterizes all three positions in the labyrinth passage doesn't finally submerge the differences among those positions that the passage had worked so hard to inscribe?[19] For finally the passage revokes a sense of agency located anywhere.

Yet will and agency do consequentially distinguish the kinds of energy by which in Weil's lexicon personality can be forfeited. Specifically, Weil differentiates between "supplementary energy" and "vegetative energy." "Supplementary energy" is that which can be sacrificed without jeopardizing egotism. Weil explains that a person could give up his life ("for Napoleon," for a lover, in the case "of a miser" for his riches), but such a relinquishment, even though it ends in death, would only illusorily count as sacrifice; it would not knowingly forfeit anything essential. If "the supplementary energy…precipitates the body into the jaws of death[,] the vegetative energy is not concerned. As soon as its concern is aroused there appears (except with the help of supernatural grace) the coldest type of egoism. This is indeed the only case in which man is egoistic" (*N* 1:283).

I take Weil to be distinguishing between sacrifice fueled by courage, love, wealth—each a different form of self-magnification, so that, notwithstanding the death of the body, egotism survives, and effectively negates, the body's destruction—and a total sacrifice that leaves nothing remaindered but need so rudimentary that it cannot be imagined. A sacrifice can exist in which nothing *essential* is lost; only for such a sacrifice can one muster enthusiasm, which is generated by a clear limit on the loss, thus by its unreality. In distinction, to arrive at vegetative energy is the task of many of these passages and the condition of their difficulty: "When the vegetative energy is laid bare and has to be drawn upon, then the universe disappears and need becomes the whole universe. The whole universe is concentrated in the soul's cry: 'I am hungry!' 'I am in pain!' 'This must stop!'…At this point, to reply: 'I don't see the necessity' is to tear the eternal part of the soul violently away from the self and fix it to the not-self" (*FL* 234).[20] In an earlier passage of the same notebook entry, Weil elaborates:

It is the supplementary energy that places the soul in the sphere of the conditional. One says "I'm prepared to go two kilometres if I can get an egg." So one has the strength for two kilometres in spite of feeling tired. But total exhaustion is the feeling: "I couldn't go ten yards, even to save my life." This corresponds to a state in which the vegetative energy is all that is left, in which walking would use up an energy which is indispensable for the maintenance of the vital functions themselves….

It is then that the soul cries "I must…!"

I must see so-and-so! I must rest! I must eat! I must drink! This pain must abate for just a moment!

One should then reply coldly and cynically, like Talleyrand to the beggar: I don't see the necessity. (*FL* 233)

Such contested identifications—in which knowledge, attention, choice, energy, and sacrifice constitute the person (even as each of these terms is itself the site of disagreement)—might explain why a religious framework, no less than a psychological one, would be unequipped to account for Weil's writing without recourse to a category outside itself. This is the case because, for instance, a concept like masochism (whether in Freud's understanding or Gilles Deleuze's) pathologizes what it is examining in terms of an individual economy,[21] while, conversely, a concept like sacrifice translates what is being examined into a religious paradigm that is, as opposed to asceticism, by definition collective, presuming a nonidiosyncratic relation to a system. Weil's formulations are inhospitable to either of these understandings ("One must not be *I*, but still less must one be *We*" [*N* 1:298]; "There is no way from the collective to the impersonal").[22] Weil's writing disallows the kind of arbitrary separation of person from collectivity, even while it preserves the demarcation between a larger human order and the single person who remains resistant to it. Moreover, there is an anomalous crossing of categories whether these be of sects with an eschatology (Christianity) and sects with no eschatology (stoicism), which Weil nonetheless characterizes as "twin conceptions" of the same thing (*NR* 276); or of disciplinary realms, as when geometry is said to be a "double language," which is addressed to matter and supernatural relations alike (*NR* 278);[23] or of domains, as when physical labor is described as the "spiritual core" of the social world (*NR* 288). Yet if disciplinary and philosophical distinctions are also violated, the result is not facile integration; Weil always remained obsessed with what is *anathema sit*—what is left out as well as what is incorrectly assimilated. In Weil's writing we are always discovering something left out, and the most opportune to omit, hardest to lay bare, is vegetable energy, that which resists its own extinction.

Thus, even in the midst of lifelong starvation (if starvation is the right name for it), a wish might persist, say for mashed potatoes "done the French way" or for "a little butter roll." I take wanting potatoes done in the French way, voiced in a conversation where what is deliberated is how much sustenance and what kind of sustenance will preserve life, as a manifestation of the desire to be, rather than as the expression of a particular or trivial preference. Wanting the potatoes is wanting being itself, in which the wanting (being or potatoes), makes hunger inseparable from taste, insofar as hunger cannot be eliminated. But even as one could imagine hunger as inseparable from taste, there would be, in Weil's distinction, some less composite need (not possible to indicate in terms of potatoes or bouillon: "because she does not want any milk" [quoted in *SW* 538]) or something further specifiable (and also further reducible). This is what the imagination can never represent to itself, for to see hunger stripped of any ideational objects and also stripped of affect (or any other accompaniment) is to see need beyond imagination. It is this "coldest type of egoism" (*N* 1:283), "this mortal cold of the *vegetative energy* that one so rarely touches," next to which "all things other than oneself cease to exist" (*N* 1:292–93), that Weil's passages touch.

iv

In Weil's passages violence is a logic that dictates consent: "One does not consent to [affliction] with abandon, but with a violence exerted on the entire soul by the entire soul" (*FL* 244). Elsewhere violence is understood as what is done *to* us: "Our soul is shut off from all reality.... God...explodes it, and makes contact with reality" (*FL* 288). But violence is also associated with a shifting from one allegiance to another (as in the labyrinth passage or as in the refinement of vegetative energy from supplementary energy). In other words violence is what enables a shattering of the unified entity thought of as the self. Weil is not committed to a shattering that involves dispersal but rather to a core or reduction that will be left once the shattering has gotten rid of the gratuitous. Violence is a form of mobility, a way to achieve mobility in relation to form. Weil more minutely locates violence in an orientation:

> Fasting, vigils, etc.,—as acts of piety, it is good if they are easy. There is something marvelous in facility, something that is reflected in the quintets of Mozart and the songs of Monteverdi. I want to suffer violence from human beings, and to be obliged to do violence to myself on their behalf; but for God I would like to do only easy things. Except for the actual orientation of thought towards God, which is the supreme and intimate violence that the soul does to itself. (*FL* 188)

Much like attention, an orientation seems too insignificant to count at all until it is counted, for both attention and orientation are mechanisms for getting outside what is inescapable. Weil sees this access less as a paradox than as an amplification. Violence inheres in making the "I" universal: "Man—a mind tied to a body—is only able to exist if this same body is an image of the universe, and if the limited portions of matter to which he has access are—some of them—images of the universe" (*N* 1:107).

Such definitions of impersonality become descriptions uttered from the vantage of discovery, when the physical becomes perceptible as an embodied sense. Thus, for instance, when Weil writes, "suffering—The universe which enters into the body" (*N* 1:134), she locates suffering as arising at the moment when the body can't escape registration of what is other than itself. Suffering is defined as what the body can't escape incorporating—the body coming into being in relation to its permeability. ("The secret of our misery lies in the fact that certain things enter into us and certain things go out from us. Food. Attachment" [*N* 1:247].) What I mean to emphasize in these examples is a drama whose violence Weil roots in the body. Hence Weil's parable of ultimate love—a drama that *registers* differentially on the body, according to changing conditions. It is not to be *understood* differentially, though (despite that prohibition's seeming to be a mere nicety of reason). "A man drinks a glass of water. The glass of water is God's 'I love you.' He is two days in the desert without finding anything to drink. The dryness in his throat is God's 'I love you.' God is like an importunate woman who clings to her lover, whispering in his ear for hours without stopping: 'I love you—I love you—I love you—I love you'" (*FL* 128). These are words whose indiscriminate meaning ("only one meaning" [*FL* 128]) and indiscriminate reference (the body) are inescapable ("in his ear…without stopping"), being situated always where we physically are.

To inhabit the physical is to see what is "irreducible." Thus:

> Milarepa and food. After having destroyed to the utmost the reality of the universe, he finally reached its irreducible point, the point where the very mind which conceives finds itself degraded to being one out of the number of appearances.
>
> Food constitutes this point. Food is the irreducible element.
>
> Fasting constitutes an experimental knowledge of the irreducible character of food, and hence of the reality of the sensible universe. (*N* 1:316)

Milarepa is the Buddhist figure who penetrates the illusory nature of reality—a process in which looking closely at phenomena (including the mind) reveals their insubstantial nature. I take the passage to mark the process by which Milarepa discovers that food alone maintains solidity, cannot be "degraded" to the status of illusion. Food is what the mind can't unthink. The mind can't unmake the necessity of food, though lack of food can unmake the mind, by showing it to be illusory. Thus food is like the atom: elemental. But food can be refused. For, according to one way of reading the end of the passage, "fasting" is a way to examine irreducibility; it might be that what was thought a definitive bottom line is itself a thought, that necessity is an appearance which fasting proves nonactual.

In other words, for Milarepa, as for the soul in Weil's earlier passage who cries "'I must...!'...I must eat! I must drink! This pain must abate for just a moment!" one "should then reply coldly and cynically, like Talleyrand to the beggar: I don't see the necessity." It's relevant to examine the value of Talleyrand's coldness and cynicism, of this detached indifference. For the moment one applies it, not to another but to oneself, one sees there *is* no imperative. There's no necessity to live; there is only a desire to do so. All of Weil's writing works toward the place from which one can redirect Talleyrand's rejoinder from the beggar to oneself. For while food is "irreducible" (in the sense of imperative), it is a limited or qualified necessity. Food is necessary for one's life. But one's life isn't necessary. Weil's writing charts a movement from illusions of necessity predicated on claims, rights, and needs ("The principal claim we think we have on the universe is that our personality should continue") to a different understanding of necessity: "Attention is what creates *necessary* connections. (Those which do not depend on attention are not necessary.)," which might or might not pertain advantageously to oneself, but which alone could assert legitimacy.

In negotiating a transfer from a false idea of necessity to a true one, hence also from the didactic to the experiential, violence instantiates itself, for in moving from prescriptions that dictate specifications of desire ("One must destroy intelligence and will"; one must love what has neither "amiability [nor] existence"; one must "go down to the source of [one's] desires in order to tear energy away from its object. It is there that desires are true, in so far as they are energy" [*N* 1:203]) to desire experienced as a lack, there is only a cry, purified of abstract imperatives: "A little child who sees something bright is so totally absorbed in his love for the shiny object that his whole body leans towards it and he quite forgets it is beyond his reach....A child does not will to obtain the bright object or the milk, he makes no plans for getting them; he simply desires, and cries" (*FL* 325). Weil abandons imperatives, we "must love," "must destroy," for the representation of the child's position is an inhabiting of that position, dictated as a cry from within its intensity. But what is the object of the cry? What object has dignity? With reference to the body can any object survive belittlement?

One loves only what one can eat. When a thing is no longer edible one leaves it to anyone else who can still find nourishment in it. Human love operates only within limits. Some change could happen to me, such that none of those who love me would pay any more attention to me....

I love a fruit, but I no longer love it when it is rotten....

There are two lines in the *Iliad* that express with incomparable power the wretched limitation of human love.

This is one:

"... on the ground [the dead] lay,

much dearer to the vultures than to their wives."

And this is the other:

"After she was worn out with tears, she began to think of eating."

(*FL* 322–23)

A constantly regulated perspective interlineates the voice that defines ("One loves only what one can eat"), the voice that is subjected to the hunger being defined ("I love a fruit"), the voice that observes ("on the ground they lay ..."), the voice that inhabits Niobe's perspective—a perspective made truly terrifying because Niobe's absolute grief at the slaying of her children can't sustain itself before thoughts of food that arise as if gratuitously (not represented as issuing from hunger), the most terrible mental affliction yielding to the most trivial one.[24] In passages like these Weil inhabits positions (as Niobe, as Milarepa, as the crying child) from which she also dislocates herself. Such a shift from an oracular perspective to a habitation from within is consonant with two analogous stances the passages attempt to realize: what must properly be embodied (must acknowledge its confinement in a body) if the universe is to be perceived as real and, conversely, what must be disembodied ("Never think of a human being, unless he is by our side, without thinking that he is perhaps dead" [*N* 1:218]) because embodiment, when a consequence of the imagination, is a mistake.

Only within the body—within Milarepa's experiment on the irreducibility of food, up close to Niobe's grief trivialized at the moment "she began to think of eating"—can abstract formulations be tested. To represent the logic behind "fasting" or to represent the experience in which grief ends (is aborted by thoughts of eating) and in which the child's crying "tirelessly" cannot come to an end (because there is no available object within reach to end it) is the work done by Weil's writing. It locates impersonality outside of human grief within desire torn from an object in a redefinition of irreducibility. Violence is a consequence of an absolute limit coolly looked beyond (Milarepa's supposition about the irreducibility of food; Niobe's grief) to some further limit that affronts human vanity. Violence is associated with adjustments in perspective that regulate how persons are seen from outside their own vantage. Thus, for example, in her essay "Human Personality" Weil attempts to sever the human personality from what is sacred: "If it were the human personality in [a man] that was sacred to me, I could easily put out his eyes. As a blind man he would be exactly as much a human personality as before. I should have destroyed nothing but his eyes" (HP 314). The intentionally shocking figure is instructive for the completeness with which it leaves intact a construct that is trivial (the person, the personality), while violating what is not trivial, indicating that "although it is the whole of [a man] that is sacred to me, he is not sacred in all respects and from every point of view" (HP 314). Blinding, being beaten, even physical obliteration, constitute experiments in the study of efficacious violence which separates the sacred from the personality that degrades it: "Affliction is a device for pulverizing the soul; the man who falls into it is like a workman who gets caught up in a machine. He is no longer a man but a torn and bloody rag on the teeth of a cog-wheel" (HP 331). This is not a metaphor, because it is not a figure; it is instead an analytic statement indicating what would in fact be left of such a man—a "bloody rag on the teeth of a cog-wheel"—which depends on the annihilation of the person experienced from within. Or rather, it is precisely the point that what is seen from without and experienced from within no longer differ. Thus what has been demolished is a privatized perspective, "pulverizing" being an optical testimony as well as a visceral one.

Although truth is rooted for Weil in the representation of the body, it is not always rooted in a body with recognizable features. For example, in the following passage, impersonality is an infusion that touches all things equally. What is canceled is a distinction among human, divine, and inert entities, rendering the beggar, the seed, and the person the same kind of featureless entity that is only animated and made sensible in relation to another kindred entity:

We cannot take a step toward the heavens. God crosses the universe and comes to us.

Over the infinity of space and time, the infinitely more infinite love of God comes to possess us. He comes at his own time. We have the power to consent to receive him or to refuse. If we remain deaf, he comes back again and again like a beggar, but also, like a beggar, one day he stops coming. If we consent, God puts a little seed in us and he goes away again. From that moment God has no more to do; neither have we, except to wait. We only have not to regret the consent we gave him, the nuptial yes. It is not as easy as it seems, for the growth of the seed within us is painful. Moreover, from the very fact that we accept this growth, we cannot avoid destroying whatever gets in its way, pulling up the weeds, cutting the good grass, and unfortunately the good grass is part of our very flesh, so that this gardening amounts to a violent operation. On the whole, however, the seed grows of itself. A day comes when the soul belongs to God.... Then in its turn it must cross the universe to go to God. (*WG* 133)

Perhaps the most curious aspect of the passage devolves from its transformation of the stanzas from Isaiah. The point about grass being part of our very flesh is that it partakes of the categorical indistinction that renders human and divine figures equally "anonymous" (*WG* 125), equally inert matter, and also renders being indistinguishable from nonbeing. In a sense the passage reverses "All flesh is grass" turning it into all grass is flesh. That is what makes "gardening" a "violent operation," as if what were being eradicated in the passage were not only the personal but also the human.

In other words, in the "gardening" passage violence is a consequence of a drama that Weil roots in the suffering of the body. At the same time she disallows any connection between this experience of pain and any recognizable person on whose behalf or in relation to whom one could have outrage. In the beating, pulverizing, blinding, starving, thirsting that permeate Weil's writing, pain is intensified until its endurance seems impossible, even as pain and what might count as stamina are cut away from any person's containment of these. Violence is a consequence of the excess of affliction, for once extracted from the person pain is in no way reduced, but is conversely unbound, as if the negation of the person didn't obviate the pain but preserved it as an entity—something without origin, without scope, and finally without reference. Yet the pain is not precisely no one's pain—disassociation is not how pain achieves its autonomy—but rather, properly conceived, must be understood each time as pain that consumes *one*. Pain is not unfelt, but, rather, it engrosses all feeling and every other aspect of the person. That is at once its triumph and its efficacy.

But pain on whose behalf? In the service of what? While one could call Weil's thinking anti-Hegelian thinking because in its delegation of pain it appears to preserve the distinction between masters and slaves, between aristocratic statesmen and beggars (as in the Talleyrand quotation), or between humans and God, exacting pain as a price or allocating pain hierarchically, the disempowerment ("[God] comes back again and again like a beggar...") and affliction ("a nail...whose head is all necessity spreading throughout space and time" [*WG* 134–35]) in fact apply to all equally: "Affliction is a marvel...a simple and ingenious device which introduces into the soul of a finite creature the immensity of force, blind, brutal, and cold" (*WG* 135), that consumes all imaginary constructs—the personality *and* God—freeing the space as it were for some authentic presence. Yet true to Weil's principle that God does not yet exist (*N* 1:151), her formulations, implying a dialectic they also resist, can never get further than the pain that is at once preparatory and uncompensated.

Therefore the writing in the passages I am describing paralyzes any response we could properly summon, since the arena on which Weil trains our observation (the de-creation of the person) is intentionally divorced from available categories of understanding, as Weil herself testifies: "To consent to being anonymous, to being human material (Eucharist); to renounce prestige, public esteem—that is to bear witness to the truth, namely, that one is composed of human material, that one has no rights. It is to cast aside all ornament, to put up with one's nakedness. But how is this compatible with social life and its labels?" (*N* 1:217).

v

Just the incompatibility of nakedness and truth with "social life and its labels" is the appeal of Weil's writing. In other words, from the formulations I have been considering it has seemed that Weil's obsession with attention was infinitely resourceful, or, if finitely resourceful, then that to follow attention had no *imaginable* end. The intrigue of Weil's formulations (speaking for myself personally) lies in the promise of an escape from the predictability of what is possible in the human world if comfort is not the driving factor. Thus Weil's writing offers an *idea* of what might be experienced if one had courage to perceive the body without consolatory illusions; if "difficulty" were a joy ("An insuperable difficulty is a sun" [*N* 1:84]) by virtue of inescapability not retreated from; if God remained a category free of belief, fear, and exclusion. Why would a life structured in relation to such reunderstandings be not impoverished, but rather rich? If there were a choice between satisfactions (call the collection of them happiness, under the best of circumstances transient) and the attempt to live in relation to a penetrable depth, to ask how one might be fully human without regard for cost, could one *thinkingly* refuse that choice? Finally, would it be possible to suppose a world in which such questions were not rhetorical? For Weil they were neither rhetorical nor apolitical; the interrelation of Weil's writing and her life demonstrates she is not manipulating phrases.[25] Thus Weil's refusals might be understood in terms of the stripping away of solaces, a sacrifice in which she claimed nothing was lost. And her abstinences, like those of Kafka's hunger artist (to whom she has been compared), could be understood as based not on a distaste for sustenance but rather on an appetite so voracious and for sustenance so rare that one could only glean it. Even if one is repelled by such an acquired taste, there is Weil's extraordinary writing, with its generation of interest at the site of value as intensity. Her obsessive attempts to distinguish the personal from some amplitude she designates variously as the "sacred," the "impersonal," the "irreducible," the "good" locate value in a discipline contoured by an ardor for what will *not* sustain her. In fact Weil's splittings of the person, characteristically dramatized by an embodying and disembodying of an "I," compose a corpus of writing about attention that enacts impersonality as a set of instructions Weil presents herself as trying to heed. Thus the cultivation of attention is less pedagogic (as "School Studies" implies) than improvisational. Attention, constitutive of impersonality, is what, at cost, Weil's language is modeling.

Attention can only be sustained moment after moment; therefore a notebook of attentive moments can only be collected without being narratively organized. What binds these attentive moments to each other is the repetitive relation between two kinds of writing: one of which issues didactic imperatives and one of which embodies those imperatives—the writing enacting a breakthrough experience in which a hypothetical position is made to give way to its instantiation. Thus something dispels the heterogeneous quality of writing in Weil's notebooks, making it seem driven. What cancels the miscellaneous quality of Weil's writing is not its history but rather its intensity, which is reiterated in exacting a transfer from what is abstract to (strange to say) the impersonality that is blooded. This intensity is underscored in the extremity of consequences (the soul "pulverized"), and it remains unmistakable in less melodramatic expressions of self-extinction: "Beauty... *tears us away from* the point of view" (*N* 1:232). Intensity is a hallmark of Weil's writing. One must insist on this because Weil actually dismissed intensity as at odds with her endeavor: "What thing in the world is most opposed to purity? The pursuit of *intensity*" (*FL* 7). Although there is a distinction between intensity and the pursuit of intensity, I would argue that Weil is as opposed to one as to the other. Nonetheless, in Weil's writing intensity produces purity. Say, rather, that in Weil's writing the person experiencing extinction is condensed to an intensity whose specific instantiation (and whose specific experience—of pain, joy, fear, what have you) becomes immaterial. Thus Weil is not only engaging in intellectual work. Weil's intellectual work has efficacy. But not for us. We view this efficacy perfunctorily from the outside. My essay concludes by examining the cost for the person to whom such writing is not perfunctory.

I first return, however, one last time to the suppositions behind Weil's writing. Weil's hostility to the category of the self had looked unassimilable to masochism and to any other punitive understanding. Yet willing life in unusual forms—forms of vitality purged of an "I"—becomes in these passages heuristically inseparable from willing death in unusual forms (may I "be insensible…like old people in the last stage of decrepitude"). Thus these positions are coupled, even though Weil's writing and her life seem to defy such linkages and conclusions. In other words, the preservation of the self in Weil's writing is not a necessary part of any commitment to self-sacrificing—however the positions might exist simultaneously in the passages examined. Conversely, the commitment to life lived at the greatest intensity seems in Weil's writing inseparable from fatality. Yet the compensation for Weil's practices of attention—and, indeed, their intelligibility—lies in preserving the difference between being dead in the sense of being without a vantage and being dead as an actual phenomenon.

It was the *mechanical* nature of the personal that Weil, in her philosophy and her political thinking, tried to contest. Yet the defiances she crafted—the sentences she wrote her way into—hurried her toward a death as catastrophically wasteful (indeed as imaginable) as the conventions that seemed moribund to her. (If one compares Weil to Sylvia Plath, whose writing against personal limits produced the same calamity, and compares Weil's project to another project differently engaged in the constitution of a world outside a pure "I," Edith Stein's dissertation on empathy—which is writing that is benign, but also writing that is passionless: without energy, and even, it might be said, without interest—a correlation seems indicated between what compels interest and what compels fatality of one's own design.)[26]

Why should it be the case that living on the highest terms (from Weil's point of view) would, in Weil's sense of necessity, coerce the lethal? That nothing would count as a sufficient answer to such a question does not obviate its urgency. To put it somewhat differently, is the causality that seems inevitable in Weil's writing—in which a commitment to attention is a commitment to death—a consequence of a thwarting of her idealism (it needn't, shouldn't have had this end), or a fulfillment of that idealism (it had to be so)? For if one regards fragments like "not to believe in the immortality of the soul, but to look upon the whole of life as destined to prepare for the moment of death" (*N* 2:469), compensation is evacuated everywhere; the space one had supposed to be opened up where the "I" obtruded is only immediately reoccupied by another predictability, as if making clear the limit on human inventiveness. Was Weil's death, then, a mistake about the inevitability of consequences? And *whose* mistake? For it is easy (when the consequences are *viewed* and not *lived*) to participate in the mistake, as it were, "empathetically."[27] To find Weil's formulations remarkable is to be struck by their amplitude, by her writing large of human will such that impossibility is always understood derisively. Weil's solution to scarcity—to the impoverishment of attention—is simply to disbelieve in it: to maximize human effort as a value to which she could commit herself without regard for success, without regard for extremity, that is, without reserve, and with no perception of threat.

At the beginning of this essay, I touched on two understandings of attention equally endorsed by Weil. In the first, "Attention consists of suspending our thought, leaving it detached, empty, waiting, not seeking anything, but ready to receive in its naked truth the object that is to penetrate it" (*WG* 112). In such an understanding the consequence of attention is waiting without grasping, in the sense of not focusing on objects, while supposing focus will come, having patience in lieu of expectation. The cost of such attention for the person would be the lack of effort which "School Studies" describes as "negative effort," or more precisely "the greatest of all efforts." In the second understanding, attention is engaged, wholeheartedly embracing or grasping an object or a truth, "in all its nakedness, behind the particular form in which it happens to have found expression" (*NR* 65). To accept truth as such is to dispense with requirements that truth assume a certain appearance (that is the "nakedness" part)—in other words, that truth adhere to a person's specification of it. However, there is a third description of attention (which

Weil here calls philosophy) in which attention is disengaged from grasping objects (as in the second passage) but is equally disengaged from relinquishing them (as in the first). Thus differentiated, attention looks like this: "The proper method of philosophy consists in clearly conceiving the insoluble problems in all their insolubility and then in simply contemplating them, fixedly and tirelessly, year after year, without any hope, patiently waiting" (*FL* 335). In the third and most difficult instance, where the prescription for attention seems most innocuous, difficulty arises from the total absence of compensation, which both other passages designate as truth—which, in this last case, is neither present nor prospective. In effect the third passage reveals a consequence hard to overestimate and equally hard to picture, for Weil's formulation of enduring the "insolubility" without lessening the attentiveness—of sustaining the attentiveness, notwithstanding the failure "fixedly and tirelessly, year after year"—provides a breathtakingly understated representation of the cost Weil implicitly affixed to her endeavor. The state of mind that would produce such endurance (in the face of such failure) is not a person's state of mind understood from any easily recognizable vantage but rather an attempt to suspend a person's state of mind, with its frustrations, expectations, and above all hopes—that is, with its distinctions. What is at issue could be gleaned obliquely by reference to a few sentences of T. S. Eliot's confession of confusion ("enlightened mystification") two years into the study of Sanskrit and Indian philosophy. Specifically, Eliot wrote, "half of the effort of understanding what the Indian philosophers were after—and their subtleties make most of the great European philosophers look like schoolboys—lay in trying to erase from my mind all the categories and kinds of distinction common to European philosophy from the time of the Greeks." Thus, he continues, "I came to the conclusion…that my only hope of really penetrating to the heart of that mystery would lie in forgetting how to think and feel as an American or a European: which, for practical as well as sentimental reasons, I did not wish to do."[28]

But what does it mean to say that the "philosophy" passage does not represent a person's state of mind understood through the "traditions and mental habits of Europe for two thousand years"?[29] If an "I" in Weil's claim "is only a motive," the image of waiting without hope seems to forfeit that motive. "Call him…hit him…beat him…he will not move" (*WG* 196) suggests a purposiveness in which the one who waits is not dissuaded by interference. The waiting has a point (the master's knock), however deferred and however we might reject it as a motive that could be ours. In distinction, contemplation without hope, "fixedly and tirelessly, year after year," issues from a position from which everything has been evacuated. There is no plenitude to any part of Weil's formulation, as she would say, "nothing supplementary." There is no differentiated sense of time, because the future is understood to be just like the past; thus there is no way to move from "insoluble" to soluble. There is only pointless waiting—which is to say, waiting that is not waiting at all, but rather waiting that has become being. For once waiting is not intelligible in terms of any goal, there is only the automaticity of an elemental state, enough to satisfy any craving for lifelessness. But there is not here even a craving for lifelessness. This is a formulation of impersonality that has been as if fulfilled without the resistance that in Weil's work customarily—from a margin or through an obliquity—marks a counterforce that makes the project of impersonality "imaginable."

Such a formulation abolishes the representation of a person's state of mind and links it to passages like these, which go one step further, eliminating not only the person but also the human:

> The vegetative energy, by which the chemico-biological mechanisms necessary for life are maintained, is below the level of time. When the former energy is exhausted and the vegetative energy has to be expended for something other than the biological functions for which it is destined, then a quarter of an hour seems like endless duration. Then it is that the cry: Enough! invades the soul, and the soul is split in two if it does not endorse that cry. It is then that the very sap of life flows away and the man becomes dead wood while still alive. (*FL* 220)
>
> …in the event of privation, [man] cannot help turning to *anything whatever* which is edible.
>
> There is only one remedy for that: a chlorophyll conferring the faculty of feeding on light.
>
> There is only one fault: incapacity to feed upon light; for in the absence of this capacity, all faults are possible and none is avoidable. (*N* 1:223)

Weil keeps performing through her writing procedures that transform a person's state of mind into "dead wood," or—since "[man] cannot help turning to *anything whatever* which is edible"—into a state, which, however improbable, by virtue of its use of chlorophyll, can feed on light (*N* 1:223). But feeding on light (through chlorophyll) or not feeding at all (dead wood) are inverse personifications that provoke by antithesis the very manifestations of a person they were meant to dispel—at their most extreme, menacing, by what can only be incompletely banished, the inhumanity of Weil's project.

In fact, one could say, the metaphors "dead wood" or "feeding on light" are too extravagant to capture the reductiveness to which Weil aspires. Better to put the reductiveness in the following terms, as Weil did:

> To know that God is the good or, more simply, that the absolute good is the good, and to have faith that the desire for good is self-multiplying.... Nothing else is needed....
>
> But it is in this simplicity that the greatest difficulty lies.... Who could endure an hour's conversation with a friend, if the friend kept on repeating nothing but: God, God, God.... (*FL* 309)

Such a passage epitomizes, it seems to me, the impoverished state of mind that Eliot rejected and that Weil cultivated, as it also clarifies the difficulty of training attention even on the representation of such a simplification. (This is why perhaps we can attend to Weil's writing—in which an adherence to difficulties often seems to alter her relation to those difficulties—while ourselves getting nothing practically useful from it.) The ellipses are the intimidating part of the proposition "God, God, God...," indicating as they do a continuity of endeavor in which the goal is to pay attention to (rather than merely to hear) this—or any—word whose repetition would quickly deprive it of significance. Even as the conditions are deemed to be intolerable ("Who could endure?"), a limit case is suggested that is literally unimaginable, there being nothing for imagination to feed on in the midst of these repetitions. Yet the other side of unimaginable is a margin, a condition, a reduction, a glimpse of what might open up through an abandonment of imagination. Specifically, it is the idea of the friend, in conjunction with the idea of a conversation, that is, the idea of the ordinary in conjunction with the presumption of benevolence (if *friend* could be assumed to imply such a connotation, and if *conversation* could be supposed to have this content), which illuminates what renders these propositions so nonplussing. For the elements do not appear to be compatible, nor could they be compatible, arising from different spheres and at different levels. It's the conjunction of the benevolent, the ordinary, and the unintelligible (or mysterious), a constellation of alien elements whose conjunction is nonetheless so compelling as almost to validate Weil's understanding of necessity ("Attention is what creates *necessary* connections") seen, that is to say, from the other side of a person's requirements.

6

"The Sea's Throat":
T. S. Eliot's *Four Quartets*

i

When in part 1 of "The Dry Salvages" the speaker says

> The river is within us, the sea is all about us....
>   The sea has many voices,
> Many gods and many voices....
>   The sea howl
> And the sea yelp, are different voices
> Often together heard[1]

he is attesting to a polyvocality in which voice can be distinguished but not individualized. Voices in Tennyson's "Ulysses" ("the deep / Moans round with many voices") also contribute to the strain that is audible. Voices keep emerging even after they appear to have been conclusively calculated.[2] For while in "The Dry Salvages" II "all sea voices" suggests the end of an accounting, that idea is ruptured in the acknowledgment "There is no end of it, the voiceless wailing," "no end, but addition." Moreover, presences which we don't associate with voice because they have no manifestation in sound,

> At nightfall, in the rigging and the aerial,
> Is a voice descanting (though not to the ear …
>   and not in any language).
> ("The Dry Salvages" III)

are nonetheless said to be voices. The point about saying something is voiced, while also saying it is audible outside of language and even sound, is that it articulates a phenomenon while dissociating that phenomenon from the properties that make it recognizable, that make it what it is. This estrangement of voice from its constitutive properties (sometimes language, always presumptively sound) is paralleled by a dissociation within the poem of voice from any individual source to which it could be attributed. The dissociation of voice from an individual entity is *opposite* to the "dissociation of sensibility" Eliot notes in "The Metaphysical Poets." The "dissociation of sensibility" resists recognizing experiential amalgamations not legible as unities—in Eliot's examples, resists seeing the relationship between reading Spinoza, falling in love, "the noise of the typewriter or the smell of cooking," whereas voice dissociated from an individual entity arises in the midst of such amalgamations, which are "always forming new wholes."[3]

Voice in Eliot's poem is unsettling because of the impression that propositions evolve which cannot be assigned to individual speakers, as if voiced propositions were emerging independently of speakers, though the latter supposition could not be true. Yet this way of phrasing it articulates the sense that while perceptions, memories, emotions are developed in relation to one another, they are not developed in relation to a motivating center. The poem as a whole represents experience and affect as independent of any person or entity to whom experience and affect could be referred. This discrepancy is not an incidental feature of Eliot's writing; the poem insists on that discrepancy as on a deep understanding. The strangeness of the poem is always subverting a question like Who is speaking? or To whose perception can this be referred? Affect or experience can never be referred to this one or that one. Or it can be assigned only tautologically or technically to the one who speaks. I shall return to this idea. But I must first examine another manifestation of compromised individuality exemplified by a set of centrally linked passages in *Four Quartets*.

At the end of "East Coker," a moment is said to derive its intensity not from any exceptionality, but oppositely from the way in which duration is distilled into the present, compelling the moment to its inevitability:

> As we grow older
> The world becomes stranger, the pattern more complicated
> Of dead and living. Not the intense moment
> Isolated, with no before and after,
> But a lifetime burning in every moment
> And not the lifetime of one man only
> But of old stones that cannot be deciphered.
> ("East Coker" V)

For the speaker, strangeness is a consequence of the fact that there is no boundary between a single moment and a lifetime of moments; something consumes the present not with light or with heat, but with reference to what preceded it. This series of moments which are recuperated in the present reaches outside the parameters of an individual life, including moments experienced by those now dead (for whom "old stones" are synecdoches). Yet although something revelatory seems promised by such an understanding, in which a speaker sees his fate as part of a history that includes other moments not recognizable in the present and other persons not recognizable as himself, when he discovers that such a history entails conceiving of others' deaths, he can't make out the meaning of what he sees. The indecipherability of the writing on those hypothesized stones or of the stones themselves (which are ciphers for meaning independent of any writing) erodes the linkage the lines set out to establish. Factual information about the dead is as unavailable as any depth connection, vainly imagined as "a deeper communion," "another intensity." In fact to return to the beginning of the passage is to see that, although the speaker first pluralizes experience (sees his experience as incorporative of that of others), he has no access to such an aggregate.

In a second passage, associated with this one by its consideration of the same problem (How is the "live" nettle related to "the dead nettle"?)[4] the speaker is drawn to a "village, in the electric heat / Hypnotised" by music he imagines he could hear from a festival of peasants dancing ("Lifting heavy feet in clumsy shoes"). Whether these peasants are ancestors (the family of Sir Thomas Elyot in the sixteenth century) or some other peasants is immaterial: "If you do not come too close, if you do not come too close, / On a summer midnight, you can hear the music." But apparently you can't see the dancing without also seeing the death in which the dancing concludes:

> Keeping time,
> Keeping the rhythm in their dancing....
> The time of the coupling of man and woman
> And that of beasts. Feet rising and falling.
> Eating and drinking. Dung and death.
> ("East Coker" I)

The spectral festival therefore fades into a noneuphoric vision and ultimately to a lament:

> The houses are all gone under the sea.
>
> The dancers are all gone under the hill.
> ("East Coker" II)

"All gone" is a child's idiom, and it is a child's whimsy which imagines a beneath to the sea akin to a beneath to the hill where the burial ground presumably is. This child's nursery rhyme is also in touch with a reality, with Victorian houses which used to be at the edge of the sea and are now under it. "Under the hill" echoes a phrase from Blake's "To the Accuser who is / The God of This World," in which Jehovah and Jesus, in the narrative appended to their names, become fully identified with ("thou art still")[5] dispossession, homelessness, unreality, and, in "under the hill," death—states drawn into Eliot's rewriting. When these lines are recalled,

> In the middle, not only in the middle of the way
> But all the way, in a dark wood, in a bramble,
> On the edge of a grimpen, where is no secure foothold,
> And menaced by monsters, fancy lights,
> Risking enchantment
> ("East Coker" II)

this seems less like a signaling of Dante than an infantilizing and (in "fancy lights") like a theatricalizing of the idea of a journey, for if "fancy lights" allude to will-o'-the-wisps, they also ask us to think of lights of fancy. Because the lines reiterate the beginning of Dante's *Inferno*, they recall a world in which the natural and the theatrical can't be separated, Dante's world being natural only insofar as it is a highly stylized depiction of a wood. In ventriloquizing a child's voice first in the lament "all gone," and then in the reduction of terror to a child's perception of it ("monsters"), it seems that, as in "old stones that cannot be deciphered," death and peril are not experienced but are rather again distanced (here by being rendered conceptually immature) so as not to be experienced. Therefore, although in the first of the passages death becomes indecipherable and in the second of the passages death *is* deciphered and even mourned in the lament of "all gone," in both instances imagining others' fates has no consequences for the understanding of one's own. Death remains something the speaker is outside of.[6]

In a third passage, when the speaker encounters a figure, a ghost, whom he can neither mistake nor identify, caught "between un-being and being,"[7] there is no longer any way to exile the dead from the living, or the stranger from himself. Thus the dead can no more be indecipherable to the living than the living can lament the dead as having suffered an experience to which they are immune. Because the ghost is not fully separable from his predecessors, and the speaker not fully separable from the ghost, the distinction between the living and the dead is reshaped to include a state recognizable as *dying*, which mobilizes the two other states earlier misconceived as autonomous and inert, so they are engaged with each other.

In a passage at the end of "Little Gidding" the speaker recurs to the stones he couldn't read and penetrates their sense. He doesn't penetrate their sense by having access to particulars (the names, the dates), but instead by understanding that the experience to which the particulars refer is equally his, something that can be described not in terms of perceiving ("the pattern" grows "more complicated") or lamenting ("all gone"), but rather of accompanying:

> any action
> Is a step to the block, to the fire, down the sea's throat
> Or to an illegible stone: and that is where we start.
> We die with the dying:
> See, they depart, and we go with them.
> We are born with the dead:
> See, they return, and bring us with them.
> ("Little Gidding" V)

Thus it would seem that when the speaker suddenly sees himself included in the death he had viewed from outside, he has corrected a mistake. But what is the mistake? I want to argue that the mistake does not have to do with regarding fate individually when it ought to have been regarded collectively. For while one sense of the lines "See, they depart...See, they return" is that all deaths are *this* death, which is also *my* death, the effect of such a recognition never involves any forfeiture of individual experience, any disowning of it so that it can be attributed to everyone. If the "we" pluralizes experience, the "See" undoes the plurality. The recognitional moment is not properly experienced as collective, though it is also not properly experienced as personal. The poem more strenuously represents a disarticulation of any kind of entity. My essay is about such a disarticulation. Voice made unrecognizable as voice in "The Dry Salvages" III ("descanting...not to the ear,...and not in any language") is made more mysterious in the whole of *Four Quartets* by the fact that it cannot be associated with a person, like Valéry's "voice who knows" itself "to be no longer the voice of anyone" ("La Pythie").[8]

In the progression of the four passages regarded above, there is an erosion of the distinction between the fate of the live man and the fate of the dead man. The basis of their commonality is not, however, that each is subject to death. Rather, the live man comes to look like the dead man because neither has discrete identity, no identity apart from the other, and, more generally, no identity represented as personal. In the passages I have touched on—which are the spine of the poem, what makes it cohere philosophically in a register distinct from the doctrinal one (discussed in the final section of this essay)—the poem strips identity from experience, so that what is represented is experience that is particularized without being particularized as someone's. That is *Four Quartets'* most radical discovery.

In the movement from one of these passages to another, a predicament is deliberated. A deliberation harks back to an earlier set of reflections (as "cannot be deciphered" harks back to "all gone"). Hence memory could be said to officiate over the development of one passage from another in a textual harking back that is not the same as a person's remembering because it is without a subjective center. For instance, "The houses are all gone under the sea. / The dancers are all gone under the hill"—a response to the "dung and death" perceived by a speaker who is hypnotized in "East Coker" I by a loss that is not *his* loss—is obliquely recalled in "Little Gidding" III: "See, now they vanish," which not only seems to *issue* from no one in particular, but also to *refer* to no one is particular. This vanishing is itself climactically recalled in *Four Quartets'* penultimate stanza: "See, they depart,...See, they return." Either the subject (and grammatical object) of such a perception is the dancers of "East Coker" or the subject—the "they"—becomes fully incidental to departing and returning—which is noticed but not referred to an individual's vision. Rather, departing and returning is distilled as its own experience, apart from any relevant particularized who. What draws these fragments together across three poems is the reiterated idiom ("See") which each time harks back to that moment in "East Coker" when death was envisioned rather than experienced, when death was *seen* (and which perhaps also harks back to Pound's "See, they return" in "The Return").[9] "See" does not hark back by way of a repeated word, but rather by way of an affective sense, a pathos that permeates "See" just as it initially permeated "all gone." And it is that affective sense which is revived in the two subsequent formulations as an echo—but not a verbal echo—of "all gone." Yet although "vanish" in "See, now they vanish" is picking up (we could say remembering) a conceptual, as well as affective, residue from the first passage's "all gone," no person is central to the remembering. Thus the passages develop affect with respect to a loss that is not a particular person's loss.

Reflections are identified with each other, but not identified with an individual person, even when a line's allusive texture implies a name, as in "Brunetto Latini," "Poe" (I shall return to these examples), "Samson," or "Dante." "Samson" and "Brunetto Latini" are characters in poems by Milton and Dante, whereas "Poe" and "Dante" are authors. Yet in *Four Quartets*, "Poe" and "Dante" are also characters. "Dante" is a character in a poem Dante, the author, is writing, and "Poe" is a character in a poem Mallarmé is writing. Moreover, "Dante" and "Samson" are names that pertain to characters while somehow releasing the experience had by those characters—the name "Dante" or "Samson" being a placeholder for a specification that Eliot's language recalls, includes, and surpasses.[10] In *Four Quartets* implicit names do not therefore individualize. Names indicated by allusion loosely bind a constellation of utterances, which presumptively issue from a shape that resembles but cannot be identified with the one who is named. Even at a moment when utterance seems attributable to "Dante" or "Samson" (as in "O dark dark dark. They all go into the dark" ["East Coker" III], or as in the colloquial rethinking "So here I am, in the middle way" ["East Coker" V]), the point is that such words could become anyone's who would claim familiarity with the state excavated by those words. In the transparent availability of "So here I am," and "O dark dark dark," a speaker discovers the expression of an emotion, in this case despair, by virtue of the fact—this is the sense of it—that he resides where it is. As with Emile Benveniste's "shifters," pronouns like "I" or "you" render reference outside an immediate context gratuitous. This capacity to penetrate an expression, to voice it, has nothing to do with the substitution of the literary for the experiential.[11] But it also has nothing to do with identity or personal ownership. Being where the experience of "Dante" is depends on mobility, on not being locked into a position that is identified as owned or disidentified as other. When an "I" is articulated, as in the speaker's meeting with the compound ghost in "Little Gidding" II, he emerges transiently through a series of novelistic self-descriptions ("I met," "I caught," "I assumed"), whose comparative density and apparent continuity make him recognizable as the representation of a person. But these amplifications of self are no sooner established than they begin to come undone, for he almost immediately disclaims the autonomy on which they are founded: "I was still the same, / Knowing myself yet being someone other."

Although voices in *Four Quartets* arise in different registers[12]—the child's voice imputing its motivation to the directive of a bird ("Quick, said the bird, find them, find them" ["Burnt Norton" I]), the voice that ponders philosophically oriented propositions about time ("that which is only living / Can only die" ["Burnt Norton" V])—no voice is closed off to another. Thus, for instance, "Quick now, here, now, always" in "Burnt Norton" opens onto "Quick now, here, now, always" in "Little Gidding," even though the child's perception of immediacy is not consonant with that of the spiritual adept who achieves immediacy not in innocence but by surrender. Thus "The complete consort dancing together" in "Little Gidding" reaches back to "Keeping the rhythm in their dancing / As in their living" of "East Coker," even though in the second instance "dancing" refers metaphorically to the harmony of words well placed—to an idealization of language—and not to an idealization of generation. Thus "the past has another pattern" in "The Dry Salvages" returns to the "formal pattern" in which they move in "a heart of light," even though "pattern" in "Burnt Norton" animates, vitalizes, even, one could say, humanizes the natural world ("for the roses / Had the look of flowers that are looked at"), whereas the "pattern" in "The Dry Salvages" abstracts and deadens it. (Needless to say, these examples could be further enumerated). One might characterize these repetitions as self-quotations, but for the fact that that there is no self from whom they are represented as originating. One way to make sense of the heterogeneity of voice is to understand it in terms of Bakhtinian polyphony or dialogicality.[13] What binds the reflections together is not a personal entity to whom a certain content could be referred, but a set of relations by which content is revised.

The voices in *Four Quartets* which have progressions without having personal origins incarnate the "extinction of personality" addressed in Eliot's 1919 "Tradition and the Individual Talent" (*SE* 7), not because they recombine "impressions and experiences…in peculiar and unexpected ways" (*SE* 9)—this is what characterizes the impersonality of the artist—but because they have a reiterative response to a single experience ("all gone," now living now dying, "we go with them") which is neither individual nor typical. Nothing uniform could constitute a type any more than it could constitute an individual. Insofar as continuities and continuances are established among voices in *Four Quartets*, it might be in relation to what thought experiments in philosophy call "person-stages"[14] or to what didactic suttas (*sutras*, in Sanskrit), in Buddhist psychology, call "aggregates," constellations in which dependent relations are not equivalent to or constitutive of a self. (I shall return to this idea.)

All voices are intermittent. All voices are from time to time. Yet Eliot emphasizes the special case for the intermittency of voices in *Four Quartets*. He does so because when representations are more than voices, when voices are said to issue from embodiments, they are embodiments which don't cohere but which, rather, "form and fade," because as the relationship between the living and the dying is worked out in the poem, it becomes defined by now living, now dying, not ultimately but rather immediately, moment after moment, so that being and no longer being are repeatedly brought together. What is intermittent in *Four Quartets* is not therefore only the manifestation of voice, but also the manifestation of being that voice describes itself as experiencing. Eliot emphasizes the intermittency of voice finally because, as discussed in section IV, being is continuously represented as nothing that could cohere, coming to be constituted by categories that are assimilable to each other ("one life," "generations," "primitive terror") without being legible in relation to individuals or types, there being no type that could include "primitive terror" as an element that is categorically commensurate with the other constituent parts, since "primitive terror" does not logically belong in the sequence.

The recurrence of the formulations I have begun to examine ("the communication / Of the dead is tongued with fire beyond the language of the living" ["Little Gidding" I], to name a further instance), which don't have the feel of propositions, and at times not even the structure of propositions ("Why should we celebrate / ...dead men more than the dying?" ["Little Gidding" III]), reside in an experiential, even heuristic register. My argument depends on taking the idea of the heuristic seriously. The affective feel, the mood of these passages, has as much to do with a repetition that could be called motivated, even obsessive—a recurring to, or a rethinking ("that which is only living can only die") and even at times a rehearsing ("You say I am repeating / Something I have said before. I shall say it again" ["East Coker" III])—as it has to do with the fact that language is often inflected as the representation of speech would be. Thus the haunted quality of these passages—what comes to seem haunted as a consequence of recurrence—raises a question about what an identifiable voice is that is no one's voice.[15]

While mobility is what anyone can have in relation to experience, experience in Eliot's poem is represented as possessing a fixity not susceptible to change.

> Now, we come to discover that the moments of agony...
>   are likewise permanent
> With such permanence as time has. We appreciate this better
> In the agony of others, nearly experienced,
> Involving ourselves, than in our own.
> For our own past is covered by the currents of action.
> But the torment of others remains an experience
> Unqualified, unworn by subsequent attrition.
> People change, and smile: but the agony abides.
> ("The Dry Salvages" II)

That a person could be said to change but the agony to abide is compatible with the representation of experience in *Four Quartets* as having that separability from persons which would make "In the middle of a dark wood" only transiently the words of "Dante." Thus experience can be identified by one's residing in a certain location ("So here I am") or by one's residing outside of a location ("We appreciate this [permanence] better / In the agony of others, nearly experienced, / ...than in our own"). Eliot attributes a fatality to the features of experience, here analogized to a rock—

in the restless waters,
Waves wash over it, fogs conceal it;
On a halcyon day it is merely a monument,
In navigable weather it is always a seamark
To lay a course by

—which confers on experience something like a discoverable essence that emerges or is unveiled so that "in the sombre season / Or the sudden fury" experience "is what it always was." As I shall argue, other representations in the poem violently contradict the idea of this inevitability and the sense of this essence, which oppose the ethos of the poem as a whole. However, it momentarily seems that, although the right conditions are required to bring out the identifiable features of experience (rage is understood to be such a condition), there is something essential about experience, suggesting that it has discrete features which are continuous over time and perceptible in space. Just such an identifiable, noncontingent essence is denied to Eliot's representation of voice and its dissociation from any person in *Four Quartets*.

ii

In *Four Quartets* all understandings of the representation of a person must make reference to the "compound ghost" ("Little Gidding" II), who is paradoxically the most fully embodied figure in the poem. Because he vividly consolidates and makes manifest the eroded distinctions between the living and the dead that are staged throughout *Four Quartets*, I must examine this section of the poem, the third of the passages discussed above, in detail. Unlike Tiresias in *The Waste Land*, who occupies a similarly privileged position, but who is autonomously fixed above a scene he can lament but not engage in, the ghost becomes who he is in relation first to the speaker; then to the figures "Dante," "Brunetto Latini," and "Virgil"; and, finally, to Mallarmé's "Poe," even as he is also constituted through reiterated dissolutions. Thus he is the model for a person's *unmaking*.

The representation of the ghost who emerges in "Little Gidding" II after the departure of the last bomber in an air raid in wartime London—rendering the scene of the meeting simultaneously infernal and purgatorial—is "modelled on Dante's encounter with Brunetto Latini (*Inferno* XV), closing with a direct translation of Dante's cry of horrified recognition, '*Siete voi qui, ser Brunetto?*'"[16] Eliot corporealizes this figure, affording

him "brown baked" features, a gait, a manner of speaking, even an irony—
that is, a particularity visible nowhere else in the poem. The appearance
of Brunetto forces us to ask how Eliot constructs a representation that is
more than voice, to ask what is essential for a being to be specific, without
being individual:

> Between three districts whence the smoke arose
>> I met one walking, loitering and hurried
> As if blown towards me like the metal leaves
>> Before the urban dawn wind unresisting.
>> And as I fixed upon the down-turned face
> That pointed scrutiny with which we challenge
>> The first-met stranger in the waning dusk
>> I caught the sudden look of some dead master
> Whom I had known, forgotten, half recalled
>> Both one and many; in the brown baked features
>> The eyes of a familiar compound ghost
> Both intimate and unidentifiable.
>> So I assumed a double part, and cried
>> And heard another's voice cry: "What! are *you* here?"
> Although we were not. I was still the same,
>> Knowing myself yet being someone other—
>> And he a face still forming; yet the words sufficed
> To compel the recognition they preceded.
>> And so, compliant to the common wind,
>> Too strange to each other for misunderstanding,
> In concord at this intersection time
>> Of meeting nowhere, no before and after,
> We trod the pavement in a dead patrol.

The passage identifies, negates, and finally reaffirms and deepens the manifestations of a presence whose origin and actuality are still disputed. The
alien, the diverse, the incomplete, the "half recalled"—but also these characteristics in a perceptible intensity (thus the "strange")—are attributes of
the ghost (what the speaker is facing), but they are also immediately made
inseparable from the speaker's attributes. The speaker regards a figure at once
different from himself and a figure whose unrecognizable elements are identifiable as his own.

What constitutes the speaker's illegibility is just what constitutes the ghost's illegibility—his heterogeneity. (Eliot retained the sense of the speaker's compound nature through the second complete draft of the poem: "I was always dead / And still alive, and always something other" [*CFQ* 185].) The appellation "one and many" does not indicate how the two characterizations of the ghost pertain to each other, for the *indefinite* number connoted by "many" prohibits any distillation to the "one" of entity. Thus while "compound" reiterates the idea of "one" as a union of elements, "many" prohibits its realization, for "one" would require the definite number that "many" leaves evasive.[17] The lines compel us to suppose that the ghost is one entity, since his speech is not choral and his form is not plural. But they equally eschew presenting a unitary conception of him, for he is made assimilable not only to the speaker but also to unnamed others.

The lines equally make mysterious the relation between voicing and listening in that the speaker is at once hearing words and recognizing himself as producing the words he hears. The speaker forms words and so does the apparition. Yet the words that are formed are not different words. This correlation between his words and its words summons up a weird verisimilitude that might peculiarly be called realistic in that it suggests the simultaneous cry of recognition when persons, in a surprise meeting, speak in unison. But even as the simultaneous greetings recall a natural meeting, the ghost's other characteristics declare the meeting visionary.

To call the status of the meeting into question is to say more than that it is dreamlike. The passage most powerfully deliberates not whether the ghost has being, but what kind of being he has—whether his being is unique as well as particularized—almost as if such a question about his being as related to the question of his identity could be separated from a question of his being as related to the question of his reality. The ghost embodies a state articulated in "Burnt Norton" V as occurring in the transition "Between un-being and being." The ghost has "features." Yet these features are not equivalent to a physiognomy, in that nothing is revealed in them—"brown baked" occludes the very particularities it could make penetrable—even as his visage is sufficient to make him recognizable within a category: "some dead master." Moreover, although he has expressiveness to generate a "look," something about his being ("still forming") is merely provisional. "Being" is more fully challenged by the speaker's characterization of him as "dead," one whose being on earth (though not in purgatory) is completed, one who has no more being, as opposed to one whose being is still only incipient. This contesting of the ghost's being from the double vantage of his not yet having fully arisen and his already having passed away is reiterated at that moment when the speaker greets the ghost and just as deliberately denies the embodiment of the one he is recognizing ("'What! are *you* here?' / Although we were not"). To say these and like assertions ("In concord at this intersection time / Of meeting nowhere") are "paradoxical" is to consolidate the antithetical claims in a way Eliot's passage refuses to. For if one aspect of the passage's peculiarity resides in its redundancy—its reiterative rehearsal of the manifestations of the ghost's existence—another aspect of its peculiarity lies in the fact that what is repeated are separable questions about the ghost's reality (does he appear in a dream?) and about his individuality (does he have one, what would constitute it?). These appear to be independent questions, which are made to overlap. What might count as the criteria of either (a separable voice, a location in time, a sustained presence, and even that capacity for mutuality that would render recognition reciprocal) are rehearsed in relation to each other.

When the ghost, urged, speaks, his words directly recall by their inversion Brunetto Latini's. While Brunetto is eager to linger to speak to Dante, so that he might rehearse and celebrate a fame toward which he also urges Dante ("If you pursue your star, / you cannot fail to reach a splendid harbor"), the ghost speaks reluctantly and self-dismissively:

And he: 'I am not eager to rehearse
   My thoughts and theory which you have forgotten.
   These things have served their purpose: let them be.
So with your own, and pray they be forgiven
   By others, as I pray you to forgive
   Both bad and good. Last season's fruit is eaten
And the fullfed beast shall kick the empty pail.
   For last year's words belong to last year's language
   And next year's words await another voice.
But, as the passage now presents no hindrance
   To the spirit unappeased and peregrine
   Between two worlds become much like each other,
So I find words I never thought to speak
   In streets I never thought I should revisit
   When I left my body on a distant shore.
Since our concern was speech, and speech impelled us
   To purify the dialect of the tribe

And urge the mind to aftersight and foresight,
Let me disclose the gifts reserved for age
    To set a crown upon your lifetime's effort.
  ("Little Gidding" III)

The lines contain a loose reworking of Dante, as for instance when "among the sour sorbs, / the sweet fig is not meant to bear its fruit" (Brunetto's trope for his own occasioned death) is transformed first into the ghost's "Last season's fruit is eaten / And the fullfed beast shall kick the empty pail" and then into the "bitter tastelessness of shadow fruit." The latter picks up fruition that has been averted in *The Inferno*, but also fruition that has been devoured without being savored in Eliot's own earlier line. The absence of fruit (of fruiting not produced and fruiting now consumed) is loosely linked to beasts—in Brunetto's tirade against them, to "the beasts of Fiesole"—"that malicious, that ungrateful people / …a people / presumptuous, avaricious, envious"—who did Brunetto Latini in, and against whom Brunetto warns Dante. Eliot softens the rancor which emanates from Brunetto's descriptions of these people. But he retains the aura of worthlessness associated with Brunetto's judgment of their motivation (essentially blind hunger: "Let the beasts of Fiesole find forage / among themselves"). Judgment is reiterated by Eliot in the ghost's derisive transference of this worthlessness to himself—seeing himself as valueless to the speaker as the empty pail is to the "fullfed beast." These reworkings are central to a didactic point implicit in Eliot's representation. Before elaborating, I must consider more directly what specifically draws Eliot to Dante's passage.

In *The Inferno*, the speaker meets Brunetto Latini, the Florentine rhetorician, whose encyclopedia, *The Treasure*, espoused the value of rhetoric in public life, and whose writing secured Brunetto's fame. In *The Inferno* Dante's relation to Brunetto is ambiguous. Brunetto, Dante's former teacher, is below Dante, and Virgil, his current teacher, is ahead of him. Dante bends his head, as with reverence, but it nonetheless remains unclear whether he is stooping out of necessity so that he can hear Brunetto, or whether he is stooping out of respect. Whether to stoop or stand straight bears on the question of Dante's relation to his two teachers. Both call him "son." The question raised by the canto is: Whose son is Dante? If he is Virgil's son, he understands civilization as based on divine legitimization. If he is Brunetto's son, he understands civilization as based on civic humanism. Brunetto makes eloquence the ultimate authority and enjoins Dante to be guided by providence and ambition. Virgil, oppositely, espouses a theocentric model of social organization in which divinity guides fate. In *The Inferno*, both Brunetto and Virgil ignore each other's presence, and there is a strong sense in the canto that Dante is being seduced by Brunetto's self-aggrandizement and by his flattery, which Dante reciprocates: "If my desire were answered…you'd still be / among…humanity." (At the canto's end, Dante is still enchanted with the splendor of Brunetto's achievement—"he…seemed like one of those / who race across the fields…. he / appeared to be the winner, not the loser"—just as he was when, at an earlier moment, Virgil turned back to instruct Dante, and the latter—ignoring Virgil—seamlessly resumed his rapt conversation with Brunetto.) What that seduction means in practical terms is that two visions of civilization and two paradigms for immortality are being invoked between which Dante must choose.[18]

In *The Inferno* Brunetto defends his fame and honor, urging Dante to emulate him: "Your fortune holds in store such honor for you." His last words to Dante recapitulate esteem for his own writing: "Let my *Tesoro*, in which I still live, / be precious to you; and I ask no more." The heart of the passage, however—the lesson which the compound ghost directly repudiates—is contained in Dante's specification of his teacher's value for him: "You taught me how man makes himself eternal; / and while I live, my gratitude for that / must always be apparent in my words." In *Four Quartets* the speaker's failure even to recognize the ghost, not to mention the common fate of death, renders the plausibility of self-eternalizing ludicrous. Eliot's critique of self-eternalizing pertains as much to false ideas about identity as to false ideas about fame and honor, for when the ghost's speech continues, its focus shifts from a question of whether identity can be *sustained* to a question of whether it can be *conferred*. In the second line of the ghost's self-derisive rumination—

> Since our concern was speech, and speech impelled us
>> To purify the dialect of the tribe
>> And urge the mind to aftersight and foresight,
> Let me disclose the gifts reserved for age
>> To set a crown upon your lifetime's effort

—Eliot is translating "Donner un sens plus pur aux mots de la tribu," from Mallarmé's "Le Tombeau d'Edgar Poe."[19] Mallarmé's poem poses an understanding of identity not as something which could be assumed but, rather, as something which could be *achieved*, or as something which *Poe* achieves when eternity makes him what he is. "Tel qu'en Lui-même enfin l'éternité le change" is not the fragment of text that Eliot incorporates. Yet one could only "purify the dialect of the tribe" (disdain for whose commonness recalls Brunetto's disdain for "the beasts of Fiesole," since purification is equally what Brunetto urges on Dante: "be sure to cleanse yourself of their foul ways"), if one's achievements were so remarkable that they distinguished one from others, a delusion the ghost exposes as his own blind vanity:

Let me disclose the gifts reserved for age
    To set a crown upon your lifetime's effort.
    First, the cold friction of expiring sense
Without enchantment, offering no promise
    But bitter tastelessness of shadow fruit
    As body and soul begin to fall asunder.
Second, the conscious impotence of rage
    At human folly, and the laceration
    Of laughter at what ceases to amuse.
And last, the rending pain of re-enactment
    Of all that you have done, and been; the shame
    Of motives late revealed, and the awareness
Of things ill done and done to others' harm
    Which once you took for exercise of virtue.
    Then fools' approval stings, and honour stains.
From wrong to wrong the exasperated spirit
    Proceeds, unless restored by that refining fire.

The speaker's recognition of the ghost as "intimate and unidentifiable" raises a question of whether being could be known without being identified, of whether being could be specific without being individual. "You taught me how man makes himself eternal" asks whether a particular being could be eternalized such that he would always be who he is. Eliot's allusion to Mallarmé's "Le Tombeau d'Edgar Poe" considers whether one could tautologically be changed into oneself, could *become* who one is. This latter conception would render the self an attainment which death, in Mallarmé's conception, confers on Poe. Although Mallarmé suggests that death triumphs over Poe and in the voice of Poe ("Que la mort triomphait dans cette voix étrange!"),[20] that triumph has the effect not of vanquishing Poe but of conferring a brilliance on him[21] which is equivalent to his realization. There is something so bizarre about Mallarmé's idea in that it supposes identity to be something *deferred* rather than something given, a unique case, in distinction to a normative one. The lines implicitly invite consideration of what Poe might have been before he was so established or so secure—of what he might have been before he was himself. This speculation returns us to the question—Who is the ghost? Is the ghost anyone?—which the beginning of Eliot's scene asks us to contemplate.

The moments I have pointed to in the passages from Dante and Mallarmé are adjacent to the ones Eliot incorporates in *Four Quartets*. I am therefore considering evidence of a phenomenon in excess of the physical description of the ghost (in lines that directly echo Dante), and in excess of the characterization of motive (in lines that directly echo Mallarmé). Narrowly, within Eliot's allusions themselves there is no emphasis on self-eternalizing, in one instance, or on being made into what you are, in the other instance, but it would be a mistake to dismiss elements of both the Mallarmé and the Dante passages which are proximate to Eliot's direct allusions, because they bear on the topic of the ghost's identity taken up at the passage's beginning. As the ghost's speech continues, Eliot provides a countervision to Dante's and Mallarmé's. The ghost disparages his prior conceptions of "virtue" and "honor" (a rebuke to a self-aggrandizement like Brunetto's), and he implicitly disparages his prior idea of eloquence—of thinking his speech better than other people's speech (a rebuke to a hubris like that which underlies Mallarmé's rapturous celebration of Poe, as well as Brunetto's dismissal of the "beasts of Fiesole," from whom one would have to purify oneself). "Gifts" in "gifts reserved for age" both ironizes the ghost's insights (they are not a gift, but a curse), and from a different vantage derides his former assessments of himself—that his capacities were extraordinary. This trivialization of achievement and speech recurs to the question of identity, since it is Brunetto's achievement that constitutes self-eternalizing, as it is in commemoration of Poe's exceptional speech that death confers identity.

We must therefore understand the questions raised in the latter half of the passage, Can identity be preserved in death, or even conferred by it? as an elaboration of the passage's initial concern: Is the ghost identifiable? When the ghost enumerates his illusions, these pertain not only to the question of honor (how other people regard you) but also to what it is they regard (to what it is you are), which, once illusion is pared away, is insufficiently individuated to be preserved as anything unique. Although the ghost repudiates his achievements and his interpretations (of his motives and his actions), these bear on the question of whether there is anything to be made immortal, since the reduction that is left is a redundancy of error, "wrong to wrong," or is "exasperated spirit" (spirit whose utmost can't transcend itself and is no more than its irritation, another kind of empty surplus). At the beginning of the passage the ghost can't be identified because the speaker does not recognize him. At the end of the passage, in the divestments Eliot underscores, the ghost cannot be identified because he has become no one.

The uncanniness of the passage lies partially in its juxtaposition of the unidentifiability of the ghost (from the speaker's point of view) with the ghost's disidentifications with his prior conceptions of himself. Although there is a difference between a failure of identity that arises from insufficient grounds for recognition and a failure of identity that emerges from a divestment of qualities seen to be illusory, the two perspectives converge when the question of whether the speaker can identify the ghost turns into a related question of whether the ghost is someone who *could* be identified. Features that don't survive their own diminishment ("expiring sense / Without enchantment, . . . / . . . tastelessness"), combined with features that have a range but not a limit, dissolve subjectivity. This conjunction is amplified by the ghost's relation to himself (his expectations to his discoveries); the speaker's relation to himself (his assimilation of what is foreign); the ghost's tutelary relation to the speaker; the relation of Poe's voice to his death (marked by Mallarmé's astonishment that "death triumphed in a voice so strange," implying as it does that death encountered in Poe's voice an eccentricity with its own weird potency that almost was victorious); Brunetto Latini's relation to Dante, but also to Virgil, who is not includable in the colloquy but also not dismissible from the colloquy, as Mallarmé is not dismissible from the Poe he posits as unintelligible to his century, for Mallarmé officiates over that unintelligibility. When the ghost distinguishes the speaker's thought from his own ("I am not eager to rehearse / My thoughts and theory which you have forgotten. / These things have served their purpose: let them be. / So with your own, and pray they be forgiven / By others"), it is unclear what individuation could mean, given the passage's reiterated undoing of anything that might constitute it.

"I mean, to be aware that it is someone you know (and to be surprised by his being there) before you have identified him," Eliot wrote to John Hayward about the speaker's encounter with the ghost (*CFQ*, 180). He added: "*Recognition* surely is the full identification of the person." Identification is just what Eliot's scene both prohibits and makes negligible. We can see the contrast to this when in his 1950 essay "What Dante Means to Me" Eliot points to Shelley's *The Triumph of Life*, in which Dante's "influence" is also "remarkable," for the passage Eliot quotes at length narrates another encounter with a ghost, a "Shape," a "wretchedness," which not only takes human form ("the grass which methought hung so wide / And white, was but his thin discolored hair, / And that the holes it vainly sought to hide / Were or had been eyes"), but also, when questioned, identifies himself as "what was once Rousseau." Such a comparison in which the Shelley is implicitly simplified, even trivialized, by naming accomplished with immediate fluency ("what was once Rousseau") raises a question about how we might understand the differences between the two scenes. What is it that resists the process we call identification in Eliot's?[22]

The most common explanatory model reiterated by criticism of Eliot's passage—but inspired by Eliot when he dropped Brunetto's name and introduced and then dismissed Yeats's ("I do not mean anything so precise as that")—is that of mixture or amalgamation. Yet the experience of the ghost, specifically when he speaks, is not primarily of an aggregate. A more powerful explanatory model is proposed by Jeffrey Perl in his discussion of Eliot's "perspectivism," which, Perl argues, evolved in relation to Eliot's study of East Asian Buddhism, in which "a multiplicity of valid views" are "merely provisional" and have "an equivalent metaphysical validity—that is, no ontic status of any kind."[23] What something is depends on the perspective from which it is viewed. Such an analysis bears on the way in which subjects emerge contrastively—as in the "two worlds become like one another," which cannot be understood in terms of "pseudodistinctions" between "appearance and reality, this world and the next."[24] Perl's argument explains the terms in which Eliot understood contingent perspectives to prohibit singularity. (Eliot, contemplating contingency, also found it in F. H. Bradley: "We are forced to the assumption that...reality is one. But...what one?... The world...exists only as it is found in the experiences of finite centres, experiences so mad and strange that they will be boiled away before you boil them down to one homogeneous mass" [*KEB* 168]).

A third way to understand the thwarted identification is exemplified by Maurice Blanchot's analysis of the neutral as issuing from a narrative voice, of a "he" that can't be made into an "I":

It is the indifferent-difference that alters the personal voice. Let us say (on a whim) that it is spectral, ghost-like. Not that it comes from beyond the grave and not even because it might represent once and for all some essential absence, but because it always tends to absent itself in its bearer and also to efface him as center, thus being neuter in the decisive sense that it cannot be central, does not create a center, does not speak from a center, but on the contrary, at the limit would prevent the work from having a center, withdrawing from it all special focus of interest, even that of afocality, and also not allowing it to exist as a completed whole, once and forever accomplished.[25]

Although the ghost's speaking could be said to center him as nothing else does—his speaking engages by antithesis self-eternalizing and self-conferring—Blanchot's discussion of the neutral's preclusion of wholeness illuminates a crucial aspect of Eliot's representation. The ghost's compositional nature prohibits his wholeness or completion—qualities all the more compromised by his self-description of being constituted through a passage, a going back and forth, in a redundancy without a closure.

A fourth way to understand the thwarted identification is suggested by Giorgio Agamben in a discussion of Deleuze's essay "Immanence: A Life." Agamben interprets Deleuze's "*a life*" or "the spark of life" in distinction to Aristotle's "nutritive" or "vegetative life" (the criterion allowing for the "attribution of life to a subject").[26] "The spark of life" is exemplified in Deleuze's discussion of Dickens's character Riderhood, when, reviving after an incident of near drowning, he hovers between life and death in *Our Mutual Friend*. Agamben quotes Deleuze: "Between his life and his death...the life of the individual gives way to an impersonal yet singular life, a life that gives rise to a pure event, freed from the accidents of internal and external life, that is, of the subjectivity and objectivity of what happens" (229). One point about this spark—this manifestation of "*a life*"—is that it has nothing to do with Riderhood's specific characteristics, the elements of his being a scoundrel, for instance. Rather, "*a life*," as the figure of absolute immanence, is precisely what can never be attributed to a subject, being instead "the matrix of infinite desubjectification" (232). "*A life*" or "immanence" is thus the opposite of Aristotle's "nutritive life," which generates distinctions. "*A life*...marks the radical impossibility of establishing hierarchies and separations" (233). Therefore "the plane of immanence...functions as a principle of virtual indetermination, in which the vegetative and the animal, the inside and the outside and even the organic and the inorganic, in passing through one another, cannot be told apart" (233). The immanence of "a" life is equivalent to a potential, "a striving that remains in itself," as a "contraction" or a "contemplation" (236–37)—a conservation not of ideas but rather of material elements, implying something like a containment. Agamben's analysis bears on *Four Quartets*, for what counts about the ghost is not his subjectivity, but rather a potential that could never be realized in subjectivity. Identification could only destroy what makes the ghost who he is.

It is not only that the features of one contributive figure can't be distinguished from the features of another contributive figure; it is that the passage additionally suggests that there is no good way to distinguish a person's features or disfigurement from the features of the street. When we are told, "In the disfigured street / He left me" ("Little Gidding" II), that personification of the street in the displacement of a word ordinarily applied to a body (or face) is more than a testimony to a cityscape marred by war. In addition, it widens the jurisdiction to which features could be attributed.[27] In view of the inclusions that make up the ghost, the near permeability of the face to the street (or rather the homology of a word that could be applied to the face with a word that could be applied to the street) is meaningful—implying that persons have features which are nonunique.

Unlike the name "Rousseau"—as discussed by Eliot—whose power of identification lies in its decisiveness (its ability to conjure up a representation whose boundaries are delimited), the power of this figure lies in his always being only almost realized. Thus the relativism which Perl addresses in a theoretical context of Eliot's philosophical views has a more immediate application to the prohibition of understanding this figure as being anyone who could be constituted independently. Contingency elements the two states between which the ghost is said to shuttle—the living and the dead—which are not legible except as they emerge in relation to each other through him. These are the states he most decisively incorporates. The ghost's forming and fading illustrate that the right way to understand the proximity of the two states' near inclusion in one another is in terms of a passage, not an entity, something that is always only emerging or declining. This is unlike Blanchot's "neutral" posited in relation to a limit and unlike Agamben's "potential" posited in relation to a diffusion, for the ghost, insofar as he is anything at all, is best expressed as a pure changing.

In *Four Quartets* the living are constantly represented as discovering their inseparability from the dead in a fate that is particularized without being owned. This discovery is made to have a formulaic inevitability, while being repeatedly represented as misunderstood. The point of the formula is not the ultimacy of the connection between the living and the dead (not the truism), but the immediacy of it. What lives and dies is not just "generations" but "intense moment[s] / ... with no before and after." The vitality of such a claim (and its confirming repetitions) raises a question of where else for Eliot a formula with this content was linked to recognition.

Both in English and in Pali Eliot had access to the Theravada Buddhist suttas, which he made famous in "The Fire Sermon" in *The Waste Land*. In the suttas,[28] Eliot encountered discourses structured by repetition, through which counterintuitive claims, patterned by varied elements within predictable sequences, representationally annihilated the construct of the person. The "method" Eliot lauded depended on a breakdown in which an illusory entity was reduced to constituent parts with which no identification could be achieved. Rather than representing a person inflamed by passion, the Fire Sermon focused on elements intrinsic to the eye and its engagements: "The eye, O priests, is on fire; forms are on fire; eye-consciousness is on fire; impressions received by the eye are on fire; and whatever sensation, pleasant, unpleasant, or indifferent, originates in dependence on impressions received by the eye, that also is on fire" (*BT* 352). The rhetoric of the suttas, characterized by exhaustiveness, is an undifferentiated assault on all the senses—for the methodological thoroughness of the above passage is systematically applied to the other senses—and by a grainy particularity so that, for instance, "mind-consciousness" could plausibly be differentiated from "impressions," "ideas," and the totality of mind itself. The point of this comprehensiveness is to "beat down, constrain, and crush mind with mind."[29] In a more benign image for the systematic assault, the training would leave no element untouched "down to the last step of the staircase" (*MN* 874).[30]

The formula Eliot admired makes visible a recurrent content: "When an untaught ordinary man is touched by feeling born of the contact of ignorance, it occurs to him 'I am' and 'I am this' and 'I shall be' and 'I shall not be'... and 'I shall be percipient'...'I shall be unpercipient.'...The ordinary man...in perceiving a percept, automatically and simultaneously conceive[s] it in terms of 'I,' assuming an I-relationship to the percept, either as identical with it or as contained within it, or as separate from it, or as owning it."[31]

One who would correct this mistake must contemplate phenomena without aggregating these to a source conceived as a self.[32] For what drives the compulsion metaphorized in the Fire Sermon as "burning" is not passion but the identification of the passion as one's own. "Aggregates" is in fact a technical term, for the parts contributive to the concept "person." There is the aggregate of material form, which is comparatively the most stable; the aggregate of feeling; the aggregates of perception, of volitional formations, and of consciousness, each consisting of independent elements. "Personal identity," one editor of an anthology of the suttas comments, in a sentence that inadvertently sounds like Parfit, "derives from the continuity and causal interconnections between the aggregates within a single stream of experience, not from a persistent self or soul at its core." Though these aggregates become the referent for the amalgamation called self, they are more like "types of events that are constantly arising and passing away."[33] Analogies expose the subtlety of misconceptions about them: "One may regard material form as self, in the way the flame of a burning oil-lamp is identical with the colour (of the flame). Or one may regard self as possessing material form, as a tree possesses a shadow; or one may regard material form as in self, as the scent is in the flower; or one may regard self as in material form, as a jewel is in a casket" (*MN* 1239–40). The remedy for conceptual solidifications is to anatomize or splinter them.[34] Splintering contests the autonomy of the object, which, reduced to parts, allows one to see: "Nothing can arise alone without the support of the things on which its existence depends."[35] Such fracturing also produces a brilliant pragmatism that disables the possibility of possession: "When…there are no hands, picking up and putting down are not discussed."[36]

The suttas equivocate about whether there is no self or no single element that, pointed to, could be said to constitute the self. Some passages represent a succession of stages that form a sequence without intermission. As in the following analogy of a light that shines all night, stages cannot be unified. Yet although the "flame of the middle watch" is not the same "as the flame of the last watch," it is inaccurate to say there was "one light in the first watch, another light in the middle watch, and a third light in the last watch." Rather, "Through connection with that first light there was light all night. In exactly the same way…do the elements of being join one another in serial succession: one element perishes, another arises, succeeding each other as it were instantaneously. Therefore neither as the same nor as a different person do you arrive at your latest aggregation of consciousness" (*BT* 149).[37] Other representations deconstruct identity temporally: "Strictly speaking, the duration of the life of a living being is exceedingly brief, lasting only while a thought lasts. Just as a chariot-wheel in rolling rolls only at one point of the tire, and in resting rests only at one point; in exactly the same way, the life of a living being lasts only for the period of one thought. As soon as that thought has ceased the being is said to have ceased....The being of the present moment of thought does live, but has not lived, nor will it live" (*BT* 150). Analogies inhabit the repetitions as experiential particulars, for the problem in the suttas is how to translate formula into phenomenological proof.[38] The analogies draw endlessly on the same formulas—nothing to justify sentimental regard for a fictitious personal identity—even as the very extremity of the plights rehearsed derides the possibility of adhering to the wisdom being advanced. The formula must be understood but, as the analogies make clear, *can't* be understood in any perfunctory way.

The imperative for understanding conjoined with the near impossibility of understanding is underscored by a form of argumentation that gives the illusion of accounting for all the categories that might pertain to a given topic. In the following inclusive formulations, the Buddha does not consider whether an enlightened being "exists after death...does not exist after death...both exists and does not exist after death...[and] neither exists nor does not exist after death" (*BT* 117). In the airtight space constructed by the compilation of all the possibilities, one's own deficient reasoning for imagining something outside this formulation is defeated. Comprehensiveness is equally visible in the "not this, not the opposite" logic of "Burnt Norton" II's "Neither movement from nor towards, / Neither ascent nor decline."[39] In the suttas the escape from propositions ("neither as the same nor as a different person"[*BT* 149]), along with constructions meant to be experienced as opaque ("I am nowhere a somewhatness for any one, and nowhere for me is there a somewhatness of any one" [*BT* 145]), reiterates formula at an experiential level which cracks understanding, revealing it to be unavailable in conventional terms (neither a person nor not a person) and also unavoidable in some other set of terms which the suttas are constructing.

At the core of *Four Quartets* there is an effacement of individuality across the poem's varied features which parallels that of the suttas. One manifestation of this effacement resides in the ghost's being rendered specific without being rendered individual. A second manifestation of this effacement resides in the poem's solecisms: "music heard so deeply / That it is not heard at all, but you are the music," indicating a juncture between perception and the nonhuman elements it assimilates, just as, in the other direction, the poem exploits tropes (in the "disfigured street / He left me"), to note qualities which, unrestricted to the human form, are absorbed into the surroundings. At such moments the representation of a person is not separable from the representation of a nonorganic entity. A third manifestation can be gleaned from the rehearsal of deictic categories—"I am here...there, or elsewhere"; "And where you are is where you are not"; "Here is a place of disaffection...Not here"—in which marks of time and place are represented as illusions that accompany the marks of identity. The most explicit parallel between the suttas and *Four Quartets* is visible in the permutations which bring the living into contact with the dead, each time compelling a distinction between them understood to be artificial or transient. The intermediate nature of experience, documented by the poem's final section ("the last of earth...which was the beginning...heard, half-heard...Between two waves of the sea"), and the conditional nature of experience ("History may be servitude, / History may be freedom")[40] deny all phenomena autonomy. Elements of experience, like elements of being, could not have autonomy, since they no sooner arise than they pass away.

As in the suttas, prescriptions become lived through a heuristic relation to them. Understandings evolve in an experimental register so that the relation to the axiomatic is one of discovery. Thus in "East Coker," the "old stones" which a speaker finds indecipherable devolve in "Little Gidding" first into "Every phrase and every sentence is an end and a beginning," a general proposition, and then into "Every poem an epitaph," a proposition which has a penetrative relation to stones the speaker initially couldn't read, for fear he would see them as his own. "Epitaph" is a synecdoche, a placeholder for the dead, in that it marks their burial. "Poem" does not exemplify the greater liveliness—the refusal of death—which would demonstrate the antithesis. Yet in *Four Quartets* poems are loosely associated in "The Dry Salvages" II with life's intensification: "beyond any meaning / We can assign to happiness." This intensification—or enlivening—is a slant contrast to the dead for whom the "epitaph" is an emblem. "Every poem an epitaph" condenses—and in its establishment of an equative relation between "epitaph" and "poem" conjoins—the two terms, demonstrating that elision between the living and the dead reiterated throughout *Four Quartets* as axiomatic. But because "poem" and "epitaph" are adjacent to true oppositions, a pattern is affirmed as a perception, not a principle.

At the end of "Dry Salvages" IV a voice utters an impersonal prayer for anonymous others: "pray for those who were in ships, and / Ended their voyage on the sand, in the sea's lips / Or in the dark throat which will not reject them." At the poem's conclusion the words of this prayer apply to oneself: "they depart, and we go with them," "down the sea's throat" ("Little Gidding" V). The erosion of distinction between the didactic and the experiential, and between others and oneself is, in *Four Quartets*, a triumph of counterpointing, which illusorily creates the sense of nothing left out—of all the terms included—even as the experiential register only reiterates the formula from that lived *sense* which the poem represents as discovered. In this way the poem produces a phenomenology of experience which is lived in the pulse as a "percept" or series of percepts. As in the suttas, however, the voice that speaks does not presume an "I-relationship to the percept." For when the speaker specifies the first-person singular, as grammar requires, that specification is neutralized by being absorbed in the poem's general claims, even as the idiomatic, self-interrupting qualities of voice insist on their representation as empirical.

iv

But how is experience constituted? In *Four Quartets* repetition takes the place of subjectivity. Repetition is an ingraining of experience, a making of it memorable. The poem establishes a store which can be drawn upon in a harking back that is seen as valuable, even as memory is not a static compiling. Memory is a repenetrating of experience thought to be understood. Consider three examples. When the ghost vanishes, abstraction appears in its wake:

> There are three conditions which often look alike
> Yet differ completely, flourish in the same hedgerow:
> Attachment to self and to things and to persons, detachment
> From self and from things and from persons; and, growing between them,
> indifference
> Which resembles the others as death resembles life,
> Being between two lives—unflowering, between
> The live and the dead nettle. This is the use of memory:
> For liberation—not less of love but expanding

Of love beyond desire, and so liberation
From the future as well as the past.…
("Little Gidding" III)

Abstraction is punctured by the analogy: "indifference" resembles attachment and detachment "as death resembles life, / Being between two lives—
unflowering, between / The live and the dead nettle." The analogy recurs—in
a brooding or dwelling on—to a repository of all the earlier instances in
the poem, where the relation between these two states is pondered. But the
analogy does not contain a redundancy. It repeats neither itself nor earlier
understandings. It seems to indicate an intermediate point between the living and the dead to which "indifference" is being likened. That is incorrect.
As Eliot wrote Hayward in a stunning revelation: The dead nettle is a kind
of live nettle.[41] There is no distinction between the *state* of the two nettles—
the dead nettle being no less alive than the live one—since the difference is
one of *species*. But there is an *absolute* distinction between indifference and
attachment and between indifference and detachment—*both* instances of
vitality casting into relief a state which is deprived of it. Thus something
is being remembered, but no less being experienced, which precipitates the
demonstrative: "This is the use of memory: / For liberation." What makes
for "liberation" is a piercing through received impressions—of which how
"death resembles life" here becomes an example that "the live and the dead
nettle" enters into and reinvigorates. For what is astonishingly made explicit
is how *in*comparable two pairs—the relation between whose terms (and
whose terms themselves) sound identical—can be.

In *Four Quartets* understandings long ago deliberated reemerge in experience—a state of affairs referred to in the notion of a "pattern" that is "changing," of a "purpose" "altered in fulfilment" "beyond the end you figured"
("Little Gidding" I). Though, for instance, the "compound" ghost would
seem to have exemplified the relation between "one and many" (and between
a speaker and preceding generations) in terms so extravagant they could not
be elaborated, these lines from "The Dry Salvages" II anticipate the amalgamations he epitomizes:

I have said before
That the past experience revived in the meaning
Is not the experience of one life only

But of many generations—not forgetting
Something that is probably quite ineffable:
The backward look behind the assurance
Of recorded history, the backward half-look
Over the shoulder, towards the primitive terror.

This passage recalls a "lifetime burning in every moment / And not the lifetime of one man only" in "East Coker." But it reexperiences that earlier moment by intuiting a prehistory—which the "half-look" gleans but cannot report—not legible in terms of either category. In "The Dry Salvages," some third entity, which does not have an equivalent status to "the experience of one life only" or to "many generations," being, rather, an emotion ("primitive terror"), at once seems to designate something prior to entity as an origin would be and also to be folded into, as a composite part of, the constellation being aggregated. Nor is it clear what it would mean for terror to be an origin that generates human history.

The lines which precede these equally recompose experience so that its elements are incompatible ones:

The moments of happiness—not the sense of well-being,
Fruition, fulfilment, security or affection,
Or even a very good dinner, but the sudden illumination—
We had the experience but missed the meaning,
And approach to the meaning restores the experience
In a different form, beyond any meaning
We can assign to happiness.

In a penetration of experience by meaning the former is heightened by a transformation ("sudden illumination") which makes experience different by making it what it is. What is strange about the permeability of these categories to each other is that "meaning" and "happiness" are extraexperiential attributes whose presence is necessary to constitute experience. Or, rather, "meaning" is first added ("the meaning restores the experience") and then subtracted ("beyond any meaning / We can assign to happiness"), but not added to and subtracted from the same phenomenon, since meaning, added to experience, can't be added to happiness. Therefore, like the constellation of "many generations"/"one life"/"terror," the formulation produces an aggregate whose parts contribute to a whole that is unimaginable as a unity—like

Bradley's "immediate experience" which might be called a "timeless unity," but which is not a unity "any*where* or to any*one*" (*KEB* 31).⁴² Although in "The Dry Salvages" II a lacerating experience, the emotion of "torment," is said to be "unqualified…is what it always was," as these examples suggest, such a fixity is unimaginable in relation to the poem's representations, which are repeatedly constituted by shifting contingencies—like William James's "pure experience," which cannot be divided into subject and object, or consolidated in any other way.⁴³ (Thus "The Dry Salvages" might attribute a fixity to emotion. But such a fixity is something the poem denies to any other phenomenon, and is virtually unintelligible in relation to the specific phenomenon of emotion.)

In the three passages I have been considering—where memory is inseparable from the freedom to re-see, and experience is an immediacy that is returned to and deepened—something is worked out through a rehearsal of positions and an inhabitation of understandings which is progressive. The poem registers a set of crucial changes in someone's understanding, from "all gone" to "vanishing" to a vision of oneself included in the vanishing. These changes constitute the action of *Four Quartets*. Thus it begins with a crude perception in which a speaker is dissociated from "old stones that cannot be deciphered" and concludes with this revised understanding:

> The end is where we start from. And every phrase
> And sentence that is right (where every word is at home…)
> Every phrase and every sentence is an end and a beginning,
> Every poem an epitaph. And any action
> Is a step to the block, to the fire, down the sea's throat
> Or to an illegible stone: and that is where we start.
> We die with the dying:
> See, they depart, and we go with them.
> We are born with the dead:
> See, they return, and bring us with them.

In their summary nature the images make inclusive without making abstract the deaths the poem has serially exemplified. Because "See" is an exclamation tied to the speaker's pathos-laden expression at deaths at which he is incredulous, its recurrence is a signature, a response recognizable as his. But since he is no longer understandable to himself as a person who could be separate from death, the response marks the vision as his own and simultaneously issues from him as a mark of pure estrangement. At the end of *Four Quartets* the speaker sees himself included in the departing and the returning attributed to the dead, whose passage back and forth seemed individuated as "Brunetto"'s.

"The block," "the fire," the "illegible stone" are condensed and cryptic, too apparently iconic to count as a death that could be experienced. "The sea's throat" punctures that unreality in that the attribution of an anatomy to a body of water in which an anatomy would seem unintelligible makes death phenomenal. The abstract emblems of death give way to a visceral sense of menace conveyed by a Dickinson-like personification in which a body is at once identified as vast, even immeasurable (a sea), and at the same time palpably narrow (a throat), thus forming a passage into which one could be fed. To submit to "the sea's throat" is to submit to a position associated with wisdom, one located in an experiential register in distinction to the poem's didactic propositions (which extrapolate wisdom *words*) and equally in distinction to subjectivity. Being internal to a wisdom position is represented as knowing you are incorporated in something that couldn't be intelligible to you, but that could be perceived. "The sea's throat...the sea's lips...the dark throat," strangely recapitulative of the end of Whitman's "As I ebb'd with the Ocean of Life" ("See, from my dead lips the ooze exuding at last"), immerses the speaker in a passage that represents "no hindrance" to death experienced. In this way an impersonality which threatened to be merely propositional becomes not simply lived but also incarnated. Like the compound ghost who is without name, without sentience, without full embodiment—but also without relinquishing these—the speaker becomes an incarnation of all those zero states the poem first makes palpable in the meeting with the ghost, and then develops along another axis.

v

Four Quartets represents barely differential *states* (now living, now dying) which are not allied with doctrinal distinctions (good, evil) or with the differential *regions* (purgatory, paradise) fundamental to doctrine.[44] Or, if the poem fleetingly engages such regions, as at the end of "Little Gidding" II, when the ghost alludes to the "refining fire" of a doctrinal purgatory whose region is mapped by dogma, Eliot sutures the "nowhere, no before and after," where the speaker meets the ghost, to a nowhere with a landscape. At the end of *Four Quartets*, however, Eliot, sacrifices the "nowhere" for a place recognizable as Dante's paradise, substituting one hypothetical region for another. Invoking the end of the *Paradiso* not as an experience ("So here I am"), but in relation to a Christian orthodoxy which Dante, along with Julian of Norwich and the author of *The Cloud of Unknowing*, is legitimating, the poem concludes like this:

> With the drawing of this Love and the voice of this Calling
>
> We shall not cease from exploration
> And the end of all our exploring
> Will be to arrive where we started
> And know the place for the first time.
> Through the unknown, remembered gate
> When the last of earth left to discover
> Is that which was the beginning;
> At the source of the longest river
> The voice of the hidden waterfall
> And the children in the apple-tree
> Not known, because not looked for
> But heard, half-heard, in the stillness
> Between two waves of the sea.
> Quick now, here, now, always—
> A condition of complete simplicity
> (Costing not less than everything)
> And all shall be well and
> All manner of thing shall be well
> When the tongues of flame are in-folded
> Into the crowned knot of fire
> And the fire and the rose are one.

There is no experiential ground on which the assurance of these lines is represented as resting. Summary and apodictic ("all shall be well...the fire and the rose are one"), the paradoxes repeat without assimilating the Christian orthodoxy they validate. Even though the passage enfolds the strands of the poem's earlier discoveries ("the children in the apple-tree") into the didactic conclusion—also authoritative because of the twining together of the vatic ("We shall not cease from exploration") and the colloquial ("Quick now")— didacticism is foreign to a voice which has rehearsed positions and inhabited understandings that are heuristic, albeit without reference to an individual's sense of things. Throughout the poem Eliot has contrasted propositional understandings of impersonality with impersonality that is incarnated. He has set dogma (what "East Coker" IV describes as "The dripping blood our only drink") against voice positions for whom testimonials of dogma are insufficient. He has established a frictive relation between the experiential and the doctrinal. This is the state of affairs relinquished by the poem's end.

Eliot would have found my claim appalling. In his 1933 *After Strange Gods* he specifically advocated "*orthodoxy*," which implies "Christian orthodoxy" (*ASG* 22) as the highest principle.[45] Its opposite is "heresy." "*Orthodoxy*" is cause for "the exercise of all our conscious intelligence" (*ASG* 31). Orthodoxy is also opposed to individuality, personality, inner light, and intuition. Eliot elaborated: "When morals cease to be a matter of tradition and orthodoxy— that is, of the habits of the community formulated, corrected, and elevated by the continuous thought and direction of the Church—and when each man is to elaborate his own, then *personality* becomes a thing of alarming importance" (*ASG* 58). Such statements could not be applied to *Four Quartets*, for they would misrepresent the way in which "orthodoxy" and impersonality are vectored in different directions in that poem.

In *Four Quartets* phenomena are liberated from personality not because they are bound by orthodoxy, but because they are bound by nothing— because they are mobile, in a vertigo that undoes the possibility of foundation. Now living, now dying marks the range of an experience that perception sequentially inhabits. That range is also comprehensible as a condensation: "Every poem an epitaph." The poem is permeable to the epitaph—*is* the epitaph once supposed to be written on a separate material object and about a separate material entity whose features could be different from one's own. Although the poem centrally rehearses this mobility in relation to the dead and the living, it is ultimately extended to neutral phenomena. When, at the beginning of "Little Gidding," the speaker asks "Where is the summer, the unimaginable / Zero summer?" the question is not fully assimilable to, but also not excludable from, the deliberation over "the pattern of living and dying." The question is not excludable from that relation because the zero state whose absence is lamented exists in a realm in which extreme states can't be extricated from each other:

Midwinter spring is its own season
Sempiternal though sodden towards sundown,

Suspended in time, between pole and tropic.
When the short day is brightest, with frost and fire,
The brief sun flames the ice, on pond and ditches,
In windless cold that is the heart's heat,
Reflecting in a watery mirror
A glare that is blindness in the early afternoon....
                    Between melting and freezing
The soul's sap quivers ...
                    This is the spring time
But not in time's covenant. Now the hedgerow
Is blanched for an hour with transitory blossom
Of snow, a bloom more sudden
Than that of summer, neither budding nor fading,
Not in the scheme of generation.
Where is the summer, the unimaginable
Zero summer?

The season is *in* nature, but not in our *concept* of nature. "Midwinter spring" violates our sense of what a natural phenomenon is, while simultaneously calling it to mind, as in "blossom / Of snow" which displaces, while eliciting comparison with, a flower blossom. A phenomenon like the snow blossom is purely natural (as snow), while seeming purely artificial (as blossom), fully in existence but outside of generation—unlike Housman's "cherry," which is "hung with snow"—without being begotten or fading as a flower blossom would, but rather conceptually made. The snow blossom is resistant to categories, for it is precisely not intelligible in terms of inclusion and exclusion.

When the speaker asks "Where is the summer?" it is not clear whether he is invoking some state other than this one, or whether he is asking where this one *is*, how it can be located if it can't be categorized. I would say the latter, in that the summer that *can* be imagined is not mysterious, lacking any capacity to torment with its strangeness. However, another way to understand the lines is to see the speaker asking where the zero summer is that *can't* be stripped of its qualities, as this summer is. Not incidental to which state is desired is the plenitude of the reduction, the intensity with which zero is achieved and sustained. There is something sensuous in the cumulative negations and subtractions—a Dickinson-like exaltation in the minus state. As with Dickinson's poem, in which negations do not dismiss the characteristics that prompted their fleeting consideration ("not Death," "not Night," "not Frost," "Nor Fire," "And yet, it tasted, like them all"),[46] the zones from which this season is dislocated ("pole" and "tropic") remain fully determinative of the passage's orientation, dictating the perception of experience, but without the capacity to make it noncontradictory.

A sense of excess and reduction, specification and its depletion, is established throughout Eliot's poem, first in relation to the ghost, who captivates by a presumed recognizability whose features are then effaced; then in relation to a voice and a set of experiences which cannot be individuated; then in relation to a state, like "Zero summer." In these different registers, the poem reiterates a failed attempt to establish essence anywhere. Although it had initially seemed possible to recognize *Four Quartets'* subject as it was specified in *The Waste Land*—What is the state of affairs that can be countenanced as true with respect to who I am ("he who [is] living") and what I might become ("now dying")?[47]—such linearity with respect to sentience and insentience is what the poem contests. When a comparable pattern of elision also emerges in relation to the question "Where is the summer, the unimaginable / Zero summer?" about a state composed of opposites, in a voice marked as colloquial, by accents of an apposition contributive to emphasis, Eliot generalizes the claim: It is not only persons who forfeit identity but all phenomena which must be seen as dependent on conditions that change.

Although in the poem there is "speech" that can't be purified, and "motive" that should be, finally the idea of purification, like that of any refinement which rests on distinction, is belied. As "Little Gidding" specifies, the only alternative is "fire or fire."[48] The one distinction that remains undissolved is that between the poem's doctrinal strain and its heuristic strain. Even if there is a way in which these could be seen as compatible—as, for instance, by suturing the Christian notion of life-in-death to the pattern of now living, now dying—they don't read compatibly. Eliot seems not to credit how thoroughly truths represented as no one's truths have been internalized as experienced, with no need to authenticate them in a separate register, even that of "orthodoxy." For the poem's formula (which harks back to tetrads like "exists after death, does not exist after death, both exists and does not exist after death, and neither exists nor does not exist after death" and to their many variations—including "neither as a person, nor not as a person") has produced a way of thinking that has become absorbed at a depth and made idiosyncratic as perception would be.

The formula, one last time, can be exemplified by the "blossom / Of snow" which has a manifestation but not an essence or, except transiently, an existence, being only *imaginable* (visually legible, but metaphoric) as an entity. Although transience is what the snow blossom is said to exist outside of in occlusion of the conditions of "budding [or] fading" that affect other blossoms, change is reintroduced in the inevitability of the blossom's passing away by melting. Thus the emblem of what is outside of change becomes a nonunique manifestation of it. The poem actualizes a realm which isn't distinction-driven, but which is rather legible in terms of degree. Eliot's word is "intensity": "We must be still and still moving / Into another intensity."[49] "Intensity" indicates a state or a space without comparison, therefore without perception of limit (like Alfred North Whitehead's "events," which seem like unities, but which are transient). The poem carves out spaces of "intensity," where something is constituted and given features, like "the sea's throat," which is a deepening, an opening, an access to a passage that is absorptive.

7

"Lines of Stones": The Unpersonified Impersonal in Melville's *Billy Budd*

In *The Confidence Man* character is "past finding out" not only because its variations and inconsistencies can't be accommodated by the "fixed principles" of "phrenology" or a "psychology"[1] (equally primitive in Melville's formulation), but also because some element determining character lies outside the conceptual borders by which we understand it to be delimited. Thus in *The Confidence Man*, one exchange—"What are you? What am I? Nobody knows who anybody is" (*CM* 165), which begins as a parody of the initial sentences of Emerson's "Divinity School Address"[2]—concludes in an irresolution that can't be dismissed as parody: "The data which life furnishes, toward forming a true estimate of" character, "are as insufficient to that end as in geometry one side given would be to determine the triangle." Melville's image raises a question of whether what is missing is more data of the same kind (more characterological data) or whether what is missing is data beyond the elements that are specific to characters and persons. While the image of the triangle suggests the former, the radical openness of that triangle, its reduction to a line without the specification of the length of the sides, suggests the latter. For although the sides must be lines, they need not be lines of the same length. And without their specification nothing closes character off from what might lie outside of it. That is my topic: how in *Billy Budd* character opens to what lies outside of it—an openness manifested by the fact that character does not seem to be an autonomous or independent entity (constituted by "something personal—confined to itself"),[3] but characters, rather, share traits we might have thought exclusively the property of one or the other.

The drama of violently different characters (or individuals) in *Billy Budd* has a counterstrain or undertow which threatens the representation of individuality. Characters like Claggart and Billy are repeatedly differentiated in terms of antithetical properties, as, for instance, "to an unvitiated taste an untampered-with flavor like that of berries" is different from the taste "of a compounded wine";[4] as the complexion of a "rustic beauty" (*BB* 51) is different from a "complexion...[that] seemed to hint of something defective or abnormal in the constitution and blood" (*BB* 64); as "virtues pristine" (*BB* 53) are different from "Natural Depravity" (*BB* 75), to name some of the descriptive contrasts which oppose Billy and Claggart. Yet the essential distinction between Billy and Claggart is effaced when Billy strikes Claggart, and we are told that "innocence and guilt personified in Claggart and Budd in effect changed places" (*BB* 103), a change accompanied by another transformation of guilt from a moral to a legal register. Although Billy is first and foremost distinguished as a peacemaker on the *Rights of Man* (*BB* 47), it is not clear what such individuation would mean when a character is dispossessed of the attribute that most distinguishes him, which is converted to its antithesis. When "quick as the flame from a discharged cannon at night, [Billy's] right arm shot out, and Claggart dropped to the deck," the "peacemaker" becomes a killer (*BB* 99). Moreover, insofar as Billy is a type before he is an individual—"the Handsome Sailor"—he is introduced by an instance of the type ("a common sailor so intensely black that he must needs have been a native African of the unadulterate blood of Ham" [*BB* 43]) that incarnates personal characteristics opposite to his own. In addition the Handsome Sailor is intensely masculine ("a mighty boxer or wrestler" [*BB* 44]), whereas Billy is feminized—analogized to "a rustic beauty...brought into competition with the highborn dames of the court" (*BB* 51). In two contexts, then, Billy is said to be equivalent to something of which he is the antithesis.[5]

In a different kind of typing, which operates in relation to a hierarchy determined by absolutes and contingents, characters are sorted into categories whose contrast is said to be explanatory—the "exceptional," the "phenomenal" (like Billy and Claggart) in distinction to the "average" (*BB* 75), the "normal" (*BB* 74) (like the Dansker and Vere). The word "phenomenal" indicates an intensification of degree—the extraordinary in either direction—distinguished less by the nature of the exceptionality (Billy's innocence, Claggart's depravity) than by its opposition to the "normal nature" or "average" mind.[6] But such distinctions are elided when Vere, closeted with Billy, is said to share with him "the rarer qualities of our nature—so rare indeed as to be all but incredible to average minds however much cultivated" (*BB* 115). How has the man of the world, initially distinguished from the exceptional or phenomenal man, become identified with him?[7]

I shall be arguing that in *Billy Budd* characters who seem constructed to represent individuals and types based on distinction (so that the features of this person or this type are alien to, and outside of, the features of that one) also reveal such individual distinctions to be negated, as when "the apparent victim of the tragedy" becomes "he who had sought to victimize a man blameless" (*BB* 103), or as when the normal man becomes phenomenal ("rare"). Claggart's passion ("passion in its profoundest" [*BB* 78]) is ostensibly opposed to Vere's impartiality ("Let not warm hearts betray heads that should be cool"[*BB* 111]). In fact, however, the absoluteness of Claggart's desire morphs into Vere's contingent judgment. For when Claggart's manipulation is thwarted by the absoluteness of Billy's blow, Vere more judiciously assumes the task of destroying Billy.[8] When the peacemaker becomes a killer, when Claggart's threat to Billy's life is made continuous with Vere's, when the type of the Handsome Sailor ostentatiously accommodates "a common sailor so intensely black" (*BB* 43) and the white man in whose face, nonetheless, "the lily was quite suppressed" (*BB* 50), character is made permeable to what lies outside it.

But I shall also be arguing (and this is my central—and the more taxing—point) that *Billy Budd* is a drama in which the category of character is more radically disturbed by the fact that the features which apply to characters (who represent individuals and types) also apply to elements that lie outside of the characterological. The drama of Claggart, Billy, and Vere is counterpointed to features of the text that have the same plastic and contradictory features that characters possess. In constructing a set of effaced distinctions which are like those that dominate persons but outside of a characterological realm, Melville treats persons as if they were not governed by a set of constraints that differentiate them from other phenomena, as if—in an extreme example to which I shall return—a person were not different from a stone or a manifestation of light.

The noncharacterological manifestations of distinction and its efface-ment—in the narrator's rhetoric and his analogies, in certain descriptions of light, in generic amalgamations and lexical incongruities, in a scriptural presence that haunts the natural world in a nondifferential way—might look miscellaneous. Only sometimes do they occur at important moments of plot. Cumulatively, however, they add up to an excess, or surpassing, of character, something that lies outside character while repeating, nonetheless, its con-tradictory attributes. My interest lies in examining this transcendence or excess, for what constitutes the compelling power and the sublimity of *Billy Budd* arises from the moments when characters seem weirdly permeable to each other, and when what explains character—distinctions which are then effaced—also seems to explain everything else. But if the erosions of distinc-tion constitute *Billy Budd*'s power, the story's coherence rather depends on the maintenance of the distinctions which are then effaced. Thus what is so haunting in *Billy Budd* is these contradictory imperatives.

Critics have remarked on the negations that punctuate *Billy Budd*'s sentences, almost indiscriminately. Thus, for instance, "[the Dansker wondered] what might eventually befall a nature like that, dropped into a world not with-out some mantraps" (*BB* 70); "Budd's intent or non-intent is nothing to the purpose" (*BB* 112); "This sailor way of taking clerical discourse is not wholly unlike the way in which the primer of Christianity…was received long ago" (*BB* 121); "This utterance, the full significance of which it was not at all likely that Billy took in, nevertheless caused him to turn…toward the speaker, a look in its dumb expressiveness not unlike that which a dog of generous breed might turn upon his master" (*BB* 107); "But it is not improbable that even such of his words as were not without influence over them, less came home to them than his closing appeal to their instinct as sea officers…" (*BB* 113).

The effect of these formulations is like that of double negatives—which in fact most are not—but like double negatives that don't add up to a positive in that the sentences identify qualities, expressions, and states, while call-ing into question the states being identified, which cannot be posited out-side the negations, but which retain their residue. One point to make about such sentences is that they at once assert and retract assertion, speak and undo speech, thereby establishing a congruence with the innocence of Billy's speechlessness. Claggart's accusation of Billy is a lie and Vere's claim about the necessity of Billy's execution is a lie. The double negatives and, I shall argue, the rhetorical constructions that identify and then negate what has been identified—constructions that can say only what things are not—are also set in opposition to those lies. But a second point to be made about such sentences is that their double imperative to identify or establish and to nullify what has been identified as an independent phenomenon is visible across all the registers of the story. This disidentifying—this erosion of what might seem the boundaries of an entity—lies at the heart of *Billy Budd*.

There are four parts to what follows. In part 1, I consider the ways in which distinctions are predicated and then effaced across registers as inequivalent as the characterological and the rhetorical. In part 2, I examine this effacing of distinction as it pervades broader registers of the story: the generic and the hermeneutic. A series of biblical allusions collectively point to a providential, sacred area that borders the historical narrative, promising a distinct space from which the latter could be read, even as finally there is something reiterative rather than differential about the two kinds of discourse. Because there is no arena untouched by the eroded distinctions, there is no outside to the problem, which unfolds in the sense of its being repeated but does not unfold in the sense of being clarified. I suggest there is something agrammatical about the same phenomenon across the domain of character and of features of the text that are extrinsic to character, an agrammaticality I touch on in relation to Melville's earlier novel *Pierre*. In part 3, I examine *The World as Will and Representation*—a book Melville was reading while he composed *Billy Budd*—specifically with respect to Schopenhauer's claim that there is a global force which negates individuality, rendering everything in essence like every other thing. I conclude by touching on the ways in which "Billy in the Darbies" more conventionally thematizes a relinquished individuality.

i

The problem in *Billy Budd* is distinguishing among elements that are at once unlike (even alien to) each other and mistakable for each other, a problem deliberated in the narrator's analogies. The following speculation pertains to whether Captain Vere, in insisting that Billy must hang, is "the sudden victim of…aberration" (*BB* 102). It pertains to Claggart's ability to cloak his "monomania" in a "self-contained and rational demeanor" (*BB* 90). And insofar as Squeak's attempt to trap Billy leads to such a triumph of "the precocity of crookedness" over "simplicity" that it is Billy, rather than Squeak, who is made to seem ignominious, it obliquely pertains to Billy (*BB* 89). For in all three instances, opposites—sanity and insanity and honor and igno-miny—are described as indistinguishable: "Who in the rainbow can draw the line where the violet tint ends and the orange tint begins? Distinctly we see the difference of the colors, but where exactly does the one first blend-ingly enter into the other? So with sanity and insanity" (*BB* 102).

The rhetoric itself makes seamless a discrepancy between the vehicle (which emphasizes *indistinguishability* figured as an invisible line between the point "where the violet ends and the orange tint begins") and the tenor (which emphasizes the substantive *irreconcilability* of "sanity and insanity"). This paradox—that sanity and insanity seem like one when they couldn't be one, or seem to be compatible with each other when they are in fact antitheti-cal—is reiterated in another register by the momentary elision of subject and object with which "Who in the rainbow" begins. For while the logical sense of "in the rainbow" suggests it is a prepositional phrase that modifies the direct object "line" (or is completed by the predicate "can draw"), the phrase's syn-tactic placement in the sentence rather suggests that "in the rainbow" be read as part of the subject, that what is being considered is not the place where tints are found, but rather the subject who is regarding them. This ambiguity about whether the prepositional phrase is part of the subject or the object is further magnified by the dreaminess of the narrative voice, which has access to spaces, like that of the rainbow, where it marks differences (like that of "the deadly space between" a "normal nature" and Claggart's [*BB* 74]), which it then disputes. I shall have more to say about this narrative voice.

In another instance of a distinction which is at once marked and eroded, the narrator's introductory characterization of Vere's pedantry, which blinds him to the fact that his historical allusions are lost on the nonbookish men to whom he is speaking, is analogized like this: Men like Vere have "honesty" which "prescribes to them directness, sometimes far-reaching like that of a migratory fowl that in its flight never heeds when it crosses a frontier" (*BB* 63). The extravagance of the analogy (the distance of its frame of reference from the obtuseness being analogized) subordinates the subject to another rendition of difference and its effacement. A distinction marked by a frontier is eroded in Vere's imperception of its crossing. These analogies in which the difference between one thing and another is marked and then effaced (the "frontier"), or effaced and then marked ("sanity and insanity"), while trivial in themselves, have rhetorical and lexical corollaries, whose cumulative effect is to leave open to question whether apparently discrete states or regions are or are not perceptibly different.[9]

More central to the plot, though no less equivocal, the incident of the Nore is introduced by the narrator as a digression, a "bypath," a "literary sin," indulgence in which brings "pleasure" in wickedness (*BB* 56). In fact the narrator's account of the Nore mutiny is not a digression, because Vere's behavior is intelligible only against the circumstances that make it legible; hence this account is central to the narrative rather than marginal to it. And "sin" is a misnomer for narrative indirection. But it is a curious misnomer for a voice which exactly isolates phrases like "mystery of iniquity'" (*BB* 76) and "moral emergency" (*BB* 70), phrases whose discrimination is incompatible with the dictional mistakes "diversion" or "sin" when measured against the literal wickedness established within the moral register drawn up by the narrator to chart Claggart's lie and Vere's judgment. The narrator's rhetorical and dictional constructions produce the identifying differences (between "evil" and "literary sin," between unqualified assertion and its equivocation) which the analogies theorize and the negations logically enact. They arrive at designations which are made to differ from prior exemplifications of the ostensible same phenomenon, so that insofar as the thing being named has deviant manifestations, it is not self-identical, from one point of view, and, from another point of view, it has no discrete essence, rather seeming assimilable to what is extrinsic to it.

So too interpretive lexicons are at once established as discrete and shown to blend into each other. In rehearsing the various lexicons that might account for Billy and Claggart, the narrator rejects the biblical one (or says he can't avail himself of it)—"If that lexicon which is based on Holy Writ were any longer popular, one might with less difficulty define and denominate certain phenomenal men. As it is, one must turn to some authority not liable to the charge of being tinctured with the biblical element" (*BB* 75)—and upholds the philosophical one. Specifically, to explain Claggart, he invokes Plato's phrase "Natural Depravity" (*BB* 75) (which he tautologically defines as something "innate"—"a depravity according to nature'" (*BB* 76). But the philosophical phrase "Natural Depravity," said to be distinct from a biblical context, inevitably calls to mind something like "original sin," suggesting that the "philosophical" concept is really a theological one.

This contesting of what something is (is it permeable to a state from which it seems distinguished or is it authentically discrete?) is crucially manifested in the narrator's attempts to delineate Claggart's evil from that of the "vulgar" villain (*BB* 75–78) he employs and to distinguish Billy's innocence from Christ's. The essential traits of both characters are established in relation to explanatory categories which are immediately exceeded. First, when Melville evokes the large-spiritedness of Claggart's "Natural Depravity," its scrupulousness and purity (there is no "vulgar alloy of the brute" in it) and, most to the point, its typicality, evil becomes detached from any individuality which could explain or motivate it. Second, this elemental evil, psychologized in terms of envy ("To be nothing more than innocent!" [*BB* 78]), typified by a series of traits shared by men whose collective nature surpasses any psychology,[10] is then defiantly made legible in terms of a source that exonerates both individuals and types: Claggart's evil is said to be "like the scorpion for which the Creator alone is responsible" (*BB* 78). But third, that quality is ultimately understandable only tautologically as something reiterative that "recoil[s] upon itself" (*BB* 78). For the pervasiveness of Claggart's evil, its manifestation as a violent force "surcharged with energy," can't be correlated with any of these explanatory accounts, being repeatedly described in terms of a boundlessness which surpasses the narrator's attempts to produce formulations about it.

Similarly, Billy's excess of innocence, its capacity to withstand the murder that should have spoiled it—for striking rather than speaking leaves Billy's innocence unmarred—and the independence of the blow from any explanatory account which could motivate it,[11] reinstates Billy's status as a type. But what kind of type? Billy's misalignment from a type of Christ, and indeed Billy's lack of interest in him, is negotiated in a series of passages. The first of these occurs when, after his closeted interview with Vere, Billy, lying on the upper gun deck of the *Bellipotent*, is visited by the chaplain. Billy refuses not just the chaplain's dogmatism, which could be integral to Christianity without being integral to Christ, but also the chaplain's message of salvation, which can't be separated from Christ. When the chaplain attempts to bring home to Billy "the thought of salvation and a Savior" (*BB* 121),

> Billy listened, but less out of awe or reverence, perhaps, than from a certain natural politeness, doubtless at bottom regarding all that in much the same way that most mariners of his class take any discourse abstract or out of the common tone of the workaday world. And this sailor way of taking clerical discourse is not wholly unlike the way in which the primer of Christianity, full of transcendent miracles, was received long ago on tropic isles by any superior *savage*, so called—a Tahitian, say, of Captain Cook's time or shortly after that time. Out of natural courtesy he received, but did not appropriate. It was like a gift placed in the palm of an outreached hand upon which the fingers do not close. (*BB* 121)

In that extraordinary last sentence Melville emphasizes the gratuitousness of Christ's compensation for Billy. The hyperbole of the image depends on a discrepancy between a gift whose preciousness can't be surpassed and Billy's indifference to it. Billy's "peace," though transcendent—"The minister of Christ...had no consolation to proffer which could result in a peace transcending that which he beheld" (*BB* 120)—is not transcendent in Christian terms. Billy's disparity from Christ is reiterated in another passage in which Billy's angelic qualities are analogized to those of angels who are "barbarous" (*BB* 120) and angels who are "beautiful English girls" (*BB* 121). The point is that Billy has more in common with barbarians and girls than, say, with Fra Angelico's seraphs—the Christian manifestation of innocence being a kind of passing stage in a beauty that both precedes and survives it.

Although Billy's dissociation from Christ seems repealed at his hanging in the narrator's language ("Billy ascended" [*BB* 124]), that repeal is not sustained. Billy can no more be understood in terms of a binarism of typology (like and unlike Christ) than he can be understood in terms of a binarism of character (good in opposition to Claggart's evil). For typology, like character, depends on identic demarcations which the narrator equivocates. Such an equivocation is visible in the narrative of shifting light which enacts a corollary drama counterpointed, as it were, to the characterological and typological one:

On the starboard side of the *Bellipotent*'s upper gun deck, behold Billy Budd under sentry lying prone in irons in one of the bays formed by the regular spacing of the guns comprising the batteries on either side....Guns and carriages...were painted black; and the heavy hempen breechings, tarred to the same tint, wore the like livery of the undertakers. In contrast with the funereal hue of these surroundings, the prone sailor's exterior apparel, white jumper and white duck trousers, each more or less soiled, dimly glimmered in the obscure light of the bay like a patch of discolored snow in early April lingering at some upland cave's black mouth. In effect he is already in his shroud, or the garments that shall serve him in lieu of one. Over him but scarce illuminating him, two battle lanterns swing from two massive beams of the deck above....With flickering splashes of dirty yellow light they pollute the pale moonshine all but ineffectually struggling in obstructed flecks through the open ports from which the tampioned cannon protrude. Other lanterns at intervals serve but to bring out somewhat the obscurer bays which, like small confessionals or side-chapels in a cathedral, branch from the long dim-vistaed broad aisle between the two batteries of that covered pier.

Such was the deck where now lay the Handsome Sailor. Through the rose-tan of his complexion no pallor could have shown....The skeleton in the cheekbone at the point of its angle was just beginning delicately to be defined under the warm-tinted skin. (*BB* 118–19)

Most curious about the passage is its theatrical "behold Billy Budd." There is in fact a dramaturgy to these shifts of light—Billy, prostrate, surrounded by dim, sullied light which is contrasted to an ecstatic play of light that emanates from within him, "a serene happy light born of some wandering reminiscence or dream would diffuse itself over his face" "in the gyved one's trance" (*BB* 119–20)—which are made additive without being codified into any unified image. Each has a particularity that resists such legibility. When the "white" of those "duck trousers" is said to glimmer "in the obscure light of the bay like a patch of discolored snow in early April lingering at some upland cave's black mouth," the enumerated differentials of this second scene are so in excess of the scene on the gun deck ostensibly being glossed as to suggest the irrelevance of any specific scene, for all scenes (including that of the bays which look like "confessionals") have become constituted of differentials of light. The multiple instantiations of light are introduced incrementally, assume the weight of something aggregated, and come to dominate the narrator's appeal to "behold Billy Budd," as if what were being beheld was not Billy but rather light. Or Billy *as* light.

Descriptions of light are ostentatiously dramatized across chapters 24 and 25 in reiterated representations of radiance and its waning—as if such brilliance (in the "snow," in the "flecks," in the "more or less soiled" whites; in the "luminous night" [*BB* 122]) and its fading ("The luminous night passed," in the "pallor" of the face, in "the pale moonshine," alliteratively made assimilable to each other) had absorbed Melville's story and rendered it contentless. Representations of light replace representations of character at crucial moments of the story, and these representations of illumination and its waning adhere to the same structure, the manifestation of a phenomenon and its effacement, visible across other registers of *Billy Budd*. Such brilliance and its extinction either replicates in visual terms the conflict enacted characterologically or—and this is the feel of it—represents suffusions of light that are incorporative of character without being restricted to it. For instance, the night before Billy's hanging, personifications are first produced—"The luminous night passed away. But like the prophet in the chariot disappearing in heaven and dropping his mantle to Elisha, the withdrawing night transferred its pale robe to the breaking day" (*BB* 122)—and then made to fade, as the depiction of light becomes progressively more naturalized at the night's disappearance: "A meek, shy light appeared in the East, where stretched a diaphanous fleece of white furrowed vapor. That light slowly waxed" (*BB* 122).

The remaindered characteristics—"meek, shy light"—occupy a position in the rhetorical trajectory that could be called natural: "meek" in the sense of mild, as in the transparence of "diaphanous"; "shy" as in receding, in the waxing of the light into "vapor," while not *being* natural. "Meek" is an attribute which also characterizes Billy—which repeatedly characterizes the "moral phenomenon presented in Billy Budd"—who lets go unreported the provocation to mutiny (*BB* 79); who is "nonplussed" when asked why Claggart should have lied (*BB* 107); who, unable to defend himself with words, looks like "a condemned vestal priestess in the moment of being buried alive" (*BB* 99). And of course "the religion of the meek" (*BB* 122) associates meekness with "the Lamb of God" (*BB* 124). Personification is the wrong term to describe this suffusion of a property across the natural, the human, the divine. For what is visible in these registers is a difference of degree or of manifestation rather than a difference of kind.

I have been arguing that the category of character is disturbed in *Billy Budd* because of the virtual indistinction of factors that govern character from factors that govern other phenomena: that rhetoric or that light. Yet Melville's erosion of characterological distinction is impressive in its own right. For in a peculiar complement to the central attribute of Billy's stutter (his "convulsed tongue-tie" when Claggart charges him with mutiny [*BB* 98]), the master-at-arms at his death is described by Vere as being in a "lasting tongue-tie" (*BB* 108). What could be the point of such an identification which gratuitously questions the distinction between Claggart's fluency and Billy's speechlessness? And when the narrator says of Claggart, who "could even have loved Billy but for fate and ban," that in his affliction "would [he] look like the man of sorrows" (*BB* 88), it is not just the providential and the social which are assimilated to each other, on either side of that "and," but also Billy and Claggart who are transiently made reflections of each other. But if Billy is like and unlike Christ and Claggart is like and unlike Christ, what could such a typology could mean?

There is something apparently agrammatical about a suffusion of like features across ostensibly discrete realms, so that what one critic claims about the character of Billy Budd ("He is not so much cut off from humanity as from normal categories of classifying it")[12] applies to the story as a whole. This categorical indistinction is all the more remarkable in view of the story's generic incongruities: In *Billy Budd* allegorical and mythic characters are placed on the same plane as realistic, historical ones. Thus Melville gives us Billy, half mythic, half folk hero, "who in the nude might have posed for a statue of young Adam before the Fall" (*BB* 94). Claggart, eaten up by his love and his hatred, which are virtually indistinguishable in him, occupies the same mythic or allegorical realm. The domain is mythic because of characters' unperplexed uniformity, their always being who they are, even when their actions betray who they are. The domain is allegorical because Billy and Claggart are transparently made intelligible in relation to Edenic prototypes (*BB* 52).[13] Vere differently inhabits an opaque historical world, where motives, actions, self-descriptions conflict with each other. ("Starry Vere" is linked less to Marvell, from whom the appellation "stellar" derives, than to the historical Spinoza, by whose "starry brow" in *Clarel* Melville denotes that of the impractical visionary.)[14] Yet although characters address each other from discrete generic spheres, this incongruity—from a certain point of view astonishing—is virtually trivialized by the fact that fate is a set of forces which sweep indiscriminately over each of them. Such forces—Claggart's evil, Billy's innocence, Vere's legal imperatives—are not owned or individuated, but play through the characters, nonuniquely.

Such nonuniqueness applies more enigmatically to scriptural and natural discourse, which, structurally discrete, in *Billy Budd* impinge on each other as if they shared each other's properties. For instance, the always looming presence of a complementary world in *Billy Budd* from whose truly different sphere one might gloss the narrated atrocities is present in the novel's biblical paradigms, which seem established as correlatives by which to judge mundane action, as in Vere's cursory vindication of Billy's killing of Claggart as an act of supernatural justice: "It is the divine judgment on Ananias!" (*BB* 100).[15] Other allusions are rife with misunderstanding of the mundane circumstance that scripture is glossing. For instance, Claggart, charging Billy with mutiny in a passage alluded to previously, seems, in Vere's implicit ruminations (or in the narrator's amplification of these), to cast "a look such as might have been that of the spokesman of the envious children of Jacob deceptively imposing upon the troubled patriarch the blood-dyed coat of young Joseph" (*BB* 96). The allusion to Joseph—"handsome," "good-looking," "loved" (as in Genesis), and about to be betrayed—both anticipates and glosses Claggart's betrayal of Vere and of Billy, but also, obliquely, Vere's betrayal of Billy.

In a parallel biblical analogy supplied by the narrator to indicate what might have occurred in the meeting between Vere and Billy which precedes the latter's execution, we are told: he "may in [the] end have caught Billy to his heart, even as Abraham may have caught young Isaac on the brink of resolutely offering him up in obedience to the exacting behest" (*BB* 115). The events of the second biblical passage are not in fact analogous to the events of Melville's tale: first because Isaac's sacrifice is averted while Billy's is not, and second because although Vere's treachery can be analogized to Claggart's, Vere cannot accurately be analogized to Abraham. Unlike Abraham before God intervenes, Vere receives no "exacting behest" to sacrifice his son (*BB* 115). Thus the invocation of scripture which initially seems penetrating—the "look" part of the first of the biblical passages in which Jacob, about to be betrayed with a lie occasioned by envy, reflects Vere's predicament—comes to seem inaccurate and even deluded in the second of the two biblical allusions. Vere is not required to sacrifice Billy, and his registration of sorrow, as the narrator hypothesizes it, does not dissipate Vere's guilt by suffusing it with the pathos of a false inevitability. Or if the narrator is the source of both biblical analogies, the near exactitude of the first is betrayed by the inequivalence of the second.[16]

In addition, biblical phrases like "mystery of iniquity" at once correctly establish the domain to which evil must make reference—if evil does not cry out for scriptural illumination, nothing does—and reveal in that reference only unremitting vacancy: in both realms, "mystery." Insofar as the scriptural and the natural are penetrable to each other, it is in the wildly incredible sense that they mirror each others' meaninglessness. The Old Testament world anticipates and echoes the passionate realities of *Billy Budd*—desire and jealousy, ambition, pitiless judgment, innocence, and power—but the violence of these relations is unredeemed and unexplained in both realms. The quotation of scripture promises a light or an opening, a penetration that would get inside sealed utterances like "Billy Budd, Billy Budd," Vere's deathbed utterance, which, naturally, in the experienced, historical world, as distinct from the providential one, can only be gleaned negatively ("These were not the accents of remorse" [*BB* 129]). But it consistently defaults on such a promise. In summoning a God world and revealing it to be empty—or full of meaning that is talismanic—Melville dispenses with the space where a God might be manifest. Or he almost does so. For there remains a tension throughout *Billy Budd* about whether there is in fact a difference between the amoral, secular, historical, experienced world and the sacred, providential one. The persistence of scriptural discourse, its enumerated instances, preserves it as a force which sometimes breaks out as a gloss on events that *is* decipherable, as when at Billy's sacrifice, his "rising" briefly figures him as "the Lamb of God" (*BB* 124). Unmistaken figuration ("the Lamb of God"), erroneous figuration (like Abraham, like Isaac), and empty figuration ("mystery of iniquity," "Natural Depravity"), are made continuous with each other, so that as with other features of the text, the providential sphere is identified as distinct from the natural, historical world and, through its devolutions, made mimetic of that world.

Melville's meditation on character inflects the last three novels which precede *Billy Budd*, novels which progressively interlineate questions of character with questions of grammaticality. For instance, *Pierre*.[17] We see correspondences between *Billy Budd* and *Pierre* in the latter novel's tortured perception that characters cannot be identified except through the positions they occupy, which are subject to reversal (for instance, Lucy and Isabel, the lover and the sister). Pierre's proleptic understanding of this logic early in the novel prompts him to say, "Oh! Lucy don't mean any thing,"[18] a transparent pun in which *does not intend* gives way more defiantly to *does not signify*. But if one claim of the novel is the sense of evacuated essence (things being nothing), another is tautology, things being redundant ("Not to dread tautology at times only belongs to those enviable dunces, whom the partial God hath blessed" [*P* 227]), as another claim still is that things are contradictory (the horologicals and the chronometricals). It is the *convergence* of these propositions (things being and meaning nothing, being undifferentiated, and being irreconcilable) that makes for "solecism" (*P* 207), a term introduced by the narrator to describe the disparity between the Sermon on the Mount and worldly pragmatism, but which in its sense of deviation, its breach of decorum, governs the novel as a whole. Either the narrator bristles at such solecism or he steps outside his defiance in effect to philosophize. Thus of Pierre, "Knowing his fatal condition does not one whit enable him to change or better his condition. Conclusive proof that he has no power over his condition. For in tremendous extremities human souls are like drowning men;

well enough they know they are in peril; well enough they know the causes of that peril;—nevertheless, the sea is the sea, and these drowning men do drown" (*P* 303).

If the narrator shuttles back and forth between a voice that rages and a voice under restraint, this divides the novel not with respect to its subject—"Lucy don't mean any thing"—but with respect to its response to that negation: on the one hand, crazed, on the other, self-effacing. In the "drowning men" passage voice swings between a pathos made inseparable from both fluency and elegance ("well enough...well enough...") and unadorned statement, which is reiterative, but only as tautology reiterates ("the sea is the sea"), with no surplus of affect—indeed with its deficit—neutralizing the pathos, or expressing it at or as a minimum. The novel as a whole is played out between differential forms of expression like this one. Thus what links *Pierre* to *Billy Budd* is first the emptiness of character; then the idea of solecism; and, finally, in the "drowning men" passage, the flattening of pathos and of any excess or differential.

In *Billy Budd* that leveling is reiterated so that no character has properties allowed to be discrete, and so that what pertains to character also pertains to aspects of the text to which character is irrelevant. The effect of this leveling is something like "the sea is the sea," embellishment without redundancy or outside. One can hear such leveling in the voice of the narrator, in which differentials are rendered empty by the fact that he has nothing to say elaboratively; everything is treated either equally or hypothetically. The narrator's punctuations of voice mimic and even caricature individuation.[19] This is not only because narrators are not usually characters, but also because, notwithstanding the fact that the plot depends on it, in *Billy Budd* nothing is allowed to have uncompromised individuality. Yet in *Billy Budd* tautology is in fact the wrong word for the hollowing-out of distinction, of individuality, of uniqueness in a way beyond repair: In *Billy Budd* it is not the *same* thing but rather *different* things which are shown to have the same essence. In *Billy Budd* distinction remains intact: It is reworked but not evaporated—if Billy is a killer, Claggart is never a peacemaker—but, as such, it is deprived of the capacity ever to mean again in a social way. In this way Melville renders individuality and its undoing coterminous. The effect, as I remarked earlier, is not a neutralization of character but rather a bafflement or haunt. Through the equivocations of the prose—Melville's most exacting—ostensibly distinct regions (the providential, the natural) and ostensibly distinct characters assume a ghostly relation. Character remains uninjured, but inconsequential—not transcended but exceeded by diffusive aspects of the prose that permeate distinction.

The novel unfolds in a space like that of the chamber where Billy and Vere are closeted, into which we see clairvoyantly without seeing penetratively (another manifestation of leveling). We are given—and lavishly—a world bright with sound ("Captain Vere's voice was far from high, and Claggart's silvery and low" [*BB* 97]), given a world gorgeous to behold ("The bonfire in his heart made luminous the rose-tan in his cheek" [*BB* 77]), given historical background embellished with supposition (Nelson "dress[ed] his person in the jewelled vouchers of his own shining deeds" [*BB* 58]), given moral discrimination whose refinements are exquisite ("To pass from a normal nature to him one must cross 'the deadly space between'" [*BB* 74]. But these polished descriptions—descriptions that have a shine to them—highlight surfaces without penetrating their meanings. Hence the word "radiance"—"the source of the radiance that suffuses"[20] *Billy Budd*, a "radiance...beyond catastrophe"[21]—a quality cryptically, but, in view of all that brilliance, unstrangely applied to Melville's last novel. The effect of such brilliance is another kind of leveling. At Vere's death, his incantatory "Billy Budd, Billy Budd" cloaks his response in a further fold of uninterpretability. That response is "inexplicable to his attendant" (*BB* 129), therefore to us, like the jeweled language discussed above.

A corollary of that reiterative brightness and that reiterative impenetrability is the suffusion of blessing that permeates the end of the novel. By light of the narrator's fantasy, Vere's catching Billy to his heart would be blessing before killing him, a blessing which by inference Billy only reciprocates: "'God bless Captain Vere!'...syllables...delivered in the clear melody of a singing bird on the point of launching from the twig." These are syllables of a bird that is free, in distinction to a bird, the goldfinch, "popped into a cage." Billy's benediction is made to sound as "some vocal current electric" in the men's "resonant sympathetic echo: 'God bless Captain Vere!'" (*BB* 123), an echo that then becomes a "murmur" hypothesized this time as "a sullen revocation on the men's part of their involuntary echoing of Billy's benediction" (*BB* 126). And restated once again by the "inarticulate sound" of "seafowl" circling the "burial spot...with the moving shadow of their outstretched wings and the croaked requiem of their cries" (*BB* 127). The mystery in all that blessing, with its natural reverberations (the bird song, the requiem of the sea fowl, the sound of the freshet wave), isn't the Christian mystery of a "personified impersonal" (Melville's name in *Moby-Dick* for the three-personed God),[22] but rather has the feel of a blind force which penetrates creatures and inanimate forms with equality. It is in relation to such a force that I must touch on a philosophical work Melville was reading when he composed *Billy Budd*.

iii

A global force, which presumes that mind and matter are made of a single substance, with different attributes, of course recalls Spinoza, whom Melville had read. But it more immediately recalls Schopenhauer, whom Melville was reading in the 1880s when writing *Billy Budd*. Thus while one could speak of novelistic or dramatic character as exceptional (in real life we have known scarcely anyone resembling certain novelistic characters), or while one could speak of dramatic or novelistic character as like our own,[23] for Schopenhauer the essence of our *own* personal characters is like the essence of all other phenomena. Schopenhauer calls this "innermost essence," "this *thing-in itself*," *will*:[24]

> Spinoza...says that if a stone projected through the air had consciousness, it would imagine it was flying of its own will. I add merely that the stone would be right. The impulse is for it what the motive is for me, and what in the case of the stone appears as cohesion, gravitation, rigidity in the assumed condition, is by its inner nature the same as what I recognize in myself as will, and which the stone also would recognize as will, if knowledge were added in its case also. In this passage Spinoza has his eye on the necessity with which the stone flies, and he rightly wants to transfer this to the necessity of a person's particular act of will....I consider the inner being that first imparts meaning and validity to all necessity...to be its presupposition. In the case of man, this is called character; in the case of the stone, it is called quality; but it is the same in both. (*WW* 1:126)

For Schopenhauer the necessity that drives the stone and the necessity that drives character are identical, because inanimate matter, plants, animals, and humans all contain the same "innermost essence"—"the kernel of every particular thing and also of the whole." For Schopenhauer, the difference between a "blindly acting force of nature" like gravity and "the deliberate conduct of man" is only the "degree of the manifestation, not the inner nature of what is manifested" (*WW* 1:110).

Melville marked this passage (and ones like it) in his copy of *The World as Will and Representation*: "All true virtue proceeds from the immediate and intuitive knowledge of the metaphysical identity of all beings....Even the weakest intellect is sufficient to see through the *principium individuationis*."[25] Such marks suggests that Melville was specifically interested in Schopenhauer's understanding that all phenomena have the same essence: The same essence manifests itself as light taking the tree, as gravitational force, and as mind. What such a claim meant for Schopenhauer was an effacement of individuality.[26] For Schopenhauer in *The World as Will and Representation* individuality is only phenomenal—manifested in time and space—but not manifested in the realm of the noumenal to which persons have access through the body as will.

(In Schopenhauer there is a contradiction between the strong claim that individuality is only phenomenal [*WW* 1:113]—and the weak claim that individuality disappears the further you go from man, a contradiction I will pass over for the purposes of this discussion[27] because it is the strong claim that the same force is everywhere and everywhere the same that constitutes the foundation of Schopenhauer's system of thought. In the strong claim, in the noumenal world of things as they are, there could be no individuality because every thing is like every other thing. Or rather, there is only *one* thing. This is not a theory of intersubjectivity, but of the absorption of all individuality into a *single* thing or will.)[28]

In positing the inner nature of the stone and the man to be the same—"the stone...has the weakest,...man the strongest, degree of visibility [of will]" (*WW* 1:126)—Schopenhauer pauses on what he calls Augustine's "naïve" formulation of this identity of will:

> If we were trees, we should not feel or aspire to anything by movement, but yet we should seem to *desire* that by which we should be more fertile and bear more abundant fruits. If we were stones, or floods, or wind, or flame, or anything of the kind, without any consciousness and life, we should still not lack, so to speak, a certain *longing* for our position and order. For it is, so to speak, a *desire* that is decisive for the weight of bodies, whether by virtue of heaviness they tend downwards, or by virtue of lightness upwards. For the body is driven whither it is driven by its weight, precisely as the spirit is impelled by *desire*. (*WW* 1:127)

What constitutes Augustine's "naïveté" is his equivocation—his "so to speak." He can only hazard identity as a form of expression, whereas Schopenhauer remains decisively committed to the idea of blind will as the single source of all phenomena.

In 1856–57, Melville, writing in his *Journal* about his impression of the pyramids, arrives at a counterintuitive conjunction of the material and the immaterial analogous to that of Schopenhauer's eroded distinction between the stone and the man: "Pyramids still loom before me—something vast, indefinite, incomprehensible, and awful.... Grass near the pyramids but will not touch them."[29] Although the demarcation between the vegetation and the stone is absolute (as "plain as [the] line between good & evil" [*J* 76]), once the eye falls inside the mass of stone, even perceptible differences become unappreciable in that they can't relieve the immensity:

> The lines of stones do not seem like courses of masonry, but like strata of rocks.... In other buildings, however vast, the eye is gradually innured [*sic*] to the sense of magnitude, by passing from part to part. But here there is no stay or stage. It is...the sense of immensity, that is stirred.... As with the ocean, you learn as much of its vastness by the first five minutes glance as you would in a month, so with the pyramid. Its simplicity confounds you.... The tearing away of the casing, though it removed enough stone to build a walled-town, has not one whit subtracted from the apparent magnitude of the pyramid. It has had just the contrary effect. When the pyramid presented a smooth plane, it must have lost as much in impressiveness as the ocean does when unfurrowed. A dead calm of masonry. (*J* 78)

Melville's journal entry concludes by asserting that if there is no affective difference within the confines of the pyramids, only unmitigated vastness, there is also no affective difference between the vision of the stones and the vision of God. For what begins as mere interlineations of qualities of vastness ascribable to both (occasioned in one instance by the materiality of the pyramids, and in the other by the immateriality of a God) evolves into an elaboration of the relation between materiality and immateriality: "Out of the crude forms of the natural earth [the supernatural priest, the Egyptian wise man] could evoke by art the transcendent mass & symmetry & unity of the pyramid so out of the rude elements of the insignificant thoughts that are in all men, they could rear the transcendent conception of a God" (*J* 78). What is at issue is not just an analogy but also a category crossing, first because the materiality gives birth to the immateriality ("the idea of

Jehovah born here") and second because the idea of Jehovah is constructed in the same way that the pyramid is. Something monumental is made out of the primitive and elemental—out of "crude forms of the natural earth" and "the rude elements of the insignificant thoughts"—becoming an amalgamation in which no discrete category is recognizable.[30]

In the *Journal* passages stone signifies neither materiality nor immateriality but some eroded place of distinction where the two are drawn together:

> We read a good deal about stones in Scriptures. Monuments & stumps of the memorials are set up of stones; men are stoned to death; the figurative seed falls in stony places; and no wonder that stones should so largely figure in the Bible. Judea is one accumulation of stones—Stony mountains & stony plains; stony torrents & stony roads; stony walls & stony fields, stony houses & stony tombs; stony eyes & stony hearts. Before you, & behind you are stones. Stones to right & stones to left. (*J* 90)

The synecdoche which represents persons' manifestations of this impenetrability—"stony eyes & stony hearts"—is granted no exceptional marking. For the point of such an enumeration is to make the includable entities equal to each other, or rather inseparable from each other, constituted "outside the possibility of plurality."[31]

iv

The erosion of a differential—effaced in Schopenhauer by the idea of seeing through the *principium individuationis*, effaced in the pyramid passage by "lines of stones" which distinguish materiality from immateriality only to hollow out any meaning this distinction could have—has a thematic corollary in "Billy in the Darbies," the ballad in which Billy consents to a fate he sees undifferentiated from anyone's. I shall conclude by considering it. But first, to reiterate one more time what I have been arguing about Melville's posthumously published story. The plot of *Billy Budd* exploits characterological distinctions as extreme as good and evil, which Melville precisely names as such. But an accompanying understanding disputes these distinctions. Melville's reworkings of the manuscript underscore this contestation.[32] In *The Confidence Man*—the last piece of fiction Melville wrote, thirty years earlier—he had proclaimed, it might seem ominously from the point of view of further fiction writing: "The difference between this man and that man is not so great as the difference between what the same man be to-day and what he may be in days to come" (*CM* 191), a proposition whose reverberations are anticipated in *Pierre*, and made boldly coherent in *The Confidence Man*'s expositions of dramatic and individual character. What is more radical in *Billy Budd* than in either of the earlier novels (though not structurally so) is that it extends this suffusion of like properties first across character and then outside of it. So, for instance, light is disseminated across the "rosebud complexion of the more beautiful English girls" (*BB* 121), across Billy's unseeing "welkin" eyes (*BB* 44) (but also through his "luminous face" and through the "luminous night" [*BB* 122]), in the breaking day with its "diaphanous fleece of white" (*BB* 122), across the supernatural sky (but also across the sky purified of the supernatural in this hint of animality: "The…vapor had vanished, licked up by the sun that late had so glorified it" [*BB* 128]), even across the look on Vere's altered face when he resolves on Billy's guilt ("as if the moon emerging from eclipse should reappear with quite another aspect" [*BB* 99–100]), for such rhetorically heightened effusions of light—which shape the experience of reading *Billy Budd* as fully as the plot does—are made intelligible as manifestations of a single phenomenon.

After Billy's hanging, the story of Billy's innocence is transferred from the narrator to an anonymous shipmate (said to be of "an artless *poetic* temperament"), who writes a ballad which impersonates Billy's voice. The impersonality is all the more striking in being parodic of a genuine anonymously authored folk ballad, and in the replication of the most conspicuously comic aspects of such a ballad—the clumsiness, the naïveté, the incongruity—out of which beauty is wrested:[33]

BILLY IN THE DARBIES

Good of the chaplain to enter Lone Bay
And down on his marrowbones here and pray
For the likes just o' me, Billy Budd.—But, look:
Through the port comes the moonshine astray!
It tips the guard's cutlass and silvers this nook;
But 'twill die in the dawning of Billy's last day.
A jewel-block they'll make of me tomorrow,
Pendant pearl from the yardarm-end
Like the eardrop I gave to Bristol Molly—

O, 'tis me, not the sentence they'll suspend.
Ay, ay, all is up; and I must up too,
Early in the morning, aloft from alow.
On an empty stomach now never it would do.
They'll give me a nibble—bit o' biscuit ere I go.
Sure, a messmate will reach me the last parting cup;
But, turning heads away from the hoist and the belay,
Heaven knows who will have the running of me up!
No pipe to those halyards.—But aren't it all sham?
A blur's in my eyes; it is dreaming that I am.
A hatchet to my hawser? All adrift to go?
The drum roll to grog, and Billy never know?
But Donald he has promised to stand by the plank;
So I'll shake a friendly hand ere I sink.
But—no! It is dead then I'll be, come to think.
I remember Taff the Welshman when he sank.
And his cheek it was like the budding pink.
But me they'll lash in hammock, drop me deep.
Fathoms down, fathoms down, how I'll dream fast asleep.
I feel it stealing now. Sentry, are you there?
Just ease these darbies at the wrist,
And roll me over fair!
I am sleepy, and the oozy weeds about me twist.
(*BB* 132)

In the ballad Billy engages with fate in words that are not his words, because they are the words of the anonymous shipmate. In a deeper sense, "Billy" engages with a fate that is not his own, in that the voice assumes a neutrality which suggests that the death could be anyone's. "Billy in the Darbies" is a realization of a fate that *is* one's own, but not *experienced* as one's own, but also not therefore *un*experienced. "Billy" is given the capacity to "think" of his death, to occupy a perspective that can acknowledge its imminence in an idiom that indicates a perception dawning on him ("It is dead then I'll be, come to think"), but not dawning on him with horror, and not dawning on him as a phenomenon which must be considered, from his point of view, unique. For "Billy" no sooner thinks of his death than he thinks of the death of "Taff the Welshman when he sank." Or rather, "Billy" thinks of beauty visible in Taff's death—of the "budding pink" of his cheek. One can hear the capacity to consider the self an object—though a beautiful object, an ornament—in "Billy's" imagining himself at his hanging to be a "Pendant pearl…. / Like the eardrop I gave to Bristol Molly." The point here is not the dehumanization but rather an image of the self as an object of beauty which others will regard, and which one speculatively regards oneself, notwithstanding the fact that beauty is created by the lifelessness exacted in the hanging—the perfect stillness, which is what makes the body like a pendant. So too in the pun, "O, 'tis me, not the sentence they'll suspend," there's a reiterated capacity to see the sacrifice of one's person as if it were not a sacrifice—there being an equivalence in "Billy's" substitution of suspending the sentence for suspending the man, though they are in fact opposite fates. The ballad registers an acknowledgment without an owning of fate: Referring to himself in the third person ("Through the port comes the moonshine astray!…But 'twill die in the dawning of Billy's last day"), Billy sees the light's dying and his own dying nondifferentially.

This capacity to see from a perspective that is not proprietary and not catastrophic is most expansive in the vision that makes combinatory and structurally equivalent a present pervaded by feeling ("I am sleepy") and a prospective future ("and the oozy weeds about me twist") in which sleepiness turns into death, or gives way to death, there being a continuity between the neutrality of the feeling and the neutrality of the fate, alike happening, and about to happen, to him, as perceiving and no more perceiving are here made equivalent. It is the capacity to feel in a way that doesn't compromise seeing which delivers Billy to a "serenity" not beholden to character but also not beholden to the God-afflicted world that elsewhere haunts *Billy Budd*. The dreamy acquiescence through which Billy visualizes his death as beautiful—a "jewel," a "budding pink," a body wrapped in weeds—throughout conveys the sense that he is viewing his life and death as natural occurrences, impersonally, even as this impersonality could be ascribed to the fact that "Billy's" words aren't Billy's. ("The sublime," Schopenhauer wrote, lies in "an exaltation beyond our own individuality" [*WW* 1:206].)[34] The sublime of "Billy in the Darbies" lies in Melville's capacity to represent the effacement of individuality with the same neutrality as "the sea is the sea," a reiteration whose further irreducibility, and whose absolute clarity, might be likened to another reiteration that makes the "rose-tan" in Billy's cheeks and the "rose" of the dawn he becomes ("Billy ascended; and, ascending, took the full rose of the dawn"[*BB* 124]) the same astonishing element.

For Walter Benjamin, fate and character, in an essay of that title, written in 1919, are separable—though not separable in the sense that they were for the Stoics, in that, for the Stoics, if there was sufficient character, there would not then be fate. For Benjamin, in distinction, character and fate apply to different regions of the nature of man. Fate applies to "the natural guilt of human life" from which no one is exempt.[35] In comedy, according to Benjamin, there is individuality and freedom: Character "is the sun of individuality in the colorless (anonymous) sky of man" (206). In tragedy, on the other hand, the response to fate is something more substantial than character; Benjamin calls it "genius." Specifically, genius manifests itself as the awareness that man "is better than his god"—an awareness which reduces him or, from another perspective, elevates him to "moral speechlessness" (203). Benjamin elaborates: "The moral hero, still dumb, not yet of age...wishes to raise himself by shaking [the] tormented world. The paradox of the birth of genius in moral speechlessness...is the sublimity of tragedy. It is probably the basis of all sublimity, in which genius, rather than God, appears." Though the sentences are enigmatic and essentially unelaborated, Benjamin implies that in tragedy, and in all sublimity, genius rather than God is the placeholder for value against forms of destruction. God could overcome destruction as well as impose it, but genius can stand up to it (Benjamin implies) with an outrage whose force is equivalent to God's, although not victoriously so. In other words, in Benjamin's opposition between genius and God, "moral speechlessness" is a contestatory presence which asserts its superiority to the fate that will vanquish it. That contestatory presence is the source of its power. *Billy Budd* revises such terms. In *Billy Budd* what stands in the presence of fate is *not* the "moral speechlessness" of an antagonist's superiority. Rather, "genius" is constituted by a speechlessness that is ultimately, if not initially, serene—by a "genius" manifested in the acknowledgment of a pure fate before which character noncatastrophically evaporates.

This is the neutral last paragraph which closes the chapter narrating Billy's hanging: "And now it was full day. The fleece of low-hanging vapor had vanished, licked up by the sun that late had so glorified it. And the circumambient air in the clearness of its serenity was like smooth white marble in the polished block not yet removed from the marble-dealer's yard" (*BB* 128). The paragraph substitutes for an apocalyptic, providential language ("glorified"), a language that is reiterative of features that aren't appropriated or differentiated—whose value lies in a beauty not compromised by possession or adaptation—in something clear, "smooth," and all-encompassing.[36] That "serenity" is "genius." But not in Benjamin's sense. Rather, in Schopenhauer's sense, genius is the capacity to view all things objectively—that is, without emotional investment or willing: "Genius is the ability to leave entirely out of sight our own interest, our willing...and to discard entirely our own personality for a time, in order to remain *pure knowing subject*, the clear eye of the world...the clear mirror of the inner nature of the world" (*WW* 1:185–86). Or, as Melville, would have it, the "smooth white marble in the polished block not yet removed from the marble-dealer's yard." Such a state—without the sun's glorification (or a God's), and equally without the bright constraint of personal will (which Benjamin called "the sun of individuality")—is what *Billy Budd* achieves in Melville's unfinished work.

Notes

1 Thomas R. Nevin, *Simone Weil: Portrait of a Self-Exiled Jew* (Chapel Hill: Univ. of North Carolina Press, 1991), 295.

2 Lawrence Buell speculates convincingly that the "First Series, Second Series" in Suzuki's titles were indebted to the titles of Emerson's essays (*Emerson* [Cambridge, MA: Harvard Univ. Press, 2003], 196; hereafter abbreviated B; further references are cited parenthetically). Asiatic influences on Emerson's thought were first documented by Arthur Christy, *The Orient in American Transcendentalism: A Study of Emerson, Thoreau and Alcott* (New York: Columbia Univ. Press, 1932).

3 Cleo McNelly Kearns, *T. S. Eliot and Indic Traditions: A Study in Poetry and Belief* (Cambridge: Cambridge Univ. Press, 1987), 67.

4 Until 1993 Peabody's translation was attributed to Thoreau, though it was signed by Peabody (Thomas A. Tweed, *The American Encounter with Buddhism, 1844–1912* [Chapel Hill: Univ. of North Carolina Press], 1992; pbk. ed., 2000), xvi–xvii, xxxi. In Bruce A. Ronda's recent biography, *Elizabeth Palmer Peabody: A Reformer on Her Own Terms* (Cambridge, MA: Harvard Univ. Press, 1999), no mention, however, is made of the translation, which Tweed called "groundbreaking" (xvii).

5 For Empson's relation to Anesaki, see John Haffenden, *William Empson*, vol. 1, *Among the Mandarins* (New York: Oxford Univ. Press, 2005), 318; for Eliot's relation to him, see Kearns, *T. S. Eliot and Indic Traditions*, 76–84; and Jeffrey M. Perl, *Skepticism and Modern Enmity Before and After Eliot* (Baltimore: Johns Hopkins Univ. Press, 1989), 49–61. Perl's important chapter "Foreign Metaphysics" (43–66) is based on two earlier essays coauthored with Andrew P. Tuck in 1985. Perl and

Tuck were the first to discuss Eliot's Asian studies with reference to an examination of his unpublished philosophical notebooks at Houghton Library, Harvard University. Eliot's manuscript and typescript essays, as well as his class notes for the years he spent at Harvard, remain unpublished.

6   See Richard Tuck's discussion of the passage from Hobbes's *The Elements of Law* (1889) in which Hobbes makes these distinctions (*Hobbes: A Very Short Introduction* [Oxford: Oxford Univ. Press, 1989], 67–68, 129). The passage which Tuck argues is "at the heart of Hobbes's moral and political philosophy" insists that "upon the occasion of some strange and deformed birth, it shall not be decided by Aristotle, or the philosophers, whether the same be a man or no, but by the laws" (*The Elements of Law: Natural and Politic,* ed. Ferdinand Tönnies [London: Frank Cass and Co., 1889], II.8.10; 2nd ed. [New York: Barnes and Noble, 1969], 189).

7   Simone Weil, "Human Personality," in *The Simone Weil Reader,* ed. George A. Panichas (Wakefield, RI: Moyer Bell, 1977), 314.

8   *The Notebooks of Simone Weil,* trans. Arthur Wills, 2 vols. (New York: Putnam's, 1956), 1:279; hereafter abbreviated *N.* Further references are cited parenthetically in the text.

9   "Philosophy...is *exclusively* an affair of action and practice," Weil observed in her notebooks. "That is why it is so difficult to write about. Difficult in the same way as a treatise on tennis or running" (*First and Last Notebooks,* trans. Richard Rees [London: Oxford Univ. Press, 1970], 362; hereafter abbreviated *FL;* further references are cited parenthetically in the text). *Four Quartets* dramatizes a process of transformation, in which one's understanding of being changes through repetitions that become a practice. Emerson's essays model forms of practice; their implicit understanding is that there are no chance results, and no results in delegation. Thus, Pierre Hadot's account of ancient philosophy as a training whose goal is perception of bare reality through the discipline of attention (rather than as a university discipline and rather than in relation to the construction of a discursive system) (*Philosophy as a Way of Life: Spiritual Exercises from Socrates to Foucault,* ed. Arnold I. Davidson [Oxford: Blackwell, 1995]) could be elaborated in relation to Weil, Emerson, and Eliot. For Jonathan Edwards, on the other hand, no practice could result in that love of the whole experienced as a *taste,* which would alone demonstrate value. That is the "true" of Edwards's "true virtue." I discuss Buddhist practices of attention in relation to William Empson's ideas about the Far East.

10 Jonathan Edwards, "Of Being," in *The Works of Jonathan Edwards,* ed. John E. Smith, 22 vols. to date (New Haven, CT: Yale Univ. Press, 1957–), vol. 6, *Scientific and Theological Writings,* ed. Wallace E. Anderson (New Haven, CT: Yale Univ. Press, 1980), 206. *The Works of Jonathan Edwards* is hereafter abbreviated *W.*

11 Ralph Waldo Emerson, "Experience," in *Essays and Lectures,* ed. Joel Porte (New York: Library of America, 1983), 480–81. "Experience" is hereafter abbreviated E. Further references are cited parenthetically in the text.

12 Ralph Waldo Emerson, "Nominalist and Realist," in *Essays and Lectures,* 580; hereafter abbreviated NR. Further references are cited parenthetically in the text.

13 Ralph Waldo Emerson, "Nature," in *Essays and Lectures,* 7.

14 Hannah Arendt, *On Revolution* (New York: Viking, 1963; repr., London: Penguin, 1990), 82; hereafter abbreviated A. Citations are to the 1990 edition. Further references are cited parenthetically in the text.

15 *The Nature of True Virtue,* in *The Works of Jonathan Edwards,* vol. 8, *Ethical Writings,* ed. Paul Ramsey (New Haven, CT: Yale Univ. Press, 1989), 540.

16 Simone Weil, "Hesitations Concerning Baptism," in *Waiting for God,* trans. Emma Craufurd (New York: G. P. Putnam's Sons, 1951; repr., New York: Harper and Row,

1973), 48, 49–50; hereafter abbreviated *WG*. Citations are to the 1973 edition. Further references are cited parenthetically in the text.

17 George M. Marsden, *Jonathan Edwards: A Life* (New Haven, CT: Yale Univ. Press, 2003), 1.

18 A theory with commensurate language in the Buddhist suttas called "dependent origination" has a foundation incommensurate with that of Edwards's idea. To see "dependent origination" is to see a law of cause and effect in which states arise and are conditioned by previous states to which they are proximate or contiguous. "Dependent origination" articulates dramatic and self-evident chains of causality (if there is birth, there will be aging and death) and subtle ones (at every moment of contact with the sensory world, if there is a birth of feeling—pleasant, unpleasant, or neutral—there will be desire; if desire intensifies, there will be attachment (wanting or not wanting); if attachment, it will give rise to another burst of existence, known as *becoming, bhava* in Pali) (see *Thus Have I Heard: The Long Discourses of the Buddha Dīgha Nikāya*, trans. Maurice Walshe [London: Wisdom Publications, 1987], 34–35). Edwards's understanding of contingency is a dependence on the creator alone.

19 *The Works of Jonathan Edwards*, vol. 2, *Religious Affections*, ed. John E. Smith (New Haven, CT: Yale Univ. Press, 1959), 383–461.

20 Ralph Waldo Emerson, "The Divinity School Address," in *Essays and Lectures*, 81, 84. "The Personality of the Deity" is the title of the response of Henry Ware, Jr., to Emerson's "Address."

21 In the margins of his copies of *Essays, First and Second Series*, Melville was openly contemptuous of Emerson's optimism. Thus, for instance, when in "Prudence," Emerson asserted, "Trust men and they will be good to you," Melville wrote, "God help the poor fellow who squares his life according to this" (*Melville's Marginalia*, ed. Walker Cowen, 2 vols. [New York: Garland Publishing, 1987], 522; hereafter cited as *MM*). Next to Emerson's sentence in "Spiritual Laws" "[Man's] ambition is exactly proportioned to his powers," Melville wrote, "False" (*MM* 521). Beside Emerson's claim in "Spiritual Laws" that "the good, compared to the evil which [man] sees, is as his own good to his own evil," Melville wrote, "To annihilate all this nonsense read the Sermon on the Mount, and consider what it implies" (*MM* 522). Next to this sentence from "Heroism," "Heroism feels and never reasons, and therefore is always right," the marginalia note, "Alas! the fool again!" (*MM* 522). When Emerson in "The Poet" affirmed "the poet...disposes very easily of the most disagreeable facts," Melville remarked bitterly, "In this sense Mr. E. is a great poet" (*MM* 524). Although Melville found certain expressions of Emerson's to be "noble," and to have clear, strong meaning (*MM* 522), for the most part his marginalia isolate "gross and astonishing errors & illusions," isolate "blindness [which] proceeds from a defect in the region of the heart" (*MM* 525).

22 Ralph Waldo Emerson, "The Over-soul," in *Essays and Lectures*, 392.

23 *The Letters of Herman Melville*, ed. Merrell R. Davis and William H. Gilman (New Haven, CT: Yale Univ. Press, 1960), 125.

24 Herman Melville, *Billy Budd, Sailor (An Inside Narrative)*, ed. Harrison Hayford and Merton M. Sealts, Jr. (Chicago: Univ. of Chicago Press, 1962), 78; hereafter abbreviated *BB*. Further references are cited parenthetically in the text.

25 William Empson, *Argufying: Essays on Literature and Culture*, ed. John Haffenden (Iowa City: Univ. of Iowa Press,1987), 40. This opinion—that Christianity is a "religion whose symbol is a torture," that God is a "torture-monster"—crops up everywhere in Empson's writing. See, for example, the chapter "Christianity" in *Milton's God* (London: Chatto and Windus, 1961), 229–78.

26 Sharon Cameron, *Writing Nature: Henry Thoreau's "Journal"* (Oxford, 1985; repr. Chicago: Univ. of Chicago Press, 1988).

27 Georg Simmel, "The Metropolis and Mental Life," in *On Individuality and Social Forms*, ed. Donald N. Levine (Chicago: Univ. of Chicago Press, 1971), 329–30.

28 The word is Adorno's. In "The Essay as Form," he wrote: "The essay...takes place not systematically but rather as a characteristic of an intention groping its way" (Theodor W. Adorno, *Notes to Literature*, vol. 1, ed. Rolf Tiedemann, trans. Shierry Weber Nicholsen [New York: Columbia Univ. Press, 1991], 16).

29 Ralph Waldo Emerson, "Spiritual Laws," in *Essays and Lectures*, 305. My two essays on Emerson were written ten years apart from each other. Their terms do not specifically address each other. In "Representing Grief: Emerson's 'Experience'" I am concerned with how attributes of a personal loss are discovered to be the attributes of all experience without exception, while in "The Way of Life by Abandonment" I examine those essays of Emerson's in which the personal disappears from Emerson's acknowledgment ("Nothing can be taken from us that seems much")—in which Emerson is conciliatory with respect to a loss that is not experientially marked as a person's loss.

30 "Men are unable to forgive what they cannot punish and...unable to punish what has turned out to be unforgivable....All we know is that we can neither punish nor forgive such offenses and that they therefore transcend the realm of human affairs and the potentialities of human power, both of which they radically destroy whenever they make their appearance" (Hannah Arendt, *The Human Condition* [Chicago: Univ. of Chicago Press, 1958], 241).

ONE

1 William Empson, *Argufying: Essays on Literature and Culture*, ed. John Haffenden (Iowa City: Univ. of Iowa Press, 1987), 578; hereafter abbreviated *A*. Further references are cited parenthetically in the text.

2 John Haffenden, Empson's biographer, in a letter to me dated May 12, 2004. For the most complete narrative of Empson's relation to Buddhism, see Haffenden's account of how Empson's interest in Buddhism developed as an alternative to both I. A. Richards's theory of value in poetry, a "humanist argument for self-fulfillment," and "the ghastly god of the Christians who was appeased by the sacrifice of his son and who will mark one down for heaven or hell" (*The Complete Poems of William Empson*, ed. John Haffenden [Gainesville: Univ. of Florida Press, 2001], 148 and, inclusively, 139–52; hereafter abbreviated *CP*). See also *Argufying*, in which Haffenden anthologizes Empson's writings on the Far East (including Empson's extraordinary 1936 "The Faces of Buddha"), as well as Haffenden's earlier discussion of Empson's relation to Buddhism in his introduction to *The Royal Beasts and Other Works*, ed. John Haffenden (Iowa City: Univ. of Iowa Press, 1986), 7–77; hereafter abbreviated *RB*. Further references are cited parenthetically in the text. Some of this material is reformulated in the first volume of Haffenden's biography of Empson, *William Empson*, vol. 1, *Among the Mandarins* (Oxford: Oxford Univ. Press, 2005).

3 One of the earliest suttas (or discourses; *sūtra* in Sanskrit) of the Pali canon, "a Middle Indic version of the Buddha's teaching as first preserved through oral transmission...and written down long afterwards in Ceylon" (*CP 139*), on the consuming power of desire. Empson produced a synthesized version of five translations of the Fire Sermon (*CP* 150).

4 The manuscript was subsequently lost in London (*RB* 45–46). Draft pages are at Houghton Library, Harvard University, William Empson Papers, bMS Eng 1401 (911). [After this book went to press, Empson's biographer, John Haffenden, reported that he had found the long-lost manuscript (*TLS*, August 9, 2006).]

5 *Thus Have I Heard: The Long Discourses of the Buddha Dīgha Nikāya*, trans. Maurice Walshe (London: Wisdom Publications, 1987), 231–77; hereafter abbreviated *DN*. Further references are cited parenthetically in the text.

6 Henry Clarke Warren, *Buddhism in Translations* (Delhi: Motilal Banarsidass, 1986).

7 In the Pali suttas, the befuddlement of Ananda often motivates the Buddha's instruction. In this sutta, contemplating the Buddha's impending death, Ananda falsely hypothesizes: "The Lord will not attain final Nibbāna [Sanskrit *Nirvana*] until he has made some statement about the order of monks"—a consolatory speculation rebuked as follows: "If there is anyone who thinks: 'I shall take charge of the order,' or 'The order should refer to me,' let him make some statement about the order" (*DN* 245). The chastisement is not a petty one. Because the Buddha has no "teacher's fist" in which he reveals doctrine to an inner circle, the teaching does not depend on a monastic order which will explicate it.

8 The supernatural participation of earth, sky, and trees in the final enlightenment (*DN* 262); the radiance of the Buddha's skin (*DN* 260); the widespread lamentation (*DN* 274).

9 Called Satipaṭṭhāna *Sutta* (The Foundations of Mindfulness), this is the practice sutta, the most important in the Pali canon (sutta 10 in *The Middle Length Discourses of the Buddha: A New Translation of the Majjhima Nikāya*, trans. Bhikkhu Ñāṇamoli, ed. and rev. Bhikkhu Bodhi [Boston: Wisdom Publications, 1995], 145–55; hereafter abbreviated *MN*; further references are cited parenthetically in the text). A more recent translation, which includes a discussion of the sutta that draws on modern scholarship, can be found in Analayo, *Satipaṭṭhāna: The Direct Path to Realization* (Birmingham: Windhorse Publications, 2003; repr. 2004). "Sati" in Satipaṭṭhāna means "attentiveness directed to the present"; "paṭṭhāna" is explained either as a shortened form of *upaṭṭhāna*, meaning an "'establishing'—here of mindfulness"—or as taking as its root *paṭṭhāna*, meaning "foundation" (*MN* 1188).

10 Bhikkhu Ñāṇamoli, *The Life of the Buddha, as It Appears in the Pali Canon, the Oldest Authentic Record* (Kandy, Sri Lanka: Buddhist Publication Society, 1972), 25–29.

11 In Buddhist psychology feelings are divided into three categories: pleasant, unpleasant, and neutral. Like the weather, feelings are impersonal: "Just as various winds blow in the sky: winds from the east, winds from the west, winds from the north, winds from the south, dusty winds and dustless winds, cold winds and hot winds, mild winds and strong winds; so too, various feelings arise in this body: pleasant feeling arises, painful feeling arises, neither-painful-nor-pleasant feeling arises" (*The Connected Discourses of the Buddha: A New Translation of the Saṃyutta Nikāya*, trans. Bhikkhu Bodhi, 2 vols. [Boston: Wisdom Publications, 2000], 2:1272; hereafter abbreviated *SN*; further references are cited parenthetically in the text). Other neutralizations involve describing the composition of body, feeling, mind states, and mind objects in terms of earth, water, fire, and air elements (*MN* 278–85), or of crude collections of psychophysical phenomena called aggregates, of which there are five: the material-form aggregate, the feeling aggregate, the perception aggregate, the formations aggregate, and the aggregate of consciousness.

12 This is sometimes translated as "the body in the body" to distinguish the contemplation of one's own body from that of others.

13 Empson was specifically referring to the repetitions in the Fire Sermon (*CP* 150). However, the same phrases are repeated in all the suttas.

14 William Empson, *Seven Types of Ambiguity* (New York: New Directions,1930; rev. and repr. 1966), 196; hereafter abbreviated *ST*. Citations are to the 1966 edition. Further references are cited parenthetically in the text.

15 Among examples of this type, Empson included the cross (*ST* 192), "the difference of sound heard by the two ears" (*ST* 193), the Freudian idea of identity in opposites (*ST* 194), primitive Egyptians writing the same sign for young and old (*ST* 194), and his climactic one: Christ in Herbert's "The Sacrifice," who is "scapegoat and tragic hero; loved because hated; hated because godlike; freeing from torture because tortured" (*ST* 233).

   In John Haffenden's introduction to *The Royal Beasts*, he discusses Empson's interest in contradiction in the expression of Buddha faces; his plans for the monograph "Asymmetry in Buddha Faces" (*RB* 45); his deliberation about whether the Buddha prototype should be acknowledged as Greco-Roman or Indigenous Indian (*RB* 47–50); and the way in which Empson, in his ballet *The Elephant and the Birds*, attempted to reconcile the specific contradictions of the Far East and the West by positing an identification between "the Greek story of Philomel and Procne, and the Indian story of what the Buddha did in his incarnation as an elephant." Empson wrote: "Both stories take for granted the idea of reincarnation between human being and animal, but the Buddha goes the opposite way round from the tormented and revengeful women who are reborn as birds....The two stories have...to be worked into a unity" (*RB* 182–83).

16 Houghton Library, William Empson Papers, bMS Eng 1401 (911); hereafter abbreviated bMS. Further references are cited parenthetically in the text. By permission of the Houghton Library, Harvard University. These are fourteen nonconsecutive typescript pages. This paragraph is also printed in Haffenden (*RB* 46).

17 Some of the differences Empson saw diffused throughout the Buddha face were contradictions ("at once blind and all-seeing"); some were oppositions—two things situated in a pair along an axis (as in "sufficient to itself and of universal charity"); some were incongruities (as in a look that is "alert" and "socially conscious" while at the same time being "ironical or complacent"); and some were "incompatibilities," as in the Buddha image said to have "puppy" ears and heroic dignity. In writing of Buddha faces, Empson did not distinguish among these differences.

18 The page from which the above quotation is taken begins in midsentence: "of desire sent in from outside, gives them the sharp (nearly rectangular) curved edges," indicating that desire is a subject continued from the previous (lost) draft page. Empson's manuscript page does not clarify to what iconic tradition his description of the lips refers.

19 "[T]he sharply defined lips," "the sharp (nearly rectangular) curved edges."

20 "[S]trength and tenderness," the "sensual" and the "infantile," alertness and peace, and so forth.

21 In his analyses of faces, it is the mouth on which Empson's descriptions lavish most attention—a focus visible in a passing sentence ("How tenderness can be put into lips, what makes the two little ridges of the Chuguji Maitreya so wonderful, I have no hope of explaining"), or in a sustained examination, as of the face of "the mask in Noh for the woman who has gone mad after losing her child....The Noh woman is acting sanity. Her madness is a fixed and passive state of horror." Empson writes: "The face has a reserve and fixity which suggests a nightmarish parallel to the Buddha's. This is mainly conveyed by the mouth; a level slit with rounded ends that would be the rectangular (pillar box) mouth of agony if the muscles were not

slack with exhaustion. The only two still working seem to be the depressors under the corners and the elevators running to the nose, where there are tight little curves as if from disgust or cutious [sic] experimental smelling. Both being vertical there is none of the breadth obvious in smiling" (bMS).

22 In the draft pages for his monograph on Buddha faces, Empson writes of a Japanese Buddha that "the will to destroy will has so far failed to destroy itself....The figure is still sitting there 'trying.' In a way this seems a failure of the sculptor, though a very revealing one." Elaborating on the "strained mouth of thin lipped sensual embarrassment" which occurs rarely on early Japanese Buddhas, Empson continues: "I should connect this more complacent form of the strained mouth with the social uses of the expression, as the English Colonel's wife in *Storm over Asia*. She is determined to look as kind and as charming as if she felt at home, but is foreseeing the ambush and has no hope whatever of a smile in return" (bMS).

23 Terry Eagleton, *The Ideology of the Aesthetic* (Malden, MA: Blackwell Publishing, 1990), 43; hereafter abbreviated *IA*. Further references are cited parenthetically in the text.

24 "Aesthetic judgments are thus, as it were, 'impersonally personal,' a kind of subjectivity without a subject, or, as Kant has it, a 'universal subjectivity'" (*IA* 93).

25 "Schopenhauer's work is thus the ruin of all those high hopes which bourgeois idealism has invested in the idea of the aesthetic....A discourse which began as an idiom of the body has now become a flight from corporeal existence....By some curious logic, the aesthetic has ended up demolishing the very category of subjectivity it was intended to foster" (*IA* 171).

26 I am not suggesting that Emerson, Weil, or Eliot would be spared the ideological critique Eagleton performs on the philosophers he discusses. But I am suggesting that there is a difference between regarding the origin of an ethical practice—even one like the categorical imperative construed as universal—as shaped independently, from within, by that principle of self-governance exacted by Kant's idealism, and, conversely, regarding it as a set of imperatives understood to be extrinsically dictated. In Kant's idealism will is crucial; will is what enables you to act as you are obliged to. Weil's idealism requires will's erosion.

27 Immanuel Kant, *Religion and Rational Theology*, trans. Allen W. Wood and George Di Giovanni, The Cambridge Edition of the Works of Immanuel Kant (New York: Cambridge Univ. Press, 1996), 7–17. Further references are cited parenthetically in the text.

28 We have no orientation about speculative or theoretical ideas of limitlessness. We are oriented only about the practical uses of limitlessness. We can orient ourselves in practical, nonempirical thinking because we have the moral law and the subjective feeling to which it gives rise. In the case of limitlessness, aware of its own lack, reason "feel[s] a need" of—generates the feeling of need for—"the *concept* of the unlimited as the ground of the concepts of all limited beings" (Kant, *Religion and Rational Theology*, 11). Specifically, this means insight into rational moral law.

29 Houghton Library, William Empson Papers, pfMS Eng 1401 (1151). By permission of the Houghton Library, Harvard University.

30 Ibid.

31 Simone Weil, *First and Last Notebooks*, trans. Richard Rees (London: Oxford Univ. Press, 1970), 129; hereafter abbreviated *FL*. Further references are cited parenthetically in the text.

32 *The Notebooks of Simone Weil*, trans. Arthur Wills, 2 vols. (New York: G. P. Putnam's Sons, 1956), 2:459. Weil is here considering a proposition from Philolaus.

33 Ralph Waldo Emerson, "The Over-soul," in *Essays and Lectures*, ed. Joel Porte (New York: Library of America, 1983), 393. See also "The Poet," in *Essays and Lectures*, 460.

34 Empson's descriptions of Far Eastern art register horror as well as fascination at the relentlessness of forms to which persons are irrelevant ("terrifying" is how he described one of the dancers in a Kabuki performance [*A* 580]): "terrific changes of scenery"; "When this sinister woman becomes violent, it means nothing; it only shows the weakness, and therefore the pathos, of her way of getting into Nirvana" (*A* 579). Of the repetitions in the Fire Sermon, it "is rather like having a steamroller go over you" (*CP* 141): "This apparently short bit of text, if you put in all the repetitions, takes more than a quarter of an hour, and to sit and listen to it is a pretty appalling experience" (*CP* 150).

35 The Wurroos, not men, are also unable to cross-breed with men; moreover, they have a breeding season, Empson claimed, so that "they have become rational without using Freudian machinery" (*RB* 29); they enjoy different music ("the merely intellectual excitement, that we find in the panchromatic scales of Bartók and of Schoenberg" is "fused into the plain drama of a popular ballad" [*RB* 168]); and they have a tail, floppy ears, and fur (Empson wrote to an anthropologist, whom he consulted about his outline for the fable, that he planned to have the Wurroos "demand the status of Royal Beasts, like sturgeon," to keep their "valuable fur" "off the market" [*RB* 33]).

36 The phrase is from Empson's description of the "ripples in the smooth wood" forming the mouth of the Chuguji Buddha, "that gives all the lightness and tenderness which will at any moment brush away the present universe as an unwise dream" (*A* 575).

TWO

1 Jonathan Edwards, "Of Being," in *The Works of Jonathan Edwards*, ed. John E. Smith, 22 vols. to date (New Haven, CT: Yale Univ. Press, 1957–), vol. 6, *Scientific and Theological Writings*, ed. Wallace E. Anderson (New Haven, CT: Yale Univ. Press, 1980), 206. *The Works of Jonathan Edwards* is hereafter abbreviated *W*. Further references are cited parenthetically in the text. Clarence H. Faust and Thomas H. Johnson reproduce Edwards's punctuation (which the Yale editors standardize) for this passage in their anthology *Jonathan Edwards: Representative Selections, with Introduction, Bibliography, and Notes*, American Century Series (1935; rev. ed. 1962, New York: Hill and Wang), 20.

2 *The Works of Jonathan Edwards*, vol. 3, *Original Sin*, ed. Clyde A. Holbrook (New Haven, CT: Yale Univ. Press, 1970), 400. Further references are cited parenthetically in the text.

3 See Norman Fiering's analysis of Edwards's idea of this continued creation in relation to Nicolas Malebranche's occasionalism, "The Rationalist Foundations of Jonathan Edwards's Metaphysics," in *Jonathan Edwards and the American Experience*, ed. Nathan O. Hatch and Harry S. Stout (New York: Oxford Univ. Press, 1988), 73–101.

4 To the question of why God created creatures, *Concerning the End for Which God Created the World*, quoting Isaiah, but adding emphasis, provides this reiterated answer: "For *my own sake*, even for *my own sake* will I do it" (*The Works of Jonathan Edwards*, vol. 8, *Ethical Writings*, ed. Paul Ramsey [New Haven, CT: Yale Univ. Press, 1989], 475; further references are cited parenthetically in the text). *Concerning the End for Which God Created the World* elaborates: his "diffusive

disposition…excited God to give creatures existence" (*W* 8:434–35). According to the Miscellanies, "God is a communicative being" (*The Works of Jonathan Edwards*, vol. 13, *The "Miscellanies" (Entry Nos. a-z, aa-zz, 1–500)*, ed. Thomas A. Schafer [New Haven, CT: Yale Univ. Press, 1994], 410; further references are cited parenthetically in the text). The idea of God's communicativeness does not negate the idea of his self-sufficiency. For God to delight in the "creature's qualifications, dispositions, actions and [happy] state [is really not] different from his delight in himself" (*W* 8:446). This self-sufficiency has its fullest expression in the idea that "the emanation or communication of the divine fullness…has relation to God as its fountain.…Here is both *emanation* and *remanation*" (*W* 8:531).

5 The context for this argument is *Original Sin* (*W* 3:396–97), where Adam and his posterity are counted as one. Edwards argues that even though God insists on this oneness, "the sin of the apostasy is not theirs, merely because God *imputes* it to them; but it is *truly* and *properly* theirs, and on that ground, God imputes it to them" (*W* 3:408).

6 Alexander Allen was the first to light up the equivocations in Edwards's theory of personal identity: "There is a contradiction in this treatise on *Virtue*.…If he had said plainly what his thought implies, that the creature has no existence outside of God, his attitude would have been clear and consistent. But he seems also to grant an infinitesimal portion of an independent existence to humanity. He halts between these two opinions, neither of which is quite acceptable to him" (*Jonathan Edwards* [Boston: Houghton Mifflin and Co., 1889], 319). Moreover, within Edwards's cosmology, although persons are continuously recreated by God from moment to moment, their attributes seem self-replicated. They have bodies (upheld by divine power and distinguished by resistance to being further divided [*W* 6:67, 204–5]). They have a natural conscience (distinct from a truly virtuous benevolence), and they have a will (the capacity to follow their own inclinations and desires). Alongside his claim of their dependent existence, then, in Edwards's writings, persons are not social constructs but rather individual or private entities.

7 *Charity and Its Fruits*, published in 1852, was a series of sermons Edwards preached on Corinthians 12:5 in 1738. *The Nature of True Virtue* (hereafter abbreviated *True Virtue*), published posthumously in 1765, was written in 1755–57 (in disagreement with Francis Hutcheson, the moral philosopher who claimed that all human beings possess a disinterested benevolence which constitutes moral sense) (in *The Works of Jonathan Edwards*, vol. 8, *Ethical Writings*, ed. Paul Ramsey [New Haven, CT: Yale Univ. Press, 1989]; further references are cited parenthetically in the text), along with a companion dissertation, *Concerning the End for Which God Created the World*, intended to precede it.

8 In "The Mind," "excellency" is defined as "the consent of being to being, or being's consent to entity" (*W* 6:336). I agree with Paul Ramsey that "Christian charity," "holy love," and "true virtue" are synonyms for Edwards (*W* 8:27–33); "being's consent to Being" is Edwards's last, most original, and most mysterious of these formulations.

The idea of more or less being contingent on love of God versus love of the self is at the heart of the two cities predicated by Augustine in books 11 and 12 of *City of God*: "So, to abandon God and to exist in oneself…is not immediately to lose all being; but it is to come nearer to nothingness" (St. Augustine, *Concerning the City of God against the Pagans* [first published 1467], trans. John O'Meara [London: Pelican Books, 1972; repr., London: Penguin Books, 1984], 572; citations are to the 1984 edition). This is because "God is existence in a supreme degree—he supremely *is*" (473). Differently construed, in St. Augustine's *Confessions* to lose the sense of

God is to become estranged from oneself. The powerful role played by harmony for Edwards will allow him to elaborate such a claim in *True Virtue*: When a being consents to Being, this better agrees with general existence, better agrees with God, puts creatures in better agreement with each other, and enables true agreement with oneself (*W* 8:620–21).

9   One way to understand the discrepancy between an earlier work like *Religious Affections* which allows for a "taste" and a "sense" of ideal love and Edwards's final treatise, which does not, is to speculate that only when Edwards was free of the effort to stamp out counterfeits and travesties among his parishioners—only when he had been dismissed from Northampton and settled in Stockbridge (1751)—could he turn his attention to disinterested benevolence. This is Perry Miller's interpretation (*Jonathan Edwards* [New York: Sloane Associates, 1949; repr., Amherst: Univ. of Massachusetts Press, 1981], 287; citations are to the 1981 edition). *True Virtue*, no longer concerned with pastoral care, adheres to an ideal, indifferent to the fact that, according to Edwards's characterizations, it could not be implemented. Edwards's pastoral theology could not have advocated such a philosophical theology—since how could Edwards tell his parishioners they were assembled for an experience that was unavailable to them? Another way to explain the contradiction among his works is to note that, in *True Virtue*, in arguing against the naturalists, Edwards is propelled by his enemies into the originality of a position that is not compatible with his earlier writings, and that, in its hard-core commitment to impersonality, even verges on Christian heresy. Thus, although Paul Ramsey indicates a Miscellanies entry in which Edwards asserts that "though a man has but a faint discovery of the glory of God, yet if he has any true discovery of him," it will be sufficient "to prize God above all" (*W* 8:553), this "faint discovery" as a "true discovery" is not the point made by *True Virtue*, where the reiterated warnings are that persons are not in a position to realize the calculations prescribed.

10   The suggestive "what sleeping rocks dream of" might have provided the title for this book, but for the fact that Edwards's insistence on the impossibility of imagining impersonality—the impossibility of imagining the "nothing" that is "you and me" signified by those words—does not apply to the state of affairs represented by Empson, Emerson, Weil, Eliot, and Melville, who countenance ways of imagining the impersonality Edwards both elicits and blocks.

11   For a section-by-section explication of *True Virtue*, see Norman Fiering's *Jonathan Edwards's Moral Thought and Its British Context* (Chapel Hill: Univ. of North Carolina Press, 1981); and Paul Ramsey's "Editor's Introduction" to Edwards, *Ethical Writings* (*W* 8:1–104).

12   Edwards had marshaled the same logical arguments against the freedom of the will. In John Smith's paraphrase, "A thing can't be before itself and hence cannot be its own cause....An act of free choice can't have an act of free choice before it" (*Jonathan Edwards: Puritan, Preacher, Philosopher* [London: Univ. of Notre Dame Press, 1992], 79).

13   The difficulty of Edwards's prose has been politely ignored as if it were an accident. For instance, of Edwards's seemingly impenetrable and ideal propositions, Fiering writes: "The geometrical method of Edwards's first chapter in *True Virtue*...has rarely been noticed. This method is indicative of the quest in the post-Cartesian period to establish a strictly deductive ethics, which even Locke believed was possible....After Edwards defined what true virtue most essentially consists in, he drew from this definition apodictically a series of eleven corollaries. These corollaries are basically geometric in nature, having to do with the logical extension and elaboration of the elements in the basic definition or axiom" (*Jonathan Edwards's*

Moral Thought and Its British Context, 323–24). But though Fiering importantly acknowledges the mathematical nature of the initial part of *True Virtue*, he neatens it up and changes its terms ("The division of the corollaries into 11 is entirely my doing. I have…changed the order of Edwards's propositions as I found necessary and convenient for clear presentation" [324]). Thus while, on the one hand, Fiering's glosses are faithful to these strange passages he correctly calls gnomic, on the other hand, he smoothes out their difficulty, disentangling, in the process, the relation of the being who consents and the Being consented to—though it is just this interrelation that Edwards's text leaves mysterious.

14 Chapter 3—which mediates the description of the unfathomable calculus and the erroneous calculus—treats an inferior sort of beauty arising from agreement, proportion, and uniformity visible in such diverse phenomena as "the mutual agreement of the various sides of a square, or equilateral triangle, or of a regular polygon" (*W* 8:562); "the harmony of good music" (*W* 8:573); the "duties of husbands and wives" (*W* 8:569); and "the virtue called *justice*" (*W* 8:569). The perception of beauty in such objects is not to be mistaken for true virtue. "For, otherwise," Edwards reasons with what might almost pass for humor, "men's delight in the beauty of squares, and cubes, and regular polygons in the regularity of buildings, and the beautiful figures in a piece of embroidery, would increase in proportion to men's virtue; and would be raised to a great height in some eminently virtuous or holy men; but would be almost wholly lost in some others that are very vicious and lewd" (*W* 8:573).

15 If he approves of a higher degree of benevolence (in Edwards's example, a man's loving his enemies), that, too, is based on self-love (*W* 8:587), though it is not entirely clear whether the operative principle behind love even to enemies is that of vanity (having so much love that it can be extended without regard for the reciprocal feelings of its object) or that of swapping places (loving even one's enemy as one would wish to be loved by all, even one's enemy).

16 Even attitudes toward abstract qualities (Hutcheson proposed "love," "compassion," "indignation," and "hatred" [*W* 8:585]) can without a great deal of metaphysical refining, in Edwards's dour formulation, be attributed to self-love. So, too, the preference for certain characters on stage, or for certain creatures over others (the "innocent" bird rather than the "pernicious" rattlesnake [*W* 8:585]), arises from self-love. Moreover, although natural conscience and true virtue might seem to intersect, Edwards remarks: "I think, the case is evidently otherwise" (*W* 8:597), since the inclinations of the heart are not coincident with the judgments of conscience.

17 *The Works of Jonathan Edwards*, vol. 2, *Religious Affections*, ed. John E. Smith (New Haven, CT: Yale Univ. Press, 1959), 208). Further references are cited parenthetically in the text.

18 Perry Miller's classic essay "The Rhetoric of Sensation," in *Errand into the Wilderness* (Cambridge, MA: Harvard Univ. Press, 1956), 167–84, established the centrality of affect to Edwards's writings. Although Miller's dependence on Lockean empiricism to describe the spiritual sense has been faulted for a modernization of Edwards's psychology (see, for instance, Fiering, *Jonathan Edwards's Moral Thought and Its British Context*; Conrad Cherry, *The Theology of Jonathan Edwards: A Reappraisal* [Garden City, NY: Doubleday and Co., 1966; repr., Bloomington: Indiana Univ. Press, 1990]; and Leon Chai, *Jonathan Edwards and the Limits of Enlightenment Philosophy* [New York: Oxford Univ. Press, 1998]), sense and affect remain at the heart of Edwards's perception of the spiritual. For the most recent summary of the debate on this issue, see the introduction to *The Works of Jonathan Edwards*, vol. 18,

The *"Miscellanies" (Entry Nos. 501–832)*, ed. Ava Chamberlain (New Haven, CT: Yale Univ. Press, 2000), 18–24.

Affect alone, of course, does not constitute spiritual understanding, which is "not heat without light." Moreover, in *Religious Affections* important discriminations distinguish gracious affections from the imagination, from reason, from invention, from speculation, from intuition, and from inspiration (*W* 2:266–91).

19 For instance, "The *first* object of virtuous benevolence is *Being*, simply considered....Being *in general* is its object; and the thing it has an ultimate propensity to, is the *highest good* of Being in general. And it will seek the good of every *individual* being unless it be conceived as not consistent with the highest good of Being in general. In which case the good of a particular being, or some beings, may be given up for the sake of the highest good of Being in general" (*W* 8:545). It is hard to wrap one's mind around sentences like these not because their calculations are complex but rather because such calculations cannot be arrived at intuitively by a person. A person could not know what would count as "the highest good."

20 The words are Wittgenstein's for the sense in which one can call expectations "unsatisfied" (Ludwig Wittgenstein, *Philosophical Investigations*, trans. G. E. M. Anscombe, 3rd ed. [New York: Macmillan Co., 1953; repr. 1970], 439; hereafter abbreviated *PI*; citations are to the 1970 edition). The numbers refer to the philosophical *remark* or paragraph numbers which Wittgenstein assigned his thoughts. For Wittgenstein the point is that the absence of something contains the proposition, which has been negated. Thus, for instance, "if I say I did *not* dream last night, still I must know where to look for a dream;...the proposition, 'I dreamt'...may be false, but it mustn't be senseless" (*PI* 448).

What connects the Wittgenstein of *PI* to Edwards is their shared concern with propositions (Wittgenstein would say grammatical propositions) to express inner states. But it is also their distinction of an idea from an experienced sense. Finally, what draws the two together is a question of what criteria can or cannot establish.

21 Edwards is quoting Psalm 119:18, in "A Divine and Supernatural Light," in *Norton Anthology of American Literature*, ed. Nina Baym, vol. A, *Literature to 1820*, 6th ed. (New York: W. W. Norton, 2003), 485.

22 Because only God has substance, immaterialism is the right word. At the same time, Edwards recognizes that in the commonplace world, spirit and matter are meaningless terms split off from each other. In the passages above, therefore, his project is to make sense of how they are related.

23 Cavell is explicating Wittgenstein's "The human body is the best picture of the human soul" (Stanley Cavell, *The Claim of Reason: Wittgenstein, Skepticism, Morality and Tragedy* [New York: Oxford Univ. Press, 1979], 400). In other words, the human body does not conceal or contain the soul but rather reveals or expresses it, but not as an entity that can be located (as for Edwards, the world does not conceal the presence of God, but reveals his presence "without figure or extension"). Cavell elaborates: "Call the belief in the soul psychism. Then a serious psychology must take the risk of apsychism. It can no more tolerate the idea of another (little) man inside, in here, than a serious theology can tolerate the idea of another (large) man outside, up there. Nor of small or large anythings....What would these be but points or stretches of etherealized matter, without doubt unverifiable? And idolatrous besides. The spirit of the wind is neither smaller nor larger than the wind; and to say it is *in* the wind is simply to say that it exists only where there is a wind.... On that understanding, then: The spirit of the body is the body."

Or as Edwards put it in "The Mind," "The spirit...perceives things where the body is...and in this sense the soul can be said to be in the same place where the body is" (*W* 6:338). Edwards, Wittgenstein, and Cavell are contesting the crudeness, even meaninglessness, of certain expressions to indicate the relation of body and soul, as in Wittgenstein's question "How can a body *have* a soul?" (*PI* 283), an idiom which highlights the absurdity of a materialism possessing an immaterialism.

24   That question also comes to mind when recalling the apparently omniscient world-propositions of Spinoza's *The Ethics*. Spinoza shares Edwards's idea that all creatures are only dependent beings created by a single substance and equally derides a determination of value based on self-interest: ideas like "*good, evil, order, confusion, warm, cold, beauty, ugliness*" arise because "men persuaded themselves that everything which happens, happens on their account" (Benedict de Spinoza, *A Spinoza Reader: "The Ethics" and Other Works*, ed. and trans. Edwin Curley (Princeton, NJ: Princeton Univ. Press, 1994), 113. In addition, Spinoza argues, analogously to Edwards's claim about the freedom of the will, that, because we are finite, we can never know all antecedent conditions (137). Thus, although Edwards had not read Spinoza, *True Virtue* and *The Ethics* (each insisting on conclusions that could be made only deductively) inhabit the same moral universe. Yet Spinoza's conclusions do not require a sacrificial logic in which consent to Being without particularity demands a recognition of being's inconsequentiality. Rather, in *The Ethics* "virtue is this very striving to preserve one's own being" (209).

25   In Miscellany 880, Edwards differently imagines an infinite series in response to the question "If it be...necessary that matter should be, Why is there no more of it?... Or why is there so much; why is there not less?" (*The Works of Jonathan Edwards*, vol. 20, *The "Miscellanies" (Entry Nos. 833–1152)*, ed. Amy Plantinga Pauw [New Haven, CT: Yale Univ. Press, 2002], 122). The question leads to a thought experiment about the improbability of the universe's not being caused by God—which posits the simplest "parcel of matter"—a particle; then two particles arranged in relation to each other along a line; then three (which form an isosceles triangle); then four particles (which form a square); then five (one particle at the center of the square); then more complex forms of organization, including animals; and then eventually mankind. According to Edwards, to entertain the likelihood that "all this came to pass fortuitously is unreasonable" (*W* 20:121–39). For example, the improbability of the fourth particle's coming into that point to make "the requisite square, at any time through eternity" without being caused to do so "is expressed by an infinite number, times infinite, times infinite, times infinite, times infinite, times infinite, times infinite, times infinite, to one" (*W* 20:134). Moreover, how could it be the case by accident, Edwards asks, that "particles that are unserviceable, and are not needed to make up the frame" of this universe "should agree to absent themselves and keep at a distance" (*W* 20:136)?

26   The absolute and the endless come together for Edwards in language like this from *Concerning the End for Which God Created the World*: "The good that is in the creature comes forever nearer and nearer to an identity with that which is in God....It must be an infinitely strict and perfect nearness" (*W* 8:443) in which all things "come nearer and nearer to him through all eternity" (*W* 8:444). And finally, "'Tis no solid objection against God's aiming at an infinitely perfect union of the creature with himself, that the particular time will never come when it can be said, the union now is infinitely perfect" (*W* 8:536).

27   Brian Rotman, *Ad Infinitum: The Ghost in Turing's Machine: Taking God Out of Mathematics and Putting the Body Back In: An Essay in Corporeal Semiotics* (Stanford, CA: Stanford Univ. Press, 1993), 158; hereafter abbreviated *AI*. Further references are cited parenthetically in the text. In *Ad Infinitum*, Rotman asks, Who is it that

counts and why has he been imagined without corporeality? (*AI* 9, 148), a question parallel to Who is it that posits a nonpersonal view of true virtue, and by what calculations? In asking who is obeying mathematical imperatives and why mathematics is haunted by a disembodied ghost ("as near to God as makes no difference" [*AI* 10]), Rotman connects the idea of God with the fantasy of infinity in classical mathematics. He proposes a "de-writing—of infinity" in which *X* is no longer a "spaceless, timeless, energyless simulacrum of ourselves," and "the replacement, the de-written *X*, is arithmetical passage to the limit" (*AI* 152–53). The result is "the introduction of the Corporeal Subject into mathematics [and] represents the lifting of the repression of the body, a repression…inseparable from the desire for endless counting" (*AI* 192). The change from an absolute to a contingent mathematics would be intelligible by comparison to the emergence of relativity and quantum theories and would have consequences for applying the concept of number to certain entities or quantities, like time (*AI* 133–36).

28 W. V. Quine, *Ontological Relativity and Other Essays* (New York: Columbia Univ. Press, 1969), 63.

29 Immanuel Kant, *The Critique of the Power of Judgment*, trans. Paul Guyer and Eric Matthews, The Cambridge Edition of the Works of Immanuel Kant (Cambridge: Cambridge Univ. Press, 2000), 135–36.

30 See Ferguson's account of how "an empirical infinite (what specifically cannot be experienced by a finite human being)" converges with an "artificial" infinite that has "no empirical correlates" (Frances Ferguson, *Solitude and the Sublime: Romantics and the Aesthetics of Individuation* [Routledge, 1992], 22–23). Her analysis considers discussions of the mathematical sublime (Neil Hertz, *The End of the Line*; Thomas Weiskel, *The Sublime*) which preserve the psychological as a category (85–87).

31 The words are Wittgenstein's, in *Remarks on the Foundations of Mathematics*, trans. G. E. M. Anscombe, ed. G. H. von Wright, R. Rhees, and G. E. M. Anscombe (Cambridge, MA: MIT Press, 1996), 195. In the following, he is specifying a distinction between an infinite deduced by a pattern and an infinite that is abstractly conceptually imposed. "'Ought the word "infinite" to be avoided in mathematics?' Yes; where it appears to confer a meaning upon the calculus; instead of getting one from it" (141); Wittgenstein is suggesting that there is a technique for carrying out something like the decimal expansion of pi so that it can go on and on. He is resisting making the infinite something that can be imagined apart from such a technique.

32 *The Works of Jonathan Edwards*, vol. 4, *The Great Awakening*, ed. C. C. Goen (New Haven, CT: Yale Univ. Press, 1972), 230.

33 The title of pt. 2 of *Religious Affections* marks Edwards's strong sense of the task of his treatise: "Shewing What Are No Certain Signs That Religious Affections Are Truly Gracious, or That They Are Not" (*W* 2:125). Only Christian practice is virtually unmistakable, being "the chief of all the signs of grace…the *principal sign*" (*W* 2:406). Yet Edwards spends almost a hundred pages describing what Christian practice is. Even this sign of signs must be painstakingly anatomized, since nothing can be certainly concluded.

34 "Think of the behavior characteristic of correcting a slip of the tongue. It would be possible to recognize that someone was doing so even without knowing his language" (*PI* 54).

35 *The Works of Jonathan Edwards*, vol. 16, *Letters and Personal Writings of Jonathan Edwards*, ed. George S. Claghorn (New Haven, CT: Yale Univ. Press, 1998), 108. Further references are cited parenthetically in the text.

36 *True Virtue's* editor, Paul Ramsey, connects such a moment with paragraph 6 at the end of chap. 1. Yet the point of paragraph 6 (*W* 8:549) is to introduce the possibility of general benevolence as necessary for loving benevolence to Being in general, while immediately considering the effects of its absence. Therefore, I take the passage considered above not to refer to this earlier paragraph. For in the paragraph discussed above the "spiritual sense" is an actual rather than a rhetorical possibility.

37 Cited in Miller, *Jonathan Edwards,* 287.

38 This substitutive economy (God's presence rather than human presence) is equally seen in a letter Edwards writes to Lady Mary Pepperell on the death of her son. "Let us think, dear Madam," he counsels her, "a little of the loveliness of our blessed Redeemer and his worthiness, that our whole soul should be swallowed up with love…whatever else we are deprived of" (*W* 16:414).

39 Even as a student at Connecticut Collegiate School (later Yale College), he quarreled with his classmates, disapproving of their rowdy behavior, while finding his own actions exemplary: "Through the goodness of God I am perfectly free of all their janglings" (*W* 16:38). On November 20, 1720, Edwards writes to his uncle of his "great surprisal [to] find my cousin Elisha…to be discontented in his dwelling with me….It cannot be because I hinder him from his studies, but…because I hinder him from a superabundance of that which he loves much better" (*W* 16:35). In 1750, Edwards remarks on a more serious matter—belief in one's good estate: "I have found with such melancholy people, that the greatest difficulty don't lie in giving them good advice, but in persuading them to take it" (*W* 16:337). Tattling to Elisha's father about what "is blameworthy in your son"—that is, the reiteration of the blameworthy—proves a consistent strain in Edwards's personal letters.

40 This was a controversy which revolved around the qualifications for communion, and which concluded by Edwards's being separated against his will from his church by the vote of one member of an ecclesiastical council. See Edwards's letter to the Reverend John Erskine, May 20, 1749, written at the time that his position paper, *Humble Inquiry,* was in press, for Edwards's explanation of the controversy (*W* 16:268–71). A letter to Reverend John Erskine on July 5, 1750, elaborates his account of the events (*W* 16:347–56).

41 Specifically, the arguments were on the question of who was equipped to run the Indian girls' school at the mission and the boys' boarding school. See the letter to Sir William Pepperell (*W* 16:552–63).

42 Cited in George M. Marsden, *Jonathan Edwards: A Life* (New Haven, CT: Yale Univ. Press, 2003), 494.

43 *Doxa* is the word in demotic Greek variously translated as "glory," "splendor," and "shining" in Second Corinthians 3:7–4:6, and Edwards's reiteration of all three words in the Miscellanies passage suggests that he is remembering it as well as the passage from Exodus 34:30.

44 *The Writings of St. Paul: A Norton Critical Edition,* ed. Wayne A. Meeks (New York: W. W. Norton and Co., 1972), 53–54.

45 Here Paul attributes a motivation to the veiling of the face—so the Israelites would not see the shine of Moses's skin (or the shine…fading)—that Exodus mysteriously withholds. What is in fact truly inscrutable about this passage is that Moses veils his face only after everyone has *seen* the shine. Paul, however, dwells on the veil, instrumentalizes it—ultimately detaching it from the countenance and making it not just a veiling of the face, but also a metaphor for the veiling of the truth: "Whenever Moses is read a veil lies over their minds; but when a man turns to the Lord the veil is removed" (*The Writings of St. Paul,* 54).

THREE

1 Ralph Waldo Emerson, "Experience," in *Essays and Lectures,* ed. Joel Porte (NewYork, 1983), 471. "Experience" is hereafter abbreviated E. Further references are cited parenthetically in the text.

2 Ralph Waldo Emerson, "The American Scholar," in *Essays and Lectures,* 53.

3 O. W. Firkins, *Ralph Waldo Emerson* (New York, 1915), 237, 341. In its entirety this book provides bracing discussions of Emerson's essays.

4 Stephen Whicher, *Freedom and Fate: An Inner Life of Ralph Waldo Emerson* (Philadelphia, 1953), designates the antithesis in terms of freedom and fate. Eric Cheyfitz, *The Transparent: Sexual Politics in the Language of Emerson* (Baltimore, 1981), situates antithetical assertions in a psychoanalytic context, illuminating the conflict between male and female, specifically with reference to *Nature.* Julie Ellison, in *Emerson's Romantic Style* (Princeton, NJ, 1984), discusses antithetical features of the essays by activating the Bloomian machinery of authority and its counters. In "Emerson's Dialectic," *Criticism* 11 (Fall 1969): 313–28, R. A. Yoder describes the dialectical moves in a number of Emerson's essays. Barbara Packer's *Emerson's Fall: A New Interpretation of the Major Essays* (New York, 1982) offers a comprehensive treatment of the unresolved dialectic established between and within essays. For one of the most compelling accounts of Emerson's language at odds with itself—considered in the context of his resistance to stabilizing moments of culture—see Richard Poirier's "The Question of Genius," *Raritan* 5, no. 4 (Spring 1986): 77–104.

5 I should immediately note that my use of "voice" is a metaphor, for Emerson's essay is written. It is discourse. But it is discourse in which assertions function as voices at odds with each other. This is the case not only in "Experience" but also in other essays. In "Self-Reliance," for example, contradictory assertions are adjacent to the essay's central argument, which is clear: Where the world thinks one thing and the self thinks another, the self is to follow its own inclinations. But while some descriptions in the essay characterize the self by the volatility of its "intuition" and "inconsistency," other descriptions in the essay characterize the self as an acrostic, which "read it forward, backward, or across,...still spells the same thing" (Ralph Waldo Emerson, "Self-Reliance," in *Essays and Lectures,* 266). From the vantage of some quotations in "Self-Reliance," you must change your way of thinking and believe in self-trust. From the vantage of other quotations in "Self-Reliance," you cannot change your way of thinking (or your changes of thinking are not up to you) because perception is not "whimsical, but fatal" (269).

A slightly different instance of the dissociation I have been describing is exemplified by "Circles," where contradiction is manifested between a self who knows that "people wish to be settled" and a self who knows that "only as far as they are unsettled is there any hope for them" (Emerson, "Circles," in *Essays and Lectures,* 413). Although the assertions could be regarded as two halves of a single utterance (the first half articulating what men desire, the second half articulating what it behooves them to desire), the consistent double terms that characterize the essay suggest that Emerson is emphasizing adversarial stances rather than the bipartite structure of a single proposition.

In essays like "Self-Reliance" and "Circles," contradictions notwithstanding, one could argue that the emphasis is clear. In "Compensation," however, it is less easy to determine the relation between contradictory voices. The positive reading of "Compensation" might be paraphrased as follows: There are no incompletions in the world; the idea of the fragmentary is a delusion—a reading substantiated by a quotation like the following: "We can no more halve things...than we can get an inside that shall have no outside" (Emerson, "Compensation," in *Essays and Lectures*, 291). But an equally plausible reading of "Compensation" might be paraphrased alternatively: Wholeness or compensation is not in fact a reassurance that all will be given; it is rather a reassurance that all will be taken away—a reading substantiated by the following quotation: "The vulgar proverb, 'I will get it from his purse or get it from his skin,' is sound philosophy" (294).

Within each of these essays it makes sense that Emerson's attitude should shift. What is unaccountable about the shifts is that they remain unremarked upon, treated as if they were nonexistent, as if the discrepant statements between which the essay vacillates occupy such different registers as never to have to come into contact at all. What is unaccountable is that in "Circles," "Self-Reliance," and "Compensation" Emerson treats contradictory statements as if they were complementary statements.

6 See Stanley Cavell's response to my claim that synthesis and contradiction are not useful terms in which to consider Emerson's "Experience," in his "Finding as Founding: Taking Steps in Emerson's 'Experience,'" in *Emerson's Transcendental Etudes: Cultural Memory in the Present* (Stanford, CA, 2003), repr. from Cavell's *This New Yet Unapproachable America* (Albuquerque, NM, 1989), 116. Synthesis is important to Cavell, as are the ideas of pregnancy and death, both of which Cavell associates with "the call for philosophy and for America" (131). In yet another formulation: "Philosophy begins in loss....The recovery from loss is...a finding of the world." Yet the terms Cavell invokes to demonstrate this synthesis seem increasingly extraneous to Emerson's "Experience," as he glancingly acknowledges toward the end of his own powerful essay: "How can philosophy—in the form of the call for philosophy—look like *Emerson's* writing? This still may remain incredible" (139). I continue to believe that something more specific than the call to philosophy is being described in Emerson's essay, as argued above.

7 *The Journals and Miscellaneous Notebooks of Ralph Waldo Emerson*, ed. William H. Gilman et al., 16 vols. (Cambridge, MA, 1960), 5:19–20; hereafter abbreviated *JMN*. Further references are cited parenthetically in the text.

8 *The Letters of Ralph Waldo Emerson, 1842–1847*, vol. 3, ed. Ralph L. Rusk (New York, 1939), 9. See also the several letters written in the days preceding this one, especially that to Elizabeth Palmer Peabody on January 28, 1842:

> In the death of my boy...has departed all that is glad & festal & almost all that is social even, for me, from this world. My second child is also sick, but I cannot in a lifetime incur another such loss. (8)

The letter in which Emerson "grieve[s] that I cannot grieve" can be seen as a retort to this one, and the discrepant responses in the letters as anticipating or duplicating those of the essay.

9 Such a disengagement is suggestive of the idea of a "person-stage"—something more or less momentary—discussed in n. 14 of "'The Sea's Throat': Eliot's *Four Quartets*."

10 The concern with "power" in Emerson's late essays—especially in *The Conduct of Life*—replaces the concern with the "present" and the "possible" in *Essays, First Series*. The shift is anticipated in the concluding sentence of "Experience," where we are told "the true romance which the world expects to realize, will be the transformation of genius into practical power" (492). If you do not believe in possibility, or if you believe the present has no possibility that you can exploit, you had better have

power—a substitution made explicit in another sentence from "Experience": "Once we lived in what we saw; now, the rapaciousness of this new power…engages us" (E 487). Other sentences in "Experience" explain the difficulty of the engagement: "Power which abides in no man and no woman, but for a moment speaks from this one, and for another moment from that one" (E 477); "Power keeps quite another road than the turnpikes of choice and will, namely, the subterranean and invisible tunnels and channels of life" (E 482); "Life itself is a mixture of power and form, and will not bear the least excess of either" (E 478); "The most attractive class of people are those who are powerful obliquely, and not by the direct stroke: men of genius, but not yet accredited: one gets the cheer of their light, without paying too great a tax" (E 483); "[Our friends] stand on the brink of the ocean of thought and power, but they never take the single step that would bring them there" (E 477). Power is most potent, most itself, "the single step" away that, at once, best defines it and marks its inaccessibility.

11 *The Standard Edition of the Complete Psychological Works of Sigmund Freud*, trans. James Strachey, vol. 14 (London, 1957), 244. Subsequent references are to this edition.

12 Perhaps the title of Emerson's essay is an allusion to Montaigne's "De l'expérience." In any case Emerson's essay, as I am describing it—in its refusal to abstract from experience, in the oblique connection between one part of the exposition and another, in the consequent imperative that the reader decipher a coherent if hidden plot—seems as clearly related to Montaigne's other essays as to other essays of Emerson's own.

13 Ralph Waldo Emerson, "Fate," in *Essays and Lectures*, 967; hereafter abbreviated F. Further references are cited parenthetically in the text.

14 Jacques Derrida, "Fors," *Georgia Review* 31 (1979): 64–116, repr. in Nicolas Abraham and Maria Torok's *The Wolf Man's Magic Word: A Cryptonymy*, trans. Nicholas Rand (Minneapolis, 1986; originally published as *Cryptonymie: Le verbier de l'Homme aux loups* [Paris, 1976]); and Nicolas Abraham's "L'écorce et le noyau," *Critique* 249 (1968): 162–81, trans. Nicholas Rand as "The Shell and the Kernel," *Diacritics* 9 (1979): 16–31.

15 My notion of the dead child's elusive relation to "Experience" is illuminated by Abraham and Torok's definition of introjection as that phenomenon which absorbs into the ego a lost object or corpse that it then preserves in a phantasmatic crypt or hermetically concealed place—a space that can't be gotten at. And it is related to Derrida's extension of this idea: that the phantasmatic space of the crypt is also a linguistic space. But in this reading of "Experience," my notion differs from theirs with respect to the question of how the introjected object is to be spatialized and with reference to its accessibility. Derrida, following Abraham and Torok, asserts that an incorporated object is always readable, whereas an introjected object never is. In "Experience," however, the antithesis of "always" with "never" misstates the case. Because the lost object remains partially or liminally visible (it is the subject of the preface, but is absent from the body of the essay), "Experience" openly invites the kind of reading I am offering, while simultaneously refusing to confirm it. Thus my idea of the marginality of the subject is not only a spatial one. Or rather, the spatialization calls attention to the fact that the magical power attached to the dead child is generated by the tension between what is visible and invisible; between the prospect of introjection conceived in terms of integration (held out by the essay's beginning) and the frustration of that prospect in the body of the essay, which only incompletely and indirectly assimilates both the subject and the loss. I shall argue that power comes from this marginality.

16 In "Self-Reliance" the self disencumbered of cursory constraints remains fundamentally bound by its sympathies and aversions—by all that involuntarily comes to define it. Thus the two assertions "I would write on the lintels of the door-post, *Whim*" and "Perception is not whimsical, but fatal" may be ideally compatible, but they are experientially at odds. The degree to which this conflict remains unacknowledged as well as unexamined is the degree to which it cannot be considered perfunctory.

17 There would be another way to understand the relation between power and marginalization. It depends upon the convention (familiar to Emerson from such works as Ben Jonson's "On My First Son" and Wordsworth's "The Thorn") in which dead children are enabling because, in terms of the oedipal drama, they don't penetrate/castrate, as the man who wards off "experiences most penetrative" fears they might. If you kill them off, however, it's not just that you avoid the negative of castration; you are also bequeathed the positive penance of grief. In the case of "Experience," of course, grief is not wholly positive, because it is not wholly felt. That escalates its value. Because grief is imperfect and glancing, you have to repeat it to keep converting your losses. Yet the oedipal drama I have scripted is only a metaphor. It is not penetration the man fears and it is not the child the man kills. Rather, these are a screen for the avoidance of all conflict—an avoidance that results in empowerment. Power depends upon the evasion of conflict, upon denaturing the psychological terms the essay provokes the reader into contemplating.

FOUR

1 Derek Parfit, *Reasons and Persons* (Oxford, 1984), ix; hereafter abbreviated *RP*.

2 Parfit's argument contains two strands which I find productive for thinking about Emerson's "impersonal." The first strand involves Parfit's claim that there is no substantial entity in virtue of which it is true to say of a person that he is the "same" person over time. (Selfhood, or what Parfit calls "the unity of our lives" [*RP* 446], is a complex relation among psychological states capable of degrees we can affect.) The second strand is more specifically ethical and pertains to the relation between self-interest and concern for other persons. Parfit links these two strands through the suggestion that a change in our view of the conditions of personal identity can rationally lead us to a more impersonal concern for the quality of human experiences, regardless of *whose* experiences they are.

3 Ralph Waldo Emerson, "Nominalist and Realist," in *Essays and Lectures,* ed. Joel Porte (New York, 1983), 580; hereafter abbreviated NR. Further references are cited parenthetically in the text.

4 Ralph Waldo Emerson, "Montaigne," in *Essays and Lectures,* 709; hereafter abbreviated M. Further references are cited parenthetically in the text.

5 Ralph Waldo Emerson, "The Over-soul," in *Essays and Lectures,* 390; hereafter abbreviated O. Further references are cited parenthetically in the text. Emerson's primary understanding of the meaning of *person* and of *personality* (hence of impersonality) originated with the sense of the three-personed God. Despite the fact that Webster, following Johnson, in 1828 never mentions that there is a millennial idea of person bound up with the idea of Christ, Emerson certainly would have known this from patristic sources. Thus although Emerson uses the idea of the impersonal as if its divinity is part of his intuitive sense of the word, rather than part of its etymology, when he brings in the idea of God, what he is bringing in is the long history of *person* associated with the theology of the Trinity.

In fact what Emerson inherits is a misunderstanding. For the word *person* when it pertains to God was not originally meant to indicate an individual, but rather to denote a way of subsisting, a way of being, a hypostasis. Not pertaining to aspects of God, or to mythological intermediaries for God, and certainly not to any modern sense of individual, the Trinity originally implied a sameness of divine essence through three modes that belied the idea of "person as individual" which Emerson found so abhorrent. See the entry by M. J. Dorenkemper, "Person (In Theology)," in *New Catholic Encyclopedia*, ed. Catholic University of America, 18 vols. (New York, 1967), 11:168–70, for the sense of *person* as Emerson would have inherited it. For the more modern, philosophical sense of person as self, as in *personality*, see J. Ellis McTaggert, "Personality," in *Encyclopedia of Religion and Ethics*, ed. James Hastings, 13 vols. (New York, 1908), 11:773–81.

For a historically nuanced account of Emerson's complex relation to "individuality," see Sacvan Bercovitch's clarifying discussion of the understanding of *individualism* Emerson inherited from the socialists, of his reconception of this idea in the 1840s as a "vision of cosmic subjectivity" (opposed to socialism), and of his ultimate understanding in the 1850s of individuality as allied with industrial-capitalist "Wealth" and "Power" (Sacvan Bercovitch, "Emerson, Individualism, and Liberal Dissent," in *The Rites of Assent: Transformations in the Symbolic Construction of America* [New York, 1993], 310, 323, 330, 340). Bercovitch charts the shifts in Emerson's understanding of individualism as it moves from the utopian to the ideological, but in doing so he fascinatingly demonstrates the dynamic relation between these impulses throughout Emerson's thought and writing.

6 Ralph Waldo Emerson, "History," in *Essays and Lectures*, 237, and "Spiritual Laws," in *Essays and Lectures*, 322; hereafter abbreviated SL. Further references are cited parenthetically in the text.

7 Ralph Waldo Emerson, "The Poet," in *Essays and Lectures*, 460, 459; hereafter abbreviated P.

8 Ralph Waldo Emerson, "The Divinity School Address," in *Essays and Lectures*, 89–89; hereafter abbreviated DSA.

9 Ralph Waldo Emerson, "The American Scholar," in *Essays and Lectures*, 64, 67.

10 All major critics of Emerson have understood that if one threat to self-reliance is conformity, the other is petty self-interest or self-cherishing. See, for instance, Barbara Packer's discussion of self-reliance and self-abandonment (self-reliance, in Packer's account, rests not on "persons but powers") (B. L. Packer, *Emerson's Fall: A New Interpretation of the Major Essays* [New York, 1982], 137–47); Harold Bloom's analysis of the dialectical relation between an "Apollonian self-reliance" and a "Dionysian influx," the latter often perceptible as ecstatic energy which transforms mere individualism (Harold Bloom, "Emerson and Influence," in *A Map of Misreading* [New York, 1975], 166); and Richard Poirier's discussion of "genius" as countering the self as a conventionally defined entity, genius being what is not psychological, not moral or political, not stable, indeed not recognizable—rather, to be seen as something "vehicular, transitive, mobile," something performed in writing (Richard Poirier, "The Question of Genius," in *The Renewal of Literature: Emersonian Reflections* [New York, 1987], 89–90). I understand Emerson's "impersonality" to be *related* to, but not identical with, Poirier's "genius," Bloom's "energy," Packer's "powers," as his corrective to the deformation of personal identity. These terms rely on a neoplatonic, upward, sublimatory movement away from material particularity, whereas Emerson's impersonal moves in the opposite direction. For in impersonality Emerson is elaborating a paradox that truth to the self involves the discovery of its radical commonness.

An important contribution to this debate is George Kateb's *Emerson and Self-Reliance* (Thousand Oaks, CA, 1995), a book notable on a number of counts: first, for its excellent discussion of how antagonism and contrast lie at the heart of Emerson's notion of identity. Specifically, Kateb claims that Emerson's self-reliance depends upon an acknowledgment of the otherness and impersonality one might suppose antithetical to it; see 17. "Impersonality registers an individual's universality or infinitude" (31). In this registration what is reduced is the "biographical ego" and one acts "at the behest of 'the grand spiritual Ego,' at the behest, that is, of one's impersonal reception of the world" (33). Second, Kateb then correctly associates Emerson's impersonality with the religious ("Emerson is ravenously religious. Anything in the world...matters and is beautiful or sublime only if seen and thought of as part of a designed, intentionally coherent totality; indeed as an emanation of divinity" [65]). But, third, Kateb then tries to divorce the idea of the impersonal from the religious (because its piety embarrasses him, and because it appears to him that the driving thrust for unity, at the heart of the religious, betrays Emerson's commitment to antagonism). Kateb approves of Emerson's sense of the "interconnectedness" of things; he likes the idea of affinity, but not the idea of an "all" or a "one" to which "interconnectedness" is integral in Emerson's thought. But the very impersonality so crucial to Kateb's explanation of self-reliance is also, I argue below, inseparable from the religiousness from which Kateb would sever it. The radicalness Kateb admires depends upon the "religiousness" that he fears trivializes it. Also central in this context is Stanley Cavell's "Aversive Thinking: Emersonian Representations in Heidegger and Nietzsche," in *Conditions Handsome and Unhandsome: The Constitution of Emersonian Perfectionism* (Chicago, 1990), 33–63, an earlier, important reading of "Self-Reliance," antagonism, and transfiguration. Cavell understands Emerson's "moral perfectionism" as specifying a structure within the self that requires constant "martyrdom" (56). In other words, in Cavell's analysis of Emerson, as in his reading of Nietzsche, the "higher" self is not elsewhere or other, but is located "within." In this idea of perfectionism the self is not fixed, but neither is it absent. Perfectionism, so defined, supposes a structure essentially more conservative than that of impersonality.

11 Ralph Waldo Emerson, "Compensation," in *Essays and Lectures*, 287, 291; hereafter abbreviated C. Further references are cited parenthetically in the text.

12 Ralph Waldo Emerson, "Self-Reliance," in *Essays and Lectures*, 270, 271; hereafter abbreviated S. Further references are cited parenthetically in the text.

13 Ralph Waldo Emerson, "Illusions," in *Essays and Lectures*, 1123.

14 Ralph Waldo Emerson, "Behavior," in *Essays and Lectures*, 1042, 1043.

15 Ralph Waldo Emerson, "Circles," in *Essays and Lectures*, 406; hereafter abbreviated Ci. Further references are cited parenthetically in the text.

16 Ralph Waldo Emerson, "Experience," in *Essays and Lectures*, 476; hereafter abbreviated E.

17 Harry Frankfurt, "Identification and Externality," in *The Identities of Persons*, ed. Amélie Oksenberg Rorty (Berkeley, 1976), 242. Frankfurt's preliminary distinction between desires that are external to a self and those that are identified with it revolves around a decision made with respect to these desires (a decision rather than an attitude, for a decision, unlike an attitude, cannot be disowned). See 243–50 for what kind of decision qualifies a desire for being situated outside the person.

18 In this connection, see also this passage in "Montaigne": "There is the power of moods, each setting at nought all but its own tissue of facts and beliefs" (M 704). This passage, and the essay as a whole, are brilliant for the way in which they ventriloquize the absoluteness of point of view conferred by a mood that another mood

undermines. Understood in terms of the "machinery" of moods registered in the essay there is only "rotation" of all the "states of mind" (M 704).

19 Ralph Waldo Emerson, "Uses of Great Men," in *Essays and Lectures*, 623, 625.

20 In Emerson's "Experience," such moments of impersonal authority are dispersed across that essay after its initial pages, which acknowledge loss as personal: "the death of my son…the dearest events…the costly price of sons and lovers." "Experience," there-fore, atypically makes visible a person's relation to impersonality. See "Representing Grief: Emerson's 'Experience,'" in this volume. In essays discussed in "Emerson's Impersonal," however, Emerson blocks such a relation.

21 Emerson echoes a line from *The Enneads* (1.6.7) but not an idea, because for Plotinus impersonality is the result of an ontological change: in Plotinus the self or personality is there to be relinquished. In distinction, Emerson's text is more radi-cal, since, however oddly, as I argue below, impersonality characterizes both sides of the conversion marked by the passages discussed. See Pierre Hadot's discussion of the "levels" of self in *Plotinus; or, The Simplicity of Vision*, trans. Michael Chase (Chicago, 1993), 23–24, as well as Arnold I. Davidson's introduction to that volume, "Reading Hadot Reading Plotinus," 1–15.

22 Ralph Waldo Emerson, "Nature," in *Essays and Lectures*, 10; hereafter abbreviated N.

23 Ralph Waldo Emerson, "The Method of Nature," in *Essays and Lectures*, 121.

24 Ralph Waldo Emerson, "Intellect," in *Essays and Lectures*, 426; hereafter abbrevi-ated I.

25 Ralph Waldo Emerson, "Love," in *Essays and Lectures*, 335.

26 Henry Ware, Jr., *Personality of the Deity* (Boston, 1838), 12. In Ware's reply to Emerson's "Divinity School Address," this happiness is directly attributable to "the interest the soul takes in persons." For Ware, to destroy personality is effectively to annihilate everything recognizable, including divinity.

27 In using the word "heroic" here I have in mind what Gregory Nagy identifies as that nobility or honor which in Homer and the Bible is a direct consequence of a face-to-face encounter with God or with another heroic human. See Gregory Nagy, *The Best of the Achaeans: Concepts of the Hero in Archaic Greek Poetry* (Baltimore, 1979). Emerson reimagines something like the idea of the heroic in the presump-tion of a direct confrontation with the Over-soul, the Superpersonal Heart, the Immeasurable Mind, while in Kant this direct access to something ultimate is epitomized by moral law, possible to realize if all empirical interest is subordinated to it. It's the direct apprehension of something supreme or ultimate that in both cases suggests what might appear a bizarre analogy to the heroic. For an analogous contemporary reimagining of the heroic as defined by the immediacy of encounter with the divine or with an ultimate reality in the human, see Thomas Carlyle, *On Heroes, Hero-Worship and the Heroic in History*, ed. Carl Niemeyer (London, 1840; Lincoln, Nebr., 1966).

28 Immanuel Kant, *Fundamental Principles of the Metaphysics of Morals*, trans. T. K. Abbott (Amherst, N.Y., 1988), 60; hereafter abbreviated *FP*.

29 Ralph Waldo Emerson, "Worship," in *Essays and Lectures*, 1062.

30 Ibid., 1076.

31 Such an erasure of distinction between container and thing contained, between self and universe, is repeatedly enacted in Emerson's off-scale representations of the human, as in this formulation from "Character": "A man should be so large and columnar in the landscape, that it should deserve to be recorded, that he arose, and girded up his loins, and departed to such a place" (Ralph Waldo Emerson, "Character," in *Essays and Lectures*, 505). Or as in this one from "Montaigne": The

universe "has shown the heaven and earth to every child, and filled him with a desire for the whole; a desire raging, infinite; a hunger, as of space to be filled with planets" (M 708). In the first example, what is human and personal is matched to the landscape, is given its dimensions, as in the second example desire is matched to the stratosphere. These reconstructed propositions of the human, the human made gargantuan, are a reciprocal gesture, an accommodation in scale to the "catholic sense" of things.

32 See, for instance, the last paragraph of "Character," where the language of ownership for what is alien is explicit. Here *identifying* (in the sense of detecting) "the holy sentiment we cherish" quickly turns into *identification with* it ("only the pure and aspiring can know its face, and the only compliment they can pay it, is to own it") (Emerson, "Character," 508, 509). Such ownership is understood in terms of a religious discovery.

33 William Ellery Channing, *Unitarian Christianity and Other Essays*, ed. Irving H. Bartlett (New York, 1957), 31, 92, 108.

34 Examples of both types of statement appear frequently in the essays. Of the first type, see, for instance, all of "Compensation" and the philosophy of "Gifts" (Ralph Waldo Emerson, "Gifts," in *Essays and Lectures*, 533–38), which presumes that all have enough; for the second kind of statement, see "Nature" for an implicit critique of "the private poor man" (13); "Intellect," which critiques anyone "who is immersed in what concerns person or place" (417); and "Prudence" (in Emerson, *Essays and Lectures*, 355–68) for a dismissal of that class which needs to be concerned with health and wealth. Finally, there is a third category of statement that deserves mention in this context—those statements that dismiss the idea of social reform because you can't reform society if you don't first reform the self (the argument of "New England Reformers," in Emerson, *Essays and Lectures*, 591–609). If suffering is one's own fault, or the fault of one's too limited identification (the argument of "Spiritual Laws"), one can, according to "Fate," rectify it accordingly: "So far as a man thinks, he is free" (Emerson, "Fate," in *Essays and Lectures*, 953).

35 Walt Whitman, "Crossing Brooklyn Ferry," in *Leaves of Grass* (New York, 1980), 144, 149, secs. 1, 9.

36 Emily Dickinson, "Our journey had advanced" (no. 453), in *The Poems of Emily Dickinson: Reading Edition*, ed. R. W. Franklin (Cambridge, MA, 1998), 209.

37 Both nostalgia and rhetorically heightened summary equally testify to an eviscerated religious sense and, I have argued, to a deficient sense of the individual. They testify to a religious sense that is dismissed incompletely, that is absent but not forgotten. In the space of that absence autobiography will ultimately link up with philosophy as a newly constructed subject. This is epitomized by Friedrich Nietzsche's *Ecce Homo*, trans. Walter Kaufman (New York, 1969) (and differently attested to by Jacques Derrida's *The Ear of the Other: Otobiography, Transference, Translation* [Lincoln, NE, 1988], on the one hand, and Stanley Cavell's *A Pitch of Philosophy: Autobiographical Exercises* [Cambridge, MA, 1994], on the other).

Nietzsche presumes a separation of autobiography and philosophy that *Ecce Homo* will rectify. The exceptionalism of his position is continuously reiterated there. For instance: "I only attack causes against which I would not find allies, so that I stand alone—so that I compromise myself alone" (Nietzsche, *Ecce Homo*, 232). Derrida, writing about *Ecce Homo*, asserts, "Let it be said that I shall not read Nietzsche as a philosopher (of being, of life, or of death) or as a scholar or scientist if these three types can be said to share the abstraction of the bio-graphical and the claim to leave their lives and names out of their writing" (Derrida, *The Ear of the Other*, 7). Cavell argues that "philosophy's arrogance is linked to its ambivalence toward the autobiographical" and that, following J. L. Austin and Wittgenstein, whose methods demand an engagement of the philosophical with the auto-biographical, he will "think about an autobiographical dimension of philosophy, together with a philosophical dimension of the autobiographical" (Cavell, *A Pitch of Philosophy*, 3, 6). The point I want to make here is that the attempt to fashion anew a connection between autobiography and philosophy occurs in just that space where, as in Augustine's *Confessions*, impersonality once *assumed* the centrality of a personal existence to a discourse of the impersonal.

These three endeavors to join the autobiographical with the philosophical raise questions about a related conjunction, the personal and the impersonal—namely the question of how the two were ever separated.

38 Emmanuel Levinas, *Time and the Other*, trans. Richard A. Cohen (Pittsburgh, 1987), 51, 57. The project in this book is to show the trajectory from "anonymous" existing to subjectivity, to the alterity of the other person, an alterity with which time is associated. What interests me about this early work of Levinas is where he locates suffering (as produced by the experience of personal identity) as opposed to where Parfit locates suffering (as produced by relinquishing the idea of personal identity).

39 Of course it could be argued that to say there is no entity that would distinguish what makes persons separate is to invent an absence. For if Parfit's point is that we can't make sense of the thought that there is such an entity, why should we expect the negation of this thought—expressed in the assertion that there is no such entity—to be any more intelligible? That is to say, someone might feel that Parfit's discussion does not adequately distinguish between what is true and false and what makes sense.

40 Such resistance is not the point of Parfit's argument; indeed, on the contrary, Parfit's "point" is the moral and personal freedom of the impersonal view he espouses. But his resistance surfaces despite the point: "I would never completely lose my intui-tive belief in the Non-Reductionist View [of identity]. It is hard to be serenely con-fident in my Reductionist conclusions. It is hard to believe that personal identity is not what matters" (*RP* 280). This perseverative intuitive view enables Parfit to speak of a "person's" response to the nonexistence of personal identity.

For a fascinating discussion of how "personality" and "persons" are differently constructed by Harold Bloom, Claude Lévi-Strauss, and Jeremy Bentham, see Frances Ferguson, "Canons, Poetics, and Social Value: Jeremy Bentham and How to Do Things with People," *MLN* 110 (December 1995): 1149–64. I am particularly interested in Ferguson's discussion of how for Bentham persons are "reciprocal" constructions, "produced" by groups (1161). No sense of this reciprocity character-izes Emerson's essays; what is missing from Emerson's account of impersonality is any sense of the persons who constitute it.

FIVE

1 Simone Weil, "Concerning the Our Father," in *Waiting for God*, trans. Emma Craufurd (New York, 1951), 223–24; hereafter abbreviated *WG*. Further references are cited parenthetically in the text.

2 Simone Weil, *First and Last Notebooks*, trans. Richard Rees (London, 1970), 90; hereafter abbreviated *FL*. Further references are cited parenthetically in the text.

3 Simone Weil, *The Notebooks of Simone Weil*, trans. Arthur Wills, 2 vols. (New York, 1956), 1:59; hereafter abbreviated *N*. Further references are cited parenthetically in the text.

4 "At fourteen I fell into one of those fits of bottomless despair that come with adolescence, and I seriously thought of dying because of the mediocrity of my natural
   faculties .... After months of inward darkness, I suddenly had the everlasting conviction that any human being, even though practically devoid of natural faculties,
   can penetrate to the kingdom of truth reserved for genius, if only he longs for truth
   and perpetually concentrates all his attention upon its attainment" (*WG* 64).

5 Although on occasion Weil reverses her understanding of attention as a natural
   phenomenon (for instance, "Supernatural love and prayer are nothing else but the
   highest form of attention" [*N* 1:311]), such an appropriation of attention to the
   apparatus of the supernatural is uncharacteristic.

6 Leslie Fiedler's introduction to *Waiting for God* provides a helpful characterization
   of the terms in which Weil's "outsideness was the very *essence* of her spiritual position" (*WG* 7). She was born into a Jewish family in 1909, but her values growing up,
   in Fiedler's words, "were simply 'French,' that is to say, a combination of Greek and
   secularized Christian elements" (*WG* 13). For a detailed account of how Weil's complex religious understanding mutated throughout her life, see Simone Pétrement,
   Simone Weil: A Life, trans. Raymond Rosenthal (New York, 1976), hereafter abbreviated *SW*, specifically, for example, "London (1942–43)," in which Pétrement discusses
   Weil's religious writings in the last year of her life. In one of these papers discussing
   the basis of human obligation, Weil does not name God, because "to gather people
   behind Christian aspirations... it is necessary to try to define them in terms that an
   atheist might adhere to completely," in terms "acceptable to Catholics, Protestants,
   and atheists" (quoted in *SW* 493). See also Peter Winch's discussion of Weil's "supernatural" in terms of situations that generate "wonder" for which no explanations can
   suffice (Peter Winch, *Simone Weil: "The Just Balance"* [Cambridge, 1989], 207, 208).
   Winch's interesting account of Weil attempts to naturalize supernatural language,
   by aligning it with philosophical language in general and Wittgenstein's language
   in particular. In this way Winch marks his understanding of the erosion of the line
   between philosophy and religion in Weil's writing.

7 The problem is not that we are voyeuristically attending to private journals that we
   have no right to see; Weil extends us that right when she takes pains to ensure the
   writings' availability. Weil entrusted her notebooks and essays indirectly to Father
   Perrin: "Who knows," she wrote to him on May 26, 1942, if the thoughts "I bear
   in me are not sent, partly at any rate, so that you should make some use of them"
   (*WG* 101). It is reasonable to suppose that when Weil instructed Father Perrin to
   make use of her thoughts (*WG* 100), she meant him to make them available for
   publication, which he did.

8 The idea that God is unrepresentable reiterates the convention of a faceless
   divine—discoverable in phenomena as dissimilar as Maimonides' "negative attributes"; Pseudo-Dionysus's plural names; Augustine's inability to place God in relation to orienting dimensions of time, place, or origin; Spinoza's undiscriminating
   Nature; and the Bible's tautological "I am that I am." Much of the prose in the
   notebooks, and in the edited essays as well, is devoted to Weil's refiguration of this
   unrepresentability in terms of an outright negation.

9 Simone Weil, *Lectures on Philosophy*, trans. Hugh Price (Cambridge, 1978), 193.

10 Françoise Meltzer's discussion of "parataxis," on the "abrupt transition of registers"
   among topics and across disciplinary boundaries (Meltzer is particularly interested
   in how Weil connects philosophy, religion, and political activism), bears on the jux-
   tapositions between different inhabitations of the subject position; and, specifically,
   on the relation between believing and not listening to believing (Françoise Meltzer,
   "The Hands of Simone Weil," *Critical Inquiry* 27 [Summer 2001]: 611–28).

11 Simone Weil, *The Need for Roots: Prelude to a Declaration of Duties towards Mankind*, trans. A. F. Wills (1952; London, 1996), 277–78; hereafter abbreviated *NR*. Further references are cited parenthetically in the text.

12 Schopenhauer would have found this an uneccentric association. In *The World as Will and Representation*, Schopenhauer associated "genius" with "the ability…to discard entirely our own personality for a time in order to remain *pure knowing subject*" (Arnold Schopenhauer, *The World as Will and Representation*, trans. E. F. J. Payne, 2 vols. [New York, 1969], 2:185–86; quoted by Jonathan Crary, *Suspensions of Perception: Attention, Spectacle, and Modern Culture* [Cambridge, MA, 1999], 315 n. 75).

And William James reiterates that the link between genius and attention is a conventional one (shared by Helvétius, Buffon, Cuvier, and Chesterfield), which James in fact reverses: "Geniuses are commonly believed to excel other men in their power of sustained attention.…*But it is their genius making them attentive, not their attention making geniuses of them*" (James would then produce an account of genius associated with an escape from habit) (William James, *The Principles of Psychology*, ed. Frederick H. Burkhardt and Fredson Bowers, 2 vols. in 1 [Cambridge, MA, 1981], 400). It's the link of genius to "being dead" that renders Weil's formulation novel.

13 "Our deep purpose should aim solely at increasing the power of attention with a view to prayer; as, when we write, we draw the shape of the letter on paper, not with a view to the shape, but with a view to the idea we want to express. To make this the sole and exclusive purpose of our studies is the first condition to be observed if we are to put them to right use" (*WG* 108).

14 The indistinction of this effort is one for which we have distaste; specifically, we have "a far more violent repugnance for true attention than the flesh has for bodily fatigue. This something is much more closely connected with evil than is the flesh. That is why every time that we really concentrate our attention, we destroy the evil in ourselves. If we concentrate with this intention, a quarter of an hour of attention is better than a great many good works" (*WG* 111). Although the formulation initially sounds Protestant in that it calls to mind faith as being better than works, it displaces that formulation by the value term *attention*, to which faith and doctrine are equally irrelevant. See the remarkable notebook entry (*N* 2:354) that elaborates the complex relation between attention and action.

15 See Revelation 21–22 as well as Song of Solomon 4:9–13 and George Herbert's "Love (III)." In Weil's adaptation of the reversal of "Love (III)," the imperiousness of master become dominating slave seems to linger ("And know you not, says Love, who bore the blame? / …You must sit down, says Love, and taste my meat"), evidence of the haughtiness of Love's service, his bad faith, which Weil simultaneously acknowledges and represses (George Herbert, "Love (III)," in *George Herbert*, ed. Louis L. Martz [Oxford, 1994], 167).

16 "There are two objects for us to love. First, that which is worthy of love but which, in our sense of the word existence, does not exist. That is God. And second, that which exists, but in which there is nothing possible to love. That is necessity. We must love both" (*FL* 324). If such love is inseparable from suffering, seeing this connection is said to be better than displacing both love and suffering: "'I am suffering.' That is preferable to: 'This landscape is ugly'" (*N* 1:200).

17 Of the use of punishment and pain in training, Weil wrote: "When you set out to train a dog…you don't whip him for the sake of whipping him, but in order to train him, and with this object in mind you only whip him when he fails in some exercise. And from time to time you see no harm in exchanging the whip for a lump

of sugar (there are even times when the sugar alone is able to produce results); what matters is not the whip or the sugar, but the training" (*N* 2:425).

18 See especially Empson's discussion of the interactions between the implications of a word which remain unassimilable to any unitary formula (see William Empson, *The Structure of Complex Words,* ed. Jonathan Culler [1951; Cambridge, MA, 1989], 1–84, 289–306).

19 In Bataille's "Labyrinth (or the Constitution of Beings)," similar figures are equally conflated: "We try to place ourselves in the presence of God, but God alive within us demands at once that we die; we only know how to grasp this by killing" (Georges Bataille, *Inner Experience,* trans. Leslie Anne Boldt [1954; Albany, NY, 1988], 88).

20 "Vegetative energy" is further defined as that which is "not mobile.…It cannot give itself a direction" (*FL* 223). The imagination is unable to represent the vegetative to itself, because "the imagination is the supplementary form of energy" (*N* 1:221). "Supplementary, voluntary energy should be used up to the point of exhaustion in performing obligatory tasks. Or else it should be burnt up in contemplation" (*FL* 223). Orpheus without Eurydice, Niobe without her children—these are examples of vegetative energy; see *FL* 234.

21 In *First and Last Notebooks* Weil comments on her dictate, "Love what is intolerable. Embrace what is made of iron, press one's flesh against the metallic harshness and chill" by insisting that "this is not any kind of masochism. What excites masochists is only the semblance of cruelty, because they don't know what cruelty is. In any case, what one has to embrace is not cruelty, it is blind indifference and brutality. Only in this way does love become impersonal" (*FL* 260). I take Weil to mean that love for that toward which one is neutral or aversive is impersonal love, all other love being generated by preferences, hence by personality.

22 Simone Weil, "Human Personality," in *The Simone Weil Reader,* ed. George A. Panichas (Wakefield, RI, 1977), 319; hereafter abbreviated HP.

23 In *First and Last Notebooks* Weil wrote: "The fixed point of view is the root of injustice. Plane geometry is an exercise in thought without a point of view. Everything is on one plane" (*FL* 270), and such a description explains the sense in which geometry could be conceived as having supernatural implications.

24 Weil might have been remembering the great lines in Sophocles' *Antigone* spoken about Niobe: "Pitiful was the death that stranger died, / our queen once, Tantalus' daughter. The rock / it covered her over, like stubborn ivy it grew. / Still, as she wastes, the rain / and snow companion her. / Pouring down from her mourning eyes comes the water that soaks the stone. / My own putting to sleep a god has planned like hers" (Sophocles, *Antigone,* trans. Elizabeth Wyckoff, in *Greek Tragedies,* ed. David Grene and Richmond Lattimore [Chicago, 1960], lines 824–31). The slippage in Sophocles' lines between body, ivy, and rock is analogous to that in Weil's lines between grieving and thoughts of eating, phenomena which are disallowed any consolatory separations. In Sophocles' lines, rain and snow both displace tears and become tears, as in Weil's lines to begin to think of eating is at once a radical break from grieving and part of the same state of being "worn out." Both passages leave *unconcealed* the prior state ostensibly left behind.

25 I am thinking not only of Weil's factory work at Alsthom, Carnaud, and Renault but of her willingness to credit factory work as serious, not only because it was productive (nonabstract, nonimaginary), but also because it was committed to taking one's own productive capacities and those of other people seriously, as well as to seriously measuring the cost—human value, human dignity—exacted for such productivity.

26 Stein—whose study of philosophy and whose conversion from Judaism first to atheism, and then to Catholicism, courts comparison with Weil by virtue of how little the two have in common outside of the biographical outline—died in Auschwitz in 1942, a year prior to Weil's death in an Ashford sanatorium.

27 Here I call to mind Edith Stein's conception of empathy as sparing one dangerous consequences: "He who has never looked a danger in the face himself can still experience himself as brave or cowardly in the empathic representation of another's situation" (Edith Stein, *The Collected Works of Edith Stein*, trans. Waltraut Stein, vol. 3, *On the Problem of Empathy* [Washington, DC, 1989], 115). How much Stein remains protected against what lies outside the "I," to the perception of which her project is committed, is indicated by her clinical designation of an other as a "foreign living body" (ibid., 92).

28 T. S. Eliot, *After Strange Gods: A Primer of Modern Heresy* (London, 1934), 42–43.

29 The phrase is Manju Jain's in glossing a letter of Eliot's (to I. A. Richards), the sentiment of which echoes the passage cited above (Manju Jain, *T. S. Eliot and American Philosophy: The Harvard Years* [Cambridge, 1992], 109).

SIX

1 Passages in *Four Quartets* are identified by poem and section number; where previous citation or the discussion itself makes the reference clear, quotations are not identified in each instance.

2   the whine in the rigging,
   The menace and caress of wave that breaks on water,
   The distant rote in the granite teeth,
   And the wailing warning from the approaching headland
   Are all sea voices....

3 T. S. Eliot, *Selected Essays* (New York: Harcourt, Brace and World, 1932; repr. 1964), 247; hereafter abbreviated *SE*. Citations are to the 1964 edition. Further references are cited parenthetically in the text.

4 "Little Gidding" III.

5 "Truly My Satan thou art but a Dunce / And dost not know the Garment from the Man / Every Harlot was a Virgin once / Nor canst thou ever change Kate into Nan. / Tho thou art Worshipd by the Names Divine / Of Jesus & Jehovah thou art still / The Son of Man in weary Nights decline / The lost Travellers Dream under the Hill" (*Blake's Poetry and Designs*, ed. Mary Lynn Johnson and John E. Grant [New York: W. W. Norton and Co., 1979], 373). Eliot's essay on Blake speaks of Blake's "gift of hallucinated vision" (*SE* 279), a description especially applicable to the last two lines, where strangeness issues from a condensation of entities that does not preclude a disconnection among them.

6 In "East Coker" II, the speaker is in fact repeatedly situated on the rim of his own experience, which he regards hypothetically. Thus, for instance, when he pontificates, "The only wisdom we can hope to acquire / Is the wisdom of humility"—adding cursorily for emphasis of how much humility is necessary "humility is endless"—he appears to be calculating humility and prescribing it to himself in terms that make it impossible for what he is particularizing and quantifying to be recognizable *as* "humility." His expression thus reveals a defective relation to experience. For one's proper relation to humility—if it is humility—could not be propositional, as one's proper relation to death could not be in the imagining of it as a calamity one remains alive to mourn. To prescribe humility to oneself (as a goal or in an amount) is to stand outside the experience of humility, to make humility a

proposition rather than an experience, just as in "all gone" death has been made an inevitability attributed to others that can be viewed without being owned.

7 This phrase in "Burnt Norton" IV anticipates the emergence of the ghost in "Little Gidding" II.

8 Paul Valéry, "La Pythie," quoted in Jacques Lacan, *The Language of the Self: The Function of Language in Psychoanalysis*, trans. Anthony Wilden (Baltimore: Johns Hopkins Univ. Press, 1968), 138: "Voici parler une Sagesse / Et sonner cette auguste Voix / Qui se connaît quand elle sonne / N'être plus la voix de personne / Tant que des ondes et des bois!"

9 Christopher Ricks notes the allusion to Pound in *T. S. Eliot and Prejudice* (Berkeley: Univ. of California Press, 1988), 260; hereafter abbreviated *EP*. I am grateful to Christopher Ricks for his generous suggestions during the writing of this essay.

10 Eliot is constantly making names strange ("Love is the unfamiliar name") either by elevating common nouns to proper names (as in the previous example), or changing names to nouns. The point and the examples are Christopher Ricks's in relation to "Grimpen," a place-name in Arthur Conan Doyle's *The Hound of the Baskervilles*, which becomes a noun in "East Coker," as the noun "love" becomes a *name* in "Little Gidding." See Ricks's discussion of "the unnaming power of *Four Quartets*" in *EP*, 248–51.

In *Knowledge and Experience in the Philosophy of F. H. Bradley*, Eliot writes: "Try to think of what anything would be if you refrained from naming it altogether, and it will dissolve into sensations which are not objects; and it will not be that particular object which it is, until you have found the right name for it" (Farrar, Straus, 1964; repr. New York: Columbia Univ. Press, 1989), 134; hereafter cited as *KEB*. Citations are to the 1989 edition. Further references are cited parenthetically in the text.

In distinction, in *The Waste Land* names proliferate ("They called me the hyacinth girl"; "And I Tiresias have foresuffered all"; Madam Sosostris; Marie; Sweeney; Mrs. Porter), as they do in Eliot's notes ("Tristan und Isolde," or *Elizabeth*, which name characters as well as the titles of works).

11 The point about impersonality in *Four Quartets* is not the substitution of writing for voice, not that aspects of writing displace, accompany, or come to constitute voice, for although the "depersonalizing...is at odds with the Romantic convention of a personal voice," Eliot's alternative to personal utterance is not stylistic or artificial. The quotation is from John Paul Riquelme's *Harmony of Dissonances: T. S. Eliot, Romanticism, and Imagination* (Baltimore: Johns Hopkins Univ. Press, 1991), 78. See Riquelme's analysis of Eliot's "ventriloquism of writing" (76) in *Four Quartets*. Such a phrase characterizes Riquelme's sense of the displacement of voice by something like "style." In Riquelme's account, "style" can have a visual character ("The voice is like the Cubist presentation of a human head made up of various geometrical shapes...which are not natural but instead call attention to their made character" [74]), or style can proliferate allusions ("The historical echolalia of poetic production and response involves reverberations through an indeterminate hollow space that existed before the particular instance of writing or reading" [75]) which preempt personal voice. Riquelme's commitment to the artificial, nonheuristic quality of voice, as well as to the fact that the "singular self [is made] multiple" (76), belies the pains taken throughout by Eliot to represent speech which is not individual or plural. For even at its limit point—"'What! are *you* here?' / Although we were not"—there are not two persons speaking simultaneously. The point about speech which cannot be precisely attributed to this one or that one is not that it is shared or owned. Rather, one speaking to another, and also *for* another, produces speech that is not fully recognizable in either paradigm.

At the same time, the strangeness of such a representation does not derive from ventriloquism. The speaker is not impersonating various figures whom in fact he is not. (This is the difference between Eliot and Browning.) Nor does understanding his speech require supposing a "dispersal of the poet's self through identification with a multitude" (77). The fault of such explanations—and here one could include Hugh Kenner's notion of "echo" and William Arrowsmith's notion of "palimpsest," to which Riquelme's discussion is indebted—is that the heuristic, probing quality of voice is sacrificed to explanatory systems that make its experiential texture inaudible.

12 In *Four Quartets* a voice can be distinguished more by a stance (in "East Coker" II incredulity, for instance: "What is the late November doing / With the disturbance of the spring?") or by a performative (for instance, there is a voice that repudiates ["Here is a place of disaffection....Not here"; "Burnt Norton" III], a voice that prescribes ["Old men ought to be explorers"; "East Coker" V], a voice that stages reflections ["You say I am repeating / Something I have said before. I shall say it again. / Shall I say it again?" "East Coker" III], and a voice distinguished by its habitation within a grammatical or metrical structure [as is the voice that is governed by the four-beat line of section 3 of each of the *Four Quartets*]) than by a presumptive subjectivity. But such descriptions have only a momentary pertinence. They refer to fleeting incarnations, not to the representation of persons.

13 A particular manifestation of voice can often seem only superficially complete, compelling an element extraneous to itself which it cannot supply from within but which it can indicate. For instance, when in "East Coker" III a speaker refers to "The wild thyme unseen and the wild strawberry, / The laughter in the garden, echoed ecstasy / Not lost, but requiring, pointing to the agony / Of death and birth," "the agony of death and birth" are the necessity—the direct object—which "requiring" specifies, even as any rigorous condition seems only technically fulfilled by the completion of the grammatical unit. For the gerund form itself, and this trisyllabic instantiation of it which stalls or breaks the meter, gestures away from, and outside of, the banality of the expression "the agony of death and birth," too laxly—too loosely—conceived to fulfill an imperative like "requiring."

14 "Person-stage" is a term introduced in response to the question of what matters in survival posited by thought experiments of a person who divides into two numerically different persons, with a persistence to a sufficient part of the brain, each of whom is qualitatively equal to the other, in order to consider whether the fission descendants are the same person as each other or as the original person. Logically, they cannot be either. Is what matters in such a division an "all-or-nothing" personal identity (which is a one-to-one relationship and does not admit of degree) or a relative mental connectedness and/or continuity? "Person-stage," indicating something more or less momentary, is a term that implies connectedness or continuity without implying identity. (See David Lewis, "Survival and Identity," in *Personal Identity*, ed. Raymond Martin and John Barresi [Malden, MA: Blackwell Publishing, 2003], 147.) In distinction, "personal identity"—whether through Locke's idea of consciousness, which is equivalent to memory; Hume's "resemblance," which "causes us to forge a succession of perceptions into a persisting object" (46); Kant's *transcendental unity of apperception*" (Kant's "I think") (61–62); or William James's "*act of appropriation*," in which a moment of consciousness is replaced by another moment that "knows its own predecessor" (69)—presumes the transformation of "successive" stages, thoughts, or temporal moments into a singularity, into an entity that is *the same*. There is no singularity—no *the same*—in the idea of Buddhist aggregates or (for Derek Parfit) in the idea of person-stages

(Derek Parfit, "Lewis, Perry, and What Matters," in *The Identities of Persons*, ed. Amélie Oksenberg Rorty [Berkeley: Univ. of California Press, 1976], 91–107).

15 Catherine Gallagher coined the evocative term "nobody's story" to indicate a web of features—"nothingness," "disembodiment," "elusiveness," "withdrawal," "dispossession," and "debt," implicated in the rhetorical constructions of authors and fictional characters among eighteenth-century women writers, in *Nobody's Story: The Vanishing Acts of Women Writers in the Marketplace, 1670–1820* (Berkeley: Univ. of California Press, 1994), xiii–xxiv. In characterizing voice and memory as "no one's" in Eliot's poem, I am pointing toward manifestations of voice in Eliot's poem not intelligible in terms of the very entities (fictional characters, authors) of whom debt and dispossession come to be constitutive in Gallagher's analysis.

16 See Helen Gardner's discussion of Eliot's exchanges with John Hayward about his revisions of the passage (Helen Gardner, *The Composition of "Four Quartets"* [New York: Oxford Univ. Press, 1978], 174–81; hereafter abbreviated *CFQ*; further references are cited parenthetically in the text). Eliot associates the speaker's meeting of the ghost with Dante's meeting of Brunetto Latini—an allusion established first by the terza rima, then by the cry of recognition, and, following almost immediately, by a characterization of the ghost's features which virtually recapitulates Dante's "I fixed my eyes upon his baked, brown features, / so that the scorching of his face could not / prevent my mind from recognizing him" (*The Divine Comedy of Dante Alighieri: Inferno, A Verse Translation*, trans. Allen Mandelbaum [Berkeley: Univ. of California Press, 1980; repr. Bantam Classic, 1982], 133; citations are to the 1982 edition). But in divesting the poem of Brunetto's name, Eliot also refuses the specificity of such an identification. Eliot, writing to Hayward about the omission of the name, explained his revision as follows: "The visionary figure has now become somewhat more definite and will no doubt be identified by some readers with Yeats though I do not mean anything so precise as that. However, I do not wish to take the responsibility of putting Yeats or anybody else into Hell and I do not want to impute to him the particular vice which took Brunetto there. Secondly, although the reference to that Canto is intended to be explicit, I wished the effect of the whole to be Purgatorial which is much more appropriate" (*CFQ* 176). Notwithstanding Eliot's erasure of the name, and his introduction of a different figure, Yeats, with whom the ghost might be associated (a figure whose relevance for the poem is equally disputed by him), Eliot's recollection of certain features of Brunetto's speech in *Four Quartets* continues to engage Dante's passage. I elaborate in my text.

Eliot's lines also suggest a relation to Yeats's play *Purgatory*, where "a dead, living…man!" (*The Collected Plays of W. B. Yeats* [London: Macmillan, 1934], 435) returns from purgatory to "re-live" his "transgressions…not once / But many times" (431).

17 Eliot, interpreting Bradley, viewed monism and pluralism as complementary (*KEB* 146).

18 In my understanding of this canto, I am indebted to a conversation with Lee Patterson. See also Leonard Barkan's discussion of self-eternalizing in this passage as an act of "educational pederasty" (Leonard Barkan, *Transuming Passion: Ganymede and the Erotics of Humanism* [Stanford, CA: Stanford Univ. Press, 1991], 58–59).

19 Stéphane Mallarmé, *Selected Poems*, trans. C. F. MacIntyre (Berkeley: Univ. of California Press, 1957), 88. This is the second stanza: "Eux, comme un vil sursaut d'hydre oyant jadis l'ange / Donner un sens plus pur aux mots de la tribu /

Proclamèrent très haut le sortilège bu / Dans le flot sans honneur de quelque noir mélange."

20 The final lines in their entirety: "Tel qu'en Lui-même enfin l'éternité le change / Le Poëte suscite avec un glaive nu / Son siècle épouvanté de n'avoir pas connu / Que la mort triomphait dans cette voix etrange!"

21 Mallarmé acknowledges the brilliance is conferred by Mallarmé's own "idée" of him ("Si notre idée avec ne sculpte un bas-relief / Dont la tombe de Poe éblouissante s'orne"), that is, on an idea of Poe that Mallarmé shares with eternity against the opinion of Poe's century.

22 Identification is also resisted in Shelley's poem—and, for instance, in Paul de Man's interpretation of it, "Shelley Disfigured," in *The Rhetoric of Romanticism* (New York: Columbia Univ. Press, 1984), 93–124. But one would not glean this from Eliot, who designates Shelley's identification of Rousseau with an ease negated by the poem.

23 Jeffrey M. Perl, *Skepticism and Modern Enmity: Before and After Eliot* (Baltimore: Johns Hopkins Univ. Press, 1989), 58–62.

24 The relativism Perl discusses pertains more to states and designations that could be identified than to persons who could be. Perl's examples are the absolute and the conventional, ontological vacancy and ontological plenitude, beginning and end, nirvana and samsara.

25 Maurice Blanchot, "The Narrative Voice," in *The Gaze of Orpheus and Other Literary Essays*, trans. Lydia Davis (New York: Station Hill Press, 1981), 142.

26 Giorgio Agamben, "Absolute Immanence," in *Potentialities: Collected Essays in Philosophy* (Stanford, CA: Stanford Univ. Press, 1999), 232–33. Further references are cited parenthetically in the text.

27 Eliot's lines contain an elision, Christopher Ricks implicitly suggests, which Eliot was recalling from pt. 7 of Tennyson's *In Memoriam*: "He is not here; but far away / The noise of life begins again, / And ghastly through the drizzling rain / On the bald street breaks the blank day" (*EP* 258).

28 In a review of Donne's sermons published in the *Athenaeum* Eliot praised "the method, the analogy, the repetition…once used by a greater master of the sermon than either Donne, Andrews or Latimer: it is the method of the Fire-Sermon preached by the Buddha" (T. S. Eliot, "The Preacher as Artist," *Athenaeum*, November 28, 1919, 1252). Eliot was extolling a formula in which repetition could enlist understanding and enlightenment. He read these suttas in Henry Clarke Warren's *Buddhism in Translations* (Delhi: Motilal Banarsidass, 1986; repr. 1998), hereafter abbreviated *BT* (citations are to the 1998 edition), and in Buddhaghosa's fifth-century explication of those Pali suttas, Bhadantācariya Buddhaghosa, *The Path of Purification (Visuddhimagga)*, trans. Bhikkhu Ñāṇamoli (Seattle: BPS Pariyatti Editions, 1975; repr. 1991) (citations are to the 1991 edition).

Cleo McNelly Kearns complements our knowledge of Eliot's familiarity with the Mahayana tradition as discussed by Perl and Tuck by her consideration of Eliot's relation to the Pali canon, in *T. S. Eliot and Indic Traditions: A Study in Poetry and Belief* (Cambridge: Cambridge Univ. Press, 1987). See Kearns's brief but excellent discussion of how Eliot's interest in the Pali canon was influenced by Irving Babbitt, as well as her discussion of which texts were compiled in the Warren anthology, and of how key words were translated.

29 *The Middle Length Discourses of the Buddha: A New Translation of the Majjhima Nikāya*, trans. Bhikkhu Ñāṇamoli, ed. and rev. Bhikkhu Bodhi (Boston: Wisdom Publications, 1995), 213; hereafter abbreviated *MN*.

30 See the discussion of kinds of repetitions in the introduction to the suttas in *MN* 52–53.

31 Bhikkhu Ñāṇamoli, *The Life of the Buddha, as It Appears in the Pali Canon, the Oldest Authentic Record* (Kandy, Sri Lanka: Buddhist Publication Society, 1972; repr. 1984), 234–35. Citations are to the 1984 edition.

32 The word "conceive" in Pali is used to indicate distorted thinking. Bhikkhu Bodhi explains: Conceiving may indicate "direct identification ('he conceives X')" or "inherence ('he conceives in X')" or "contrast or derivation ('he conceives from X')" or "simple appropriation ('he conceives X to be "mine"')." Bodhi goes on: "The activity of conceiving thus seems to comprise the entire range of subjectively tinged cognition, from the impulses and thoughts in which the sense of personal identity is still inchoate to elaborate intellectual structures in which it has been fully explicated" (*MN* 1163).

33 *Numerical Discourses of the Buddha: An Anthology of Suttas from the Aṅguttara Nikāya*, trans. and ed. Nyanaponika Thera and Bhikkhu Bodhi (Walnut Creek, CA: Altamira Press, 1999), 19.

34 A "man with good eyes" contemplating the body is to see elements, not a composed entity: "head-hairs, body-hairs, nails, teeth, skin, flesh." He is enjoined to regard these with as much neutrality as if he were looking at a vessel full of various sorts of grain, "such as hill rice, red rice, beans, peas, millet, and white rice." He is to "review" what he sees thus: "This is hill rice, this is red rice, these are beans" (*MN* 147). In the same way he is to review the elements of the body as independent of each other.

35 Nanomoli, *The Life of the Buddha*, 225. The core teaching of the conditionality at the heart of Buddhist doctrine is dependent origination, which subtly anatomizes, for instance, the eye, the visible forms that constitute its objects, and the consciousness of those objects resulting in sensation (the technical term is "contact")—which, in its turn, is productive of feeling (a reaction that is either pleasant, unpleasant, or neutral) and in response to which there is either identification with the feeling as a property of self (and suffering) or no identification with the feeling (and freedom). The teaching is so central that it is said, "one who sees the Dhamma [*Dharma*, in Sanskrit] sees dependent origination" (*MN* 283). *The Path of Purification* (526–604) explains.

36 *The Connected Discourses of the Buddha: A New Translation of the Saṃyutta Nikāya*, trans. Bhikkhu Bodhi, 2 vols. (Boston: Wisdom Publications, 2000), 2:1236.

37 Some passages more uncompromisingly deconstruct component parts so that it is impossible to transpose mentality and materiality into any kind of entity: "Just as when a space is enclosed with timber and creepers and grass and clay, there comes to be the term 'house,' so too, when a space is enclosed with bones and sinews and flesh and skin, there comes to be the term 'material form.'...Just as when the component parts such as axles, wheels, frame poles, etc., are arranged in a certain way, there comes to be the mere term of common usage 'chariot,' yet in the ultimate sense when each part is examined there is no chariot,—...just as when trunk, branches, foliage, etc., are placed in a certain way, there comes to be the mere term of common usage 'tree,' yet in the ultimate sense, when each component is examined, there is no tree,—so too, when there are the five aggregates [as objects] of clinging, there comes to be the mere term of common usage 'a being,' 'a person,' yet in the ultimate sense, when each component is examined there is no being as a basis for the assumption 'I am' or 'I'; in the ultimate sense there is only mentality-materiality. The vision of one who sees in this way is called correct vision" (*The Path of Purification*, 612–13).

38 For instance, "Even if bandits were to sever you savagely limb by limb with a two handled saw, he who gave rise to a mind of hate towards them would not be carrying out my teaching....If you keep this advice on the simile of the saw constantly in mind, do you see any course of speech, trivial or gross, that you could not endure?" The analogy secures understanding by translating the didactic content into an experiential imagining, the point of whose extremity is to insist nothing should assail the mind (*MN* 223). In a variant sutta on the simile of the saw, to be savagely severed "limb by limb" might have physical consequences, but it should not have mental consequences. When "unremitting mindfulness [is] established" mind will remain tranquil, even when "fists, clods, sticks, and knives assail this body" (*MN* 280). In the case of both physical and mental pain, if one can't remain immune to the hurt, one must remain immune to the reaction which takes the hurt personally, dispassionately understanding: "This is not my self" (*MN* 279).

39 Critics have glossed the paradoxical features of Eliot's poem by recapitulating his interest in Herakleitos and John of the Cross, interests which certainly complemented his study of Buddhist cosmology. The paradoxes of the Book of Common Prayer could also be included in such a formative repository. Although Eliot's text invites explanations which are combinatory, the fact that the poem's parts issue from origins which are technically inhospitable to each other, while nonetheless being intermingled, is contributive to the illusion of its being a systematic whole, even as it defies any attempt to say which system might be the governing one.

40 The passages are from "The Dry Salvages" V; "Little Gidding" II; "East Coker" II; "East Coker" III; "Burnt Norton" III; "Little Gidding" V; and "Little Gidding" III.

41 When Hayward proposed revising the line to read "the live nettle and the dead," Eliot replied: "I cannot fall in with your suggestion....The dead nettle is the family of flowering plant[s] of which the White Archangel is one of the commonest....If I wrote 'the live nettle and the dead' it would tend to suggest a dead stinging nettle instead of a quite different plant" (*CFQ*, 200).

42 Eliot glossing Bradley: "The real world is not inside or outside; it is not presented in consciousness or to consciousness as a particular group of entities, for as presented it is not in or to consciousness at all: it simply is" (*KEB* 139).

43 Another acknowledgment of a constellation which could not but be fugitive is voiced in "The Dry Salvages" V, in counterpoint to the idea of fixity: "But to apprehend / The point of intersection of the timeless / With time, is an occupation for the saint— / No occupation either, but something given / And taken, in a lifetime's death in love, / Ardour and selflessness and self-surrender." Here the qualifications and negations so modify our sense of what is being constructed ("an occupation...No occupation...selflessness and self-surrender") that although something is said to be "incarnated" ("the gift half understood, is Incarnation"), there would be no way to imagine embodiment, which cannot even be conceived of outside of the evanescence that is its changing conditions.

44 In the 1933 *After Strange Gods,* a book Eliot never reprinted, it was the adherence to dogma—specifically to original sin—which differentiated one set of writers (Lawrence, Pound, Arnold, and Hardy) from a superior set of writers (Sophocles, Conrad, and Henry James). Specifically, "with the disappearance of the idea of Original Sin" the human beings represented by the first set of writers "become less and less real" (T. S. Eliot, *After Strange Gods: A Primer of Modern Heresy,* Page-Barbour Lectures at the University of Virginia [New York: Harcourt Brace, 1934], 45–46, 62; hereafter abbreviated *ASG*).

45 Orthodoxy, in that book's estimation, is elevated above tradition, which Eliot associated with "habitual actions, habits and customs, from the most significant religious rite to our conventional way of greeting a stranger" (*ASG* 18).

46 Emily Dickinson, "It was not Death, for I stood up" (no. 355), in *The Poems of Emily Dickinson: Reading Edition,* ed. R. W. Franklin (Cambridge, MA: Harvard Univ. Press, 1998).

47 *The Waste Land,* "What the Thunder Said."

48 "Little Gidding" IV.

49 "East Coker" V.

SEVEN

1 Herman Melville, *The Confidence Man: His Masquerade,* ed. Hershel Parker, Norton Critical Edition (New York: W. W. Norton and Co., 1971), 59; hereafter abbreviated *CM.* Further references are cited parenthetically in the text.

2 "What am I? and What is?" (Ralph Waldo Emerson, "Divinity School Address," in *Essays and Lectures,* ed. Joel Porte [New York: Library of America, 1983], 75).

3 "Original character," Melville writes in *The Confidence Man,* in a passage suggesting another image for the surpassing of characterological limits, contrary to what "is popularly held to entitle characters in fiction being original," namely, "something personal—confined to itself," is "like a revolving Drummond light, raying away from itself all round it—everything is lit by it, everything starts up to it (mark how it is with Hamlet), so that...there follows upon the adequate conception of such a character, an effect, in its way, akin to that which in Genesis attends upon the beginning of things" (*CM* 205). Though in *The Confidence Man* characters are being discussed as metacritical concepts, and in *Billy Budd* characters are being depicted as persons, in both cases characters are represented as nonindependent entities, for "original" in relation to the Genesis metaphor implies something initial, not something otherwise unique.

4 Herman Melville, *Billy Budd, Sailor (An Inside Narrative),* ed. Harrison Hayford and Merton M. Sealts, Jr. (Chicago: Univ. of Chicago Press, 1962), 53; hereafter abbreviated *BB.* Further references are cited parenthetically in the text.

5 Nothing is known of Billy's or Claggart's background. Billy is a "foundling" though "noble descent was as evident in him as in a blood horse" (*BB 52*), while Claggart, who also "looked like a man of high quality, social and moral" (*BB* 64), is rumored to be "a *chevalier*" (*BB* 65). That is, he is a swindler by one definition, and a member of nobility by another—like Billy, his opposite, of unknown origin ("About as much was really known...of the master-at-arms' career before entering the service as an astronomer knows about a comet's travels prior to its first observable appearance in the sky" [*BB* 67]), but presumed aristocratic.

6 The Dansker would be included in the category of "normal" (*BB* 74) because his "guarded cynicism" (*BB* 71) is implicitly associated with "the ruled undemonstrative distrustfulness" (*BB* 87) by which "men of the world" are characterized, even though the Dansker is not a man of the world. Vere is associated with such a category because of his "pedantry" (*BB* 109), his "ambition" (*BB* 129), and his "sterling" non-"brilliant" qualities (*BB* 61).

7 Hershel Parker explains the discrepant descriptions of Vere in chaps. 21 and 22 with reference to the novel's incompletion (*Reading Billy Budd* [Evanston, IL: Northwestern Univ. Press, 1990], 142–47). Hayford and Sealts interpret the same ambiguities in terms of Melville's "deliberately...throwing 'cross-lights' on

Vere" (*BB* 38). I agree with the latter: Vere, like Billy and Claggart, is consistently described in contradictory terms.

8 Such erosions of characterological distinction are elaborated in Barbara Johnson's discussion of the story's establishment and dissolution of binaries in that tale in terms of kinds of readers: Billy is a naive reader, Claggart is a paranoid or ironic reader, and Vere is a reader who must judge impartially in relation to martial law ("Melville's Fist: The Execution of *Billy Budd*," repr. in *Herman Melville: A Collection of Critical Essays*, ed. Myra Jehlen [Englewood Cliffs, NJ: Prentice Hall, 1994], 238–40). In Johnson's analysis, these distinctive ways of reading are not sustained. "Billy takes every sign as transparently readable" when it is "consistent with transparent peace, order, and authority," and "Claggart, for whom every sign can be read as its opposite, neglects to doubt the transparency of any sign that tends to confirm his own doubts" (238). Moreover, although Vere judges to avoid a murder—to avert a mutiny like that of the Nore—this judgment produces the murder from which it becomes indistinguishable. In "*Billy Budd*: After the Homosexual," Eve Sedgwick examines more sweeping, social binarisms, noting comparable elisions between the mutiny plot and the homosexuality plot, between the "normal" and the homosexual, between Vere's erectly rigid posture and Billy's lack of muscular spasm, and between Claggart's partiality and Vere's impartiality, which relate as part to a whole (in *Epistemology of the Closet* [Berkeley: Univ. of California Press, 1990]). My essay considers such dissolution of binaries in terms of Melville's critique of personal identity.

Edgar Dryden's *Monumental Melville: The Formation of a Literary Career* (Stanford, CA: Stanford Univ. Press, 2004) importantly examines the ways in which figures in Melville's poetry throw into question characterological individuation.

9 In minor ways, the rhetoric of *Billy Budd* continuously establishes and disestablishes, asserts what things are and undoes those assertions. Thus in the following the narrator identifies and then equivocates the Dansker's motive in calling Billy "Baby": "There was a vein of dry humor, or what not, in the mastman; and, whether in freak of patriarchal irony touching Billy's youth and athletic frame, or for some other and more recondite reason…he always substituted *Baby* for Billy" (*BB* 70). The hedging on a rationale is both insignificant, a mere manner of speaking, and, in its gratuitous departure from the narrator's unqualified assessment, remade as significant, made to seem strange. Similarly, when Billy explains to the forecastleman why he dismissed the afterguard who attempted to bribe him into aiding in a mutiny, we are told that the forecastleman accepts Billy's explanation because he is disposed to believe the worst of afterguardsmen, of whom forecastlemen have "a sorry opinion," since they "never [go] aloft except to reef or furl the mainsail, and [are] in no wise competent to handle a marlinspike or turn in a deadeye, say" (*BB* 83). Such a sentence both establishes a point of view identified as the forecastleman's and erodes what is established by rendering it approximate in that exemplary "say"—something that might instantiate the forecastlemen's scorn but whose illustrative nature is reframed as hypothetical, thus creating a distance between the contempt the forecastleman is said to feel and the narrator's equivocations about how it should be exemplified.

10 "Not many are the examples of this depravity which the gallows and jail supply.… Civilization, especially if of the austerer sort, is auspicious to it. It folds itself in the mantle of respectability.…It never allows wine to get within its guard.…It is never mercenary or avaricious. In short, the depravity here meant partakes nothing of the sordid or sensual.…These men are madmen, and of the most dangerous sort, for their lunacy is not continuous, but occasional, evoked by some special

object....Now something such an one was Claggart, in whom was the mania of an evil nature, not engendered by vicious training or corrupting books or licentious living, but born with him and innate, in short 'a depravity according to nature'" (*BB* 75–76).

11 Billy explains his violence thus: "Could I have used my tongue I would not have struck him" (*BB* 106). Yet this explanation is called into question by the narrative of a previous incident on the *Rights-of-Man*. When Red Whiskers gives Billy a dig under the ribs, "Quick as lightning Billy let fly his arm" (*BB* 47). Because the language which describes the initial blow prefigures the language which represents Billy's murder of Claggart ("Quick as the flame from a discharged cannon at night, his right arm shot out" [*BB* 99]), it associates both impulsive blows, only one of which is said to be occasioned by speechlessness.

12 Paul Brodtkorb, Jr., "The Definitive *Billy Budd:* 'But Aren't It All Sham?'" in *Critical Essays on "Billy Budd,"* ed. Robert Milder (Boston: G. K. Hall, 1989), 117.

13 Allegorical correspondences also leak into the rest of Melville's narrative. For instance, the *Rights- of- Man*, the ship from which Billy is "elected," and the *Athée*, the ship from which Captain Vere receives his fatal wound, both contain within the economy of their names a second sphere of reference: Thomas Paine's 1791 *The Rights of Man*, and atheism as a state of disbelief, rather than as a denomination. Yet while in one sense allegorical features pervade the whole novel (the Dansker, called "an *Agamemnon* man," speaking "Delphic deliverances," is loosely associated with oracular presence in Greek tragedy [*BB* 69, 86]), in another the allegorical register rigidly excludes characters like Squeak and Vere. It also excludes Horatio Nelson, who before his "glorious death" wrote a will and testament in which "a sort of priestly motive led him to dress his person in the jewelled vouchers of his own shining deeds" (*BB* 58). Thus, virtually by his own description, Nelson, "the greatest sailor since our world began," occupies the ground of historical legend.

14 Herman Melville, *Clarel: A Poem and Pilgrimage in the Holy Land*, ed. Walter E. Bezanson (G. P. Putnam's Sons, 1876; repr. New York: Hendricks House, 1973), 214. Citations are to the 1973 edition.

15 This allusion correctly aligns the biblical passage with the narrated one, since Ananias (Acts 5:5), like Claggart, conspires to deceive and, upon uttering falsehood, immediately falls dead.

16 The independence of natural and providential realms is repeatedly compromised. Thus Vere, at Claggart's death, legitimately recognizes Billy's angelic, godlike character: "Struck dead by an angel of God!" But he illegitimately invokes, on his own behalf, in response to Billy's action, God's imperative: "Yet the angel must hang!" (*BB* 101). The "mystery of iniquity," from Thessalonians 2:7, which the narrator associates with Claggart's "Natural Depravity," is appropriated by Vere to demonstrate its irrelevance to mundane circumstances (the "mystery of iniquity" is "a matter for psychologic theologians to discuss. But what has a military court to do with it?" [*BB* 108]). As these examples indicate, Vere invokes biblical discourse only when it is serviceable to him.

17 In *Moby-Dick* fate is contingent on differences of character: The good man and the evil man are segregated from each other so that one might live and the other might die. In *The Confidence Man* there is no such thing as character (whether this applies to figures in plays, men "of straw," or the persons of which they are mimetic, men "of flesh" [*CM* 151]), since no core or consistency identifies persons. *Pierre* mediates the *absoluteness* of discrete character that distinguishes *Moby-Dick* and the *absence* of discrete character that distinguishes *The Confidence Man*.

18 Herman Melville, *Pierre; or, The Ambiguities*, ed. Harrison Hayford, Hershel Parker, and G. Thomas Tanselle (Evanston, IL: Northwestern Univ. Press), 29; hereafter abbreviated *P*.

19 One could speak, for instance, of the narrator's staccato style: "In a legal view the apparent victim of the tragedy was he who had sought to victimize a man blameless....Yet more. The essential right and wrong...the clearer that might be, so much the worse for the responsibility of a loyal sea commander, inasmuch as he was not authorized to determine the matter on that primitive basis" (*BB* 103). The terse "Yet more" challenges as preposterous the idea of right and wrong as irrelevant to judgment, even as that challenge is empty of consequence. Elsewhere feigned surprise punctuates the narrator's sentences. About Billy in petty trouble, he says: "So heedful in all things as he was, how could this be?" (*BB* 69). "Was Captain Vere suddenly affected in his mind?...What then can the surgeon do?" (*BB* 101–2). But the narrator's mock incredulity at an ostensibly unthinkable predicament (Billy in trouble) and at the surgeon's complacent idea that his own action would be unthinkable exhausts its point or has no point outside of exclamation and its iterability.

When the narrator reports Captain Radcliffe's election of Billy to the *Bellipotent*, a vehemence is infused into an apparently neutral description: "Any demur would have been as idle as the protest of a goldfinch popped into a cage" (*BB* 45). The implications of that transitive verb—suddenness, dexterity, even furtiveness—touch on an intentionality that introduces the question of a fate. The simile interjects the idea of a doom into an action implemented by Captain Radcliffe but not initiated by him. This excess of implication—which is both only a passing inflection in the rhythm of a single sentence and an insinuation which becomes the point of that sentence—is made fully incidental to further exposition.

In each of these instances the narrator makes his presence felt in the marking of a distinction between a state of affairs and something in excess of its conventional understanding, which gives the lie to that state of affairs construed nonironically. This marking of discrepancy in its numerous instantiations is virtually indistinguishable from the narrator's exclamatory individuality, the way in which he interjects his presence as *his*. But the iterability I am describing is curiously evacuated of further specification and therefore renders the individuality a formality. As the narrator is no one whose contours could be further identified, he disallows our understanding that Billy is someone—a particularity—whose contours could be identified. When Billy does not report the attempt to implicate him in a mutiny, "Shrewd ones may opine that it was hardly possible for Billy to refrain from going up to the afterguardsman....Shrewd ones may also think it but natural in Billy to set about sounding some of the other impressed men....Yes, shrewd ones may so think. But something more, or rather something else than mere shrewdness is perhaps needful for the due understanding of such a character as Billy Budd's" (*BB* 89–90). In view of these operatic challenges, insight by any means (not just shrewdness) seems included in the derision of the narrator's outbreak, even as these dramatizations—which epitomize a kind of exclamatory fullness, or exclamatory frenzy—are themselves vacant of anything revelatory about Billy, about our defective understanding of Billy, or about the *narrator's* understanding of Billy.

20 Joyce Sparer Adler, "*Billy Budd* and Melville's Philosophy of War," in Milder, *Critical Essays on "Billy Budd*," 171.

21 Warner Berthoff, "'Certain Phenomenal Men': The Example of *Billy Budd*," in Milder, *Critical Essays on "Billy Budd*," 80.

22 Herman Melville, *Moby-Dick; or, The Whale*, ed. Charles Feidelson, Jr. (Indianapolis: Bobbs Merrill, 1964), chap. 119, "The Candles," p. 641.

23 The first position would be exemplified by a psychological critic like A. C. Bradley; the second by a philosophical critic like Stanley Cavell. "Hamlet's melancholy," Bradley writes—"something very different from insanity" (120)—accounts for his "'lethargy'" (123); "from the psychological point of view, it is the centre of the tragedy" (125) (*Shakespearean Tragedy: Lectures on* Hamlet, Othello, King Lear, Macbeth [(Macmillan and Co., 1904; repr. London: Penguin, 1991]). Bradley's sense of character rests on an idea of conflict which he inherited from Hegel, a sense of conflict which—in distinction to Hegel—he saw as internal to character rather than played out between characters (32). "Characters" in Shakespeare are often treated by critics, misleadingly, as mere "human beings" "confronting each other," Stanley Cavell writes (in *Disowning Knowledge in Seven Plays of Shakespeare* [Cambridge: Cambridge Univ. Press, 2003], 44), presupposing a psychology that, in its philosophical sophistication, is far from Bradleyan, while nonetheless recalling Bradley in its analysis of affect: "Lear is not maddened because he had been wrathful, but because his shame brought his wrath upon the wrong object" (59); "He cannot finally face the thing he has done;...he cannot bear being seen" (68). Such an analysis treats characters as psychologically legible representations of persons with whom identification is possible and even imperative, and in relation to whom our proper response is acknowledgment (90). Melville's understanding of character is not the psychological one differently instantiated by Hegel, Bradley, and Cavell.

24 Arthur Schopenhauer, *The World as Will and Representation*, trans. E. F. J. Payne, 2 vols. (New York: Dover, 1969), 1:110; hereafter abbreviated *WW*.

25 Arthur Schopenhauer, *The World as Will and Idea*, trans. R. B. Haldane and J. Kemp, 2nd ed., 3 vols. (London: Trubner, 1888), 3:417–18, Houghton Library, Harvard University, AC85.M4977.Zz888s. In addition, Melville owned and marked copies of Schopenhauer's *Councils and Maxims; Being the Second Part of...Aphorismen zur Lebensweisheit*, trans. T. Bailey Saunders (London: Sonnenschein, 1890), Houghton Library, AC85.M4977.Zz890s2; *Religion: A Dialogue, and Other Essays*, trans. T. Bailey Saunders (London: Sonnenschein, 1890), Houghton Library, AC85. M4977.Zz890s; *Studies in Pessimism: A Series of Essays*, selected and trans. T. Bailey Saunders, 2nd ed. (London: Sonnenschein, 1891), Houghton Library, AC85.M4977. Zz891s2; and *Wisdom of Life; Being the First Part of...Aphorismen zur Lebensweisheit*, trans. T. Bailey Saunders (London: Sonnenschein, 1891), Houghton Library accession no. AC85.M4977.Zz891s. Walker Cowen (*Melville's Marginalia* [New York: Garland Publishing, 1987]) reproduces the passages Melville has marked, not the full text, along with page numbers of the books in Houghton Library where the passages with Melville's markings can be found. The page numbers cited in my text are from Melville's editions of Schopenhauer's books (AC85.M4977), not from Cowen's transcriptions from those editions. By permission of the Houghton Library, Harvard University.

26 Walter Sutton, the first critic to note Schopenhauer's importance for Melville, argues that the influence of Schopenhauer on *Billy Budd* can be seen in Melville's reading of *Councils and Maxims*, where "euthanasia," understood as "an easy death," is similar to the death "free from all pain and struggle" which Melville provides for Billy (in "Melville and the Great God Budd," *Prairie Schooner* 34 [Summer 1960]: 128–33, repr. in *The Merrill Studies in "Billy Budd,"* compiled Haskell S. Springer [Columbus, OH: Charles E. Merrill Publishing Co., 1970], 83–90).

Marginalia in Melville's copies of Schopenhauer suggest other possible echoes. First, in the distinction between "the normal man" and "the genius" (*The World as Will and Idea* 3:151–2), a distinction Melville marked with a line, which recalls *Billy Budd*'s discrimination between a normal and an exceptional nature. Second, in Schopenhauer's discussion of the envy occasioned in a person by another's "decided superiority" such that he "thirst[s] for vengeance, and generally look[s] about for an opportunity of taking it by means of insult" (*Councils and Maxims*, 97), in relation to the spilled-soup episode which "justified Claggart's animosity into a sort of retributive righteousness" (*BB* 80). Melville also marked a passage associating inferiority and envy in *The Wisdom of Life*, 46. Third, in Schopenhauer's claim in *World as Will and Idea* that "undiminished infinity is always open for the return of an event or work that was nipped in the bud," which obliquely echoes Melville's description of Billy Budd as "nipped in the vice of fate" (*BB* 119). The echo lies not only in the transformed cliché ("nipped in the bud," "nipped in the vice"), but also in the imperviousness of infinity in one case and serenity in the other to a fate that would appear to compromise each. That Melville valued what he was reading is indicated by his checking of this introductory remark to *Wisdom of Life*: "To be outraged by Schopenhauer means to be ignorant of many of the facts of life" (xxi). Melville also put a check next to Schopenhauer's claim in the introduction to *The World as Will and Idea* that if "the effect [Kant's writings] produce in the mind...is very like that of the operation for a cataract on a blind man...the aim of my own work may be described by saying that I have sought to put into the hands of those upon whom that operation has been successfully performed a pair of spectacles suitable to eyes that have recovered their sight" (xi–xii).

27 The strong claim insists that organic and inorganic nature are identical; only in the world of appearances can things be different from each other. The weak claim locates individuality in persons but not in animals, and not in inorganic nature: "The farther down we go, the more completely is every trace of individual character lost in the general character of the species, and only the physiognomy of the species remains. We know the psychological character of the species, and from this know exactly what is to be expected from the individual" (*WW* 1:131).

See Christopher Janaway's analysis of another contradictory aspect of Schopenhauer's theory: "What I am in myself ought to be no different from what you are in yourself, or indeed from what any phenomenal object is in itself. But then if the intelligible character [which is unique and is present in all the acts of an individual] of a thing determines its empirical character—the way it observably behaves under various causal influences—why is it that every object does not behave in the same way?" ("Will and Nature," in *The Cambridge Companion to Schopenhauer*, ed. Christopher Janaway [Cambridge: Cambridge Univ. Press, 1999], 150).

28 For lucid examinations of the notion of a single principle or force with many manifestations, see Christopher Janaway, *Cambridge Companion*, 147; Janaway, *Self and World in Schopenhauer's Philosophy* (Oxford: Clarendon Press, 1989); and Bryan Magee, *The Philosophy of Schopenhauer* (Oxford: Clarendon Press, 1983).

29 Herman Melville, *Journal of a Visit to Europe and the Levant, October 11, 1856–May 6, 1857* (Princeton, NJ: Princeton Univ. Press, 1955), 75–76; hereafter abbreviated *J*. Further references are cited parenthetically in the text.

30 What emerges is a third category, not only, however, to designate the kind of immateriality/materiality God and the pyramids instantiate, but also to designate the figure who officiates over both constructions. It is the priest who is "supernatural," because his constructions straddle categories in the transcendence of stone

that comes to look like rocks, and in the transcendence of human thought that comes to look like divinity.

31 This is Schopenhauer's language: "The will is one not as a concept is one, for a concept originates only through abstraction from plurality; but it is one as that which lies outside time and space, outside the *principium individuationis*, that is to say, outside the possibility of plurality" (*WW* 1:113).

32 Thus, for example, in the original version of the ballad (in the first of the three distinct manuscript stages, drafted in 1886), Billy is unambiguously associated with the figure of Christ, "hung and gone to glory" (*BB* 5), whereas in the third and last of the manuscript stages (drafted after November 1888), in Billy's meeting with the chaplain, as discussed above, that association is challenged.

33 In assigning the ballad to sailor folklore the narrator is shifting away from the rarified and disputed ground of theological discourse to a common discourse grounded in a group character. Benjamin Britten preserves this folkloric quality in the choral scenes of his opera *Billy Budd*, which (except, paradoxically, for the set piece "Billy in the Darbies," in the opera sung by Billy) have a power far in excess of the recitative-like passages.

34 Melville is not responding to Schopenhauer as such. Yet it would be interesting to think whether—if he were—the ballad would be a parody of Schopenhauer (since pure will-less knowing is impossible to achieve through an act of will: To turn against the will is itself an act of will) or a disagreement with Schopenhauer (serenity, will-lessness, is possible to achieve). Melville seems at once to be insisting on the fact of serenity as a negation of egotism, even as he is leaving intact the conditions that guarantee serenity's difficulty. To place this contradiction in the context of my analysis, Melville is shockingly suggesting that serenity and resistance are manifestations of the same force.

35 Walter Benjamin, "Fate and Character," in *Walter Benjamin: Selected Writings*, vol. 1, *1913–1926*, ed. Marcus Bullock and Michael W. Jennings (Cambridge, MA: Harvard Univ. Press, Belknap Press, 1996; repr. 2004), 206. Citations are to the 2004 edition. Benjamin elaborates: "Fate shows itself, therefore, in the view of life, as condemned, as having essentially first been condemned and then become guilty" (204).

36 That "smooth white marble" hints at the antithetical possibilities of both a statue and a headstone, which marble removed from the marble-dealer's yard might be used to form.

Index

Abraham, Nicolas, 75
absolute(s), in Edwards, 26, 45, 51–52
abstraction: in Eagleton, 12; in Eliot, 170–71, 173, 174; in Emerson, 61, 65, 67, 72, 222n12; in Weil, 133
action, in Emerson, 76, 77
Adorno, Theodor, 208n28
aesthetic, the, Eagleton on, 12–13
affect
    in Edwards, 215n18
    in Eliot: as independent of person, 145; and repetition, 153
    in Emerson: transformation of, 76
    in Weil, 113–15; irrelevance of, 117
    See also emotion; mood
affliction, in Weil, 109, 121–23, 131, 134, 135
Agamben, Giorgio, 164–65
agency, in Weil, 119, 121, 128
aggregate/aggregation: in Buddhism, 152, 167–68, 209n11, 234n14, 237n37; and Eliot, 146, 152, 163, 167–68, 172–73; and Empson, 18; and Melville, 189. *See also* amalgamation
allegory, in Melville, 191, 241n12

altruism, in Edwards, 24, 30
amalgamation: in Edwards, 51; in Eliot, 145, 163, 171; in Empson, 15, 18; and Fire Sermon, 167; in Melville, 183, 199. *See also* aggregate/aggregation
analogy: in Buddhism, 167, 168; in Channing, 100; in Edwards, 27, 30, 35; in Eliot, 153–54, 171; in Emerson, 74, 91; in Melville, 181, 184–85, 186, 188, 192; in Weil, 110, 134
Anesaki, Masaharu, viii, 8
antithesis: in Eliot, 157, 164; in Emerson, 55, 60, 222n15, 224n10; in Melville, xiii, 16, 181, 185; in Weil, 128, 142. *See also* contradiction; discrepancy
Arendt, Hannah, xi–xii, xviii
Aristotle, 164
Arnold, Edwin, *The Light of Asia,* vii–viii
asceticism, in Weil, 126, 127, 130
attention, in Weil, 230n14; and being dead, 139, 140; as bondage, 120–21; as compelled, 119–20; as creative, 117; and desire, 124, 125; as disengaged from grasping and relinquishing

attention, in Weil (*Continued*)
    objects, 140–41; and distinction, x–xi; as focus on vs. release from objects, 109; as freedom vs. bondage, 124–25, 128; as genius, 117; as grasping truth, 140; and happiness, 114; and impersonality, 138; as natural, 110; and necessity, 133; and orientation, 131; to reality, 116; as regard without motive, 115–16; and religion, xiv–xv; and repetition, 138; significance of, 119; as stupefying, 124; as substance of prayer, 118; as suspending thought, 140
Augustine, 197–98, 213n8, 227n37, 229n8
Austin, J. L., 227n37
authority, in Emerson, 99–100, 101–2
automaticity, in Weil, 116
autonomy: in Buddhism, 5, 7, 167; in Eagleton, 12; in Edwards, xiv; in Eliot, 148, 151, 154, 169; in Emerson, 82, 83; in Empson, 7; in Kant, 96; and Melville, 181; in Weil, 136

Bakhtin, Mikhael, 152
beauty: in Edwards, 27, 29, 37, 39, 46, 215n14; in Emerson, 72; in Empson, 9, 10; in Melville, 188, 202; in Weil, 122–23, 138
Behmen, Jakob, 92
being
    in Edwards: as absolute, 51–52; amount of, 28, 29; calculation of degrees of, 45; and calculation of love, xii; as continuously created, 22, 23; as dependent, xiv; dependent vs. independent, 21, 207n18; and identity, 32; and love, 24, 213n8; as momentary, ix; and value, 30
    in Eliot: of ghost, 156–57; and identification, 160; and individuality, 160; as intermittent, 152; as momentary, ix; as specific vs. individual, 155; and unbeing, xi
    in Emerson: identity and ownership of, 80; as momentary, ix; as real, 96
    in Empson: as momentary, ix
    in Melville: mercurial quality of, ix; as momentary, ix
    in Weil: as anonymous, 117; desire for, 130; as momentary, ix; and personality, 109

Being in general. *See* God: in Edwards
benevolence, in Edwards: and access to the real, 37; as based on self-love, 215n15; toward Being in general, 216n19; in beings, 28, 29; disposition toward, 35; idea of, 34, 35; and love, 47; and love to Being in general, 33; and moral sense, 31; and private sphere, 38; and value, 30
Benjamin, Walter, 203–4
Benveniste, Emile, 151
Bercovitch, Sacvan, 223n5
Bhagavad Gita, xiv
Bible: in Edwards, xiv, 34, 50–51; God in, 229n8; in Melville, 183, 184, 186, 191–93, 241n16
Blake, William, 147, 232n5
Blanchot, Maurice, 163–64, 165
blessing, in Melville, 195–96
Bloom, Harold, 224n10
body
    in Eagleton: and the aesthetic, 13
    in Edwards: and calculation, 41, 43; expulsion of from thoughts, 21; of person vivified from within, 50
    in Eliot: features of, 165; of water, 174
    in Emerson: as conferred, 97, 98; connection of father to son's, 70; and grief, 73; and impersonality, 81, 89, 90–91, 95; liberation from, 103; loss as registering on, 66, 67, 74; loss vs. wholeness of, 75; nourishment of, 74; and Over-soul, 85–86; as prison, 102
    in Empson: and Buddha faces, 9
    in Schopenhauer, as will, 197
    in suttas, 5, 6
    in Weil: and dignity, 133; and "I," 138; and imagination, 134; and impersonality, 132; perception of without illusion, 137; in prayer to God, 126; and reality, 134; and truth, 135; violence to, 136
    See also embodiment
Böhme, Jakob. *See* Behmen, Jakob
Bradley, A. C., 243n23
Bradley, F. H., 163, 173, 238n42
Brodtkorb, Paul, Jr., 241n12
Buddha, 168; faces of, xi, xv, xvii, xviii, 3–5, 7–12, 14–15, 16, 17, 18, 20, 210n15, 210n17, 210n21, 211n22; in suttas, 209n7

denuding, in Weil, 111, 112
Derrida, Jacques, 75, 222n15, 227n37
description, in Melville, 181, 183, 185, 187, 189, 190, 191, 193, 195
desire: in Edwards, 38; in Emerson, 62, 86; in Empson, 3, 9; in Weil, 109, 114, 124, 125, 133
dialectic, in Emerson, 55, 72, 73
Dickens, Charles, *Our Mutual Friend,* 164
Dickinson, Emily, 102, 104, 174; "It was not Death, for I stood up," 177–78; "Our journey had advanced," 101
didacticism, in Eliot, 175–76
differentiation/distinction, in Melville, xiii, 181–83, 184–90, 191, 194, 195, 198, 199
difficulty, in Weil, 127–28, 137, 143
discrepancy: in Eliot, 145; in Emerson, 55, 71, 87, 97. *See also* antithesis; contradiction
discrimination, in Edwards, 25–26, 41, 43, 47–52
disintegration, and impersonality, viii, ix
displacement, in Emerson, 66, 69, 71
dissociation
    in Eliot: of sensibility, 145; of voice, 154
    in Emerson: and contradiction, 71, 220n5; and death, 64, 76; and death vs. power, 71; and experience, xvii, 72; and grief, 58, 61, 68; and impersonality, xiii; and power, 64, 73, 76; and present time, 63; as reflecting divergent claims of self, 55; as replacing tears, 57; and style, 59–60; as sustaining, 77; thematization of, 71
    in Melville, from Christ, 188
dramatization, in Emerson, 87, 89, 93, 98, 99, 103, 104
Dryden, Edgar, 240n8

Eagleton, Terry, *Ideology of the Aesthetic,* 12–13
ecstasy: in Edwards, 38, 50; in Emerson, xv, 92, 94
Edwards, Jonathan, xii, 21–52; *Charity and Its Fruits,* 23–24, 213n7; *Concerning the End for Which God Created the World,* 217n26; "The Distinguishing Marks of a Work of a Spirit of God," 43; "A Divine and Supernatural Light," 40, 43; and Emerson, xv; "Heaven Is

a World of Love," 48–49; letters of, 47–48; "The Mind," 22–23, 32, 213n8, 216n23; *Miscellanies,* 38, 40, 47, 50–51; *The Nature of True Virtue,* xvii, 23, 24, 25–52; "Of Being," 21–22; *Original Sin,* 213n5; *Religious Affections,* xiv, 32, 43; "Sinners in the Hands of an Angry God," 49; and Weil, xiv, xv, 110
egotism: in Emerson, 80, 83, 86, 94; in Weil, 129, 131
elegiac, the, in Emerson, 56, 65
Eliot, T. S.: *After Strange Gods,* 176, 238n44; and Arnold, vii–viii; "Burnt Norton," 151, 156, 168, 234n12; "The Dry Salvages," 144–45, 149, 151, 153, 169, 170, 171–74, 238n43; "East Coker," 146–48, 149, 150, 169, 172, 232n6, 234nn12–13; *Four Quartets,* ix, xi, xv, xviii, 144–79, 233n11; *Knowledge and Experience in the Philosophy of F. H. Bradley,* 163, 173, 233n10; "Little Gidding," 148–50, 151, 153, 154–58, 159, 160, 161–65, 169, 170, 171, 174, 176, 178; "The Metaphysical Poets," 145; "Tradition and the Individual Talent," 152; *The Waste Land,* 154, 166, 178, 233n10; and Weil, vii, 141, 143; "What Dante Means to Me," 163
Elyot, Sir Thomas, 146
embodiment
    in Edwards, of perceptions, 41
    in Eliot: of ghost, 154, 156, 157, 174; voices that issue from, 152
    in Emerson: of ideas in nature, 98; and impersonality, 95; of religious experience, 91; of soul, 85–86
    in Empson, of generic features of Buddha, 9
    in Weil: in attention after imagination is dispelled, 124; and impersonality, 132
    See also body
Emerson, Ellen, 58
Emerson, Ralph Waldo, xi, 208n29; "The American Scholar," 82; "Behavior," 87–88, 89; and Channing, 100; "Character," 226n31, 227n32; "Circles," 88–89, 94, 95, 220n5; "Compensation,"

Ferguson, Frances, 42, 218n30, 228n40
Fiedler, Leslie, 229n6
Fire Sermon, 2, 166, 167, 210n13, 212n34, 236n28
Firkins, O. W., 55
Foucault, Michel, 102, 103
Fourier, Charles, 90
Fox, George, 92
Frankfurt, Harry, 88
Freud, Sigmund, 70–71, 75, 130; "Mourning and Melancholia," 65. *See also* psychoanalysis

Gallagher, Catherine, 235n15
Gardner, Helen, 235n16
genius: in Benjamin, 203; in Emerson, 73, 76, 92; in Melville, 203, 204; in Weil, 117–18
genre, in Melville, 184, 191
ghost(s)
   in Eliot: abstraction following, 170–71; amalgamations epitomized by, 171–72; dance of, 148; and individual effacement, 168–69; recognition and effacement of, 178; representation of, 151, 154–58, 159, 160, 161–65, 174
   in Shelley, 163
God
   in Benjamin, and moral speechlessness, 203
   in Channing, 99–100
   in Edwards: as alone real, 50; as Being in general, 26, 27, 28, 29, 32, 33, 52; and calculation, 45–46; communicativeness of, 212n4; as continuous Being, 22; as continuously creating being, xi, 22–23, 24; and death, 47; and delusion, 32; happiness from, 37; heaven as presence-chamber of, 48–49; idea of, 35–36; and identity, 23; imagination of by self-reference, 39; knowledge of, 46; love for, 23, 24, 28, 29, 33, 213n8; love for saints by, 49; love to, 52; and real existence, 32; and sleeping rocks image, 26, 27; splendor of revealed in Jesus, 51; and true virtue, 38; virtue as love/benevolence to, 27, 28, 29, 33; virtue from, 46
   in Emerson: life with, 83; openness to, 86; and pantheism, xv; and person,

223n5; relationship to, 82; replacement of, 106–7; self as, 88, 89
   in Kant: as limitless being, 14
   in Melville: and materiality, 198–99; and morality, xv; presence of, xv; responsibility of, 187
   and Trinity, viii
   in Weil: affliction from, 137; annihilation in, 110, 111–12; and attention, xi; captivation by, 120; as consuming, 123, 127; and de-creation, xi, 112; distance from, 121–22; existence of, 137; experience of, 122; as faceless divine, 229n8; as good, 143; hatred of, 15; infusion by, 135–36; as inhospitable to identification, 112–13; love for, 119; love of, 132; naming of, 229n6; as not-yet-existing, 113; prayer to, 126–27; and secrecy, xiv; and violence, 131
   See also Jesus
good will, in Edwards, 30
grace, in Weil, 110, 129
grammaticality, in Melville, 184, 191, 193
grief, in Emerson: as begetting other subjects, 65, 74; and body, 73; at death and daily loss, 58; and deficient vs. overwhelming feeling, 69; delegated vs. owned, 70; denial of, 55; disavowal of, 73; and dissociation, 58, 61, 68; emblematization of, 69; empowerment of, 78; equivocal expression of, 64; as gratitude, 73; as gratuitous, 74; and idealism, 54, 59, 60, 76; identity as defined by claim to, 70; as imperfect, 223n16; imperviousness to, 69; as lacking effect, 66; marginalization of, 77, 78; mind as unconscious of, 56–57; personal experience of, xiii; relation to, 73; repetition of, 70, 71; representation of, 56; savoring of, 70; self as unpenetrated by, 67–68; as shallow, 54, 59, 67–68. *See also* mourning

Haffenden, John, 208n2, 210n15
happiness: in Edwards, 23, 37–38, 49; in Kant, 101; in Weil, 114
Hawthorne, Nathaniel, xv
Hayford, Harrison, 239n7
Hayward, John, 162–63, 171, 235n16

heart, in Edwards, 23–24, 32, 33
heaven, in Edwards, 48–49
Hegel, G. W. F., 99, 136–37, 243n23
Herbert, George, 120; "Love (III)," xiv, 230n15
heroic, the, in Emerson, 96, 101, 102, 226n27
heuristics, in Eliot, 153, 169, 176
Hobbes, Thomas, viii, 206n6
Housman, A. E., 177
humility, in Eliot, 232n6
Hutcheson, Francis, 30, 213n7, 215n16

"I"
    in Eliot: and disclaimed autonomy, 151; and suttas, 166–67
    in Emerson: and impersonality, 95; as lacking point of view, 94
    in Weil: abandonment of, 111, 124; and attention, x–xi; and body, 138; as deprived of particularity, 111–12; liberation from, 121; as migratory, 128; as motive, 116, 141; and suffering, 113; and violence, 131; vitality purged of, 139; well-being of, 114
    See also identity; person; self
idealism
    in Edwards, and calculation of virtue, 42
    in Emerson: and experience, 56, 62, 67, 71, 76–77; and grief, 54, 59, 60, 76; and impersonality, 106; and loss, 59; as unjust, 100
    in Kant, 42, 211n26
    in Rotman, 41
identification: in Eliot, 151, 160, 161–65, 166; in Emerson, 96, 103; in Melville, 184; in suttas, 6; in Weil, 117
identity
    in Edwards: and continuous creation, xi, 22–23, 24; dependent vs. independent, 22; and equivocation, 213n6; and reality, 32; and sleeping rocks, 27
    in Eliot: and experience, 149; false ideas about, 159; forfeiting of, 178; of ghost, 156, 161–62; lack of discrete, 149
    in Emerson, xi, 84; and being, 80; as defined by grief, 70; erasure of, 89; and experience, 62; as fixed, 87;

and impersonality, 87; and mental experience, 88–89; as misrepresenting self, 96; in variety, 55
    in Mallarmé, 159–60, 161
    at moment of disintegration, viii
    in Parfit, 79–80, 104–5
    in suttas, 5, 167, 168
    in Weil, xi
    See also "I"; person; self
illusion: in Edwards, 23; in Eliot, 161, 166; in Weil, 132, 133, 137
imagination: in Edwards, 26, 44, 45; in Eliot, 179; in Emerson, 76, 77; in Weil, 124, 134
impersonality
    and disintegration, viii, ix
    in Eagleton, 13
    in Edwards: calculation of, 39; disappearance of, 41; as impossible, 110; and love, xii; and the nonhuman, x; resistance to, xvi; valuation from, 25
    in Eliot, 233n11; of artist, 152; and extinction of personality, viii–ix; incarnated, 176; propositional understanding of, 176; recognition of, ix, 206n9
    in Emerson: access to, 82; as annihilating the personal, 93; appeal of, 95; and body, 81, 89, 90–91, 95; at death of Waldo, 69; as detached from religion, 104; and disintegration of syntax, ix; and dissociation, xiii; dramatization of, 99; emergence of, 87, 94; and emotion, 87; ethics of, 81; and the heroic, 101, 102; and ideals, 106; and identity, 87; as incompletely realized, 104; as inconsequential, 110; and individual, 104–5; and inhuman, xvi; and interest of self vs. other, 101; invocation of, 95; and lack of suffering, 106; and law, 90, 91; and mind, 81, 91; and nonhuman, x; and Over-soul, 80–81, 87; of ownership, 100; and person, 107; and the personal, xvii; person as annihilated by, 94; recognition of, ix, 206n9; and religion, 106; and society, 85; and soul, 92, 95; and totality, 86; transformation to, 103; unsystematic presentation of, 92

living, the, in Eliot, 152, 154, 165, 166, 168, 169, 174, 176, 178

Locke, John, 22, 234n14

loss, in Emerson: accommodation of, 63; in all experience, 208n29; concession to, 74; endurance vs. suffering of, 62; and experience, 61; generation of succeeding, 65; grief over, 56, 57, 58; and idealism, 59; as particular, 81; preservation of, 77–78; as registering on body, 66, 67; as scarring body, 74; source vs. expression of, 69; and time, 62–63; and transformation of affect, 76; and understanding of self, 68–69; as unjust, 100

love
in Channing, 99–100
in Edwards, 27–32, 48, 214n9; and amount of being, 28; and being, 24, 213n8; to Being in general, 52; and benevolence, 47; as blind to consequence, 30; calculation of, xii; and calculation of virtue, 42; and death, 49–50; as disposition, 33; experiential ground for, 25; for God, 23, 24, 213n8; for God vs. benevolence in beings, 28, 29, 33; and impersonality, xii; of Jesus, 49–50; as lacking gratitude or anger, 30–31; in others, 39; and particularity, 24–25; of self, 30, 215nn15–16; as way to heaven, 49; without particularity, 23
in Weil, 231n21; as coexisting with pain, 122; and food, 134; of God, 132; in prayer to God, 126

Mallarmé, Stéphane, 150, 162; "Le Tombeau d'Edgar Poe," 159–61

Marvell, Andrew, 191

masochism, in Weil, 122, 123, 125, 126, 127, 130, 139, 231n21

Meltzer, Françoise, 229n10

Melville, Herman, 102, 104; *Benito Cereno*, xviii; *Billy Budd*, ix, xi, xii, xv, xvi–xvii, xviii, 16, 180–204, 239n3; "Billy in the Darbies," 199–204; *The Confidence Man*, xviii, 101, 180, 199–200, 239n3, 241n17; and Emerson, xv, 207n21; *Journal*, 198; *Moby Dick*, 101, 241n17; *Pierre*, 101, 184, 193, 200,

241n17; and Schopenhauer, 196–98, 199

memory
in Edwards, and continuous creation, 22–23
in Eliot: and experience, 171; liberation through, 171, 173; motivating center for, 145; as officiating, 149; and person, 150; as repenetrating of experience, 170
in Emerson: divorced from wisdom, 62; lack of, 60

mental states, in Emerson, 88–89

Milarepa, 132–35

Miller, Perry, "From Edwards to Emerson," vii

mind
in Edwards: speculative faculty of, 32–33; spiritual enlightenment of, 36; and virtue from God, 46
in Emerson: as immeasurable, 82; and impersonality, 81, 91; influx of Divine mind into, 92, 93, 103; and inhabiting powers, 86; as property, 80; as unconscious of grief, 56–57
in suttas, 5, 6
in Weil: and food, 132–33; suspension of state of, 141, 142
See also thought; understanding

mistake/error: in Edwards, 26, 33, 44, 45; in Eliot, 149, 162, 167

Montaigne, Michel de, 222n12

mood: in Emerson, 80, 88–90, 225n18; in Weil, 114, 115, 116, 117, 121. *See also* affect; emotion

morality/ethics
in Arendt, xi
in Edwards: and love, 31, 32; and ultimate value, xii
in Emerson: absence of, 97; authority concerning, 99, 100; of impersonality, 81
in Kant: and happiness, 101; and orientation to God, 14; and personal worth, 96; and will, 211n26
in Melville: and Bible, 186, 192, 193; and character, xvi; distinctions in, 186, 199; and God, xv; and individuality, 187; and judgment, xviii; and violence, xi, xii
in Parfit, 223n1

moral speechlessness, in Benjamin, 203
mourning, in Emerson: of affect vs. son, 54, 63; at all experience, 65, 69; and body, 73; confusion in, 69; inability vs. refusal to, 74; and introjection, 75, 76; of loss of feeling vs. feeling's effects, 66; and object mourned, 69; as process, 75, 76, 78; refusal of vs. imperative to, 70; as relinquishment, 66; repetition of, 75. *See also* grief, in Emerson

Nagy, Gregory, 226n27
narrator, in Melville, 184, 185, 186, 187, 192, 193–94, 195, 242n19. *See also* speaker, in Eliot
nature, in Emerson, xv, 87, 91–92, 98
necessity: in Emerson, 73; in Schopenhauer, 196; in Weil, 108, 129, 133, 137, 140
negation: in Edwards, 26; in Melville, 183–84, 194
Nietzsche, Friedrich, 107, 227n37
Niobe, 134, 231n24
Noh theatre, 1, 8, 17–18
nothing/nothingness, in Edwards, 21, 26, 51–52

obliquity, in Emerson, 64, 68, 77, 78
opposites, in Empson, 7
orientation: in Kant, 13–14, 16, 211n28; in Weil, 131
Over-soul, in Emerson, xv, 80–81, 85–86, 87, 96, 97
owning/ownership: in Buddhism, 167; in Eliot, 166, 167; in Emerson, 80, 89, 93, 94, 99, 100, 102, 103

Packer, Barbara L., 55, 224n10
pain
    in Edwards, at annihilation, 49
    in Emerson: and all outside self, 97; as particular, 81; and pleasure, 98; as unjust, 100
    in Empson, and pleasure, 3
    in Weil: as coexisting with love, 122; expulsion of, 108–9; as inseparable from beauty, 122–23; purpose of, 136–37
Pali suttas. *See* suttas
paradox, in Eliot, 157, 175, 238n39
Parfit, Derek, 228nn39–40, 234n14; *Reasons and Persons*, 79–80, 104–6, 107

Parker, Hershel, 239n7
particularity: in Eagleton, 13; in Eliot, xiii, 166; in Emerson, xvii, 93, 97; in Melville, 189; in suttas, 166, 168
Paul, St., 50–51, 219n45
Peabody, Elizabeth, viii
perception
    aggregate of, 167
    in Eagleton, and the aesthetic, 12
    in Edwards: and calculation, 41, 43; language of, 46; by measurement and evidence, 47; in others, 39; of saints, 33; of value, 26; of virtue, 46
    in Eliot, 148; as alone valid, xv; and experience, 170, 176; and individual effacement, 169; motivating center for, 145
    in Emerson: of death, 67; impermanence of, 88–89
    in suttas, 5, 6
    in Weil: affect as irrelevant to, 117; of body without illusion, 137; and impersonality, 111; and understanding, 116, 117
Perl, Jeffrey, 163, 165, 236n24
person
    as aggregate, 167
    in Edwards: and continuous creation, 22, 23; disappearance of, 40; obliteration of value of, 34; as one who can calculate, 39–40; value of, 27; as vivified from within, 50–51
    in Eliot: annihilation of, 166; and individual effacement, 169; and memory, 150; nonunique features of, 165; unmaking of, 154
    in Emerson: as annihilated by impersonal, 94; as convenience, xii, 80; as egotistical, 86; forfeiting of, 94; and God, 223n5; and the heroic, 102; and impersonality, 87, 107; lack of situational givens of, 95; nature of, 83; nostalgia for, 104; personal as defining of, 90; as separate and integral, 80
    in Empson: and Buddha faces, 8, 12; demotion of, xii; features of, xvii; in *The Royal Beast*, 19
    in Melville, as undifferentiated from phenomena, 182
    as term, viii
    in Weil: and collectivity, 130; de-creation of, 137

See also "I"; identity; self
persona, viii
personal, the
    in Edwards: and calculation, 40; and
        continuous creation, 24; deficien-
        cies of, 44; as illusory, 23
    in Eliot: and binding relations, 152;
        lack of, 149; and voice, xiii, 151
    in Emerson: and authority, 101–2; as
        defining of person, 90; as dismissed
        for Over-soul, 96; and experience,
        62; and grief, 69; impersonal annihi-
        lation of, 93; and impersonality, 87;
        and loss, 208n29; and mental states,
        89; as misrepresenting self, 96; oblit-
        eration of, 93–94; transformation
        from, 103; within universal, 88
    and impersonality, xvii
    in Melville, and impersonality, 16–17
    Parfit on, 79–80
    unbinding of, xiii–iv
    in Weil: and intensity, 138; mechanical
        nature of, 139
personality, viii
    in Edwards, taint of, 38
    in Eliot: extinction of, viii–ix, 152; and
        orthodoxy, 176
    in Emerson: erasure of, 81; and imper-
        sonality, 87, 89; and moods, 89
    in Empson, and Buddha faces, 12
    in Melville, expressions in excess of, xiii
    in Weil: abolition of, xiii; attention as
        freedom from, 121; and being, 109;
        destruction of, 111; forfeiting of,
        109, 128–29; and impersonality, ix;
        and violence, ix, 135
personification: in Edwards, 52; in Eliot,
    165; in Emerson, 77; in Melville, 181,
    190, 195; in Weil, 142–43
person-stage(s), 152, 221n9, 234n14
perspective: in Eliot, 163; in Emerson, 88, 95,
    106; in Melville, 202; in Weil, 134–35
Pétrement, Simone, 125, 229n6
Plath, Sylvia, 139
Plato, 89
Plotinus, 87, 92, 93
"Poe," 150
Poe, Edgar Allan, 160–61, 162
poet, the, in Emerson, 81, 102–4
point of view, 14; in Emerson, 94; in Weil,
    xi, 113, 117–18, 138

Poirier, Richard, 224n10
Pound, Ezra, "The Return," 150
power, in Emerson: approaches to, 73; and
    cancellation of particularity, 97, 98;
    and death, 63–64, 65; and dissociation,
    71, 76; from evasion of conflict, 223n16;
    genius transformed into, 76; impor-
    tance of, 221n10; obliquity as source of,
    77; of poets, 102; sources of, 72
prayer, in Weil: attention as substance of,
    118, 119; example of, 126–27
preference, in Weil, xi, 117, 119, 130, 231n21
proposition(s), in Eliot, 145, 153, 168, 174,
    176, 232n6
prose/prose style: in Edwards, 28, 214n13; in
    Emerson, 91–99, 97, 100; in Melville,
    xvi, 183–84, 185, 194; in Weil, 111. *See
    also* analogy; rhetoric, in Melville
Pseudo-Dionysus, 229n8
psychoanalysis: and Emerson, 55, 70, 75, 76,
    78, 79. *See also* Freud, Sigmund
psychology: Buddhist, 152, 209n11; and
    continuity, 79, 105; and Edwards, 25,
    38, 43, 215n18, 216n23; and Emerson,
    79, 223n2, 224n10; and Kant, 42; in
    Melville, 180, 187, 241n16, 243n23; in
    Schopenhauer, 244n27; and Weil,
    125, 130

Quine, W. V., 41

ravishment, in Emerson, 17, 92–93, 94, 95,
    103, 107
reality
    in Edwards: experience of, 32, 34, 35,
        37; and God, 32, 50; and identity, 32;
        reference of virtue to, 40
    in Eliot, as one, 163
    in Emerson, 96; encounter with, 99; of
        grief, 57; and the heroic, 102; lack of
        contact with, 58; poet's invitation
        to, 102; as questionable, 65; unme-
        diated contact with, 96–97
    in Kant, 96
    in Weil: attention to, 116; and body,
        134; bondage to, 124; and desire, 124;
        illusory nature of, 132, 133; as not
        given, 116; penetration of, 113–14;
        and understanding, 125
recognition: in Edwards, 33–34; in Eliot,
    149, 162, 163, 166; in Weil, 117

redundancy: in Eliot, 162, 164, 171; in Melville, 193. *See also* reiteration; repetition

reiteration: in Eliot, 152, 178; in Emerson, 69; in Melville, 184, 187, 194, 195. *See also* redundancy; repetition

religion: in Eliot, 174, 175, 176; in Emerson, 87, 91, 92, 102, 104, 106; in Weil, xiv–xv, 130

repetition
    in Eliot, 171; as motivated and obsessive, 153; and reality of ghost, 157; as replacing subjectivity, 170; as self-quotation, 151–52; and suttas, 166
    in Emerson: absence of, 97; of grief, 70, 71; of mourning, 75
    in suttas, 6, 166
    in Weil, and attention, 138
    See also redundancy

revelation, in Emerson, 97

rhetoric, in Melville, 183–84, 185, 186, 190, 200, 240n9

Ricks, Christopher, 233nn9–10

Riquelme, John Paul, 233n11

rocks, sleeping. *See* sleeping rocks, in Edwards

Rotman, Brian, 41–42

Rousseau, Jean-Jacques, 163, 165

sacrifice
    in Edwards, 49–50
    in Emerson, 72–73, 74; authority concerning, 100; lack of, xvii–xviii, 94
    in Melville, 193
    in Weil, 126, 127; and self-preservation, 139; and solace, 138

saints, in Edwards, 32–33, 49

"Samson," 150

school studies, in Weil, 118–21

Schopenhauer, Arthur, x, xvii, 196–98, 199, 204, 211n25, 245n31, 245n34; *Councils and Maxims*, 243n26; Melville's copies of, 197, 243nn25–26; *The Wisdom of Life*, 243n26; *The World as Will and Idea*, 243n26; *The World as Will and Representation*, 184, 197, 230n12, 243n26

Sealts, Merton M., Jr., 239n7

self
    in Edwards: love of, 24, 25, 30, 31, 47, 215nn15–16; reference to, 39, 45; transcendence of, 25

in Eliot: and attachment vs. detachment, 170, 171; description of, 151; disclaimed autonomy of, 151; as distinct from others, 170; eternalization of, 161; and source of phenomena, 167

in Emerson, 103; abnegation of, 96; and cancellation of particularity, 97; claims of, 55; death of, 66, 67, 74; and dissociation, 55; and experience, 62; exteriorization by, 69–70; as God vs. weed, 88, 89; loss of, 93–94; and nature, 98; and Over-soul, 86; personal identity as misrepresenting, 96; personal perspective of, 81; power given up by, 86–87; and private vs. public for poet, 81; questioned as fixed, 99; reliance on, 83, 224n10; separateness of, 68; and social world, 77; as stable entity, 89; in subject position, 94; trust vs. abolition of, 95; understanding of loss by, 68–69; unethical interest of, 101; and unpenetrated by grief, 67–68

identity from, 167

in Mallarmé, 160

in Melville, as object of beauty, 202

Parfit on, 79, 223n1

separately existing, 79

in suttas, 5, 7, 167–68

in Weil: abnegation of, 126; annihilation of, 109–10, 127; effacement of, 119, 121; extinction of, 138; hostility toward, 139; loss vs. preservation of, 112; preservation of, 139; and sacrifice, 129; and violence, 131

See also "I"; identity; person

sensation
    in Eagleton, and the aesthetic, 12
    in Edwards, 35; of reality, 34; of saints, 33
    in suttas, 5, 6

sense: in Edwards, 45, 46, 47, 52; in suttas, 166

sensibility, dissociation of, in Eliot, 145

Shelley, Percy Bysshe, *The Triumph of Life*, 163, 236n22

Simmel, Georg, "The Metropolis and the Mental Life," xvi

slavery, in Weil, 119, 120, 121, 123, 137